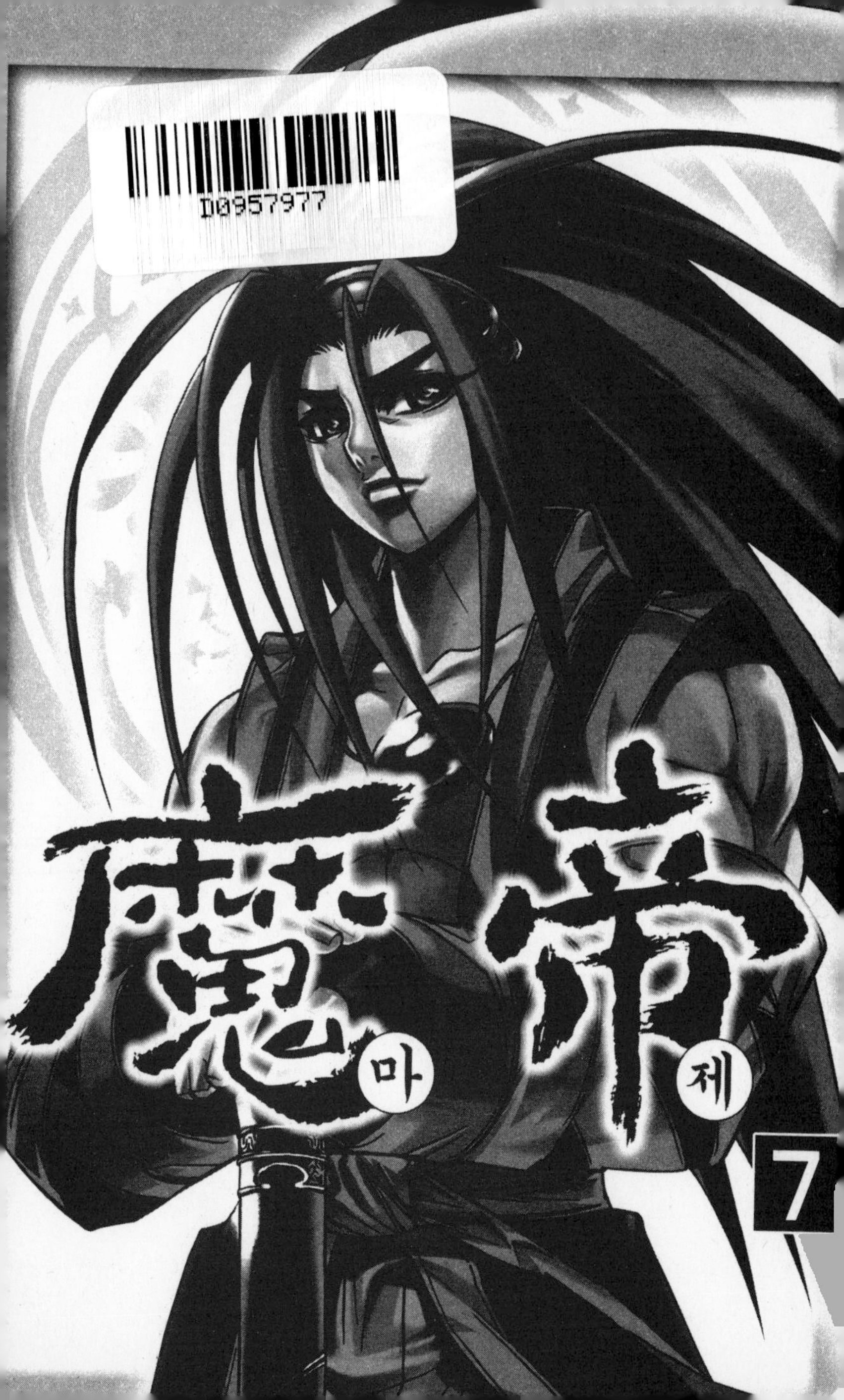
魔帝
마제
7

KING OF HELL

King of Hell Vol. 7
Written by Ra In-Soo
Illustrated by Kim Jae-Hwan

Translation - Lauren Na
English Adaptation - R.A. Jones
Copy Editor - Suzanne Waldman
Retouch and Lettering - Tom Misuraca
Production Artist - Vicente Rivera, Jr.
Graphic Designer - James Lee
Cover Design - Patrick Hook

Editor - Rob Tokar
Digital Imaging Manager - Chris Buford
Pre-Press Manager - Antonio DePietro
Production Managers - Jennifer Miller and Mutsumi Miyazaki
Art Director - Matt Alford
Managing Editor - Jill Freshney
VP of Production - Ron Klamert
President and C.O.O. - John Parker
Publisher and C.E.O. - Stuart Levy

A **TOKYOPOP**®Manga

TOKYOPOP Inc.
5900 Wilshire Blvd. Suite 2000
Los Angeles, CA 90036

E-mail: info@TOKYOPOP.com
Come visit us online at www.TOKYOPOP.com

ISBN: 1-59182-867-8

First TOKYOPOP printing: October 2004
10 9 8 7 6 5 4 3 2 1
Printed in the USA

KING OF HELL

VOLUME 7

BY
RA IN-SOO
&
KIM JAE-HWAN

HAMBURG // LONDON // LOS ANGELES // TOKYO

WHO THE HELL...?

MAJEH:
A feared warrior in life, now a collector of souls for the King of Hell. Majeh has recently been returned to his human form in order to carry out the mission of destroying escaped evil spirits upon the earth. There are two catches, however:
1. Majeh's full powers are restrained by a mystical seal.
2. His physical form is that of a teenage boy.

CHUNG POONG NAMGOONG:
A coward from a once-respected family, Chung Poong left home hoping to prove himself at the Martial Arts Tournament in Nakyang. Broke and desperate, Chung Poong tried to rob Majeh. In a very rare moment of pity, Majeh allowed Chung Poong to live...and to tag along with him to the tournament. Chung Poong's older brother--Chung Hae--is also a student of the martial arts and is the "nephew" (martial arts inferior) of Poong Chun.

THE MARTIAL ARTS CHILD PRODIGIES

"BABY":
A 15-year-old from the infamous Blood Sect, Baby is several warriors in one...thanks to his multiple personality disorder. Baby is his shy, gentle, blushing side. Hyur is his intense, unforgiving, murderous side. The question is: how many sides does this young man have?

CRAZY DOG:
A 6-year-old hellion who is partial to using a club, this wild child hails from a remote village...and he definitely lives up to his name.

SAMHUK:
Originally sent by the King of Hell to spy on the unpredictable Majeh, Samhuk was quickly discovered and now--much to his dismay--acts as the warrior's ghostly manservant.

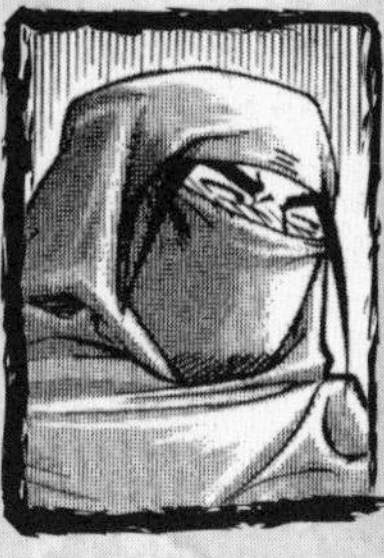

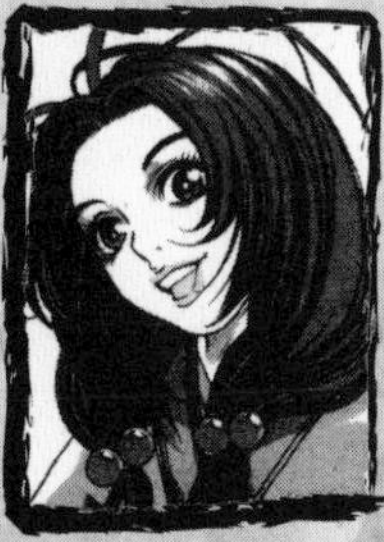

DOHWA BAIK:
A vivacious vixen whose weapons of choice are poisoned needles. She joined Majeh and Chung Poong on the way to the tournament.

KING OF HELL:
You were expecting horns and a pitchfork? This benevolent, otherworldly ruler reigns over the souls of the dead like a shepherd tending his flock.

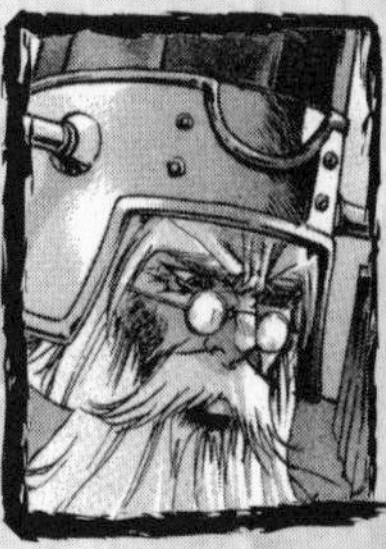

DOHAK:
A 15-year-old monk and a master at fighting with a rod, he is affiliated with the Sorim Temple in the Soong mountains.

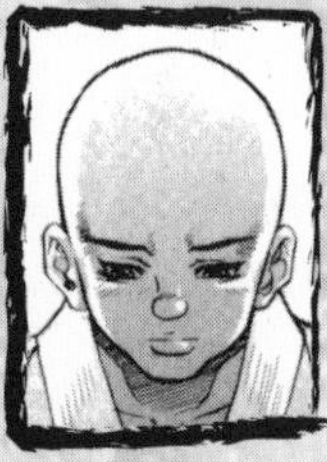

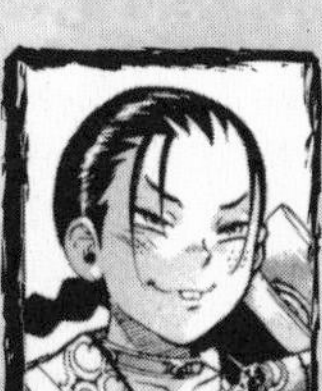

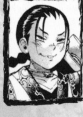

POONG CHUN:
A 12-year-old expert with the broadsword, he is affiliated with the Shaman Sect. Poong Chun is the "uncle" (martial arts superior) of Chung Hae--Chung Poong's older brother.

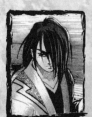

YOUNG:
A 15-year-old sword-master, possessing incredible speed, he is affiliated with Mooyoung Moon-- a clan of assassins, 500 strong.

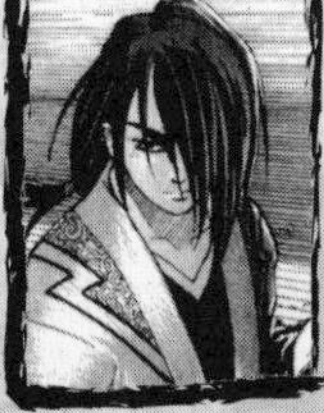

Hell's worst inmates have escaped and fled to Earth. Seeking recently-deceased bodies to host their bitter souls, these malevolent master fighters are part of an evil scheme that could have dire consequences for both This World and the Next World. It is believed that the escaped fiends are hunting for bodies of martial arts experts, as only bodies trained in martial arts would be capable of properly employing their incredible skills.

To make matters even more difficult, the otherworldly energy emitted by the fugitives will dissipate within one month's time...after which, they will be indistinguishable from normal humans and undetectable to those from the Next World. The King of Hell has assigned Majeh to hunt down Hell's Most Wanted and return them to the Next World...but Majeh doesn't always do exactly what he's told.

Majeh was a master swordsman in life and, in death, he serves as an envoy for the King of Hell, escorting souls of the dead to the Next World. Majeh caught Samhuk--a servant for the King of Hell--spying on him and, after making the appropriate threats, now uses Samhuk as his own servant as well.

The King of Hell has reunited Majeh's spirit with his physical body, which was perfectly preserved for 300 years. Due to the influence of a Superhuman Strength Sealing Symbol (designed to keep the rebellious and powerful Majeh in check), Majeh's physical form has reverted to a teenaged state. Even with the seal in place, however, Majeh is still an extremely formidable warrior.

Along with the young, wannabe-warrior called Chung Poong Namgoong and a beautiful femme fatale named Dohwa Baik, Majeh has made his way to the heralded Martial Arts Tournament at Nakyang--the most likely place for the warrior demons to make their appearance.

Shortly after arriving in Nakyang, Majeh and company met Chung Hae-- Chung Poong's older brother--though it was far from a happy reunion. Chung Hae berated his younger sibling and ordered Chung Poong to return home. With Majeh backing him up, Chung Poong was able to stand his ground and stay for the tournament.

With the start of the tournament, Majeh's behavior only got more out- rageous as he easily bested his first opponent. Chung Poong was well on his way to his first victory over the hulking 13-year-old Abaek...until Chung Poong succumbed to his worst enemy: his own fear. After the fight, even the ultra-insensitive Majeh was consoling Chung Poong...until Chung Hae dropped by with a heaping helping of scorn for his younger brother. Always happy to give as good as he gets, Majeh delivered an extremely humiliating (and painful) defeat to Chung Hae's "uncle" (martial arts superior) when they met in the tournament.

Though Majeh seemed to have forgotten his mission to capture Hell's Most Wanted, the escaped evil souls certainly had not forgotten him! While Majeh faced off against Crazy Dog, the tournament was suddenly interrupted. An elderly, one-armed, martial arts master--whose body was inhabited by one of the fugitive demons--forced his way into the arena and effortlessly killed Crazy Dog and Abaek. Despite his best efforts, Majeh also seemed on the verge of total defeat...though, as his life-force dissipated, the Superhuman Strength Sealing spell that limits his abilities was broken!

Now, Majeh is rising again...and you'd better believe there's Hell to pay!

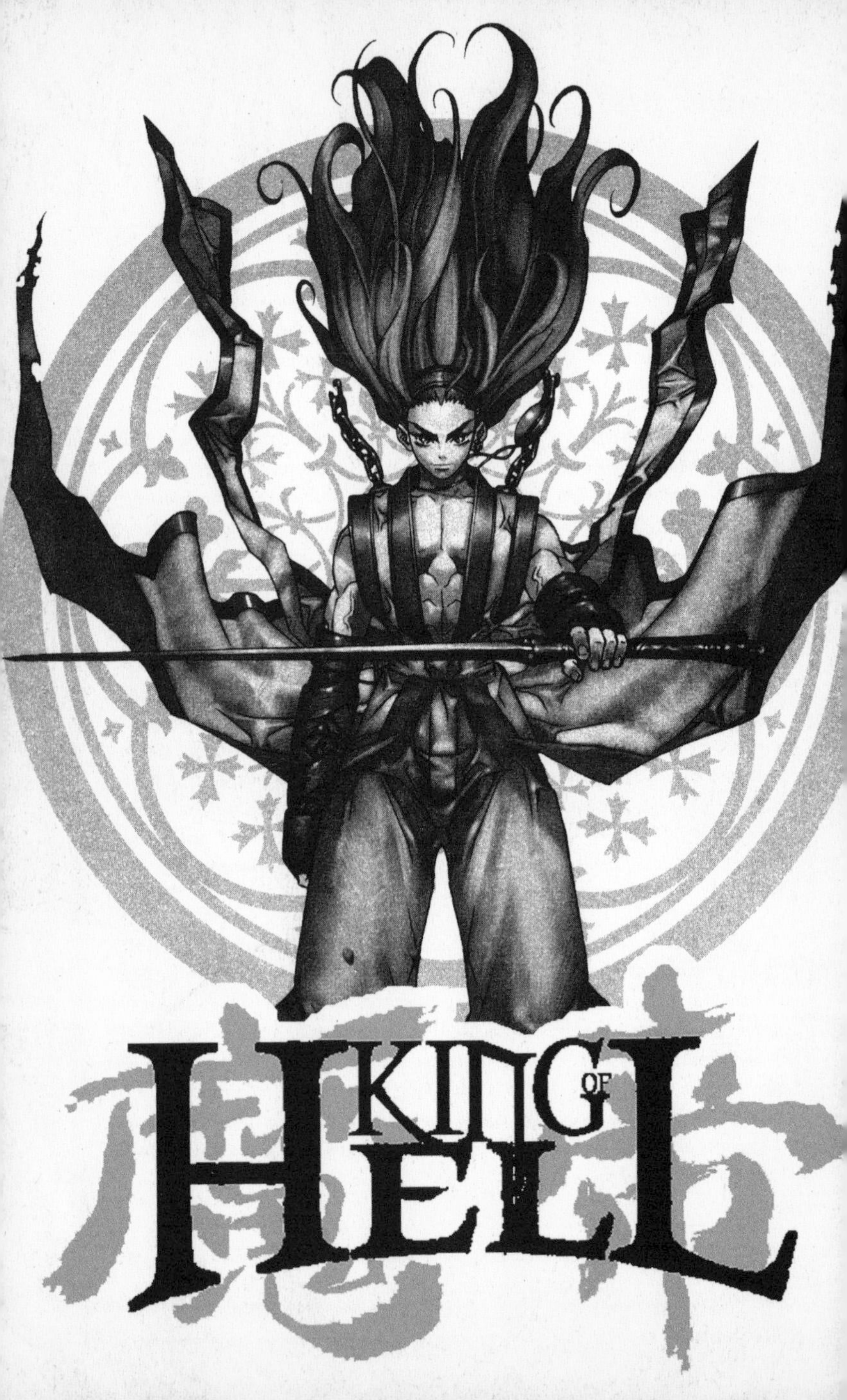
KING OF HELL

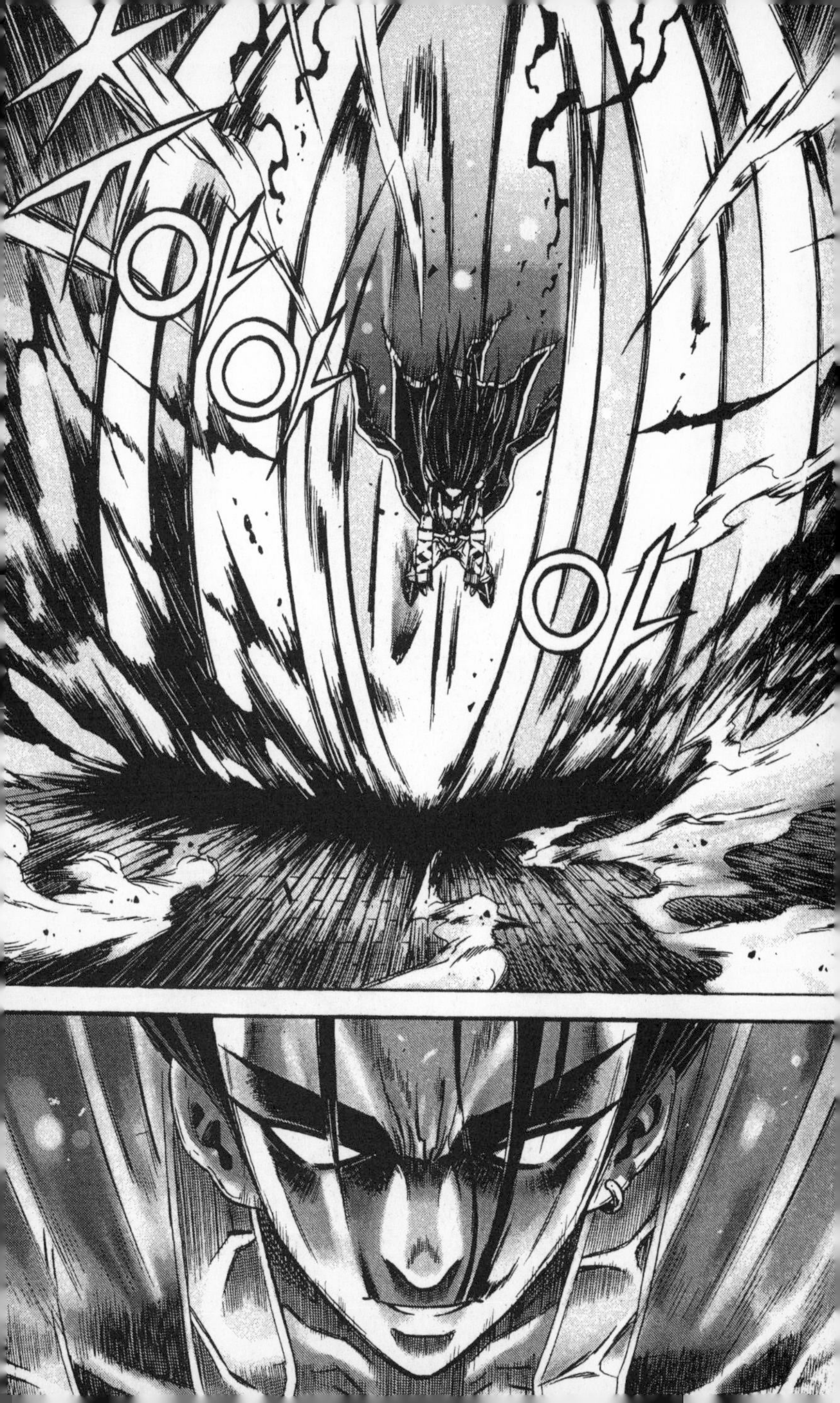

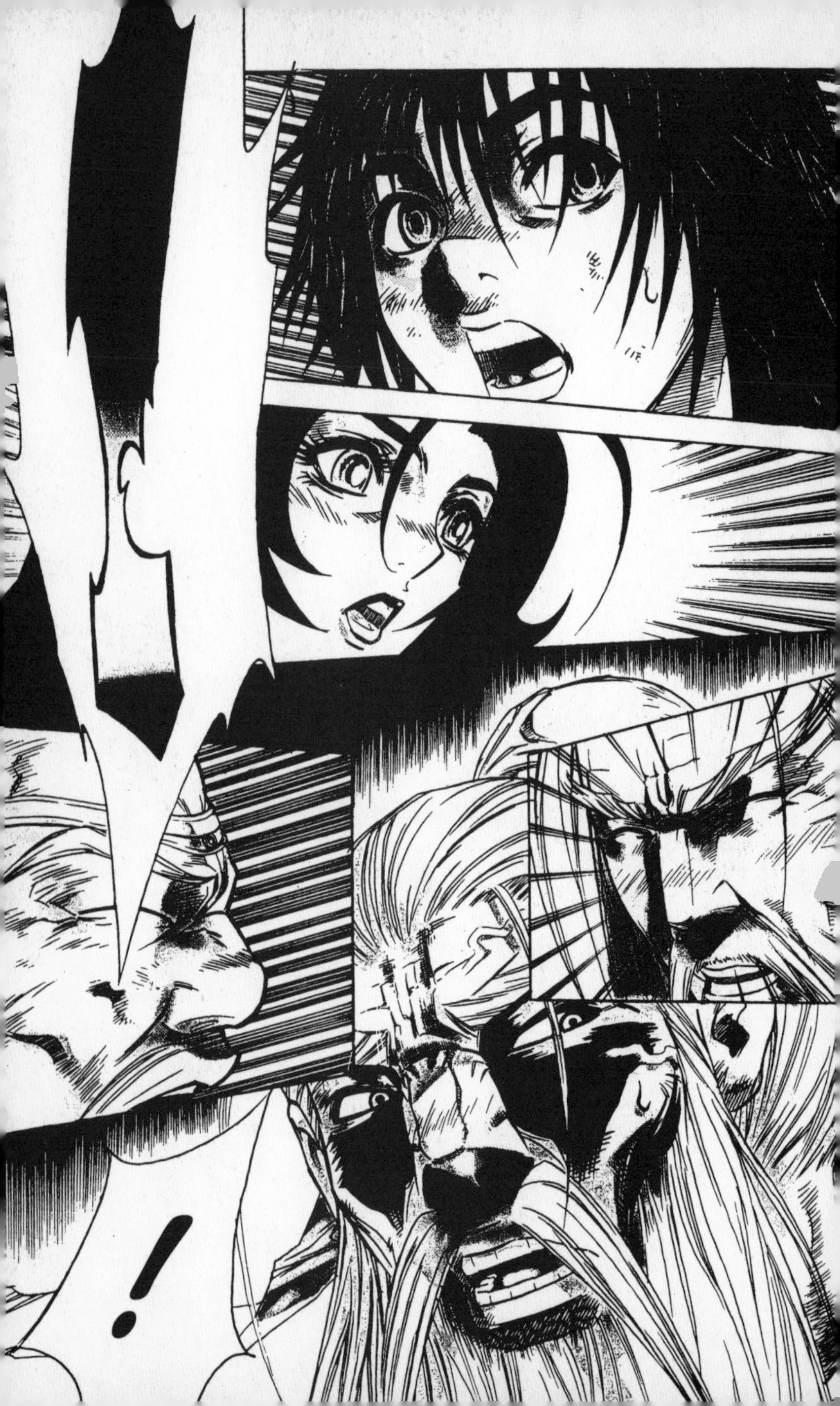
!

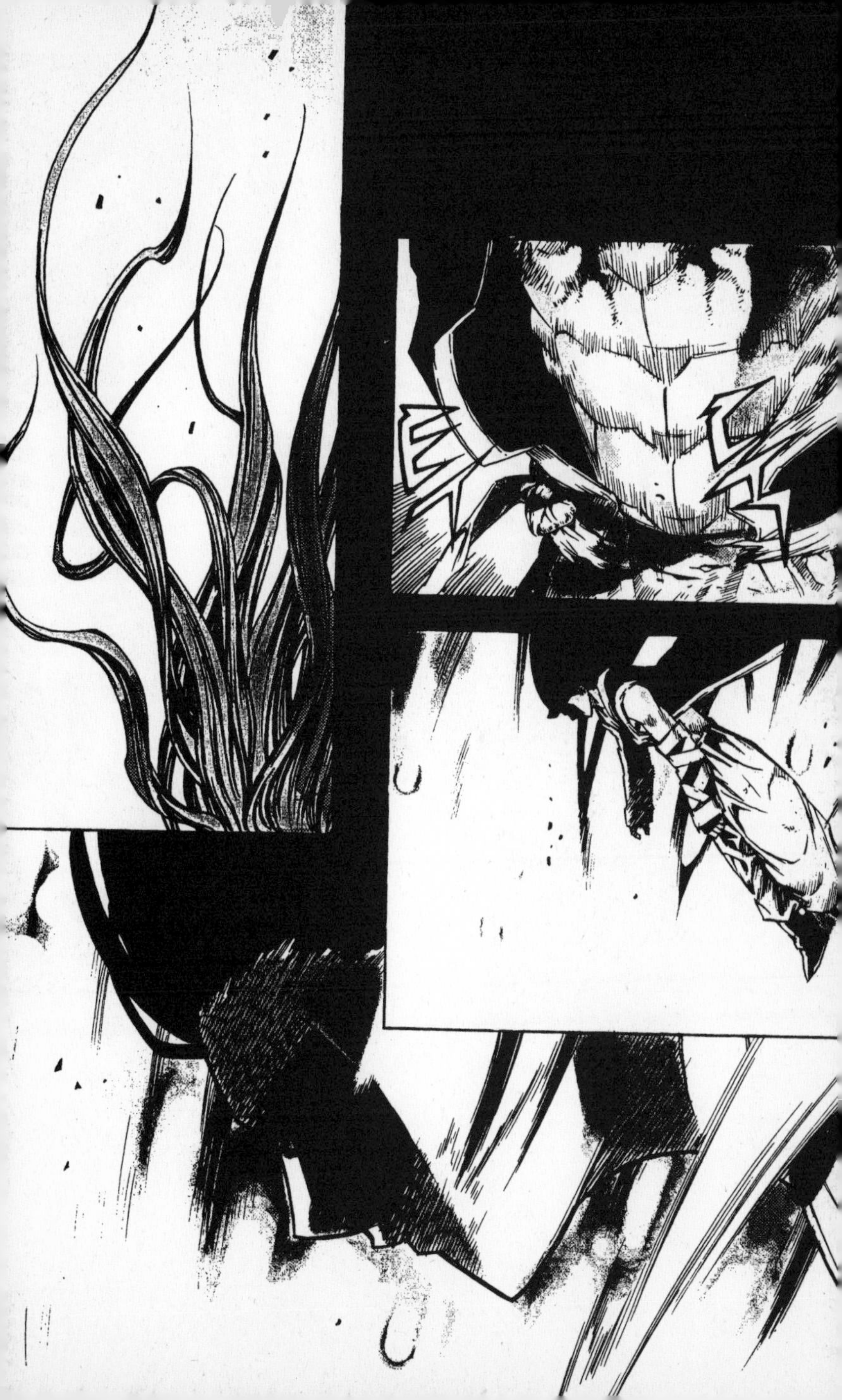

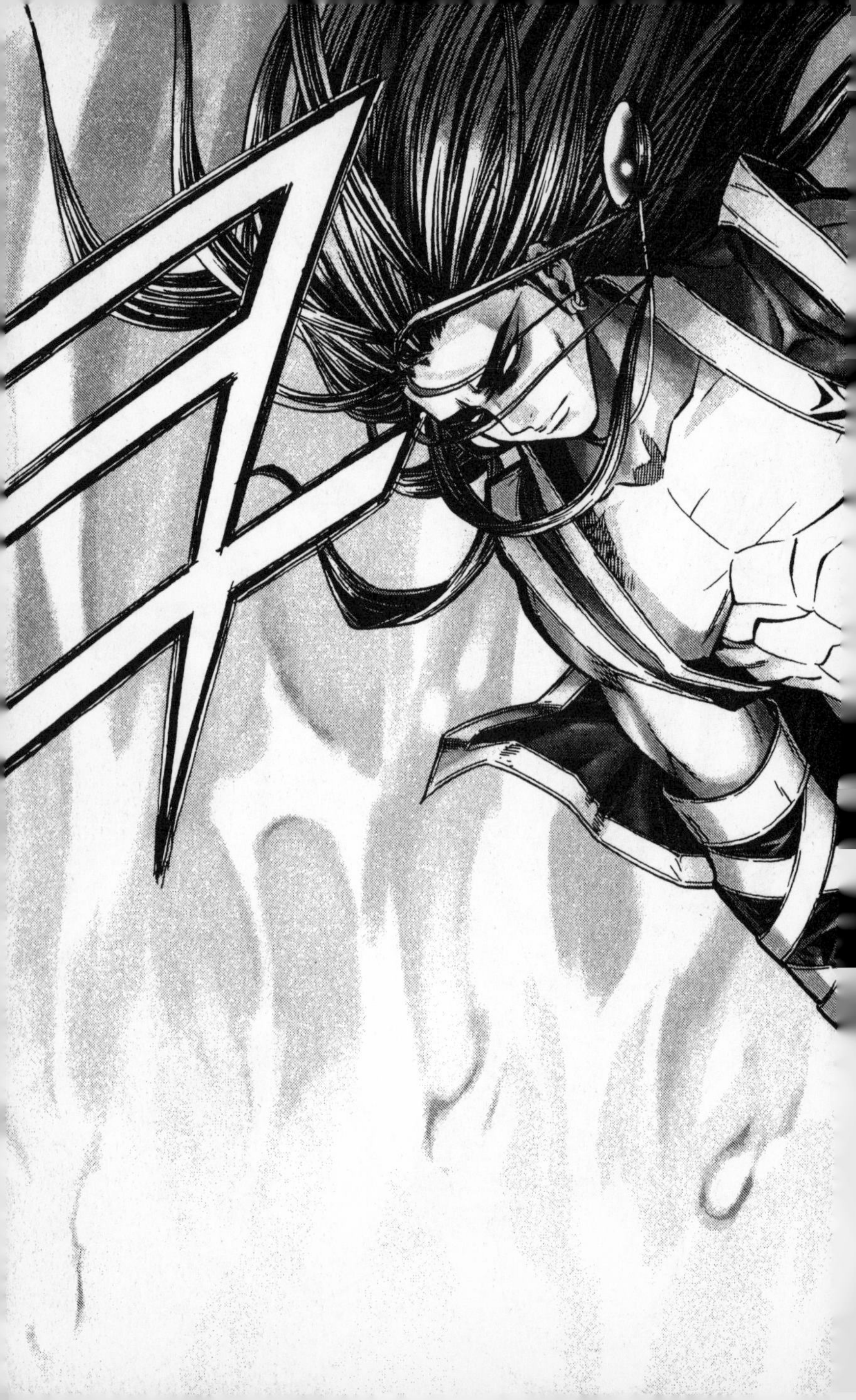

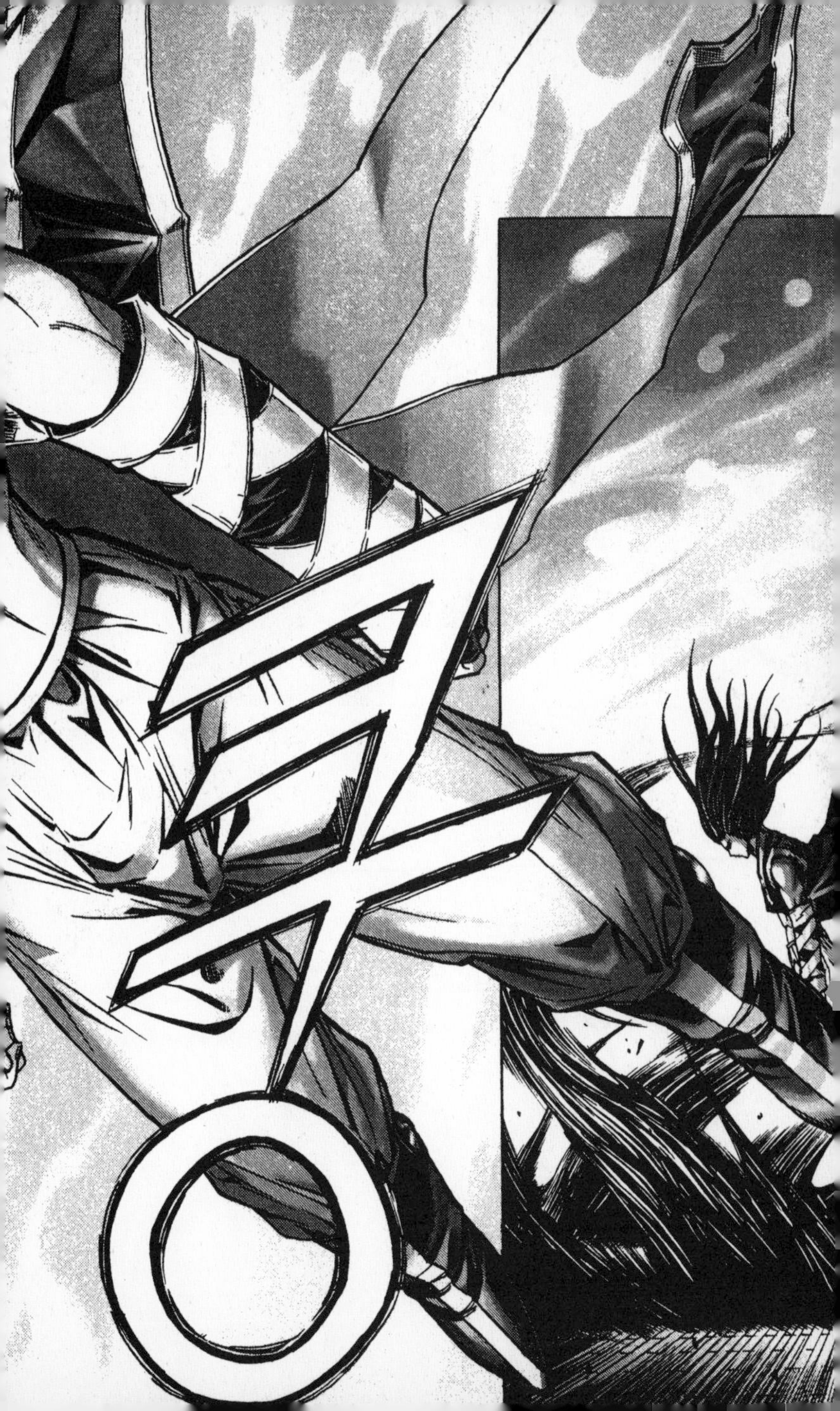

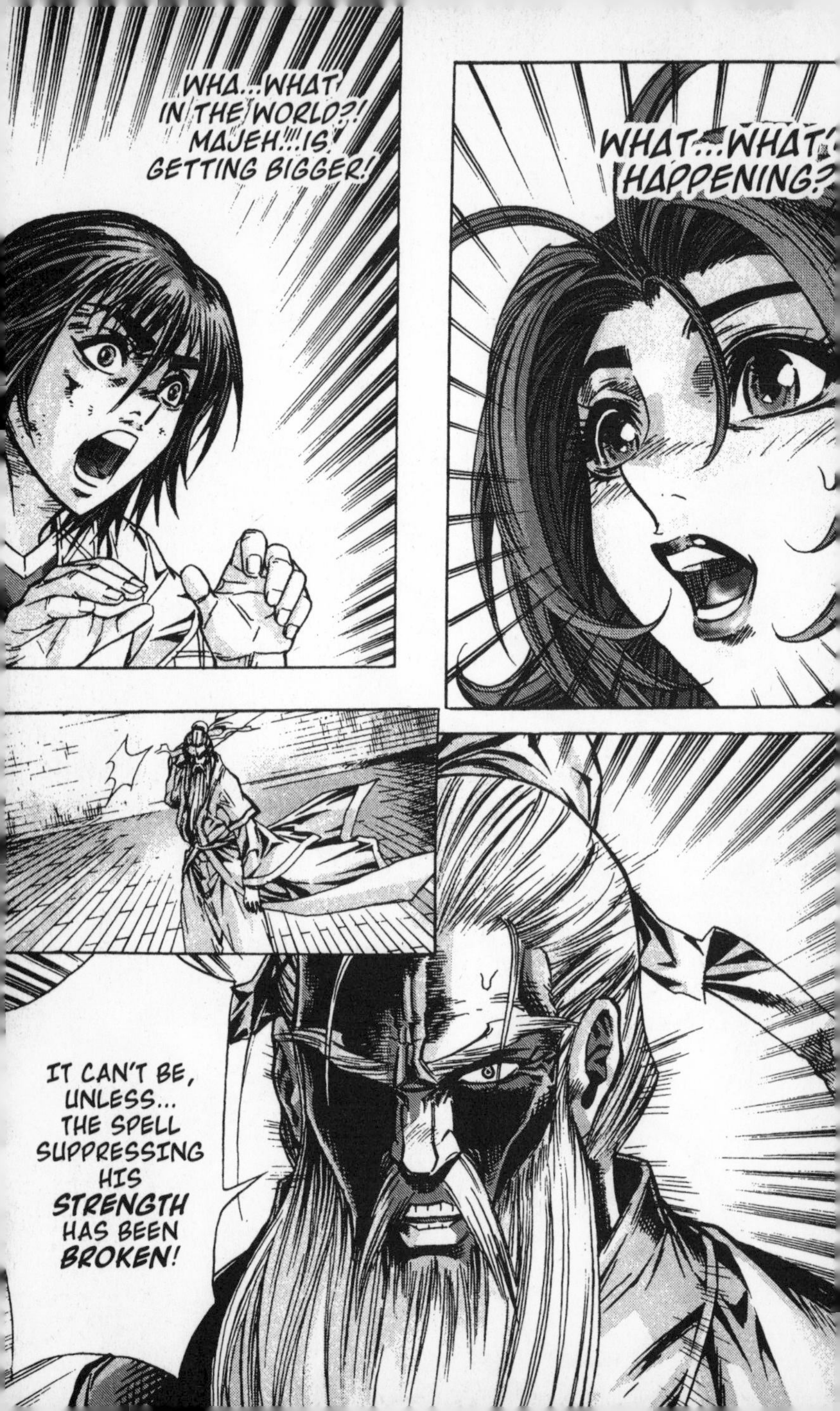
WHA...WHAT IN THE WORLD?! MAJEH...IS GETTING BIGGER!
WHAT...WHAT'S HAPPENING?
IT CAN'T BE, UNLESS... THE SPELL SUPPRESSING HIS STRENGTH HAS BEEN BROKEN!

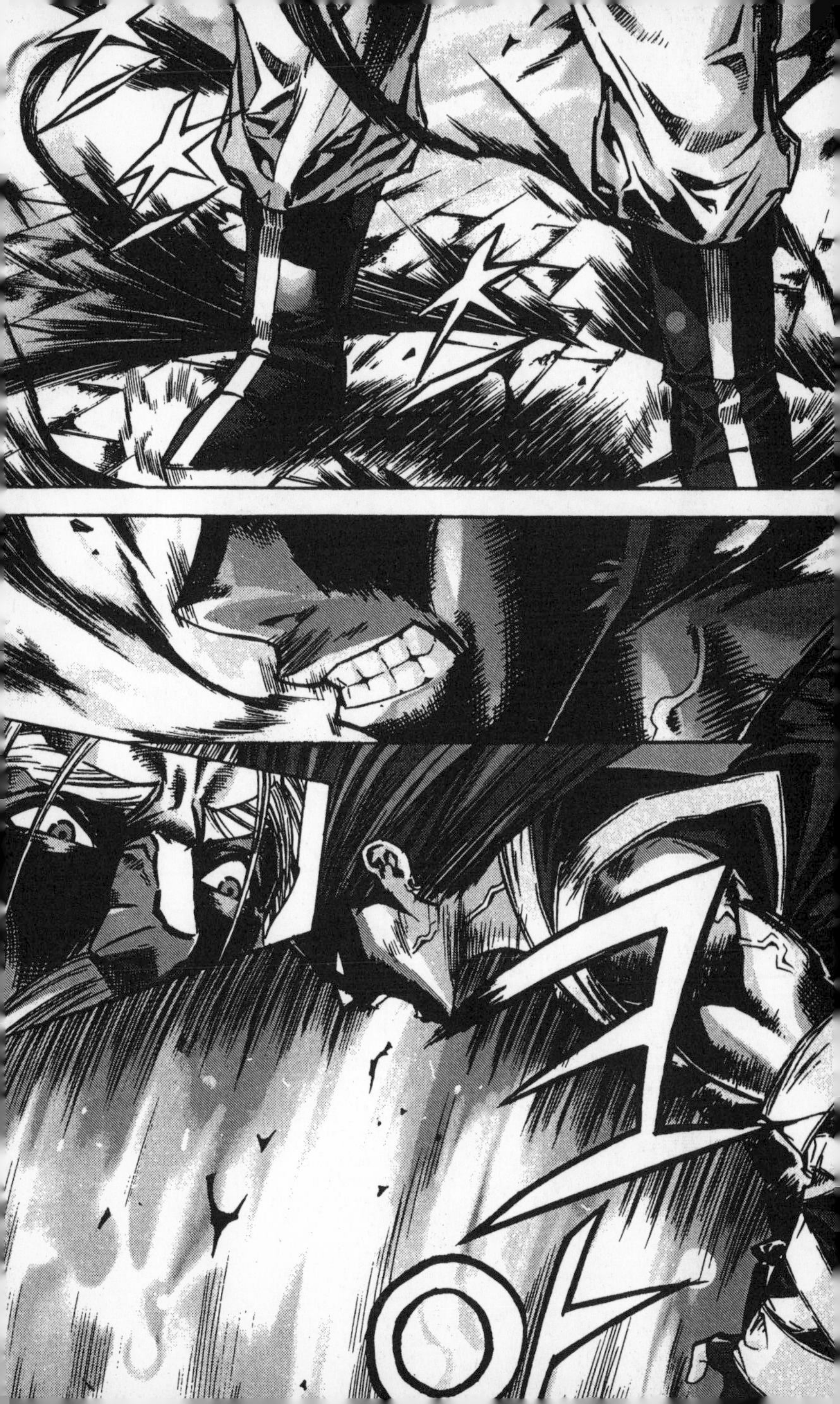

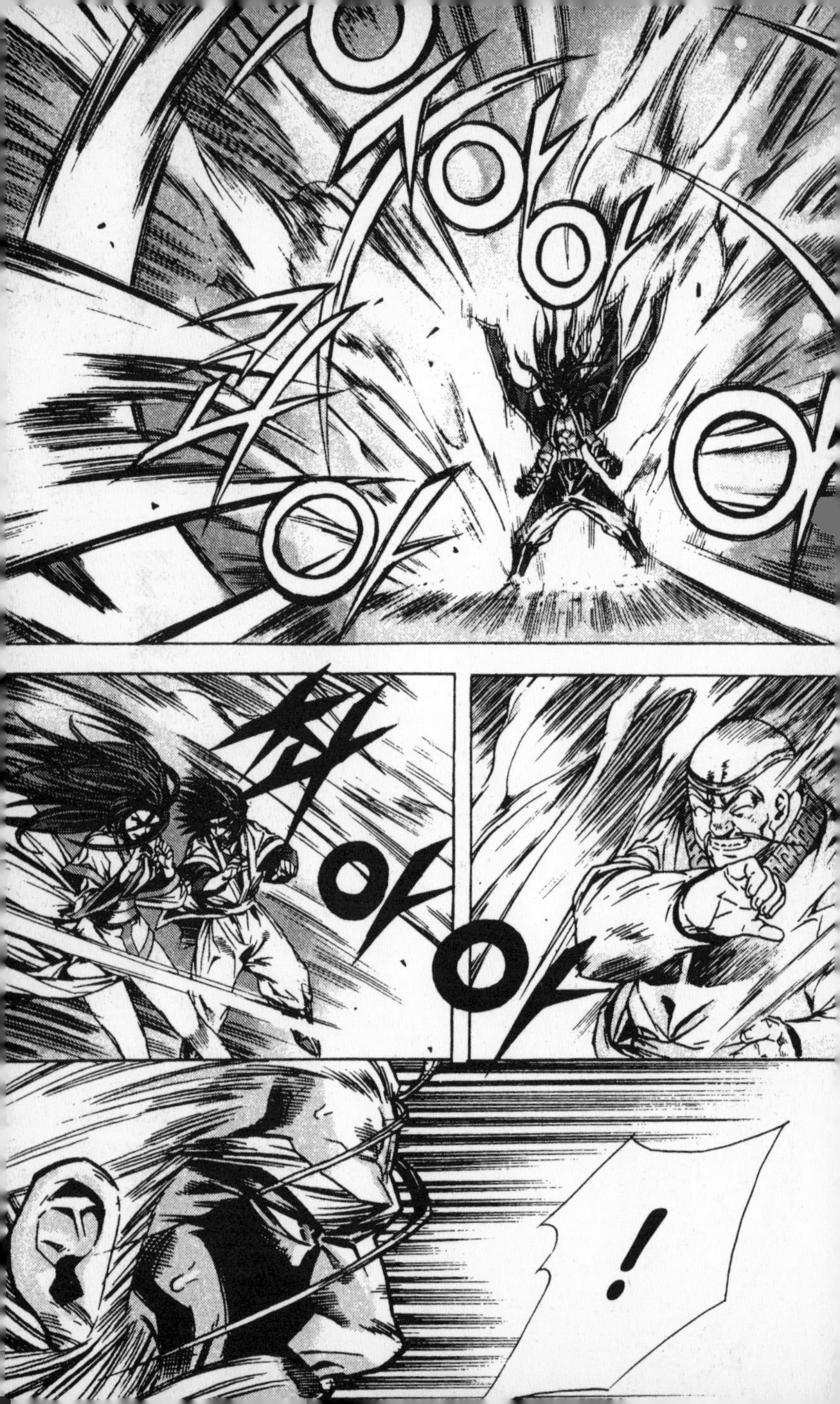
!

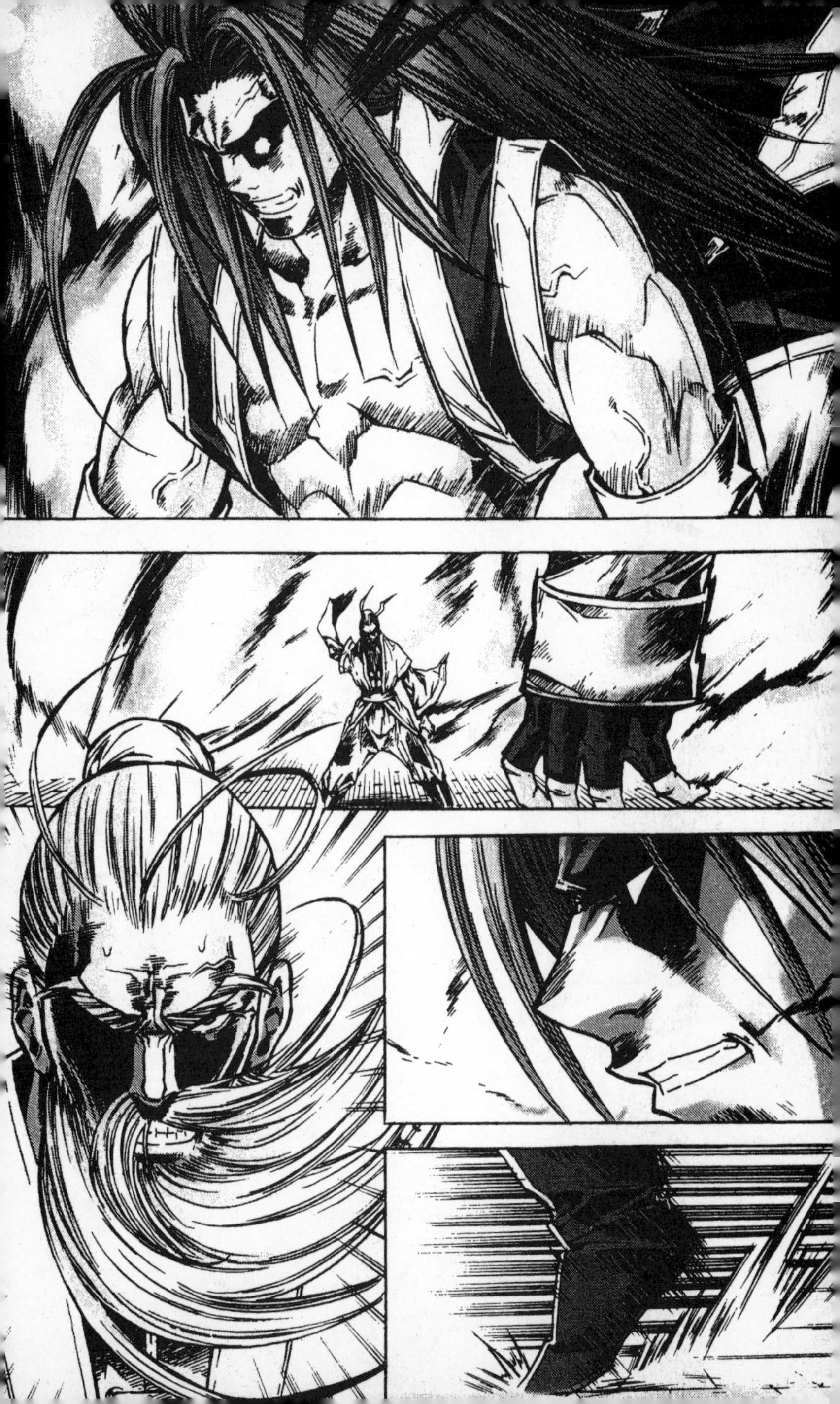

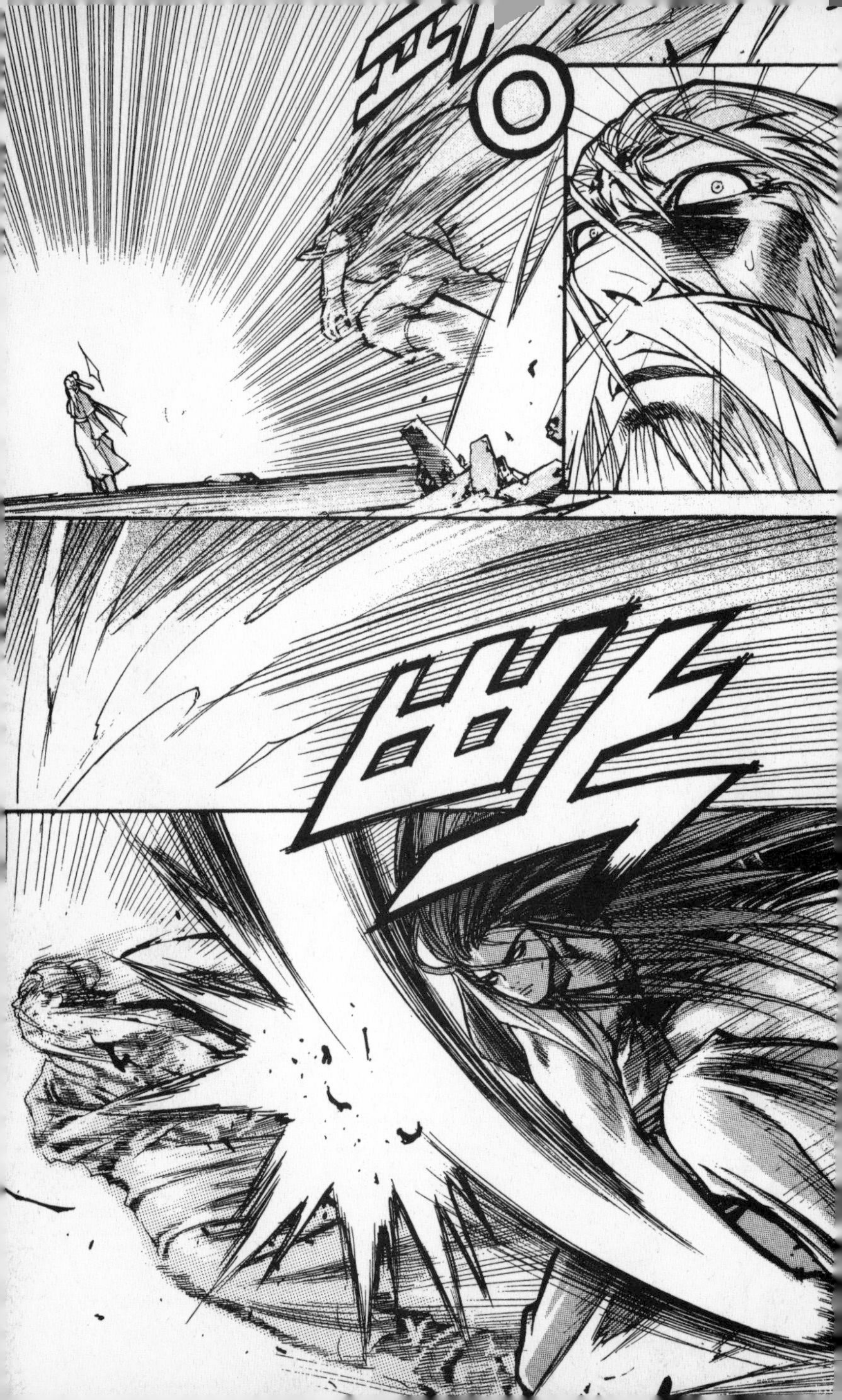

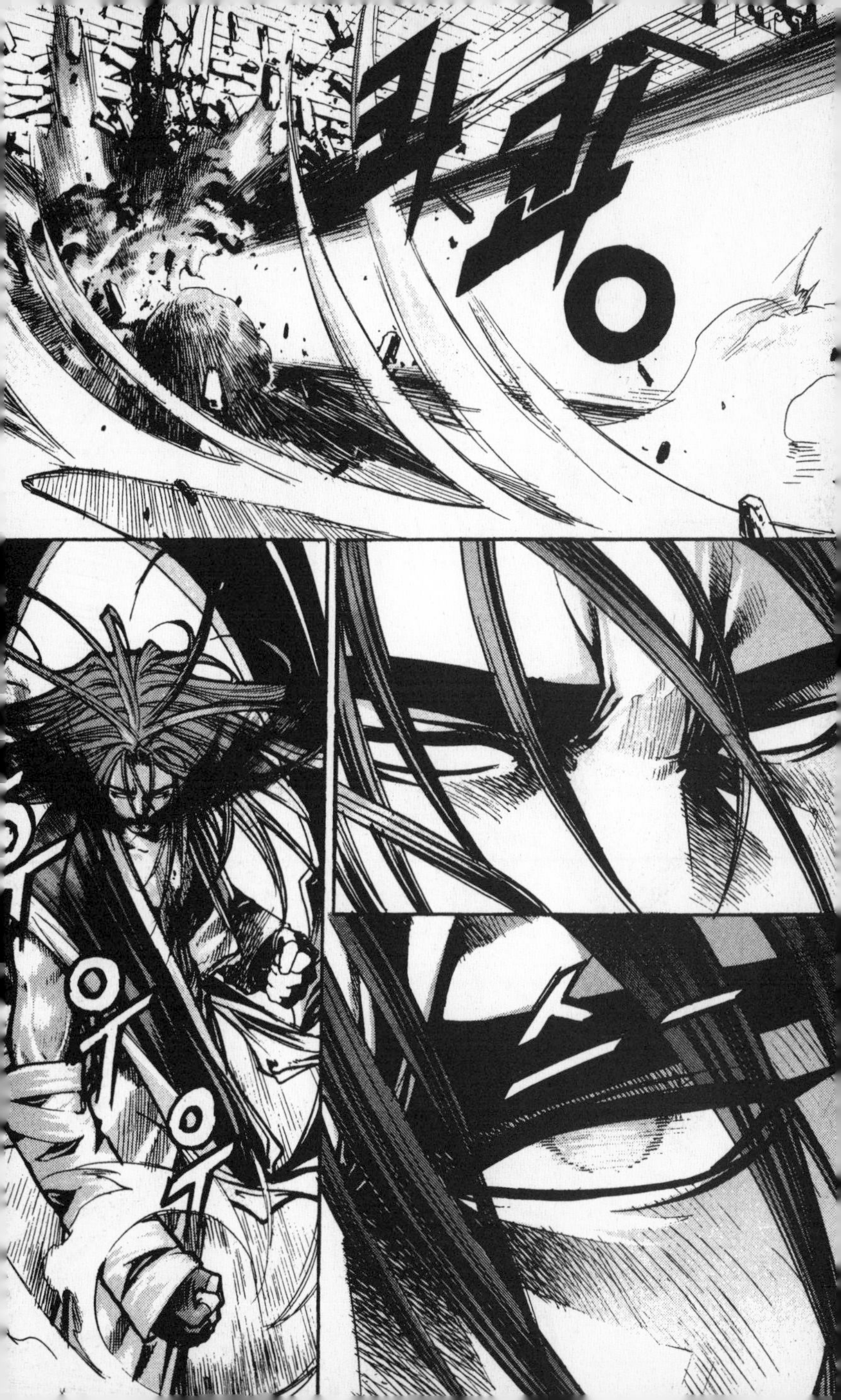

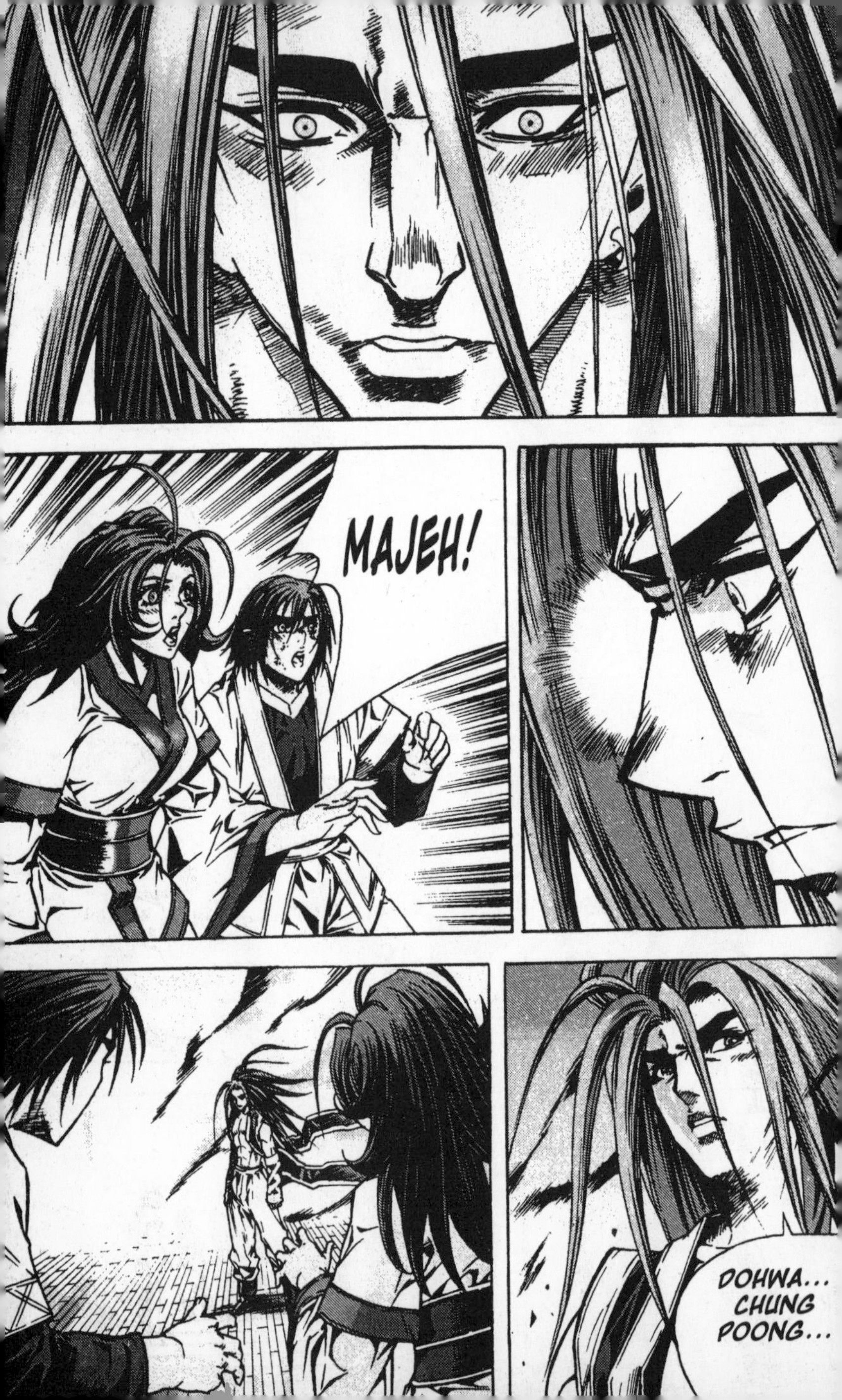
MAJEH!
DOHWA... CHUNG POONG...

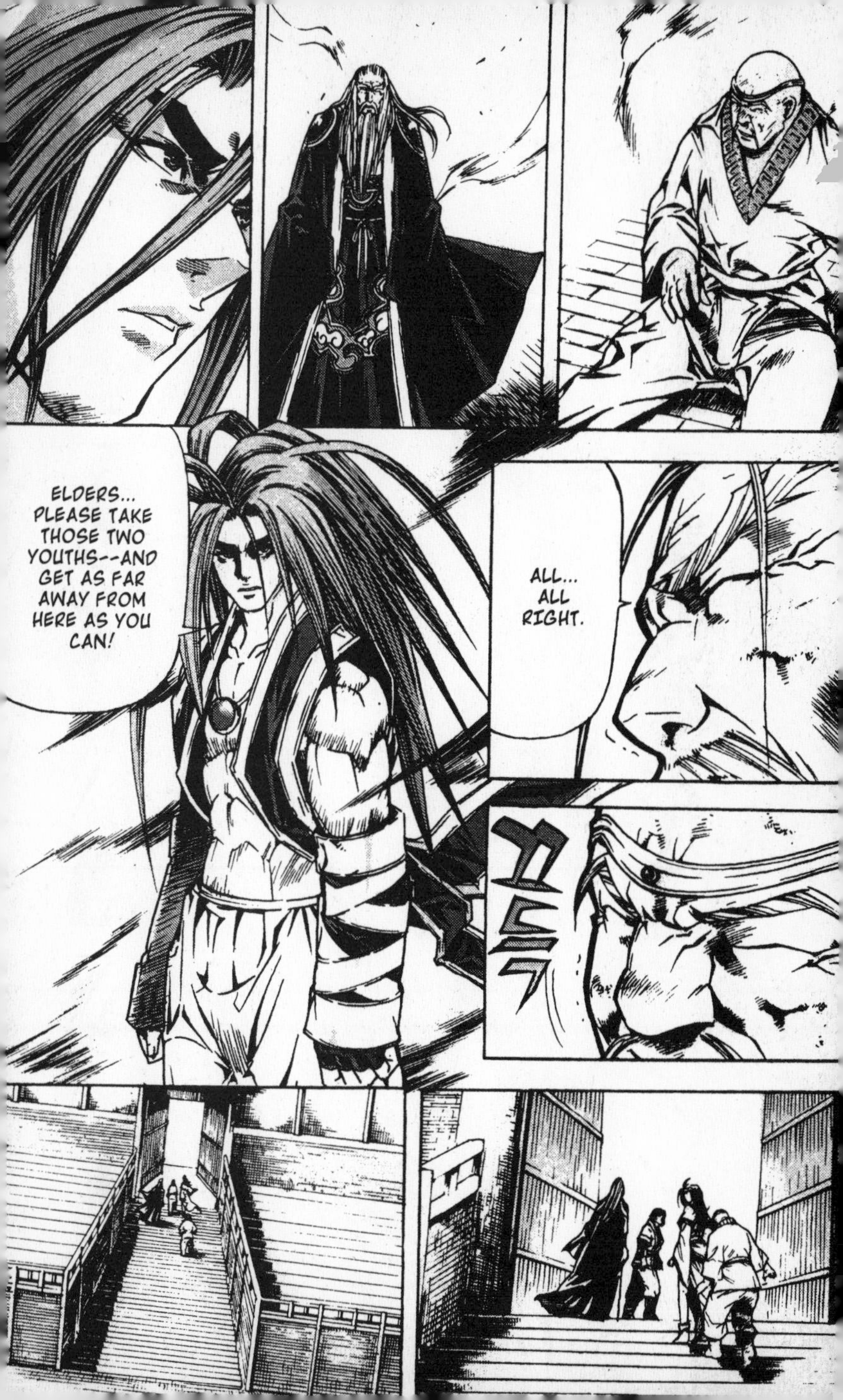
ELDERS... PLEASE TAKE THOSE TWO YOUTHS--AND GET AS FAR AWAY FROM HERE AS YOU CAN!
ALL... ALL RIGHT.

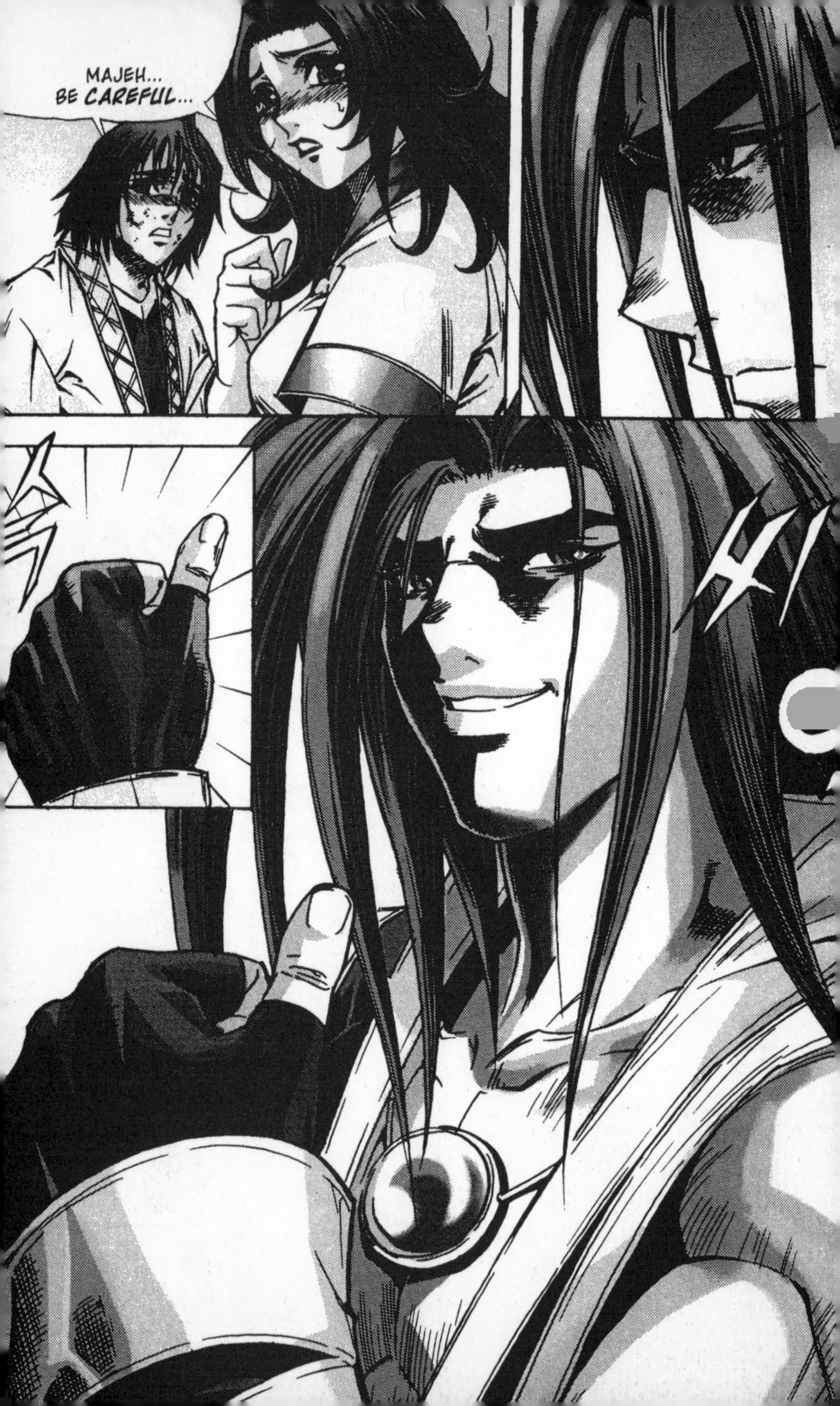
MAJEH...
BE CAREFUL...

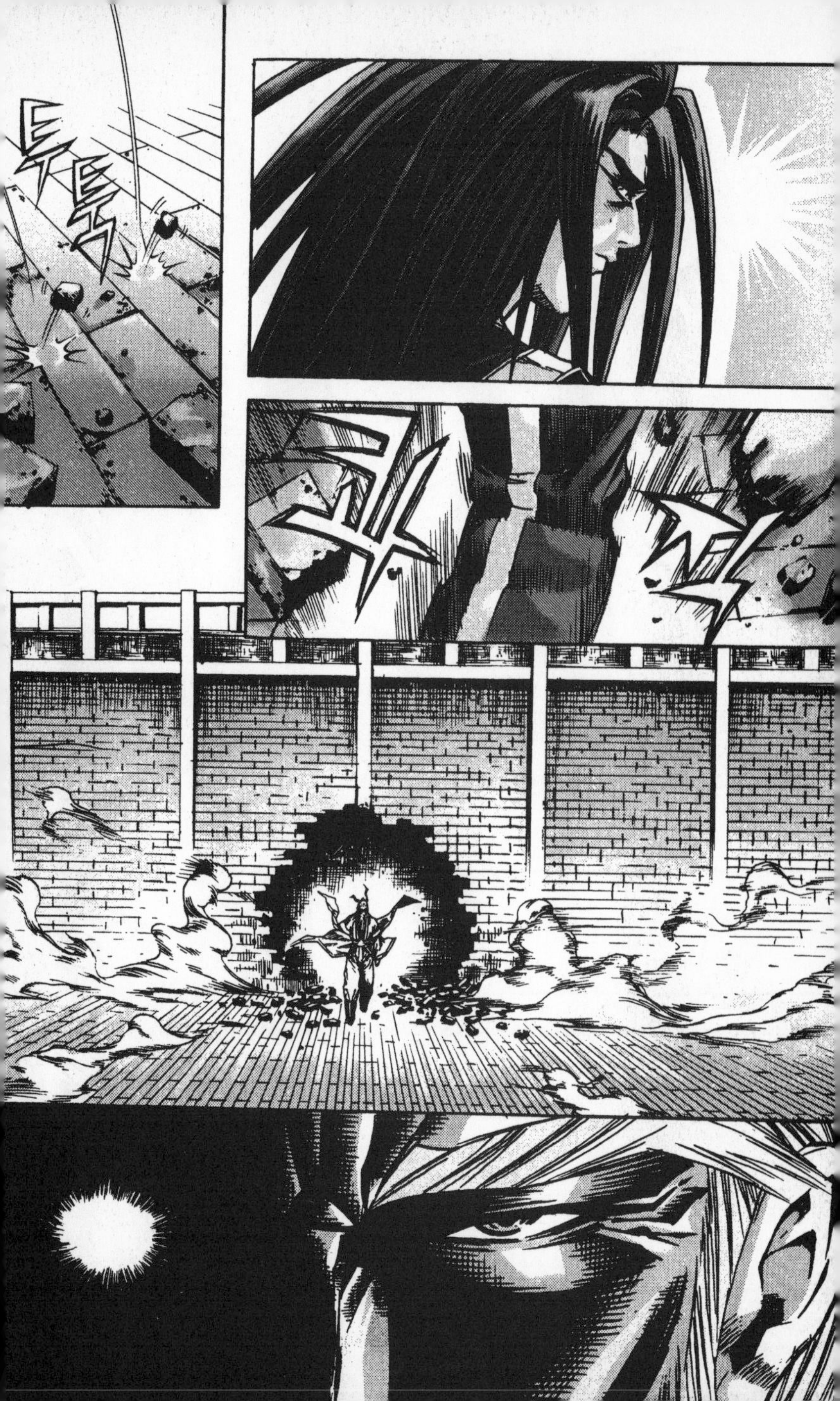

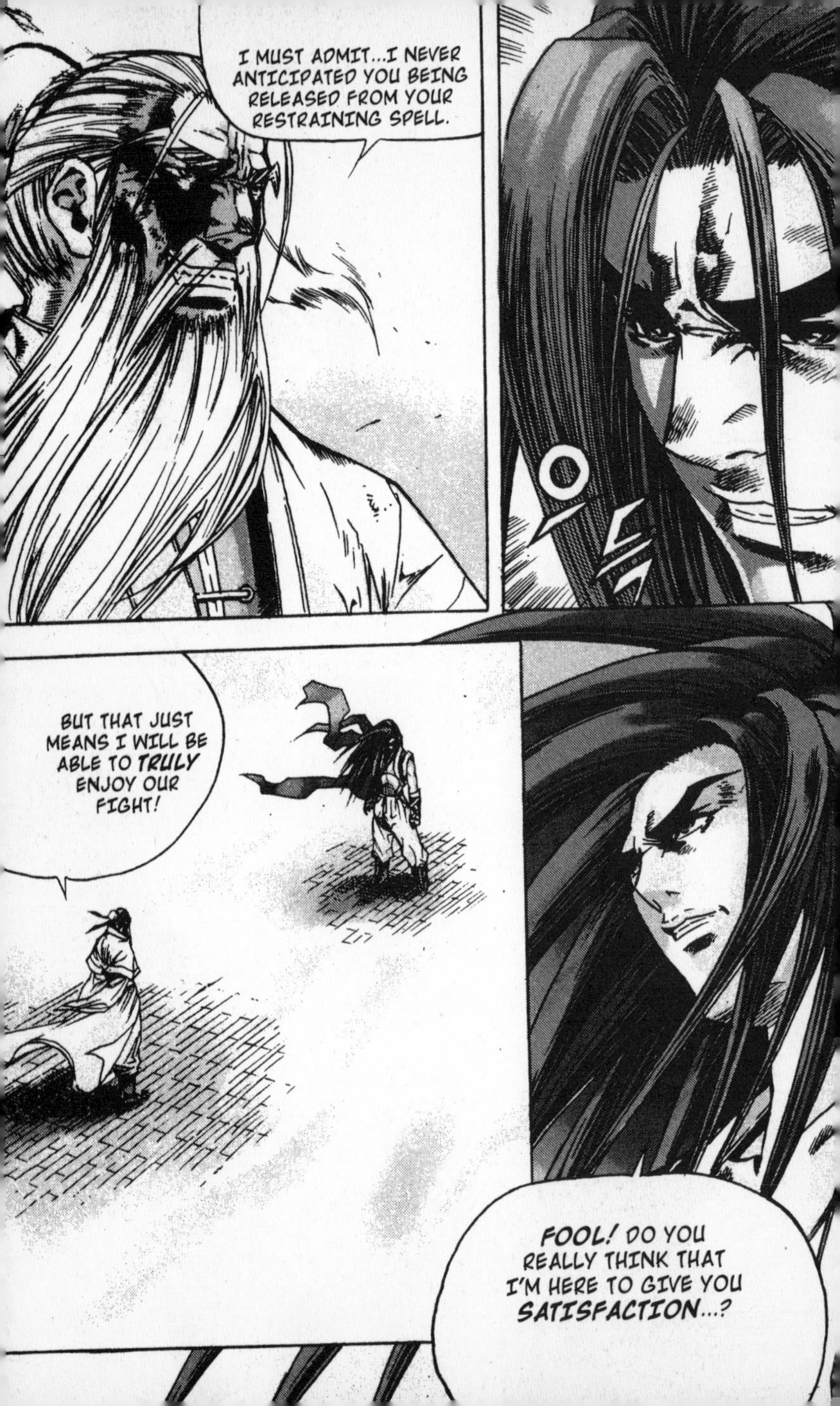
I MUST ADMIT...I NEVER ANTICIPATED YOU BEING RELEASED FROM YOUR RESTRAINING SPELL.
BUT THAT JUST MEANS I WILL BE ABLE TO *TRULY* ENJOY OUR FIGHT!
FOOL! DO YOU REALLY THINK THAT I'M HERE TO GIVE YOU *SATISFACTION*...?

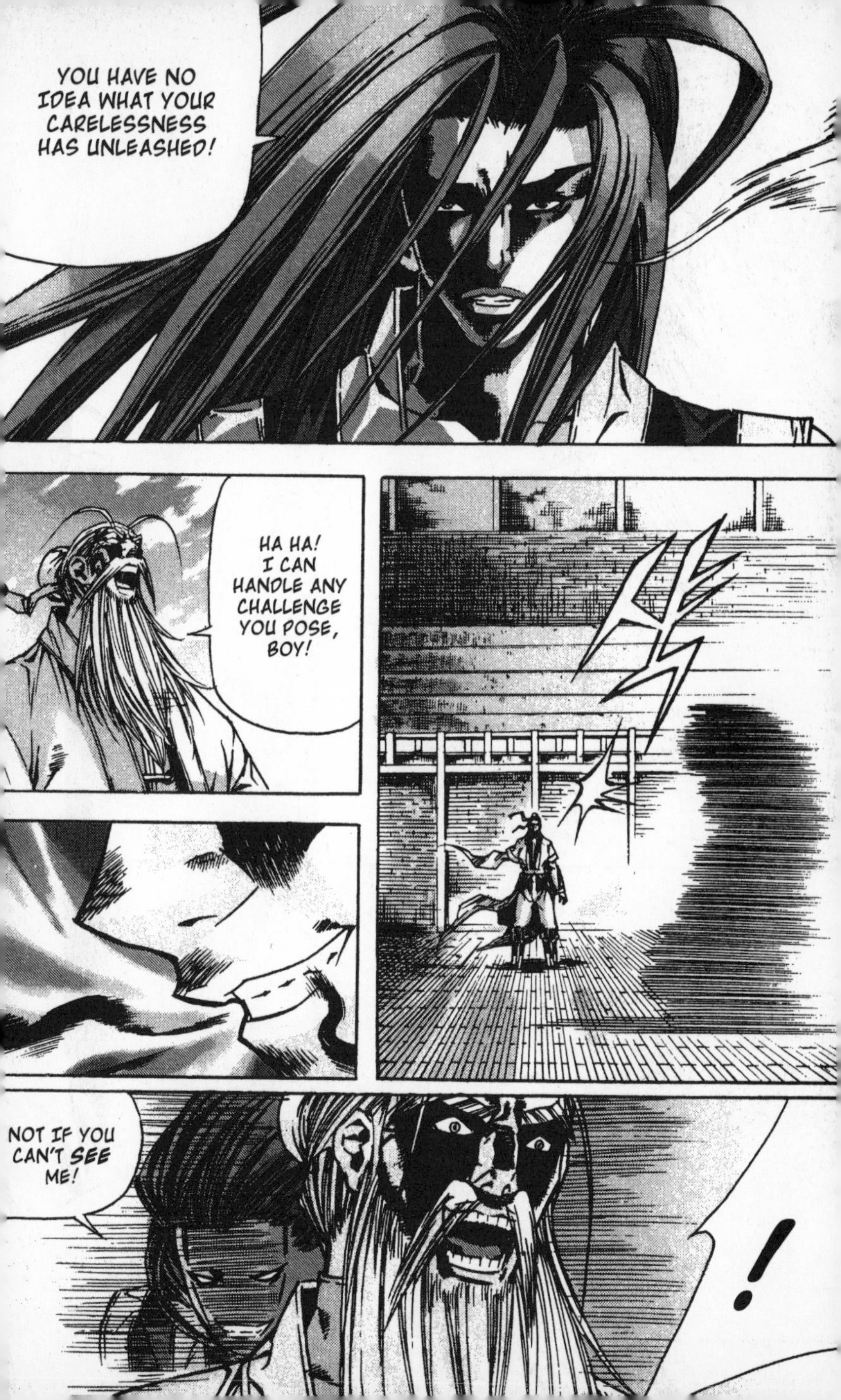
YOU HAVE NO IDEA WHAT YOUR CARELESSNESS HAS UNLEASHED!
HA HA! I CAN HANDLE ANY CHALLENGE YOU POSE, BOY!
NOT IF YOU CAN'T SEE ME!
!

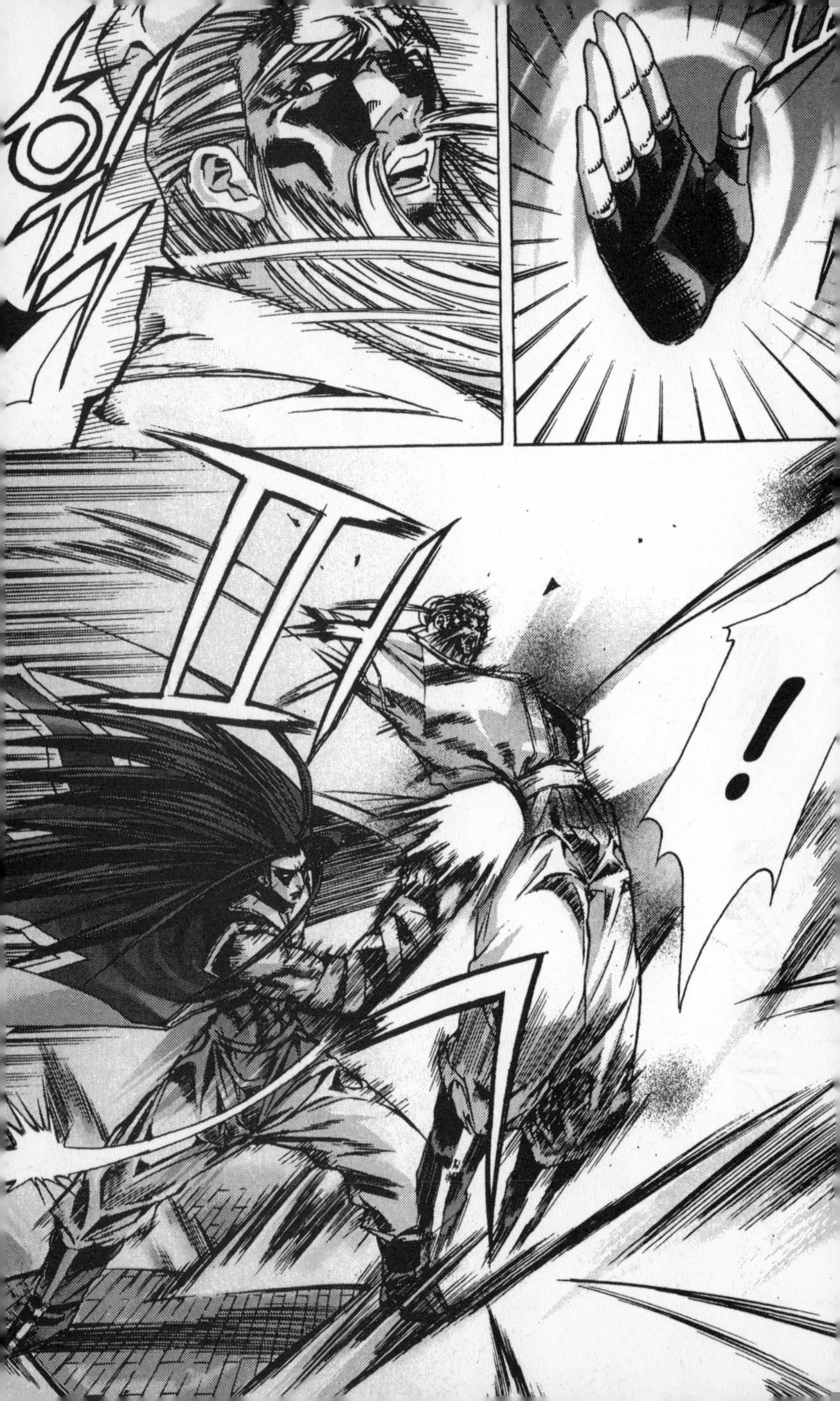
!

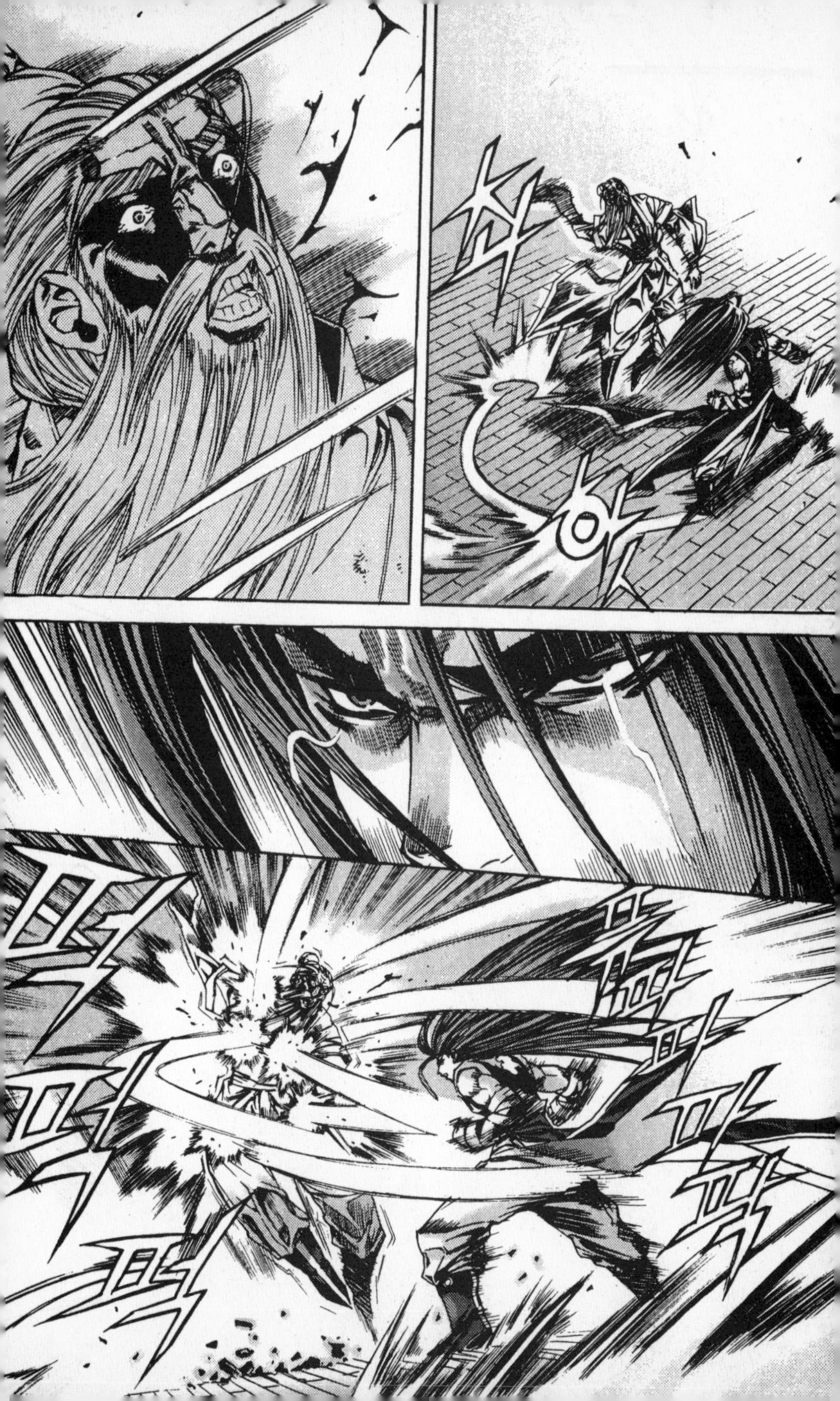

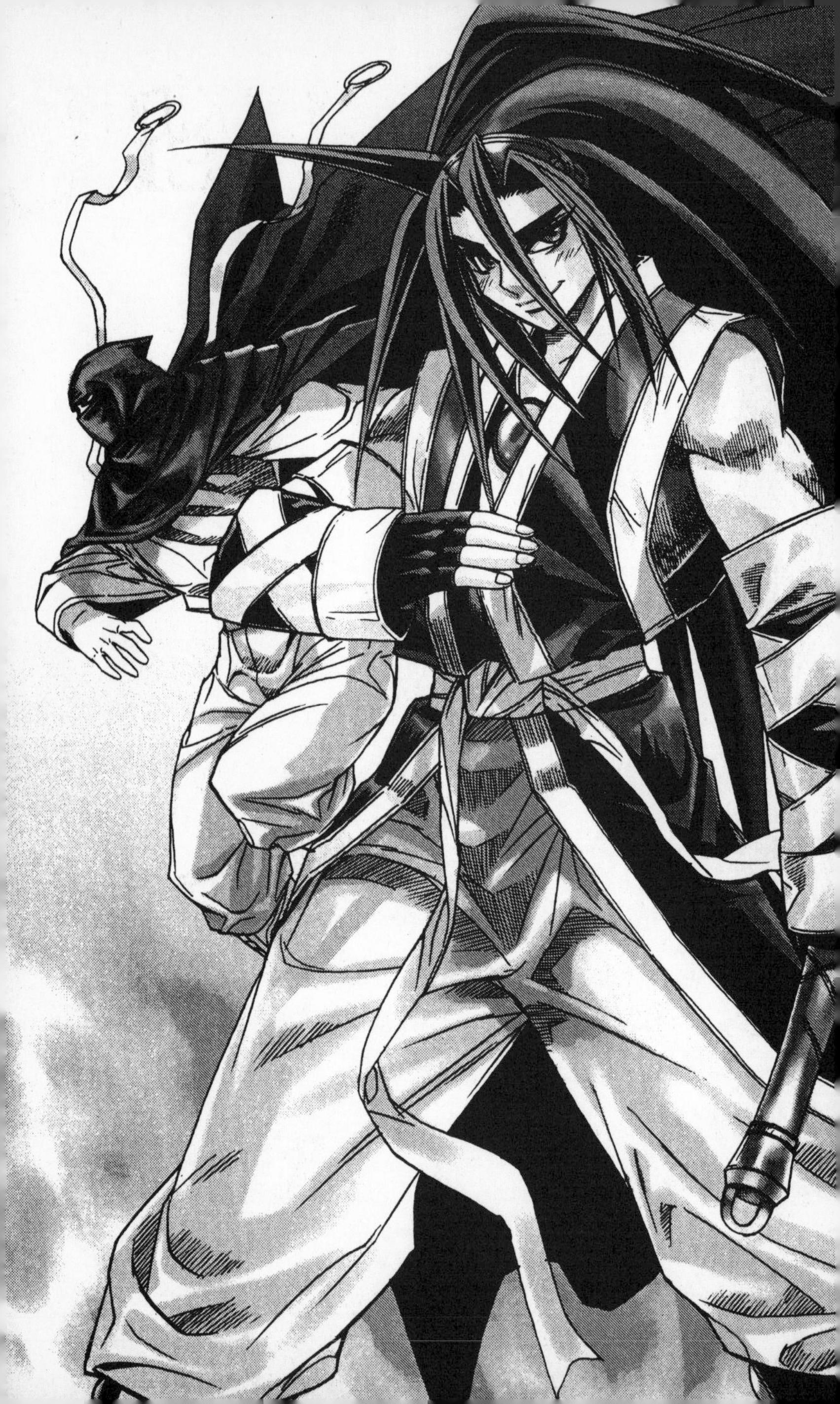

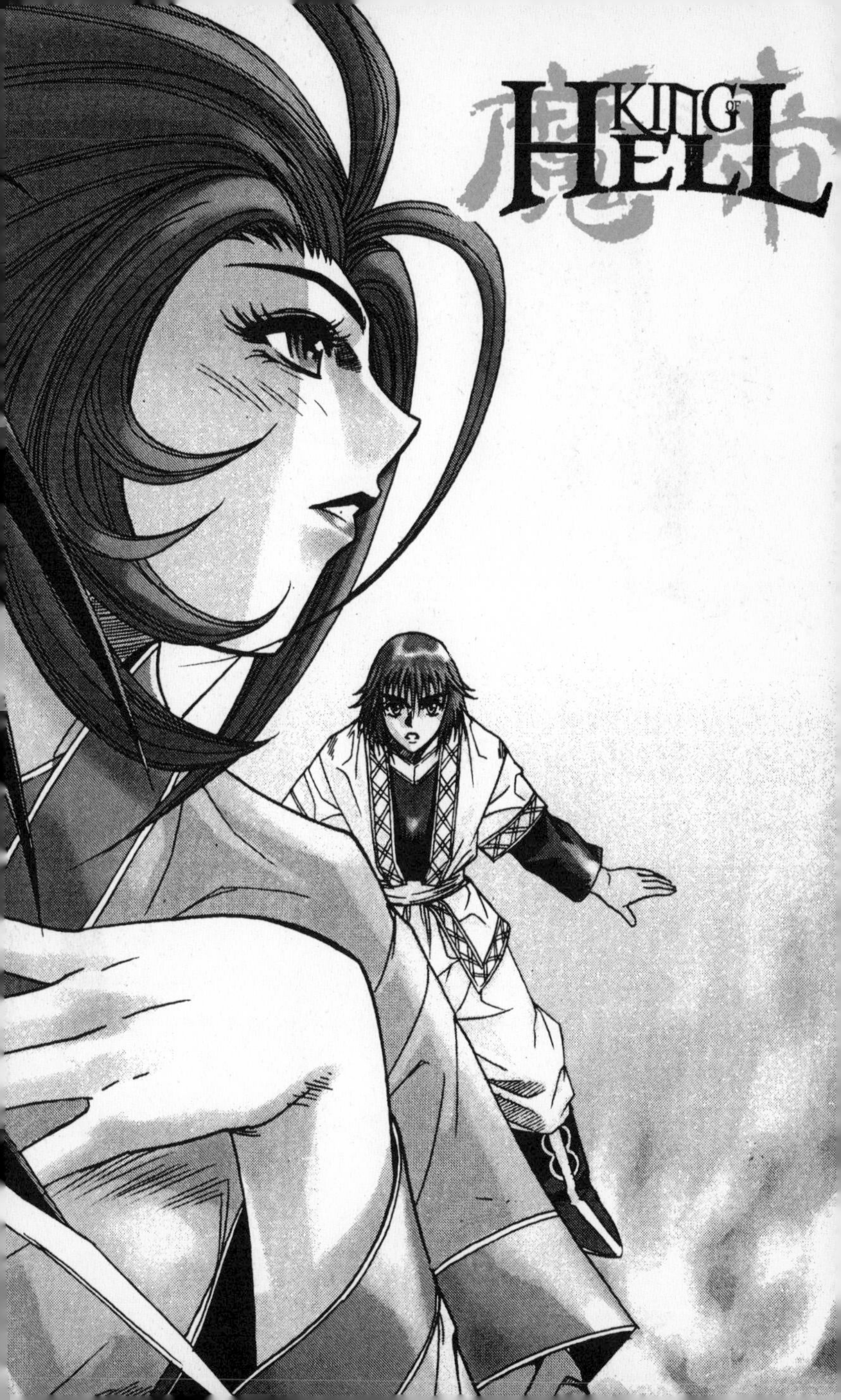
KING OF HELL

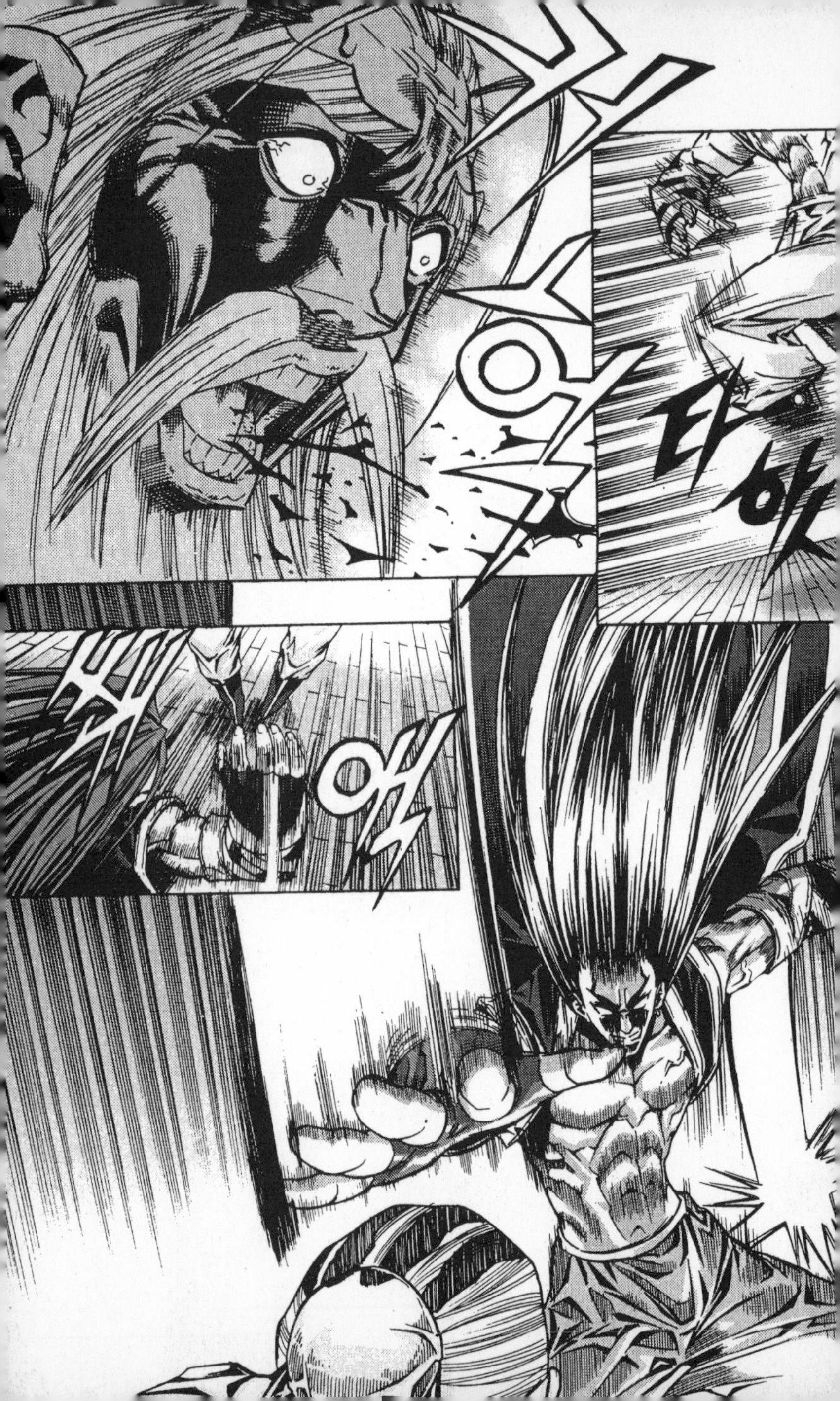

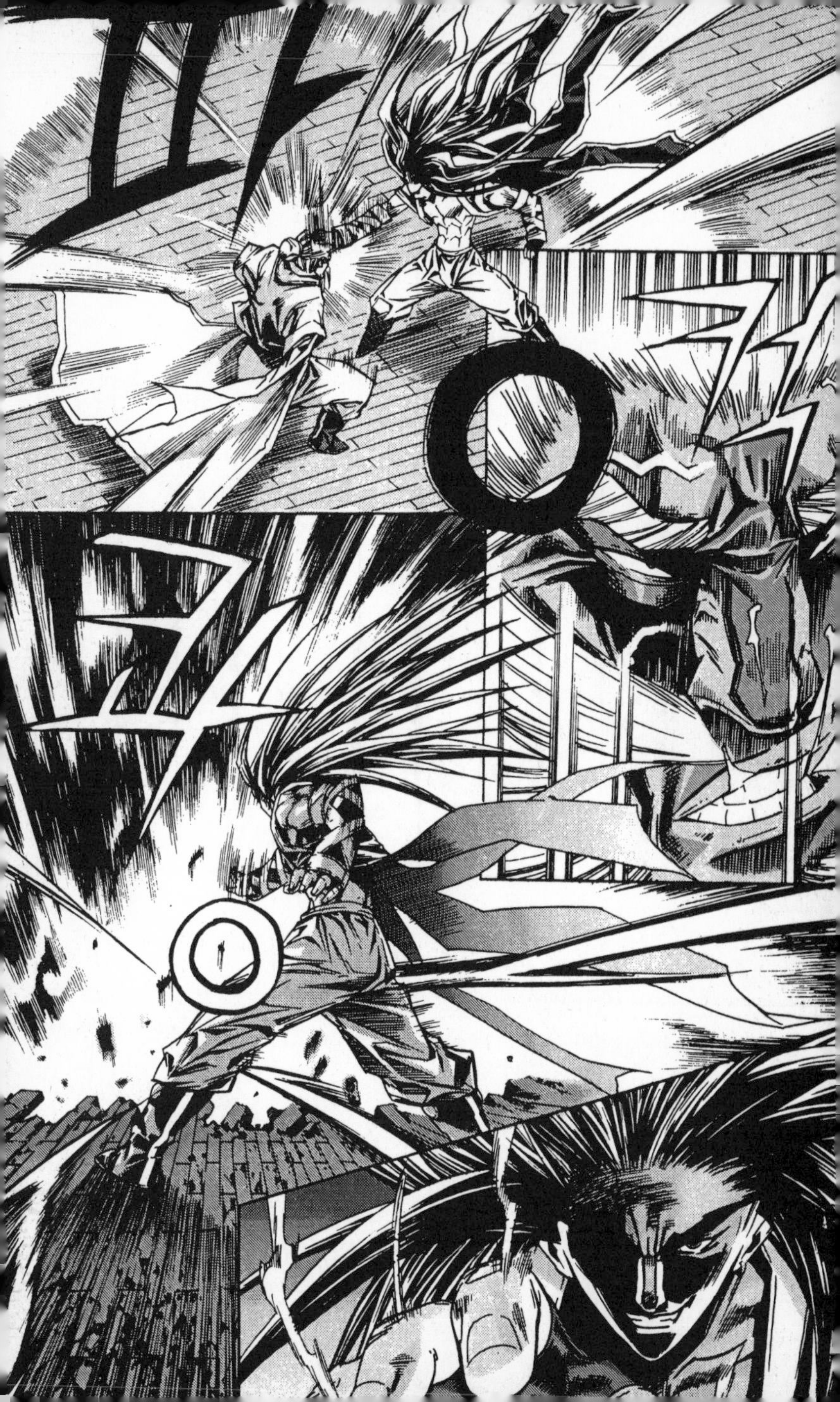

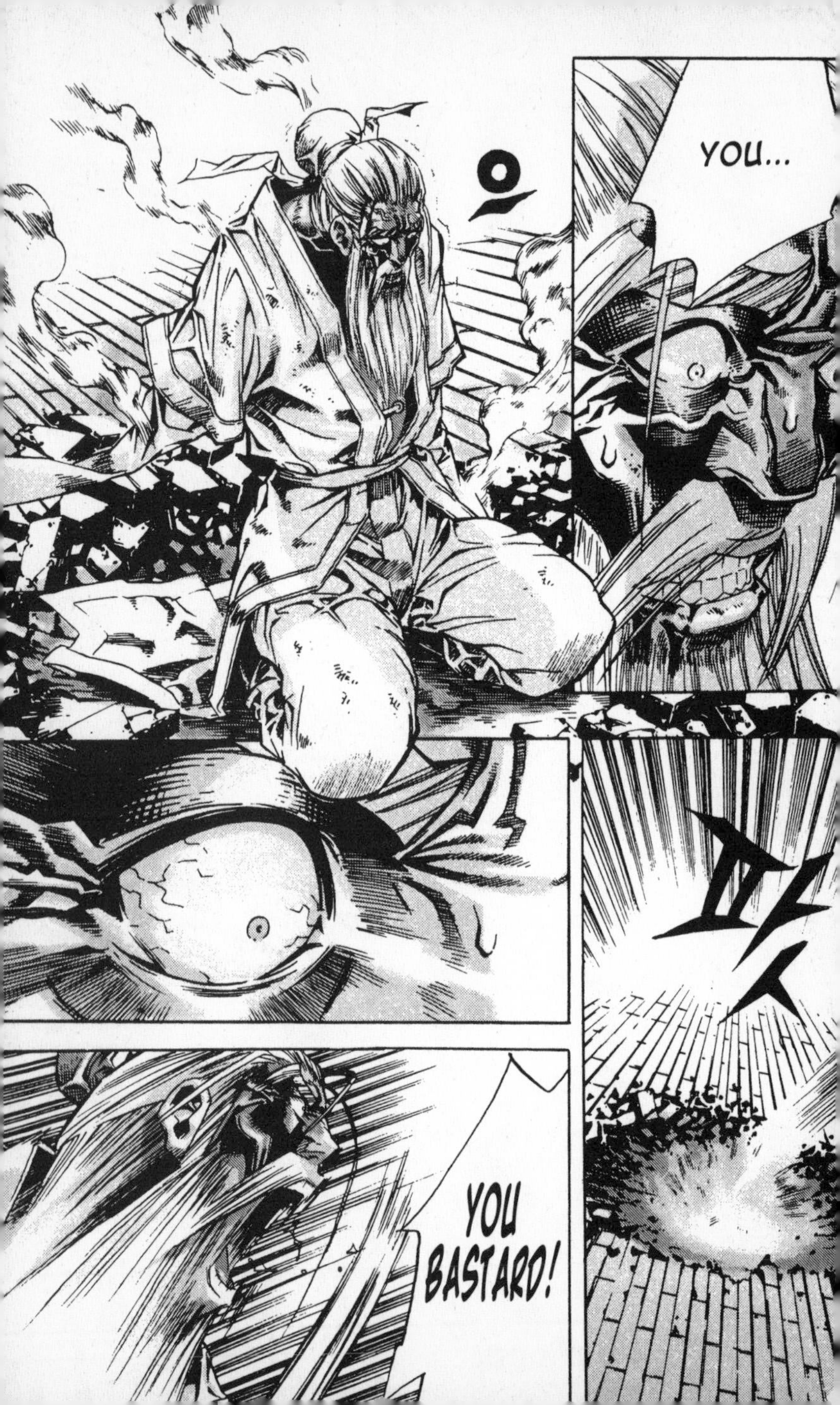
YOU...
YOU BASTARD!

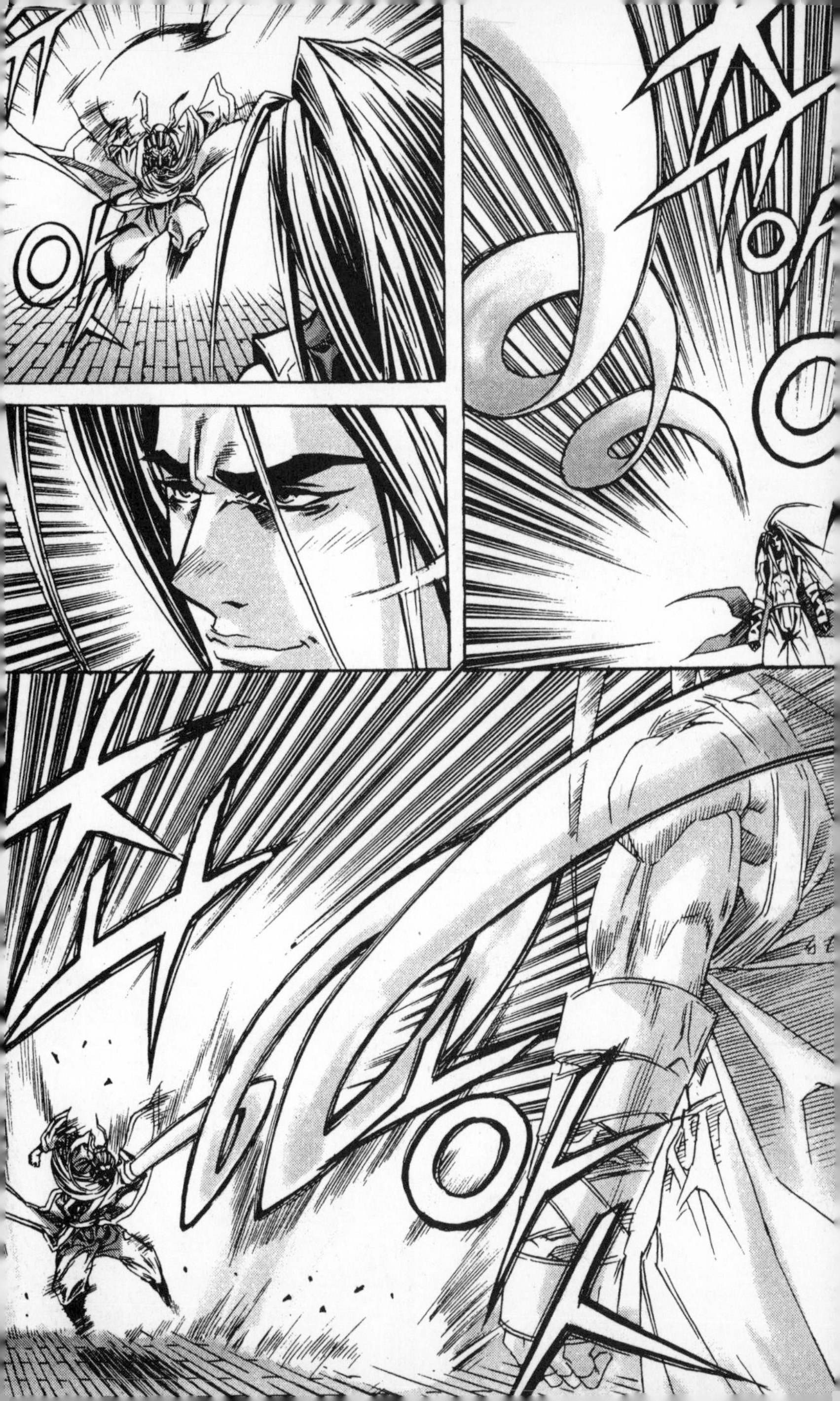

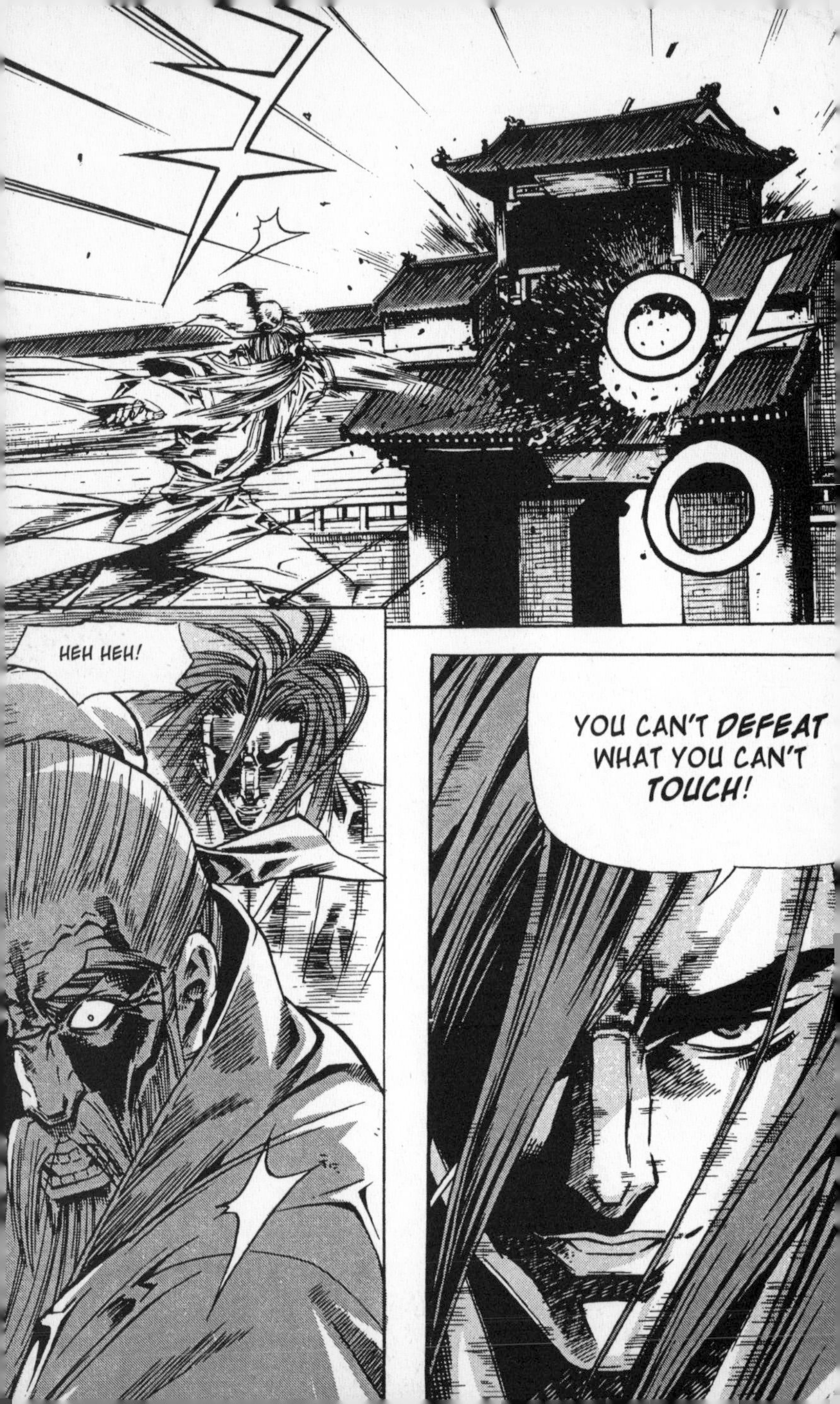
HEH HEH!
YOU CAN'T DEFEAT WHAT YOU CAN'T TOUCH!

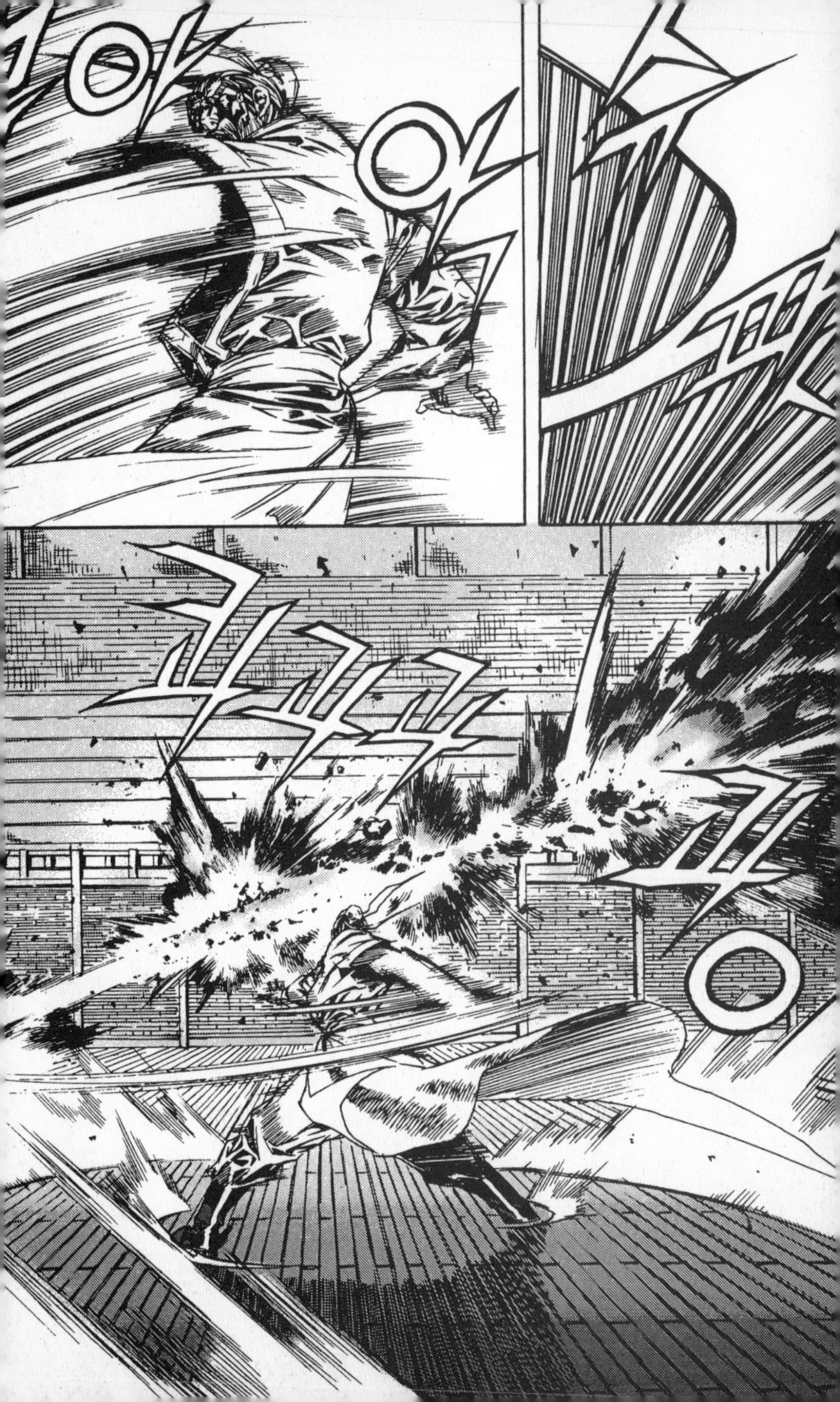

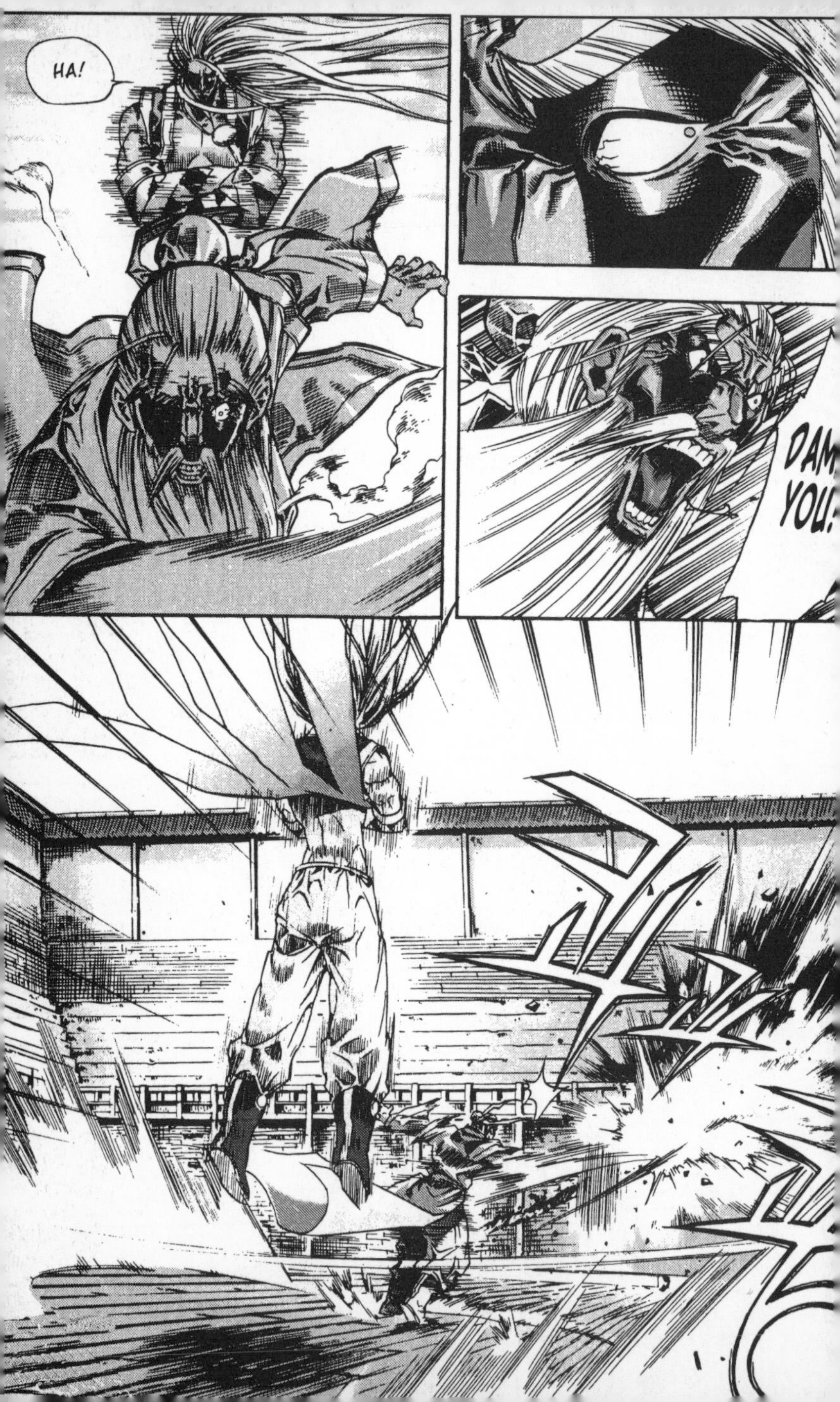
HA!
DAMN YOU!

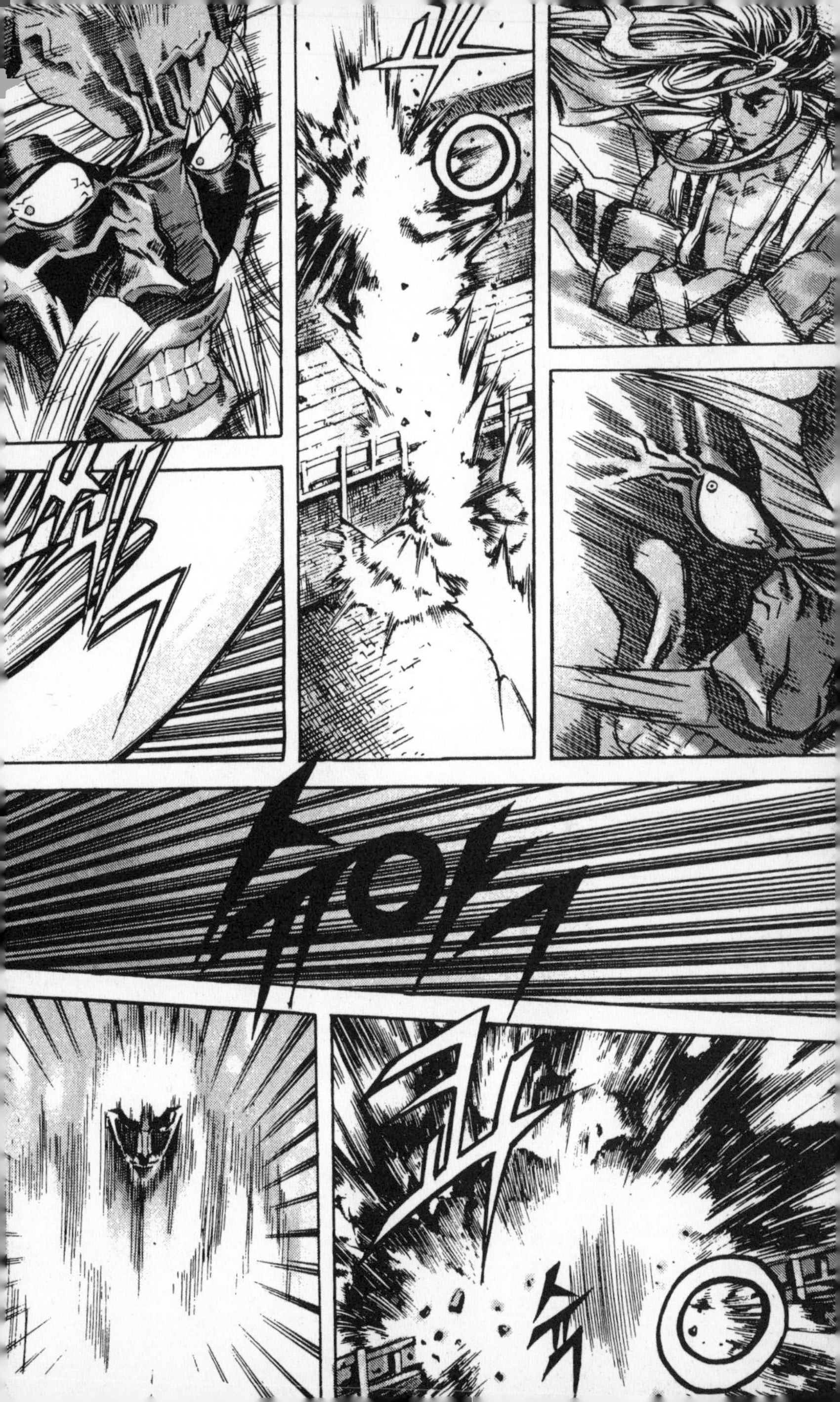

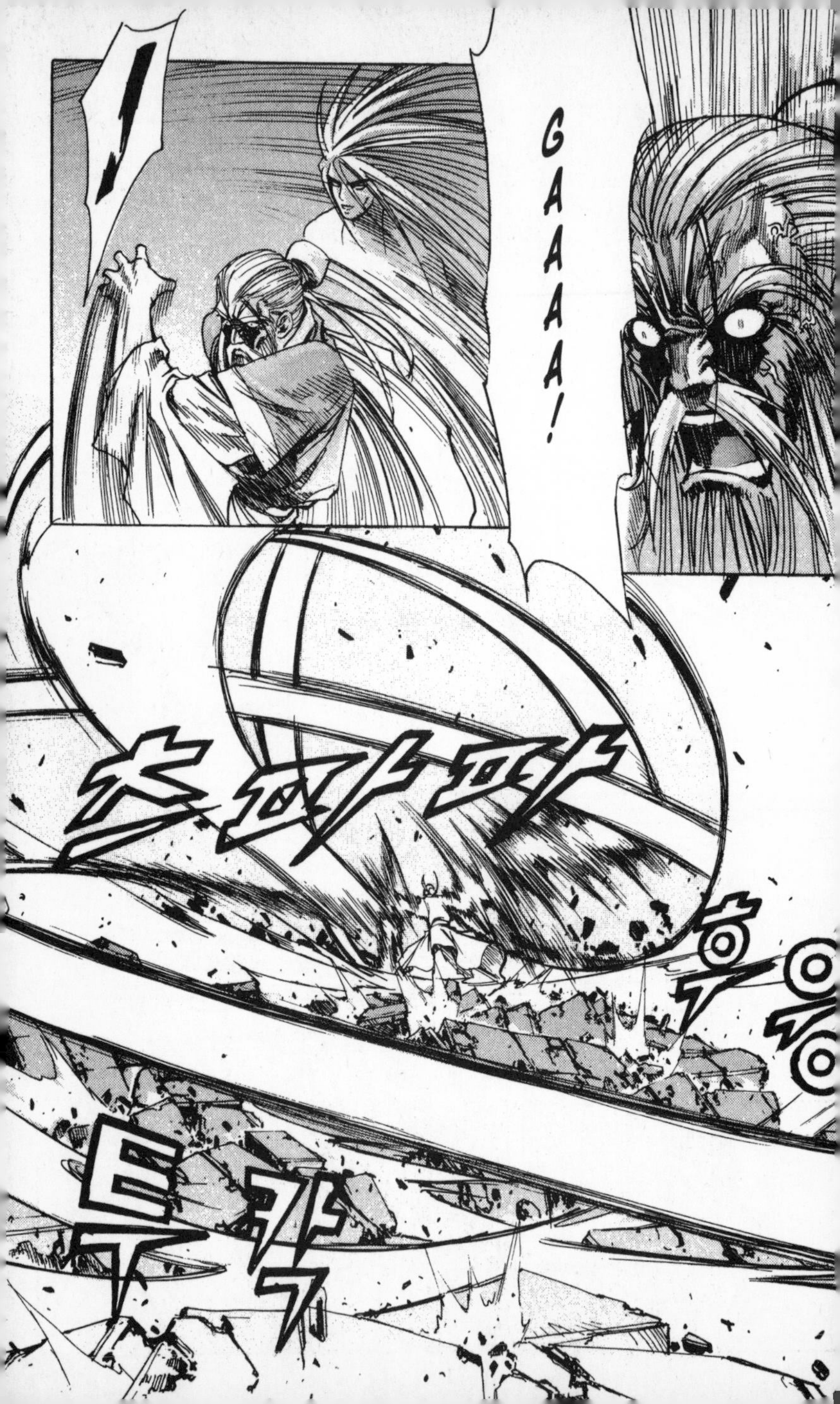

!
GAAAAA!

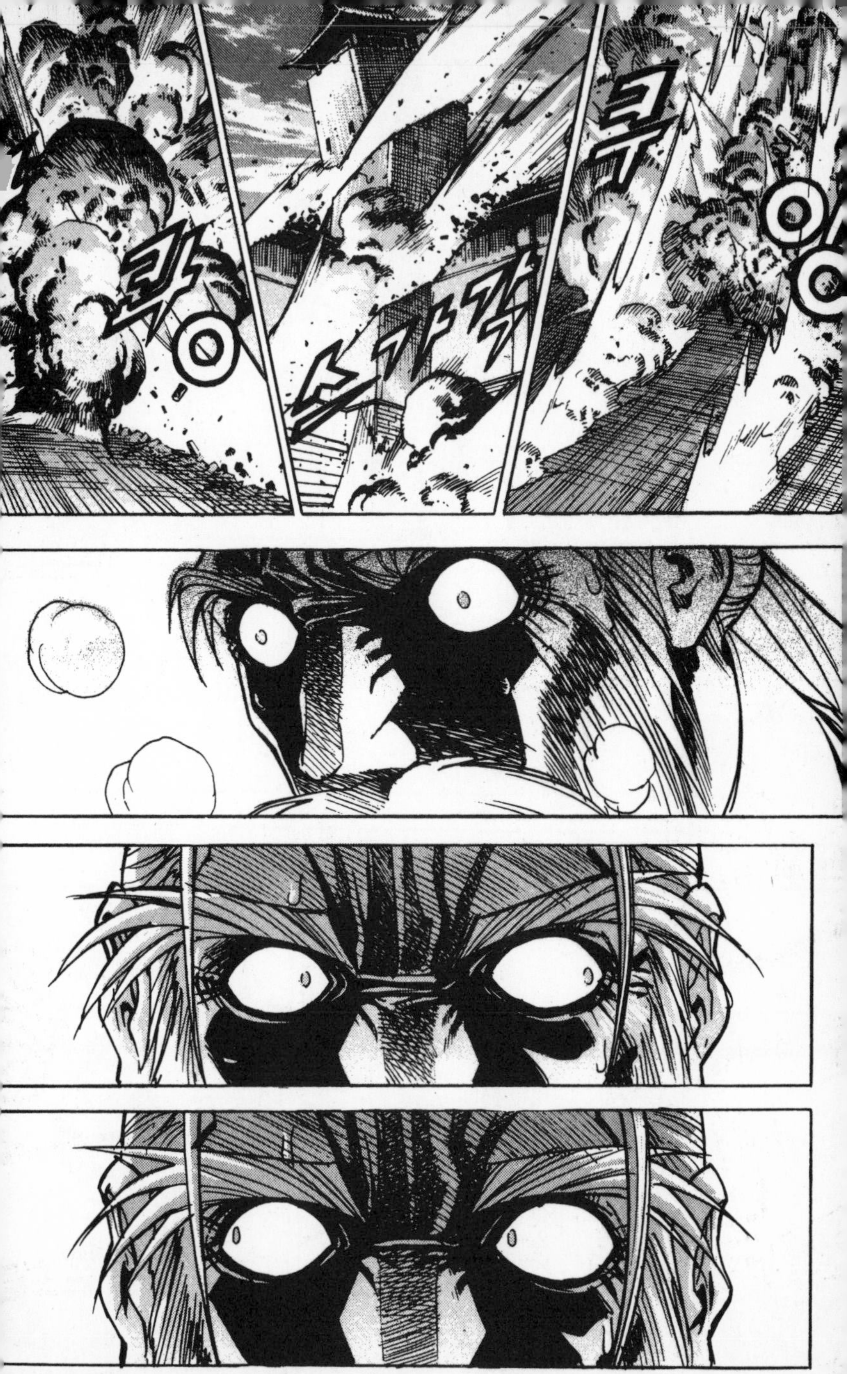

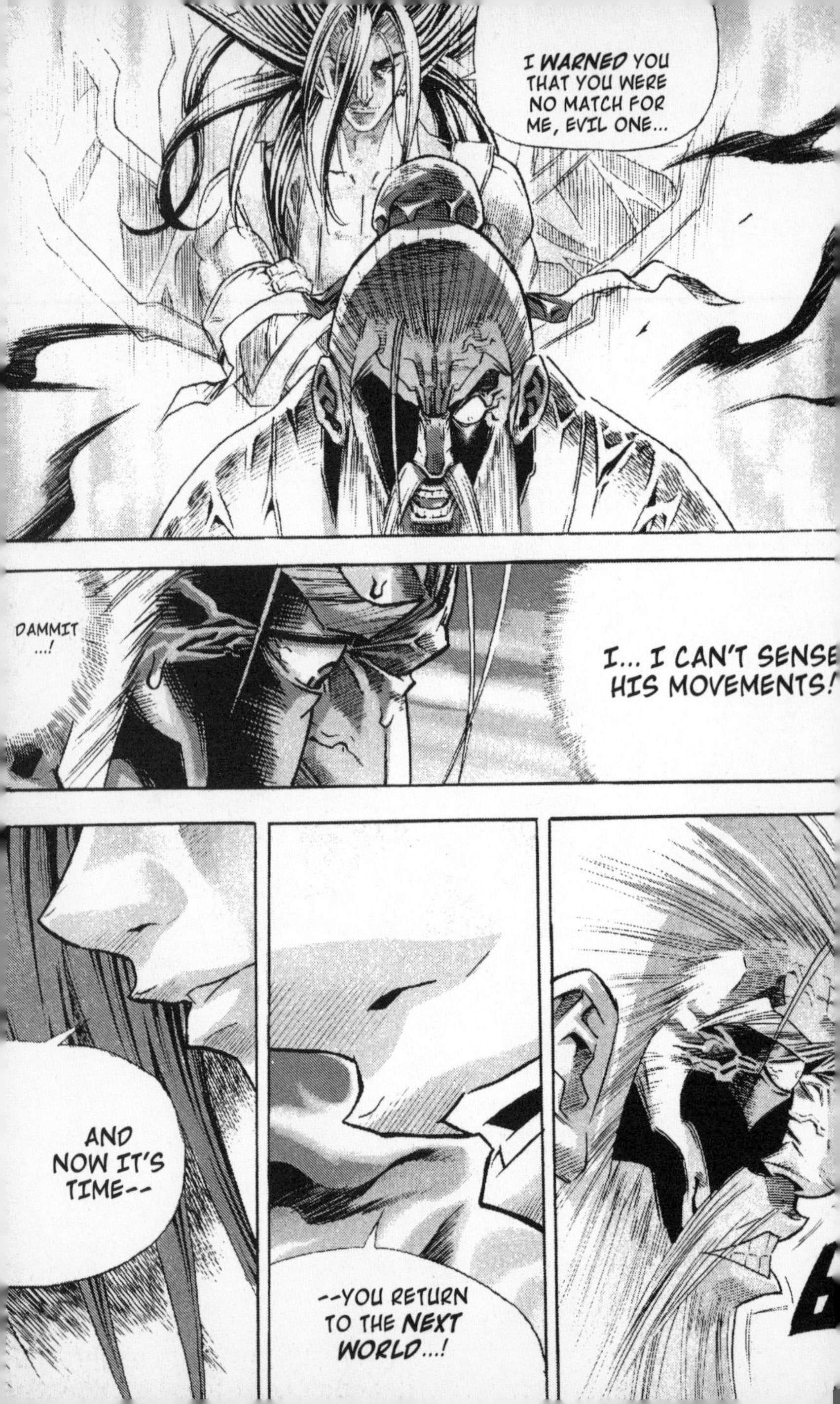
I WARNED YOU THAT YOU WERE NO MATCH FOR ME, EVIL ONE...
DAMMIT ...!
I... I CAN'T SENSE HIS MOVEMENTS!
AND NOW IT'S TIME--
--YOU RETURN TO THE NEXT WORLD...!

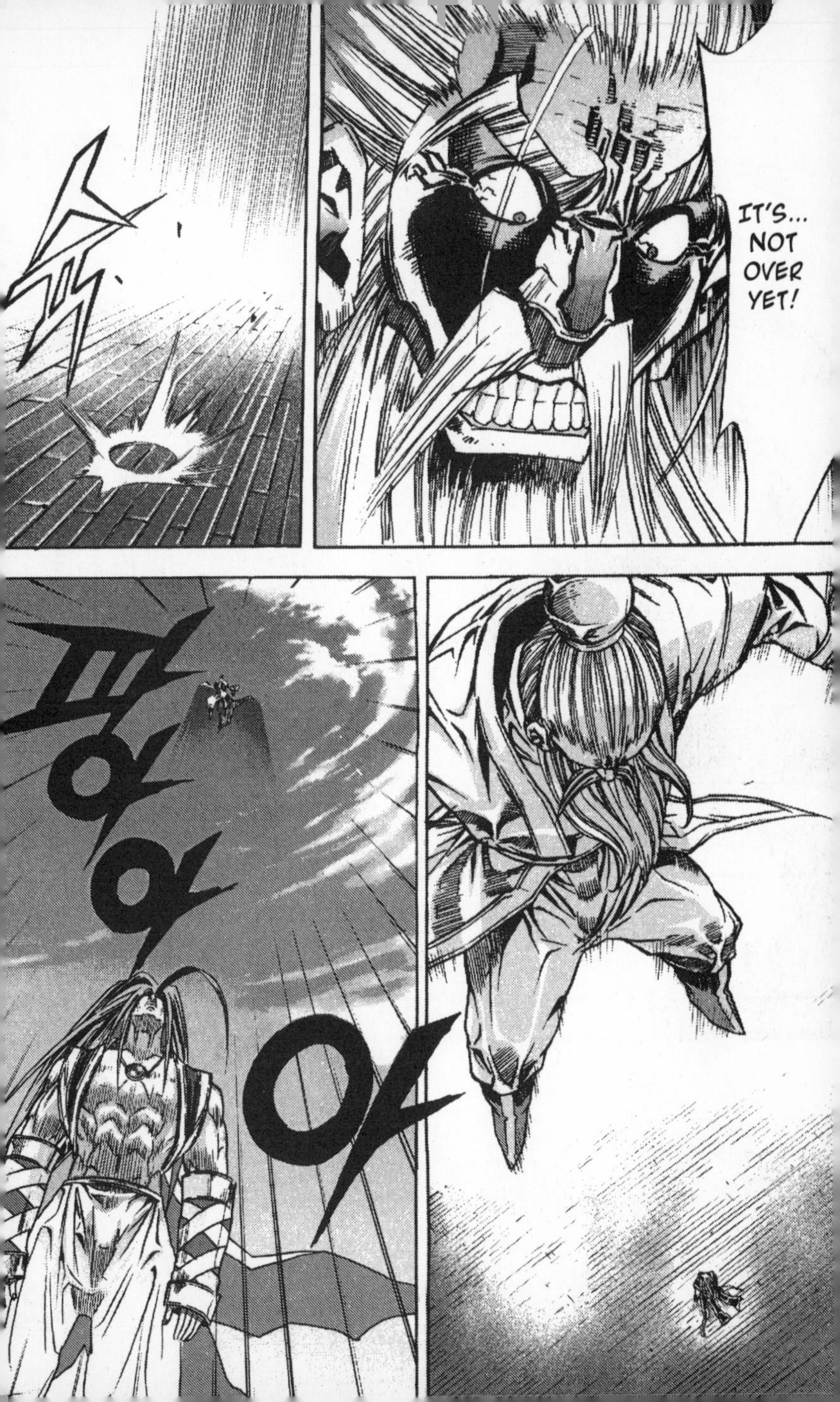
IT'S... NOT OVER YET!
파아아아

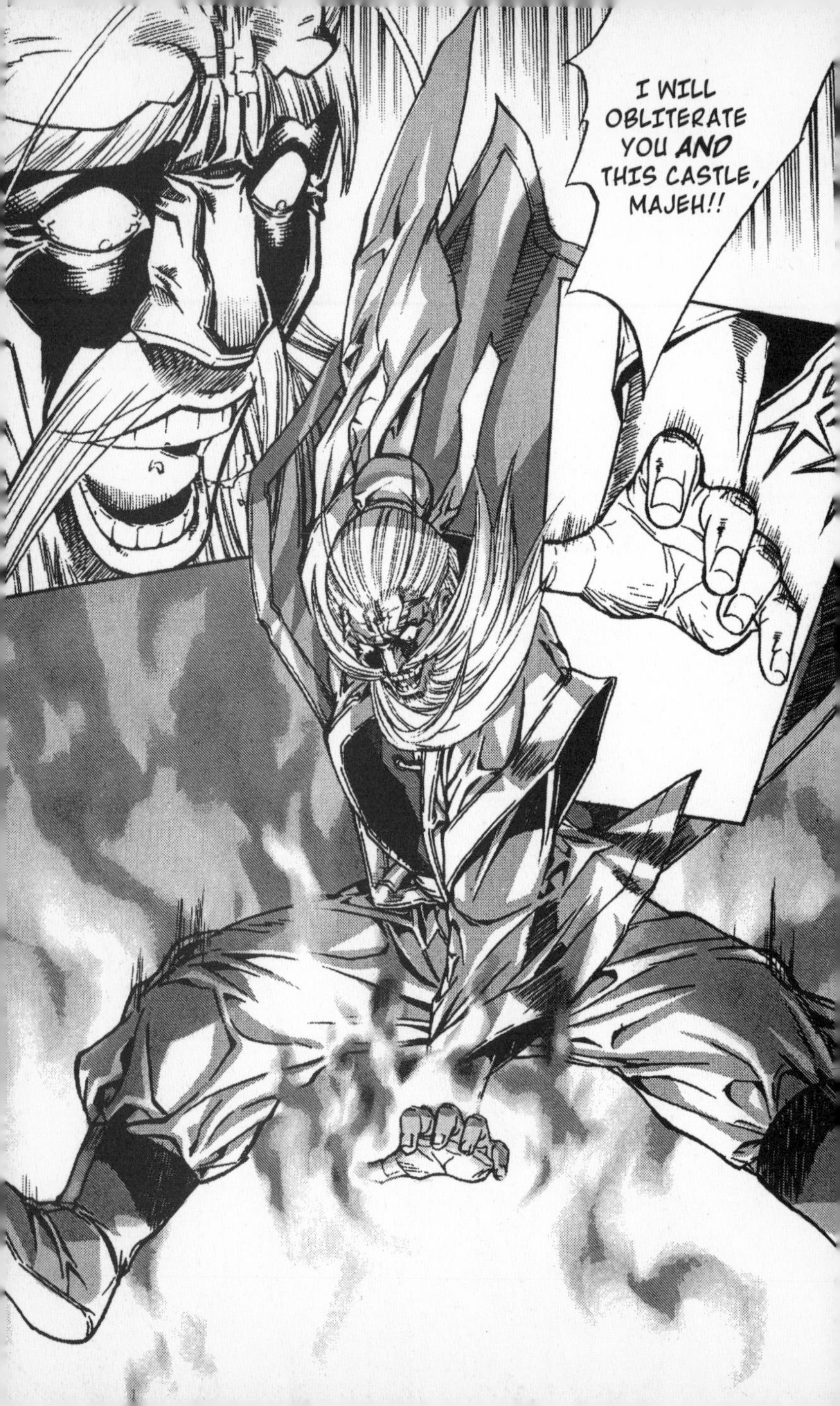
I WILL OBLITERATE YOU AND THIS CASTLE, MAJEH!!

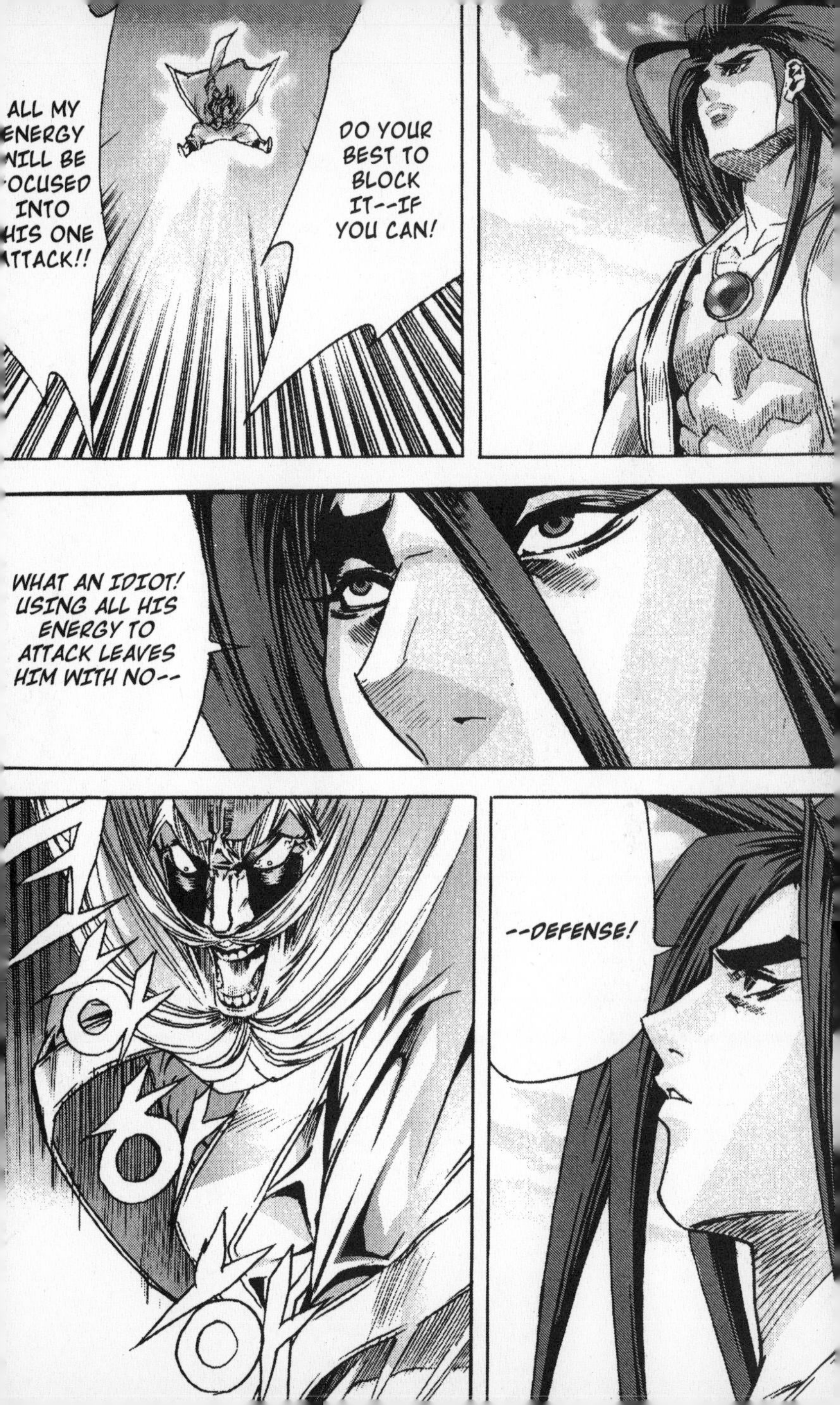
ALL MY ENERGY WILL BE FOCUSED INTO THIS ONE ATTACK!!
DO YOUR BEST TO BLOCK IT--IF YOU CAN!
WHAT AN IDIOT! USING ALL HIS ENERGY TO ATTACK LEAVES HIM WITH NO--
--DEFENSE!

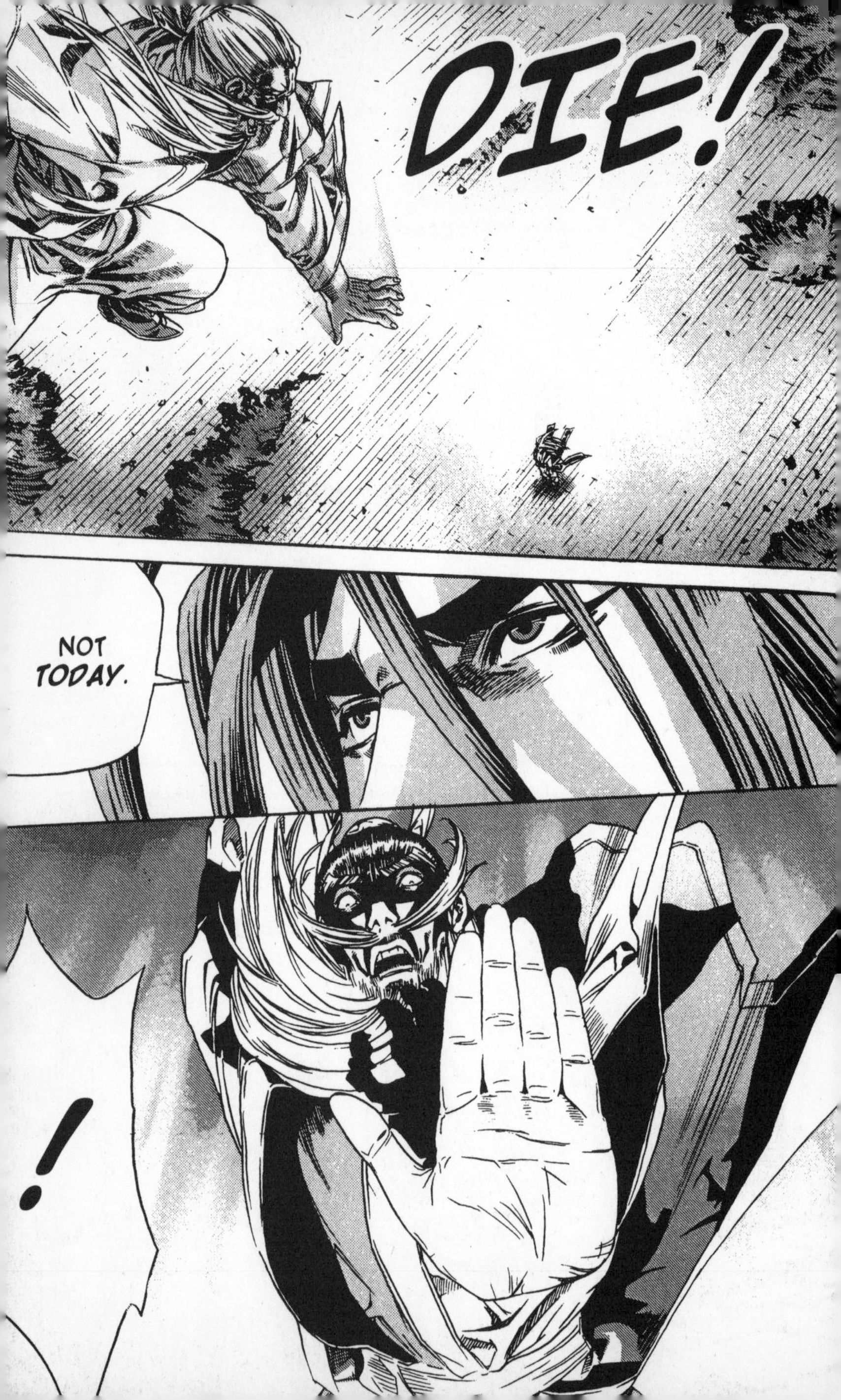
DIE!
NOT TODAY.
!

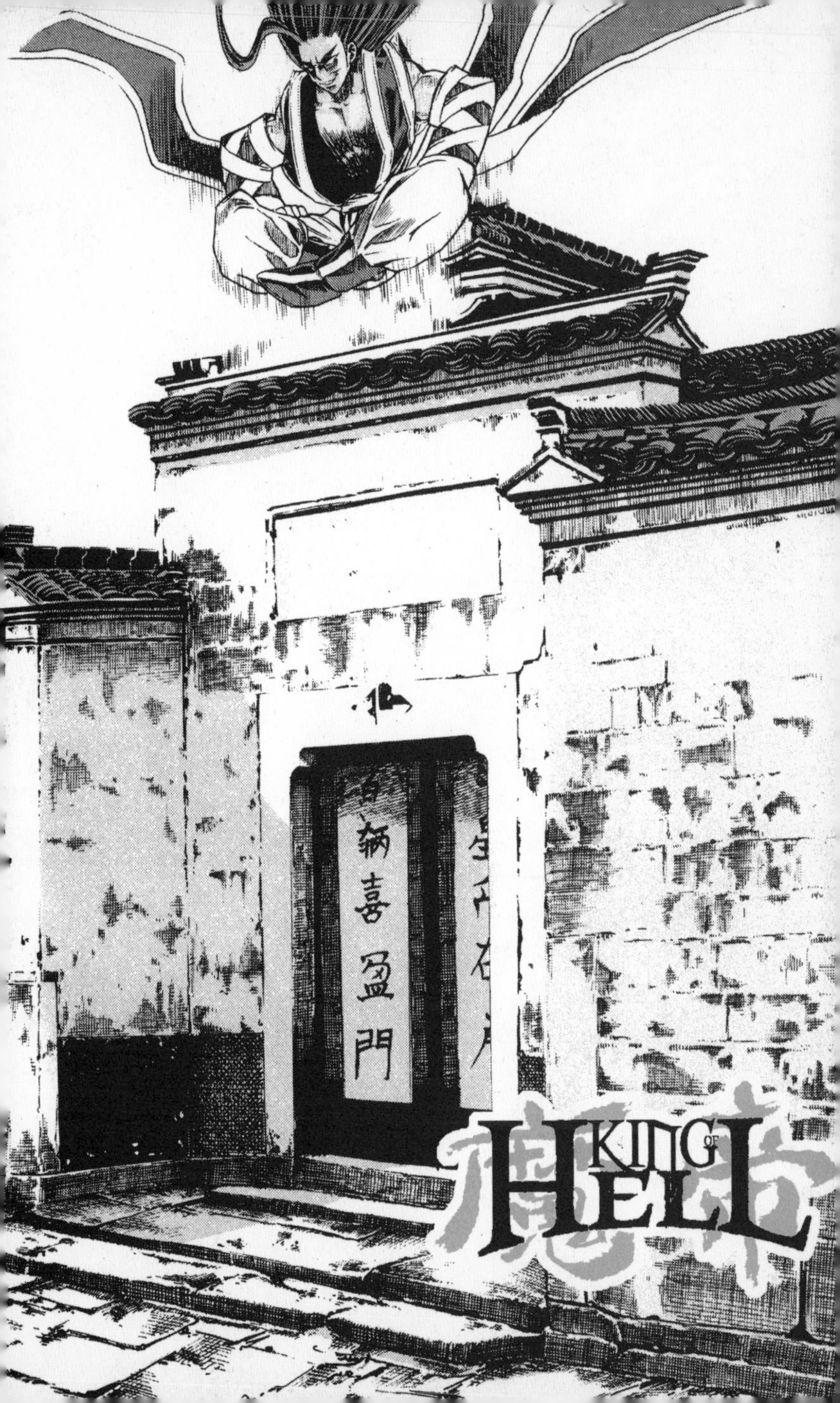
KING OF HELL

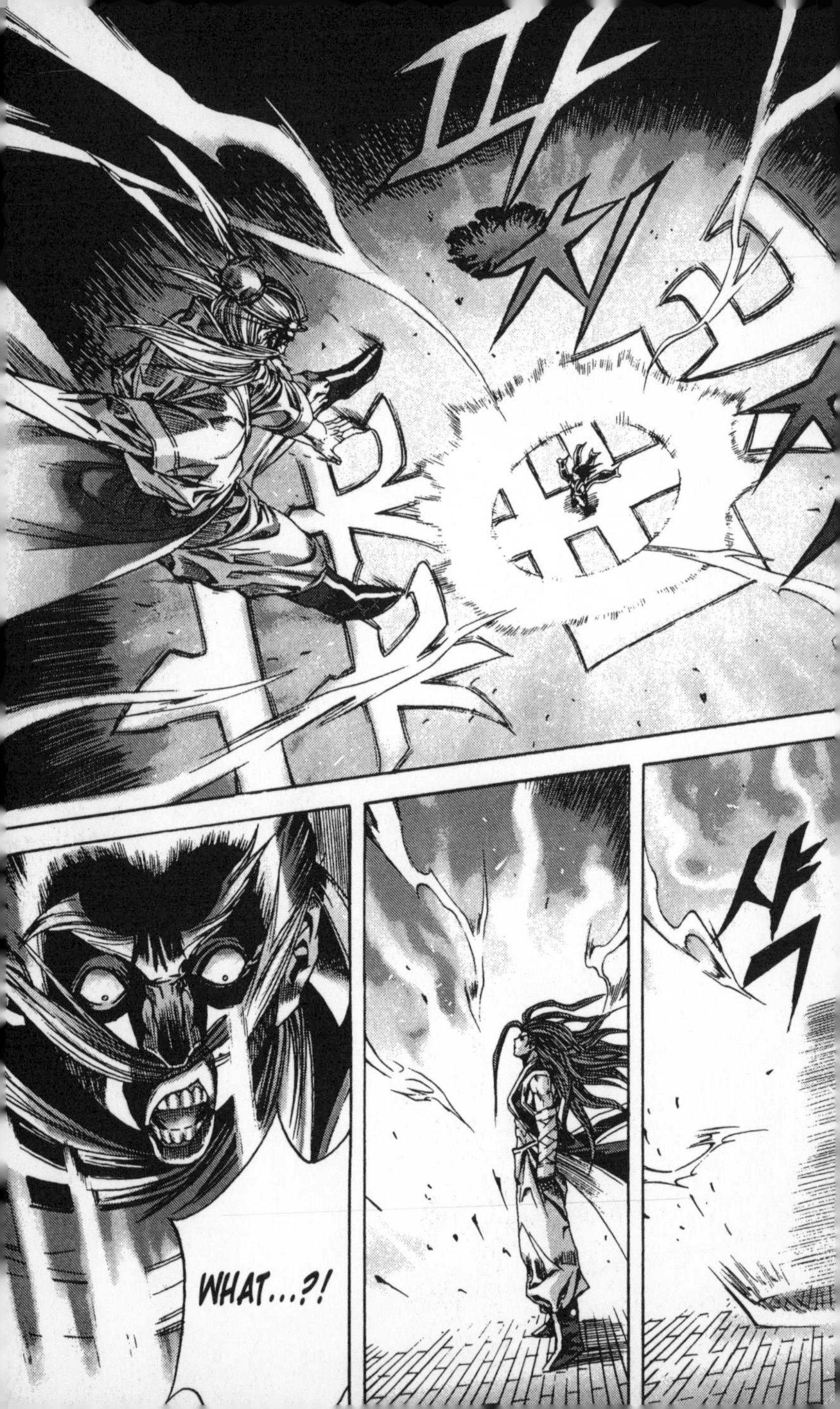
WHAT...?!

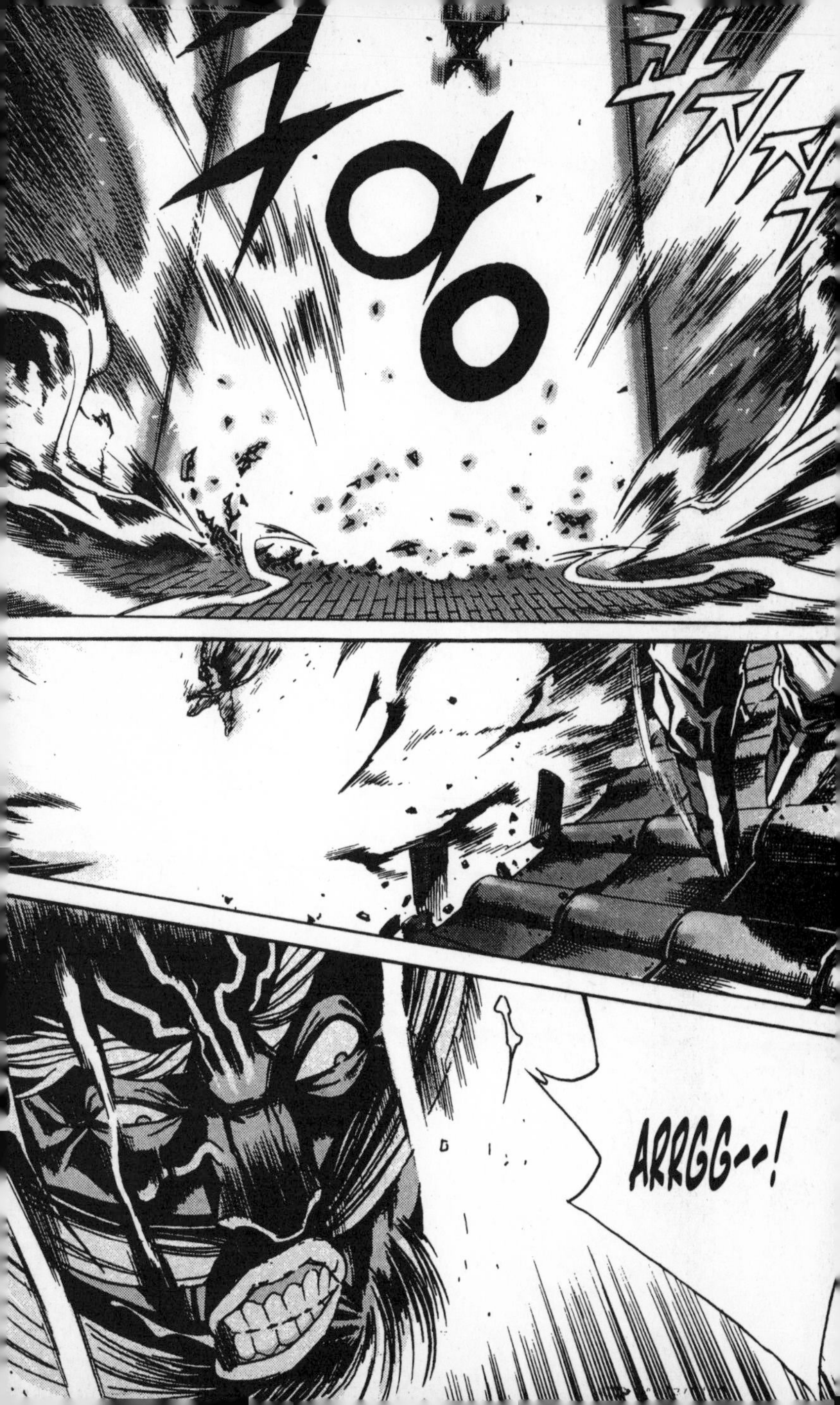
ARRGG--!

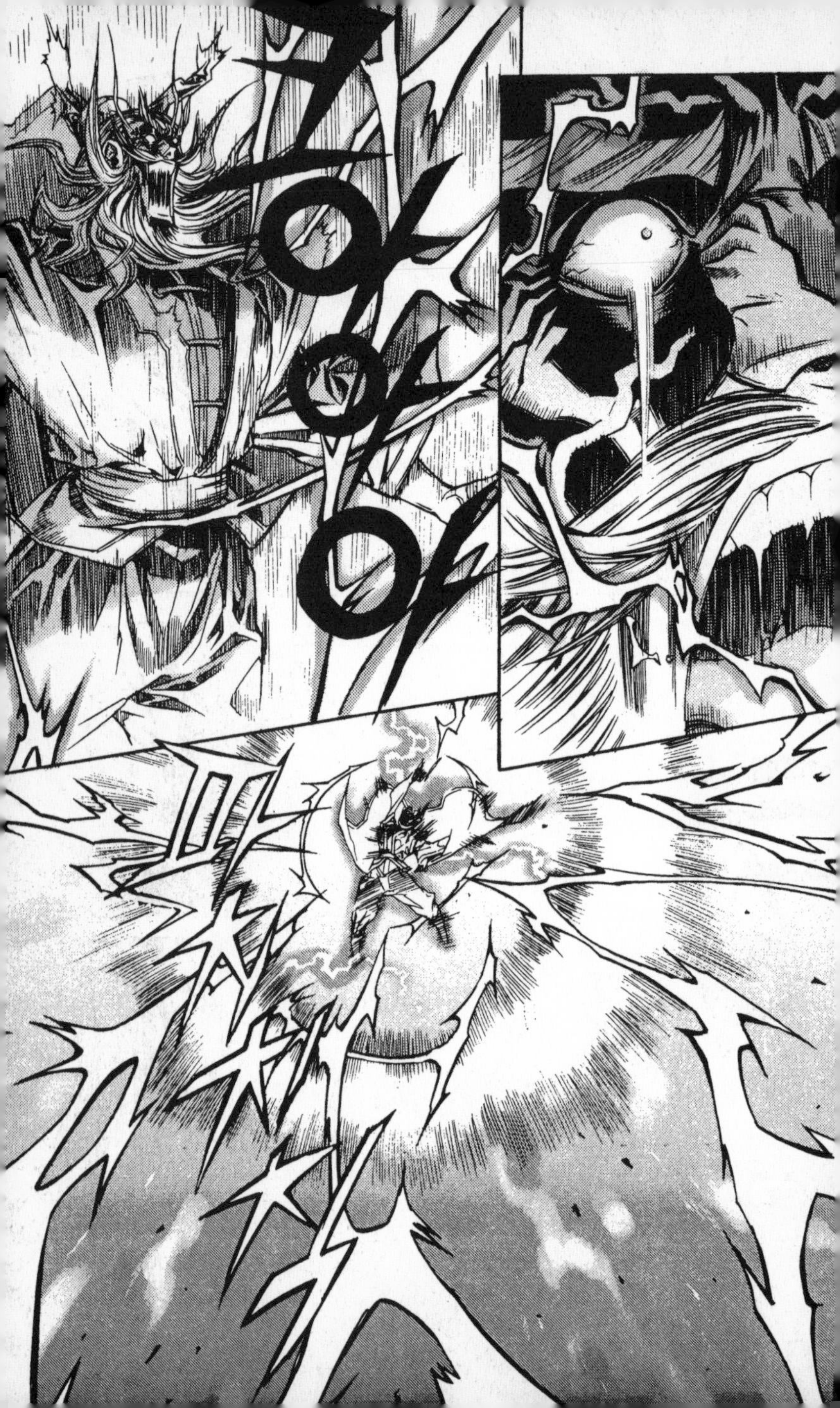
ZOKOKOK

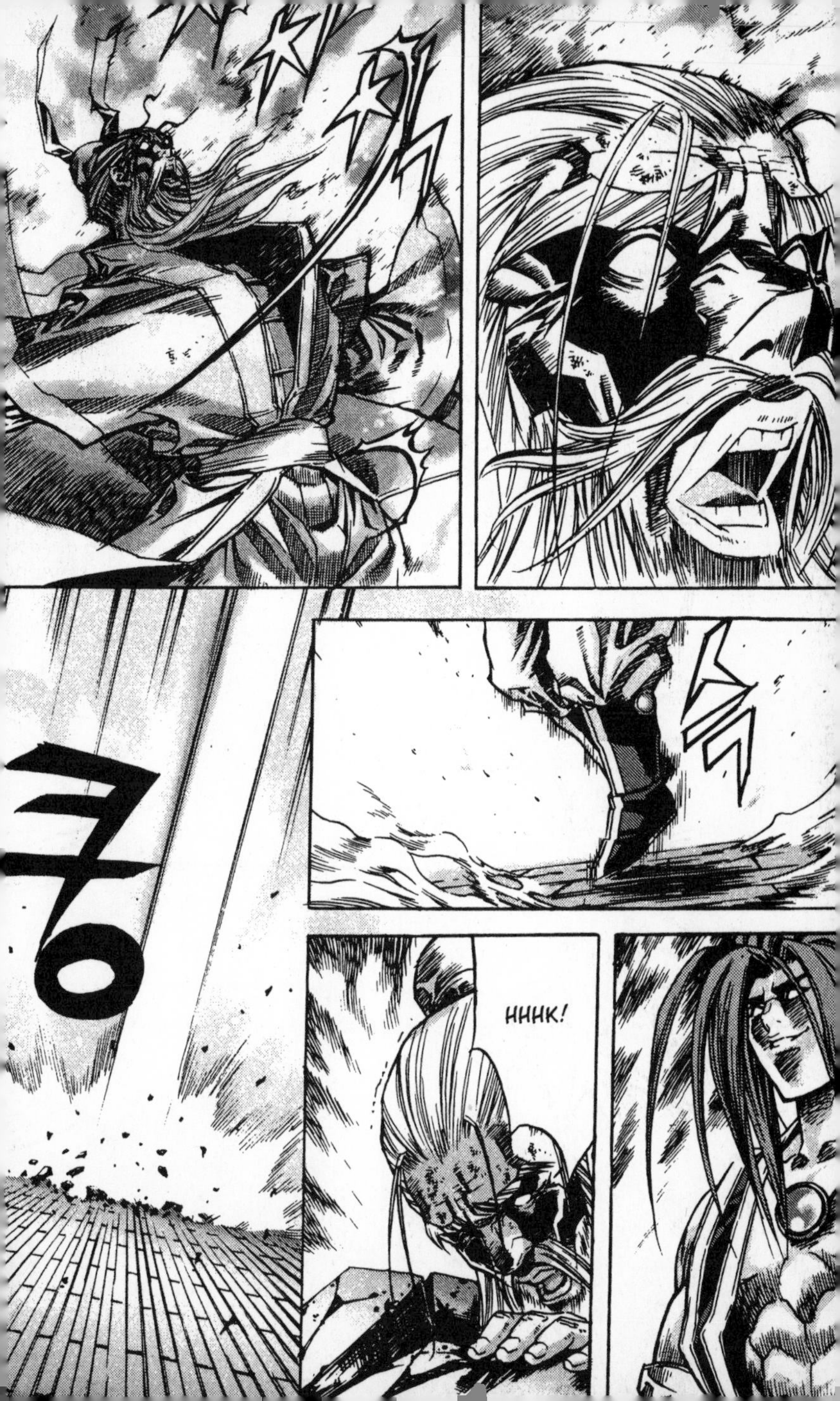
HHHK!

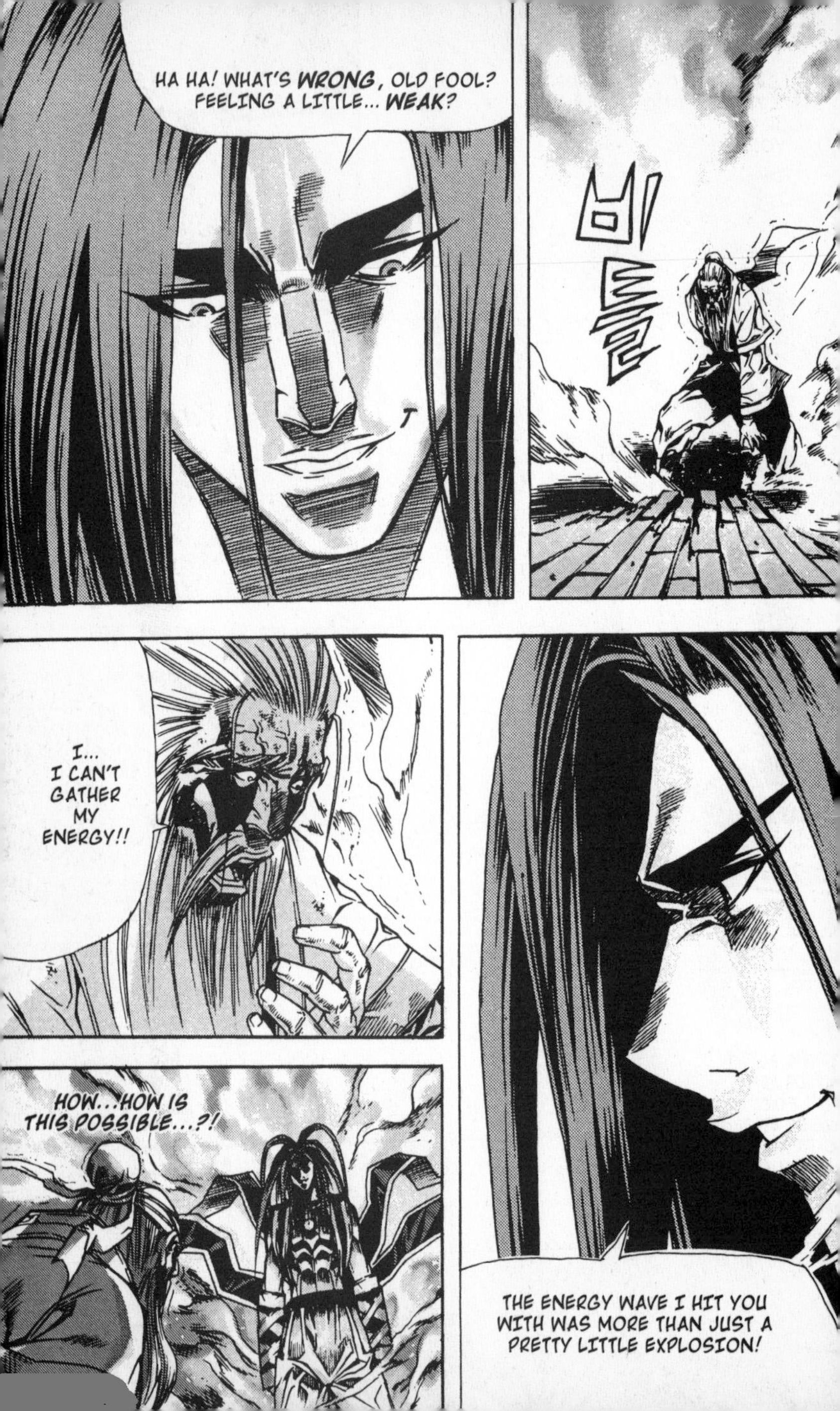
HA HA! WHAT'S **WRONG**, OLD FOOL? FEELING A LITTLE... **WEAK**?
비틀
I... I CAN'T GATHER MY ENERGY!!
HOW...HOW IS THIS POSSIBLE...?!
THE ENERGY WAVE I HIT YOU WITH WAS MORE THAN JUST A PRETTY LITTLE EXPLOSION!

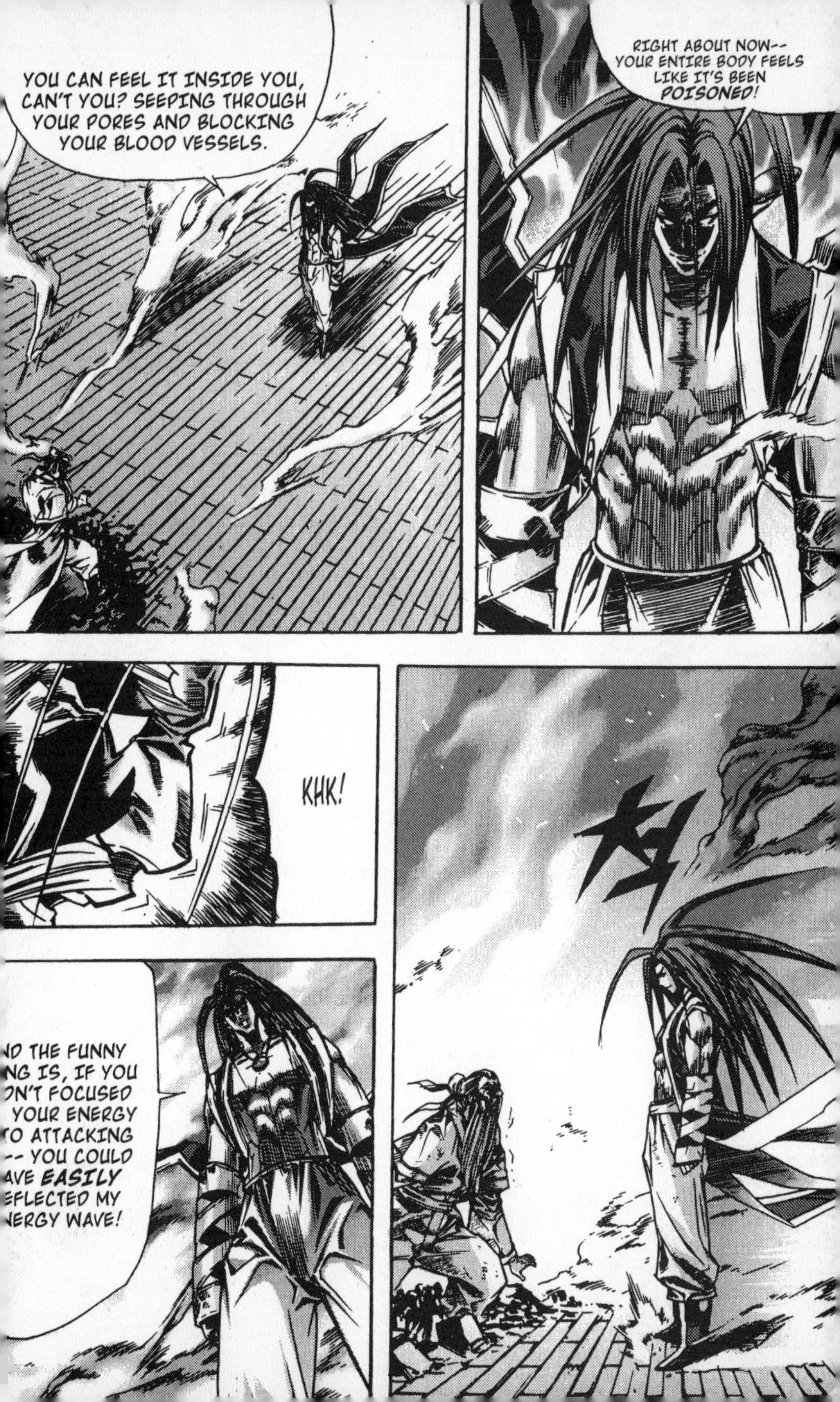

YOU CAN FEEL IT INSIDE YOU, CAN'T YOU? SEEPING THROUGH YOUR PORES AND BLOCKING YOUR BLOOD VESSELS.
RIGHT ABOUT NOW-- YOUR ENTIRE BODY FEELS LIKE IT'S BEEN POISONED!
KHK!
ND THE FUNNY NG IS, IF YOU N'T FOCUSED YOUR ENERGY O ATTACKING -- YOU COULD AVE EASILY EFLECTED MY NERGY WAVE!

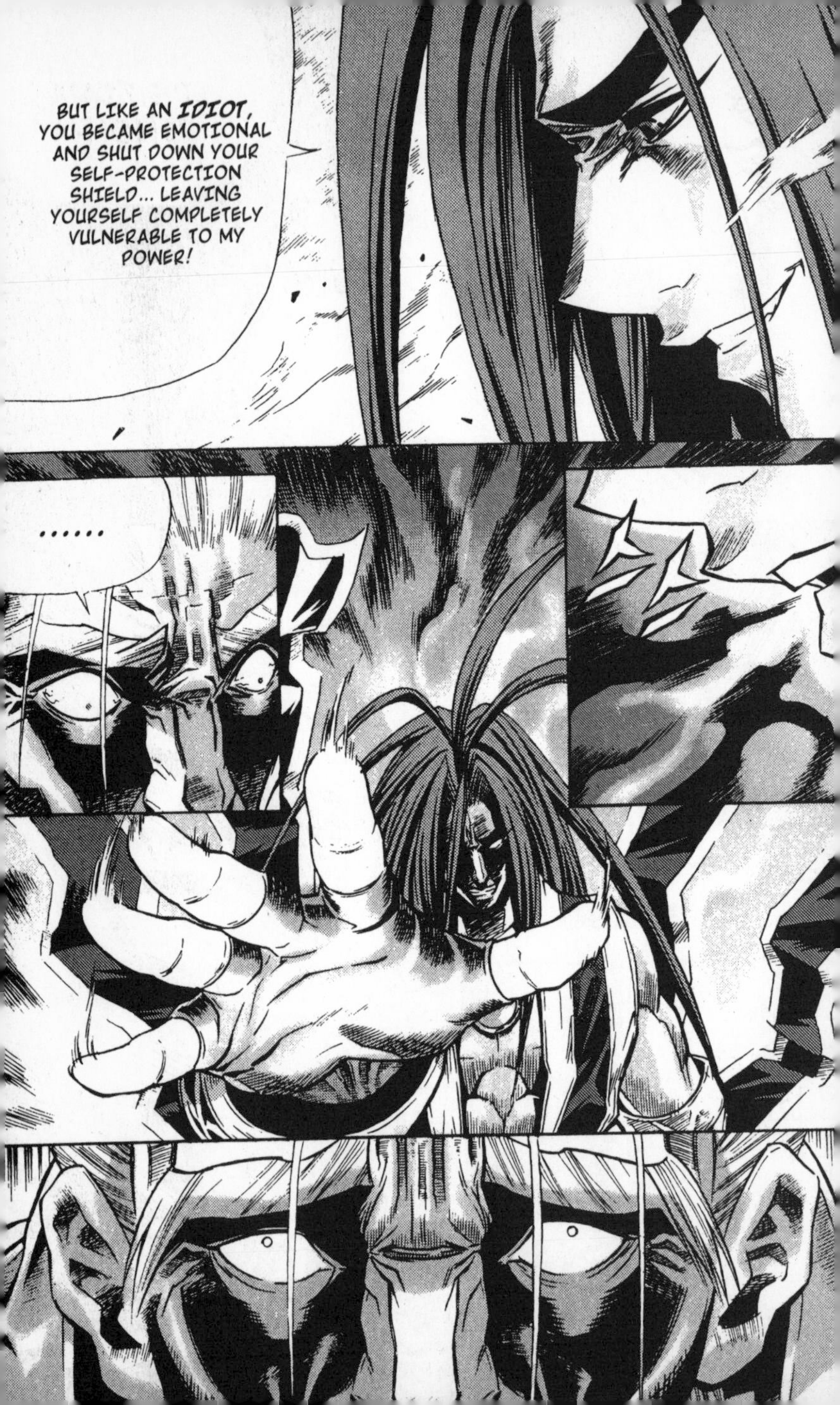
BUT LIKE AN *IDIOT*, YOU BECAME EMOTIONAL AND SHUT DOWN YOUR SELF-PROTECTION SHIELD... LEAVING YOURSELF COMPLETELY VULNERABLE TO MY POWER!
......

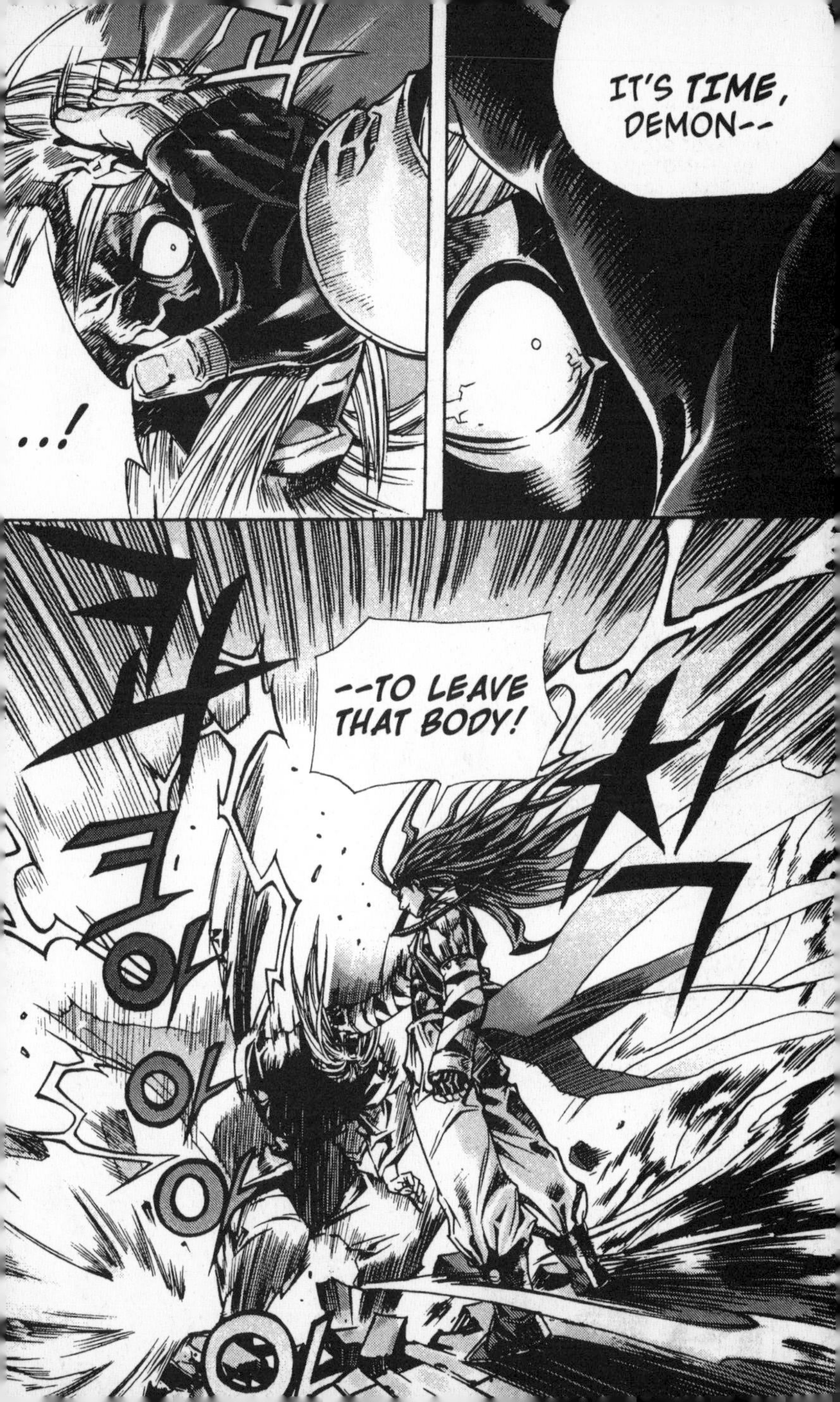
...!
IT'S TIME, DEMON--
--TO LEAVE THAT BODY!

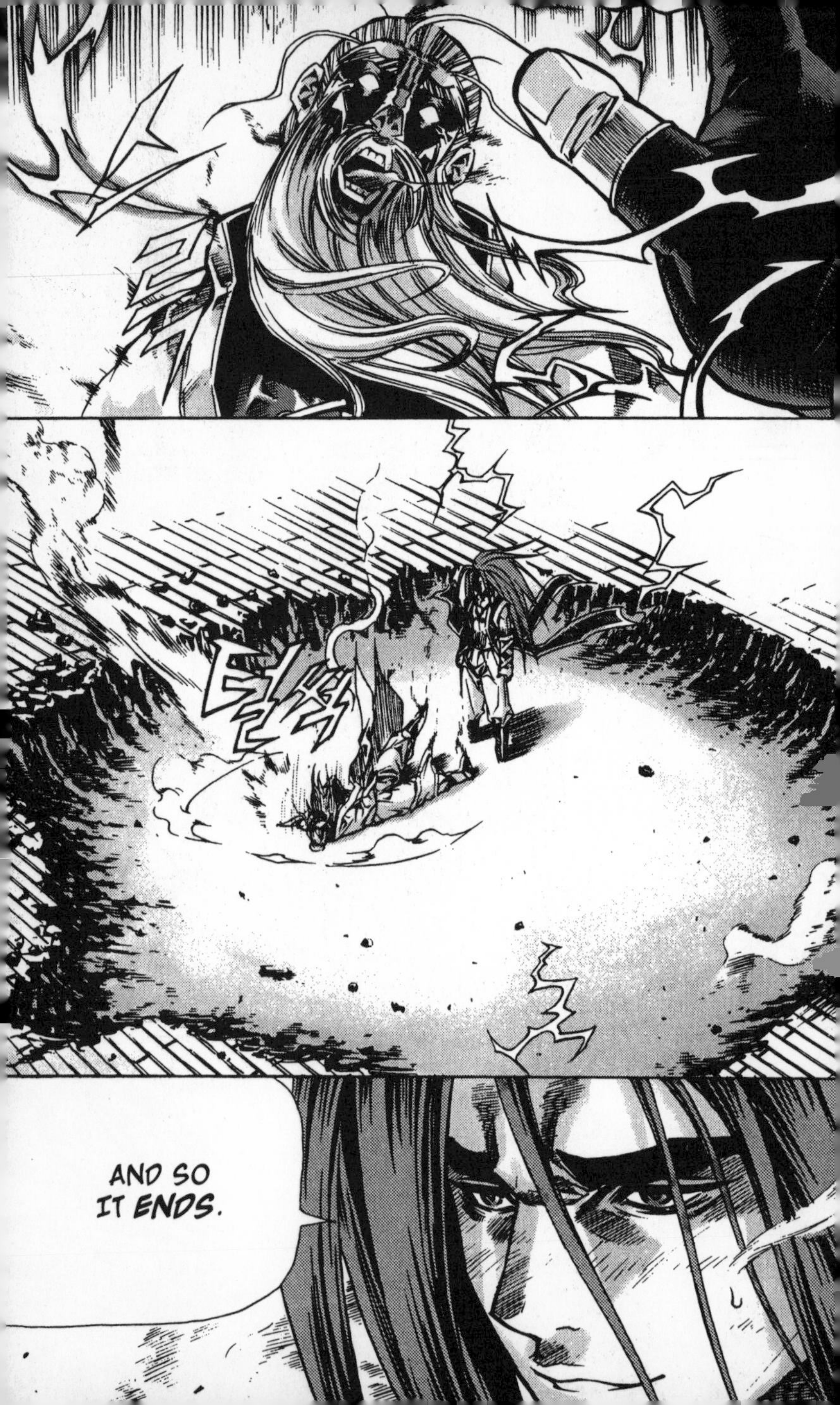
AND SO
IT ENDS.

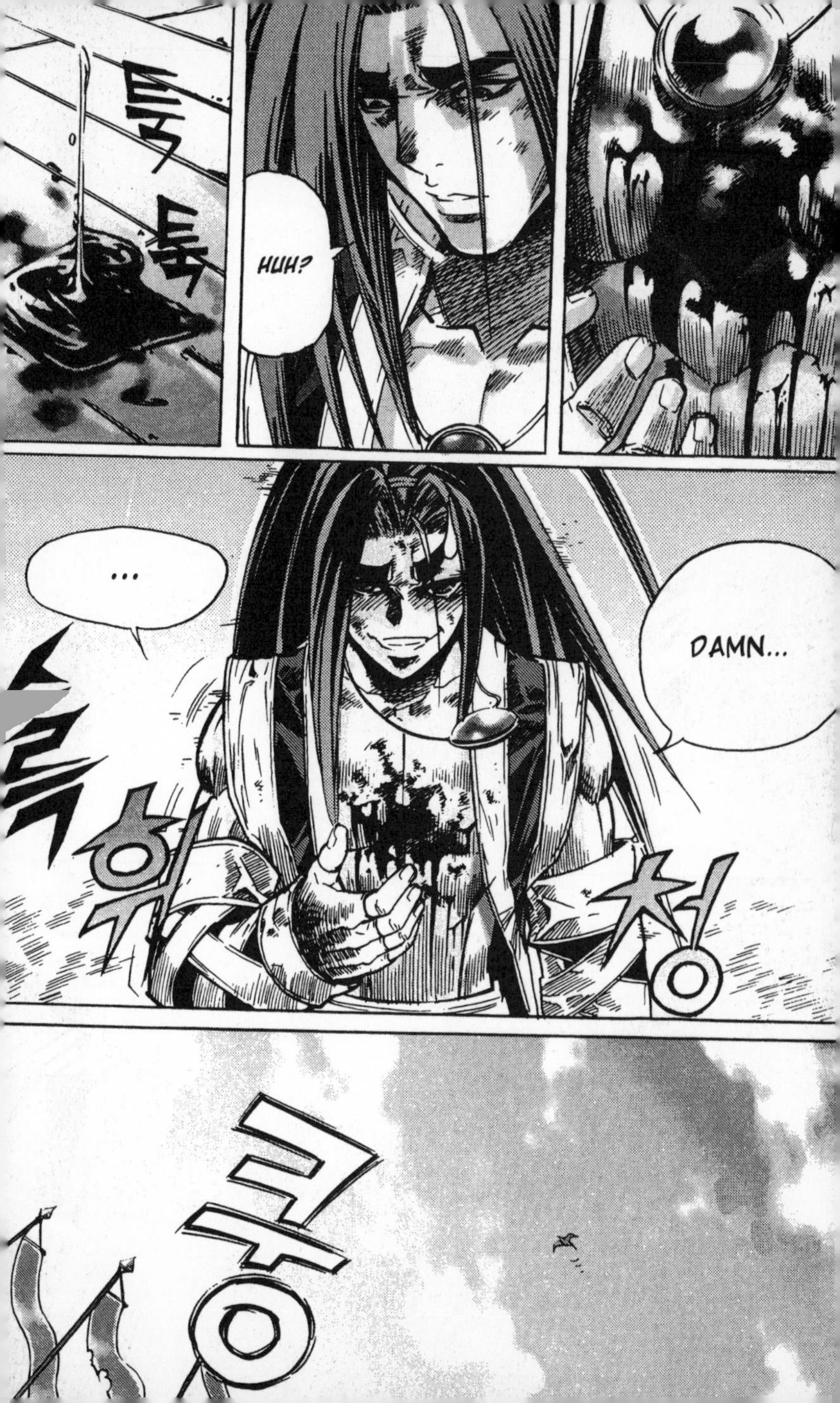
HUH?
...
DAMN...

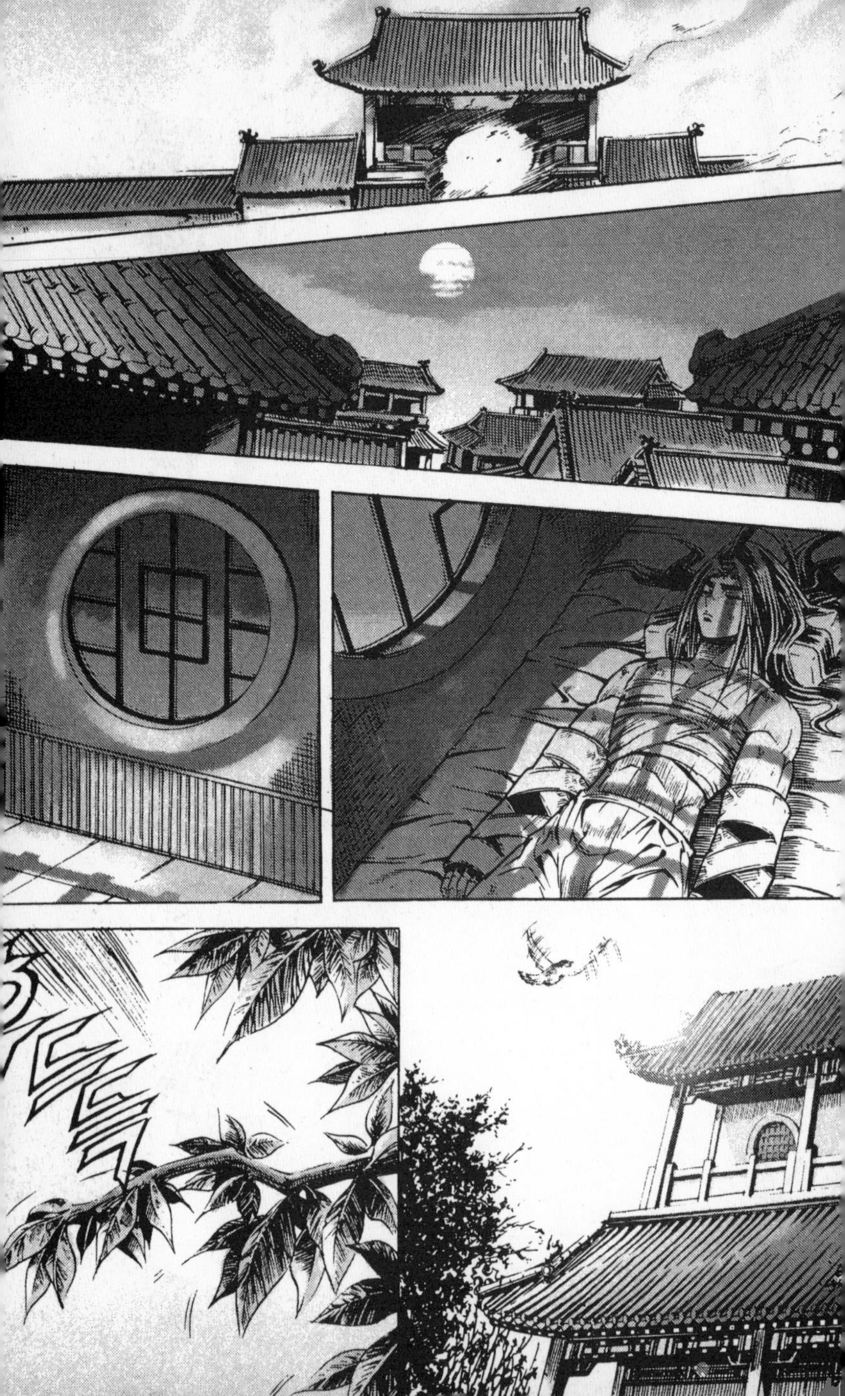

HMM...

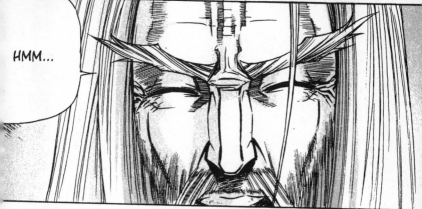

YOU TWO REALLY DON'T KNOW ANYTHING *ABOUT* MAJEH, DO YOU?

NO, WE DON'T.

WE TRAVELED TOGETHER, BUT... WE JUST RECENTLY BECAME ACQUAINTED, AND HE NEVER REALLY TALKED ABOUT HIMSELF... SO THAT'S WHY WE...

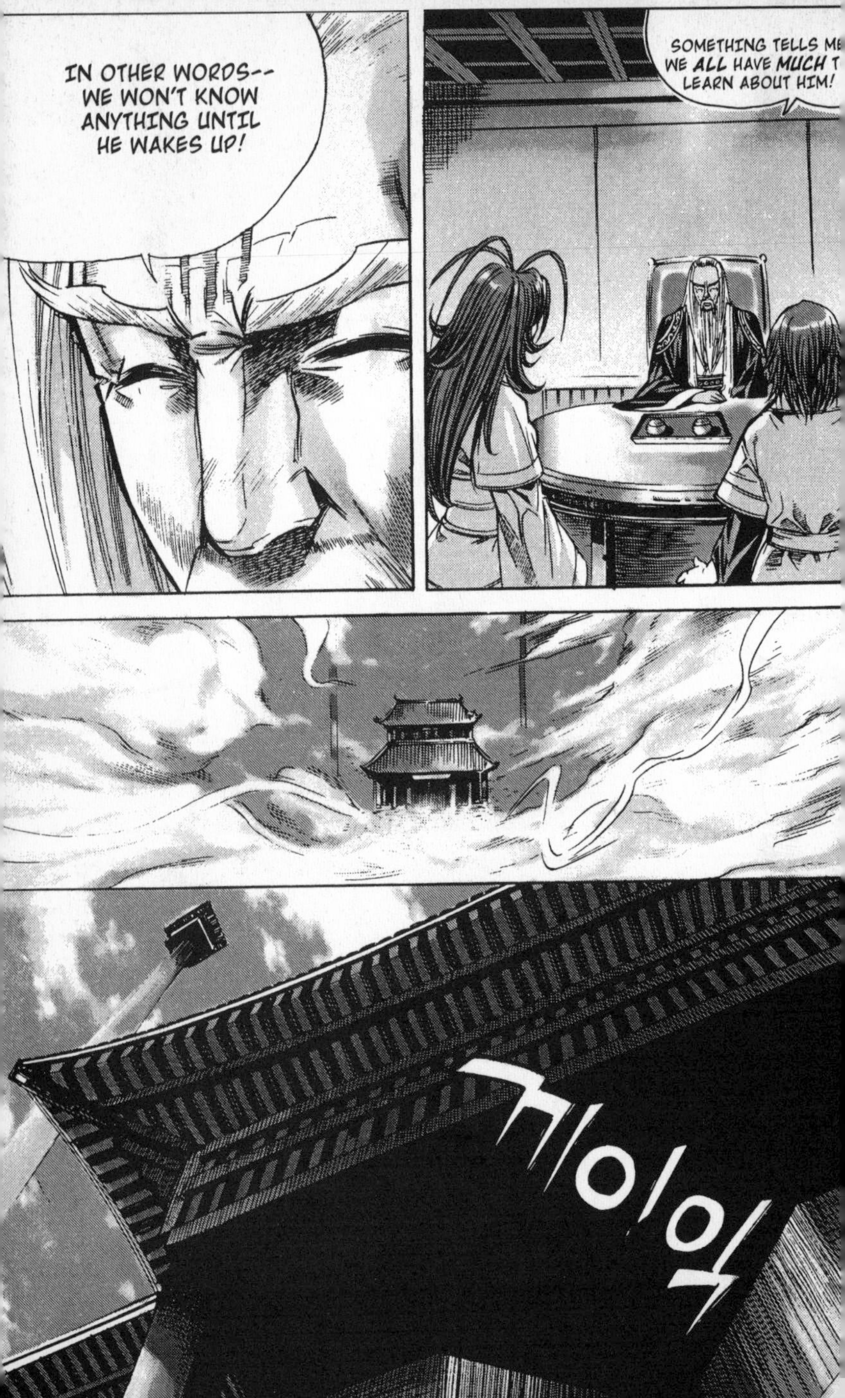
IN OTHER WORDS-- WE WON'T KNOW ANYTHING UNTIL HE WAKES UP!
SOMETHING TELLS ME WE **ALL** HAVE **MUCH** T LEARN ABOUT HIM!

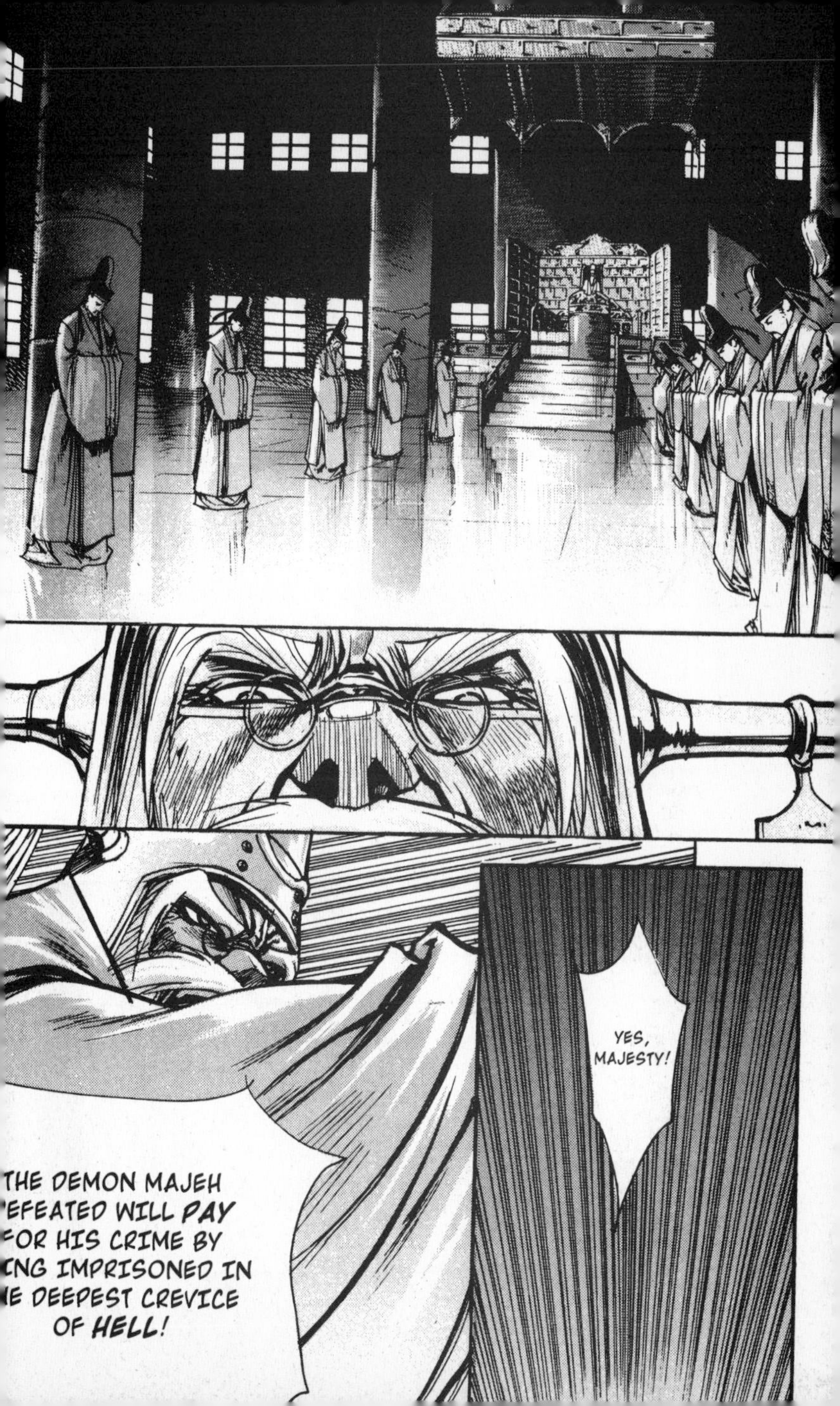
THE DEMON MAJEH
EFEATED WILL *PAY*
FOR HIS CRIME BY
ING IMPRISONED IN
E DEEPEST CREVICE
OF ***HELL!***
YES, MAJESTY!

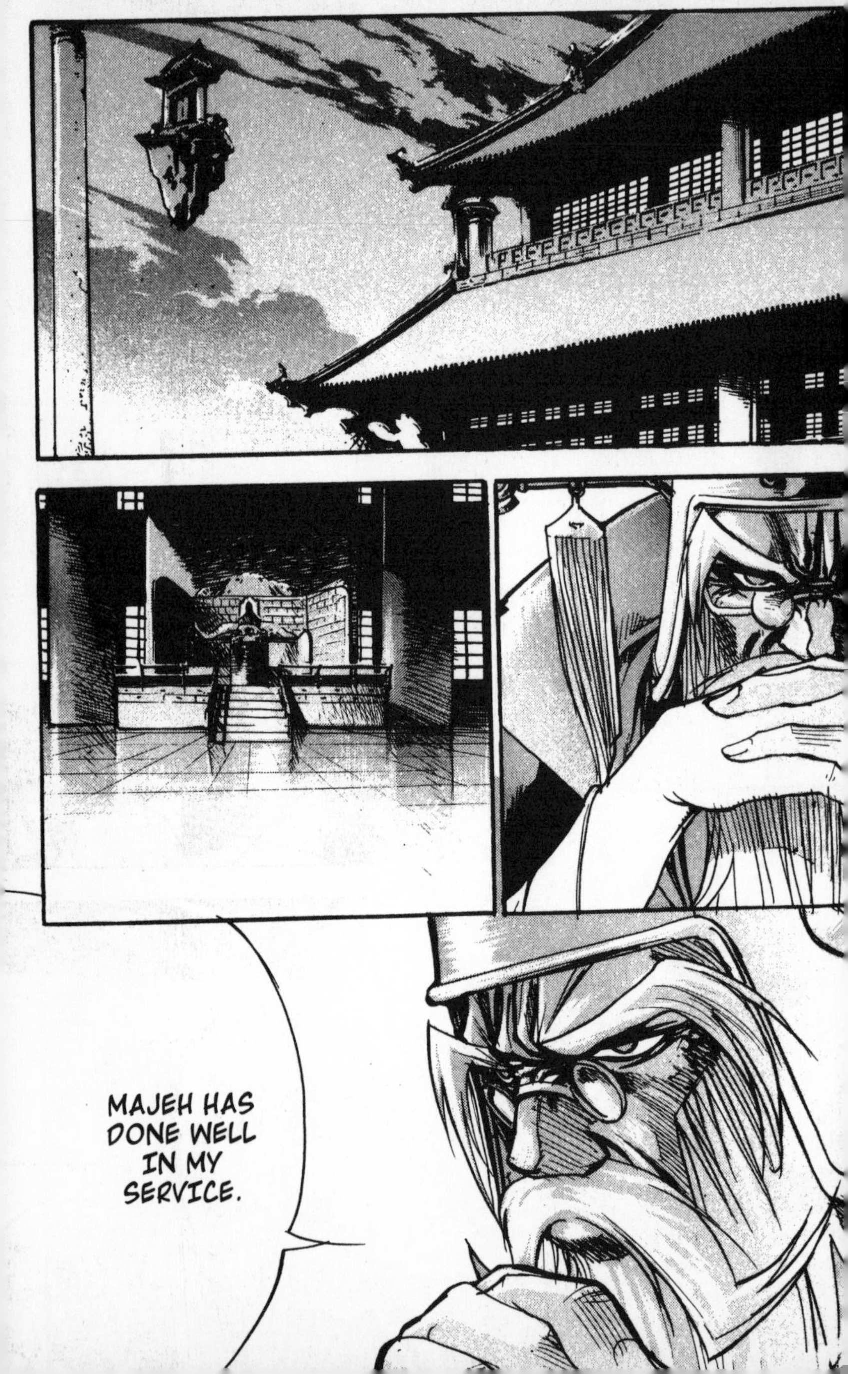
MAJEH HAS DONE WELL IN MY SERVICE.

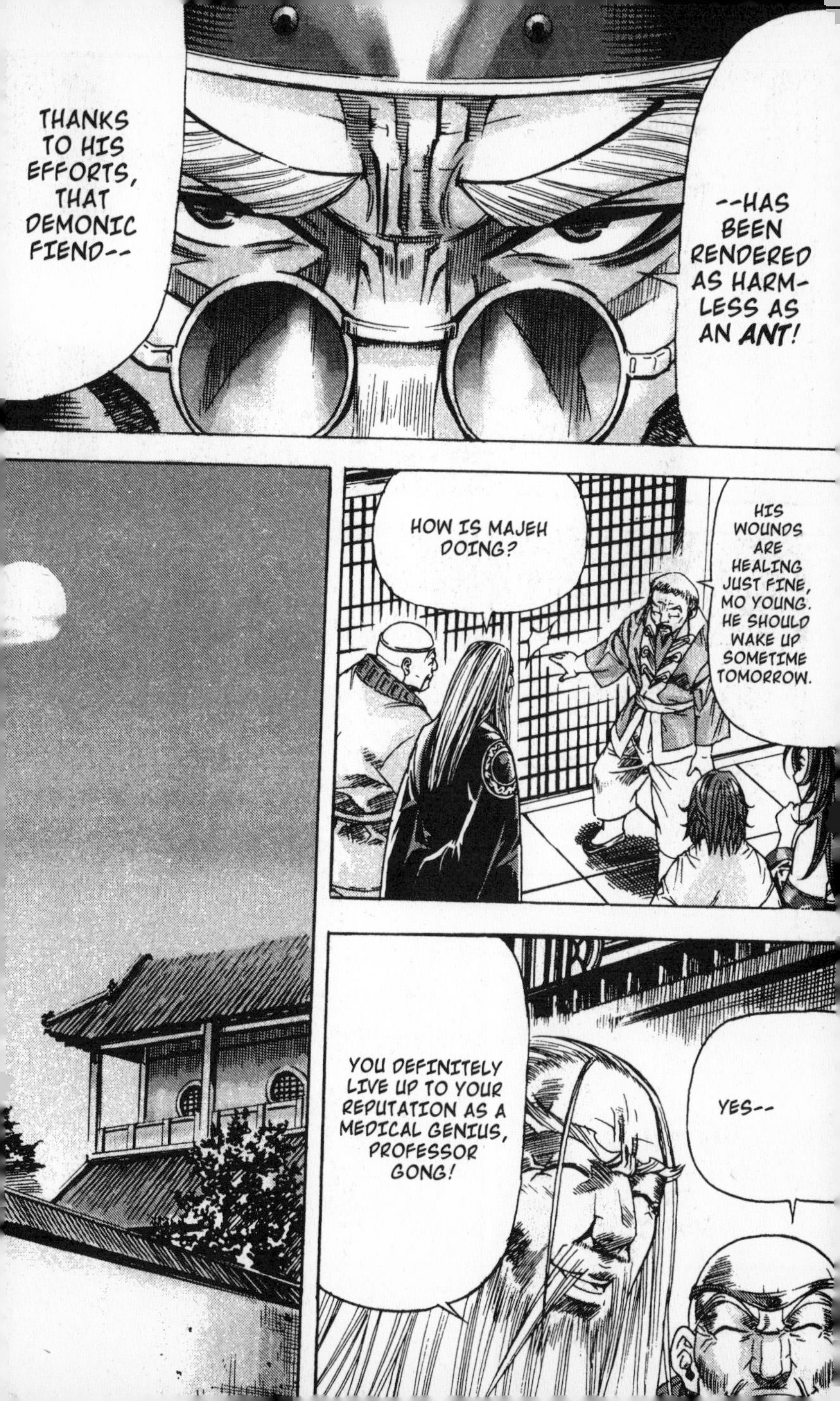
THANKS TO HIS EFFORTS, THAT DEMONIC FIEND--
--HAS BEEN RENDERED AS HARMLESS AS AN **ANT**!
HOW IS MAJEH DOING?
HIS WOUNDS ARE HEALING JUST FINE, MO YOUNG. HE SHOULD WAKE UP SOMETIME TOMORROW.
YOU DEFINITELY LIVE UP TO YOUR REPUTATION AS A MEDICAL GENIUS, PROFESSOR GONG!
YES--

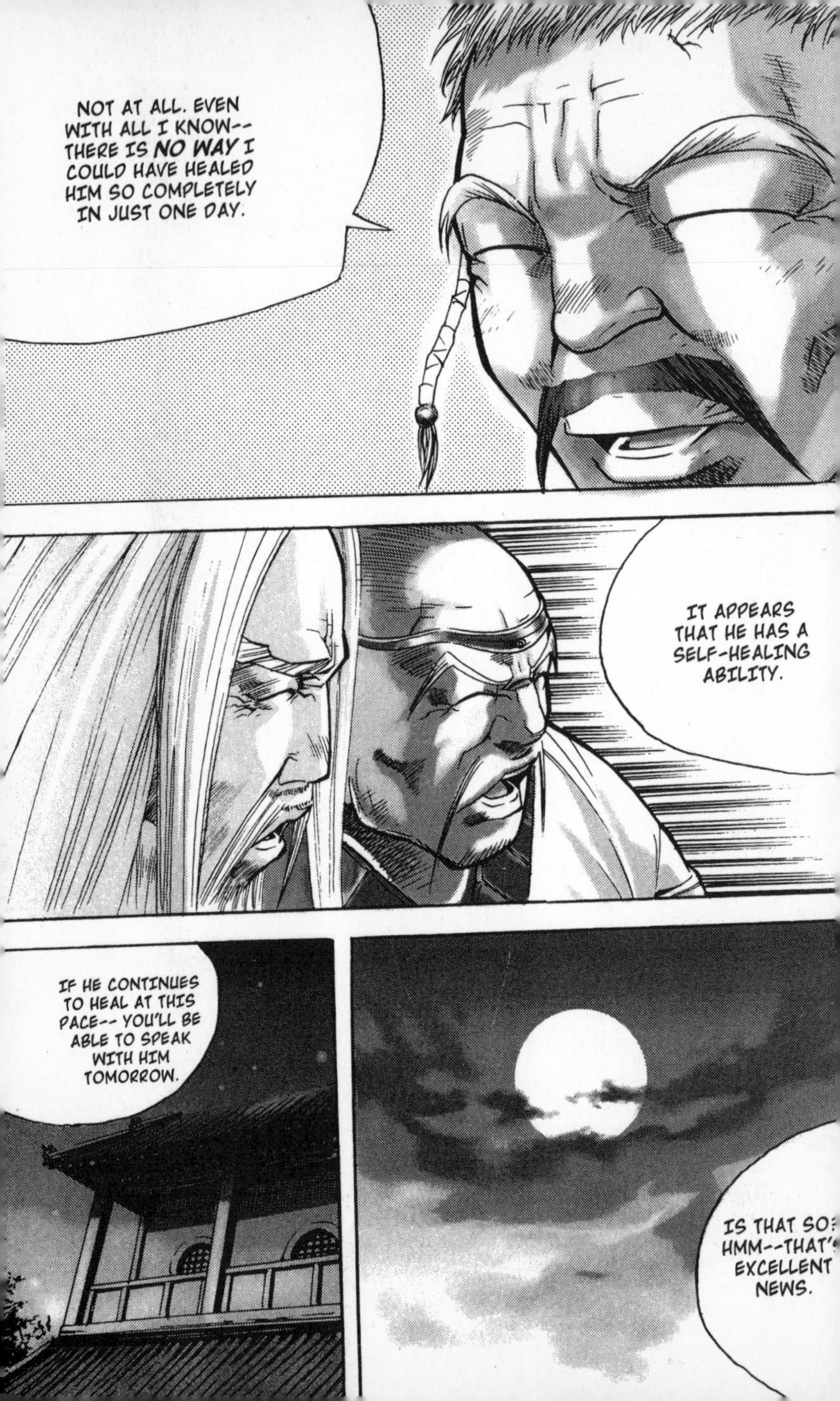
NOT AT ALL. EVEN WITH ALL I KNOW-- THERE IS **NO WAY** I COULD HAVE HEALED HIM SO COMPLETELY IN JUST ONE DAY.
IT APPEARS THAT HE HAS A SELF-HEALING ABILITY.
IF HE CONTINUES TO HEAL AT THIS PACE-- YOU'LL BE ABLE TO SPEAK WITH HIM TOMORROW.
IS THAT SO? HMM--THAT'S EXCELLENT NEWS.

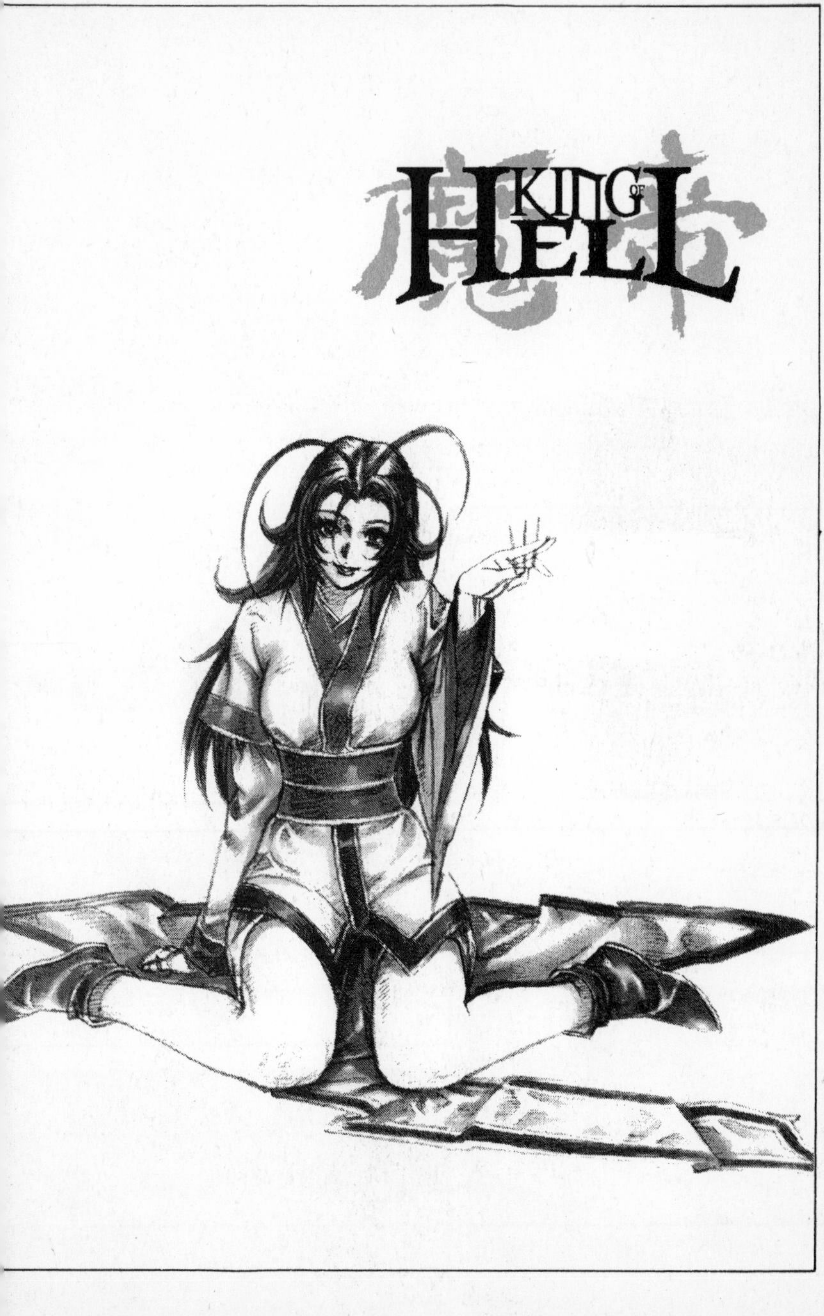
魔帝
KING OF HELL

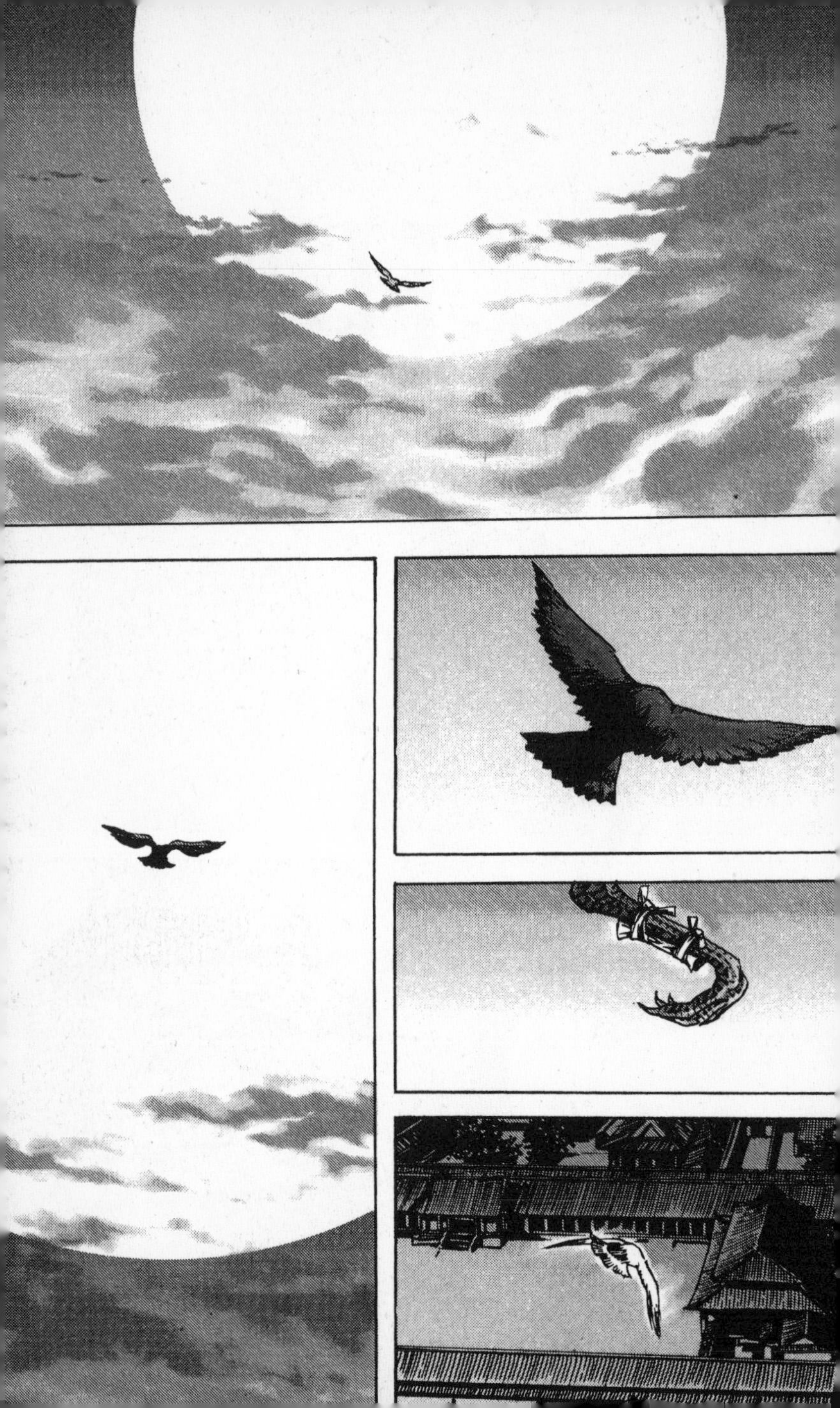

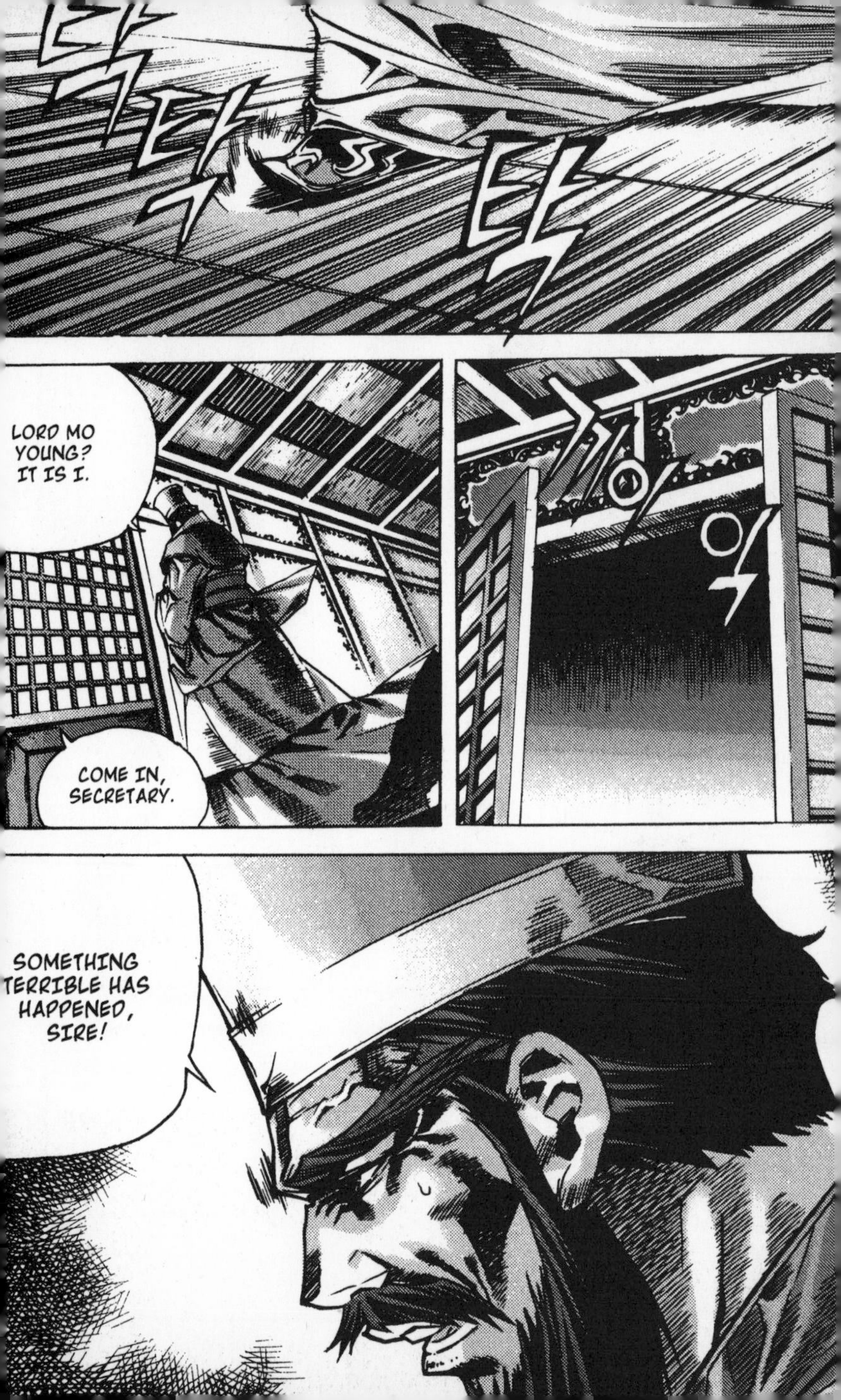
LORD MO YOUNG? IT IS I.
COME IN, SECRETARY.
SOMETHING TERRIBLE HAS HAPPENED, SIRE!

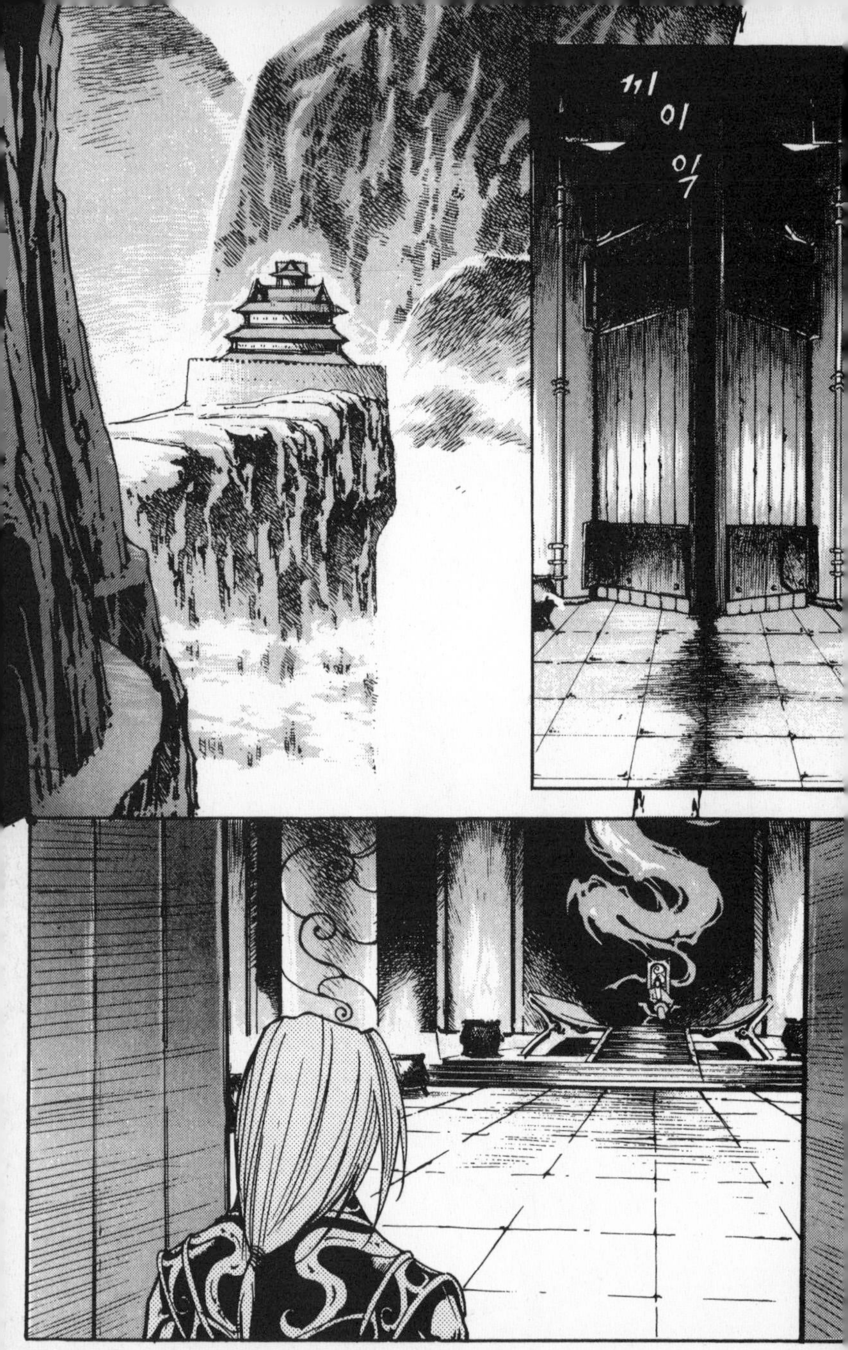
끼이익

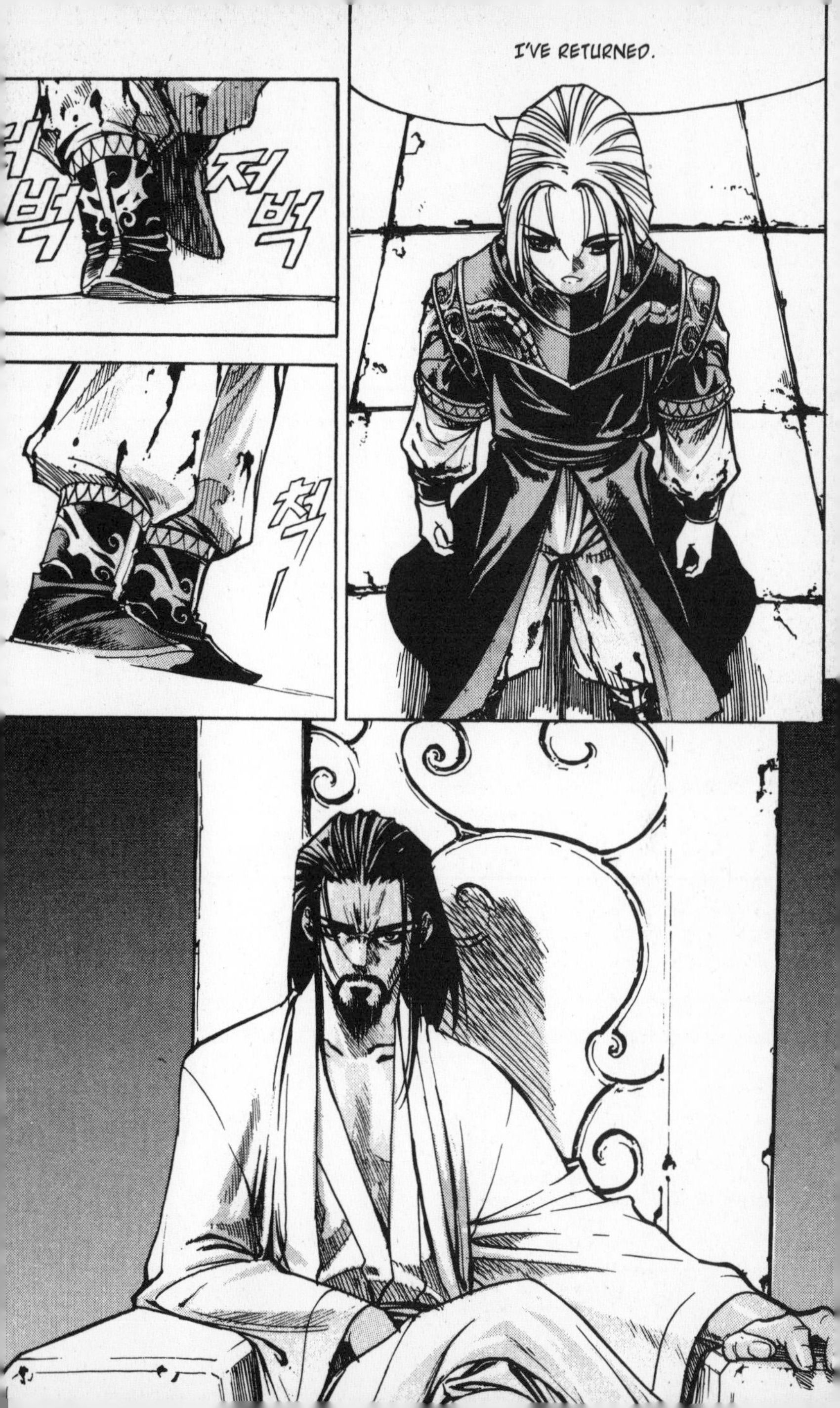
저벅
척
I'VE RETURNED.

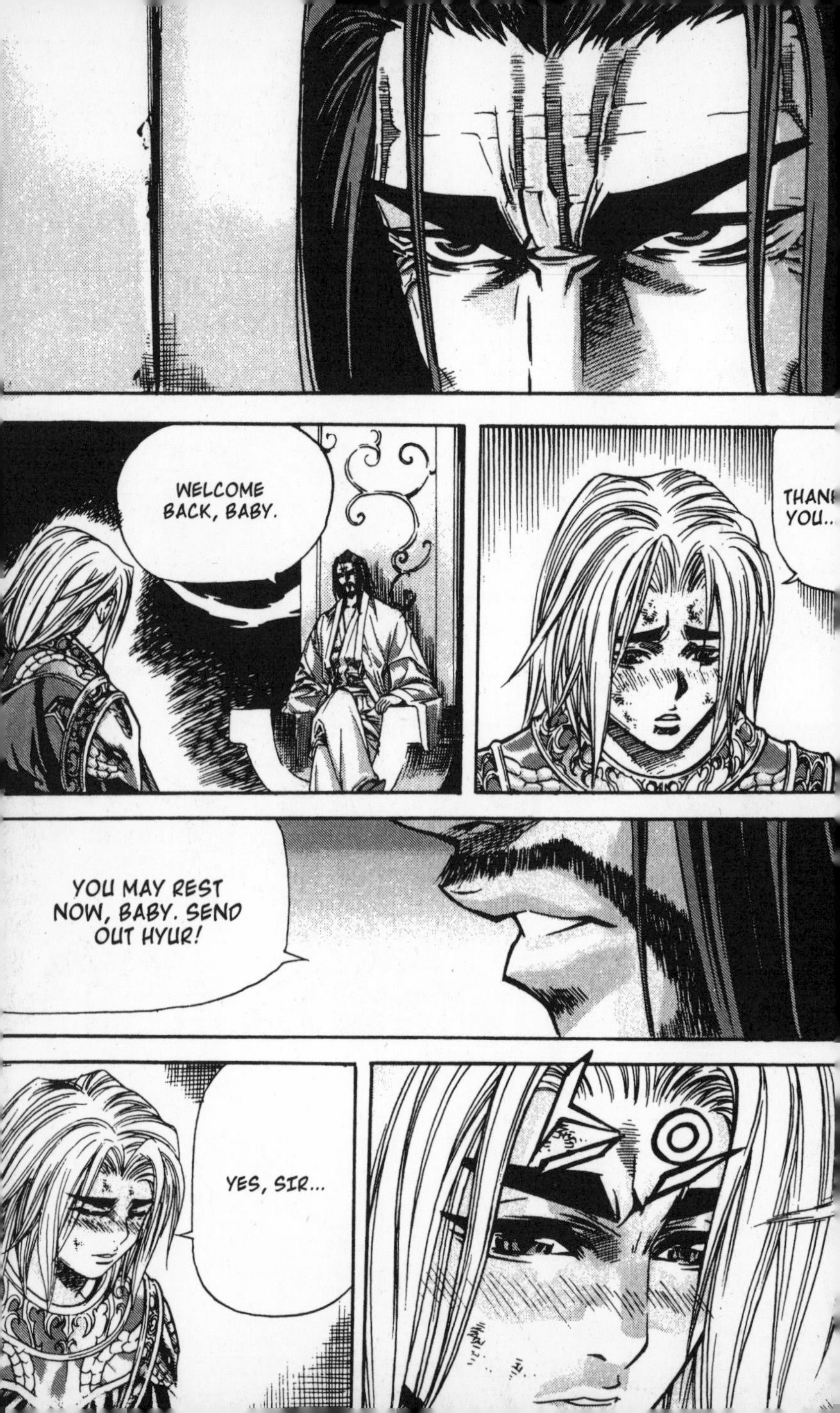
WELCOME BACK, BABY.
THANK YOU...
YOU MAY REST NOW, BABY. SEND OUT HYUR!
YES, SIR...

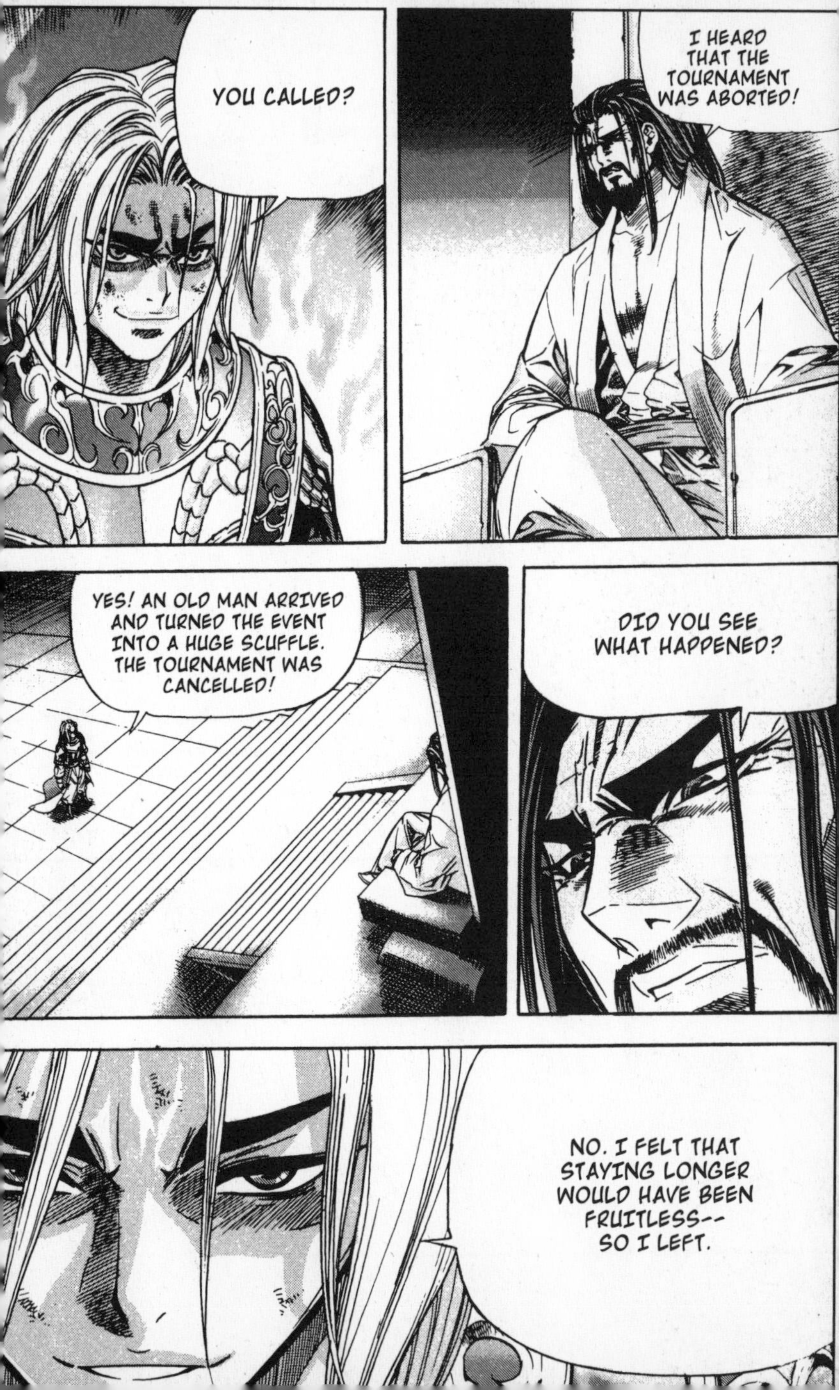
YOU CALLED?
I HEARD THAT THE TOURNAMENT WAS ABORTED!
YES! AN OLD MAN ARRIVED AND TURNED THE EVENT INTO A HUGE SCUFFLE. THE TOURNAMENT WAS CANCELLED!
DID YOU SEE WHAT HAPPENED?
NO. I FELT THAT STAYING LONGER WOULD HAVE BEEN FRUITLESS-- SO I LEFT.

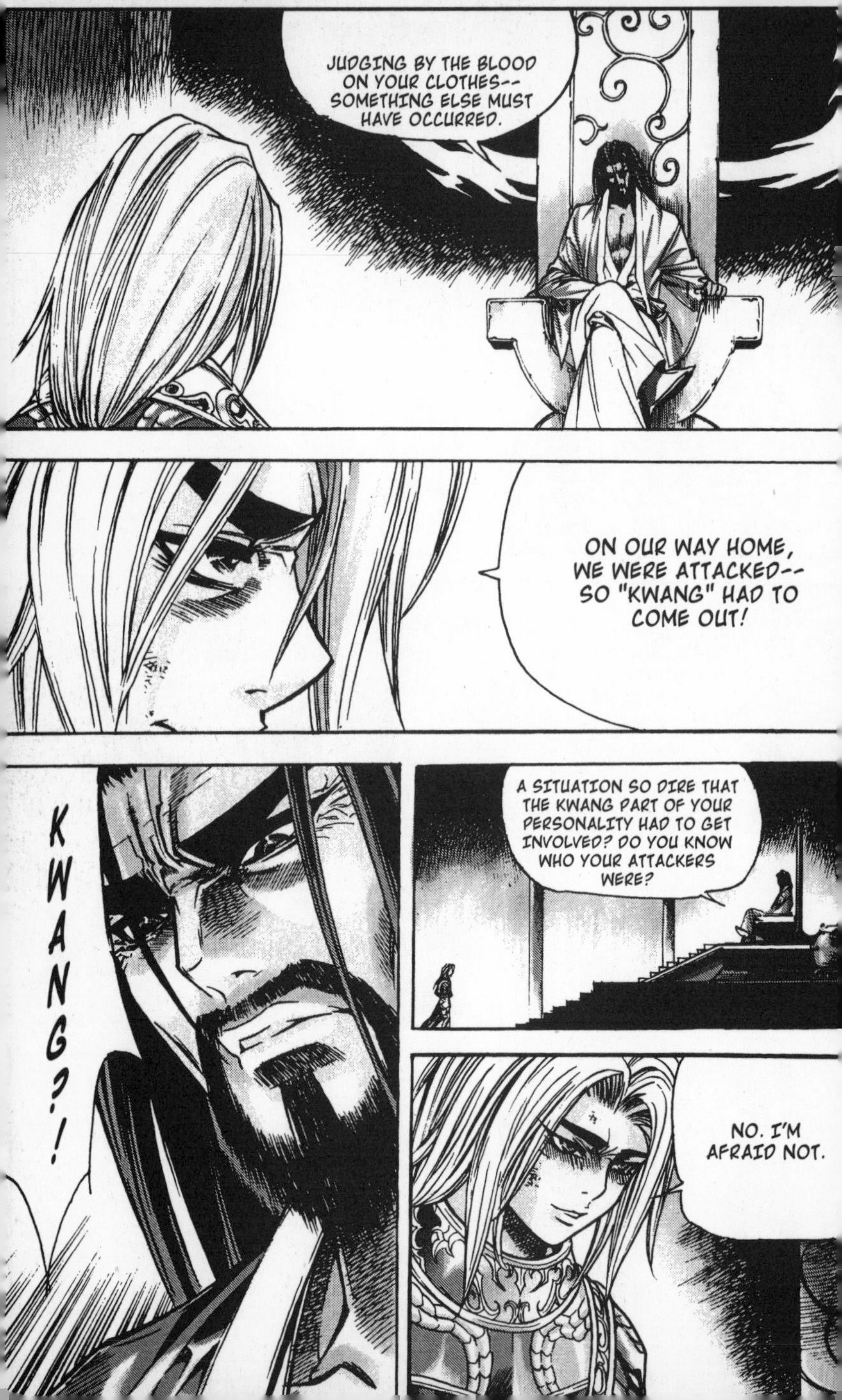
JUDGING BY THE BLOOD ON YOUR CLOTHES-- SOMETHING ELSE MUST HAVE OCCURRED.
ON OUR WAY HOME, WE WERE ATTACKED-- SO "KWANG" HAD TO COME OUT!
KWANG?!
A SITUATION SO DIRE THAT THE KWANG PART OF YOUR PERSONALITY HAD TO GET INVOLVED? DO YOU KNOW WHO YOUR ATTACKERS WERE?
NO. I'M AFRAID NOT.

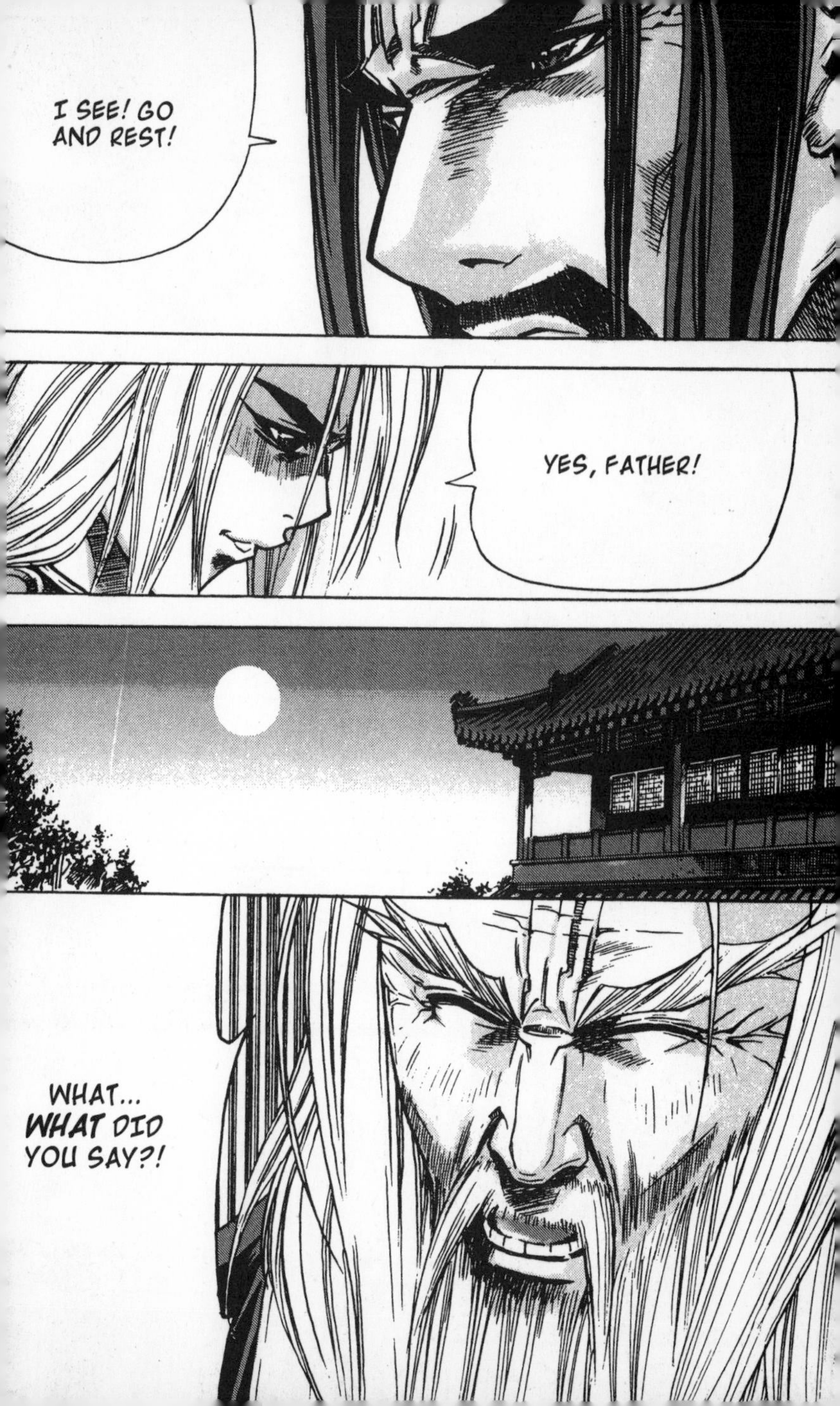
I SEE! GO AND REST!
YES, FATHER!
WHAT... **WHAT** DID YOU SAY?!

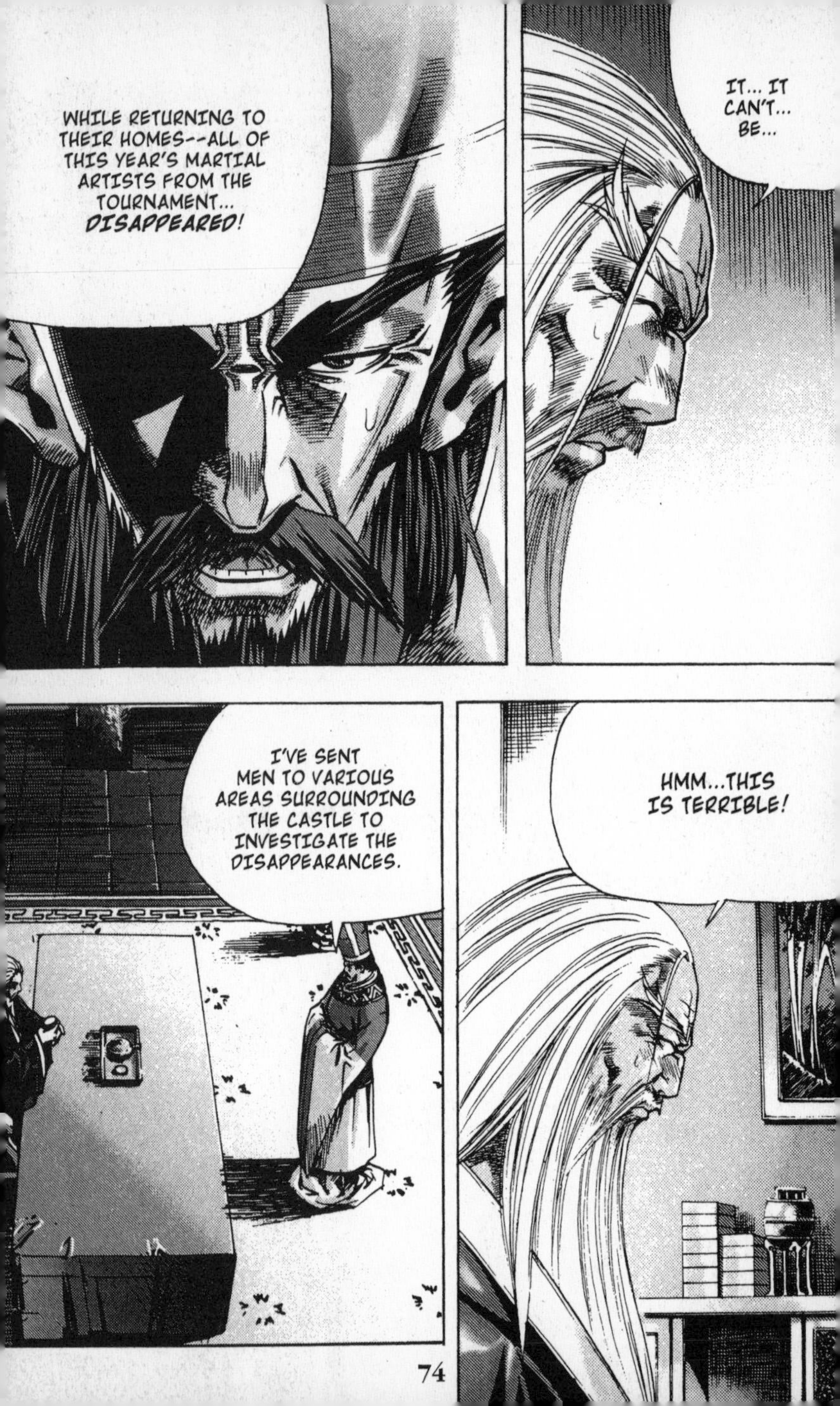

WHILE RETURNING TO THEIR HOMES--ALL OF THIS YEAR'S MARTIAL ARTISTS FROM THE TOURNAMENT... **DISAPPEARED!**
IT... IT CAN'T... BE...
I'VE SENT MEN TO VARIOUS AREAS SURROUNDING THE CASTLE TO INVESTIGATE THE DISAPPEARANCES.
HMM...THIS IS TERRIBLE!

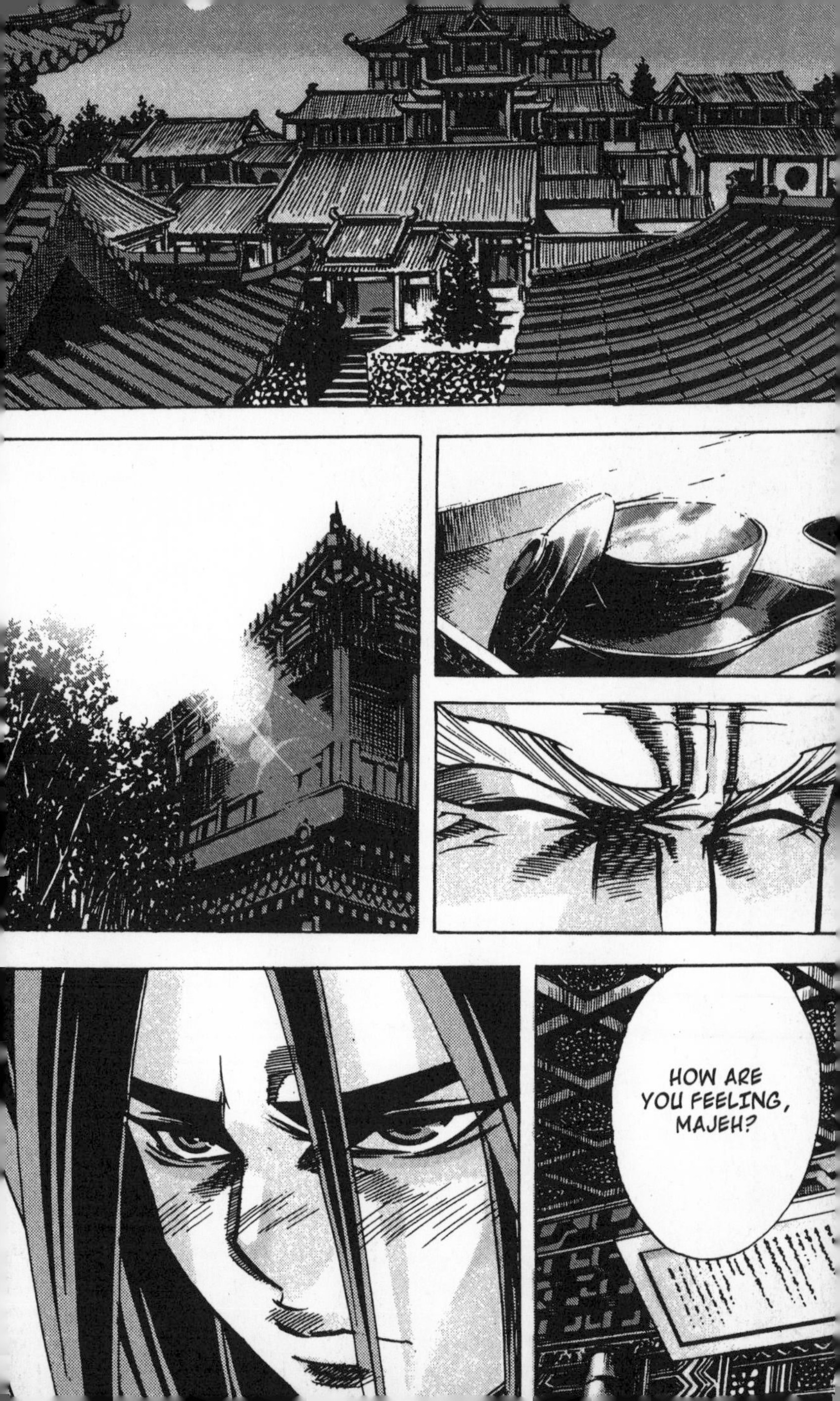
HOW ARE YOU FEELING, MAJEH?

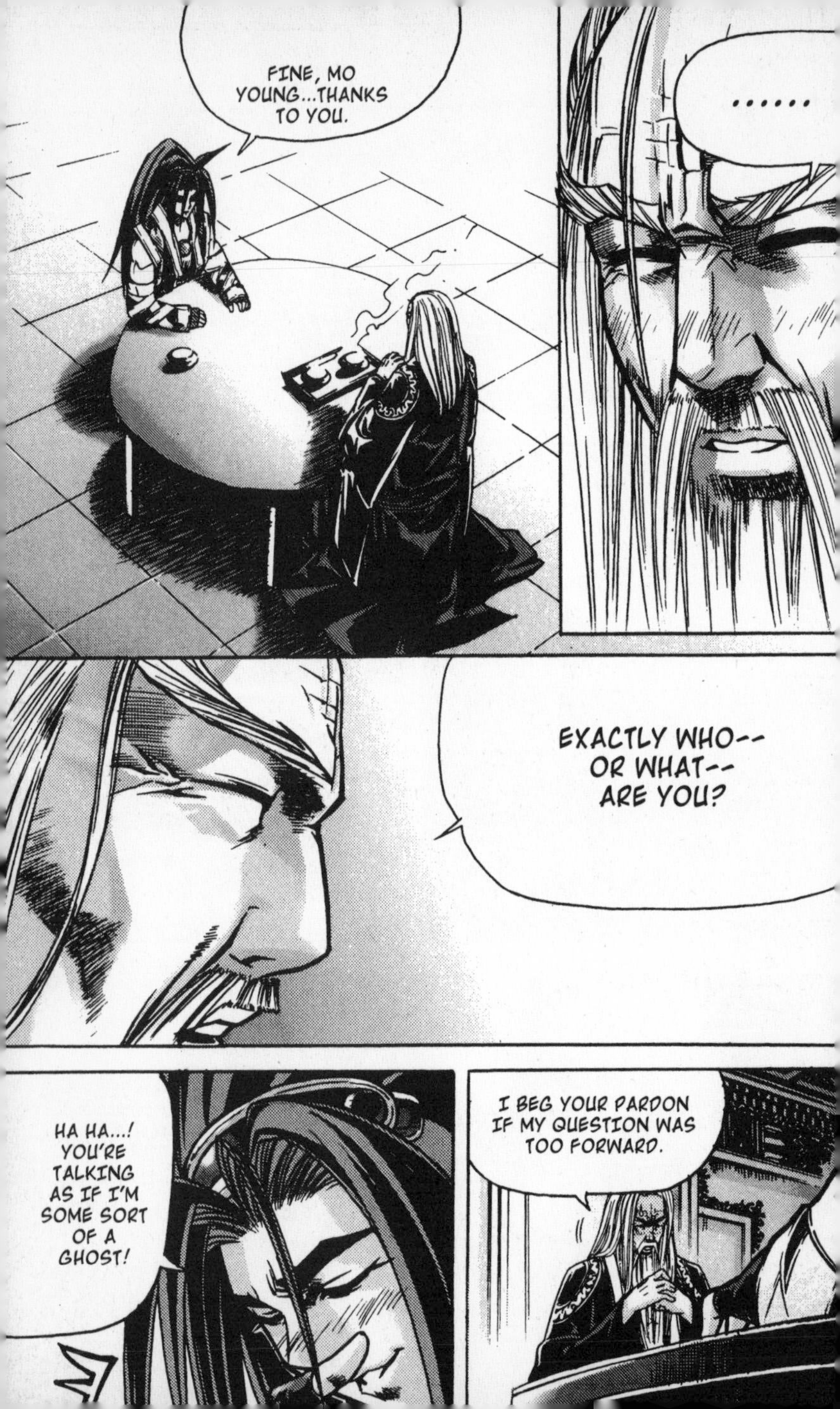
FINE, MO YOUNG...THANKS TO YOU.
......
EXACTLY WHO--OR WHAT--ARE YOU?
HA HA...! YOU'RE TALKING AS IF I'M SOME SORT OF A GHOST!
I BEG YOUR PARDON IF MY QUESTION WAS TOO FORWARD.

WITH WHICH GROUP ARE YOU AFFILIATED?

· · · · · ·

I WITNESSED YOU GROWING LARGER IN SIZE. CAN YOU EXPLAIN THAT?

EVEN THOUGH THEY NO LONGER EXIST... I'M STILL NOT AT LIBERTY TO SAY.

AS BEFORE... I CANNOT.

VERY WELL.

ONE FINAL QUESTION, THEN.

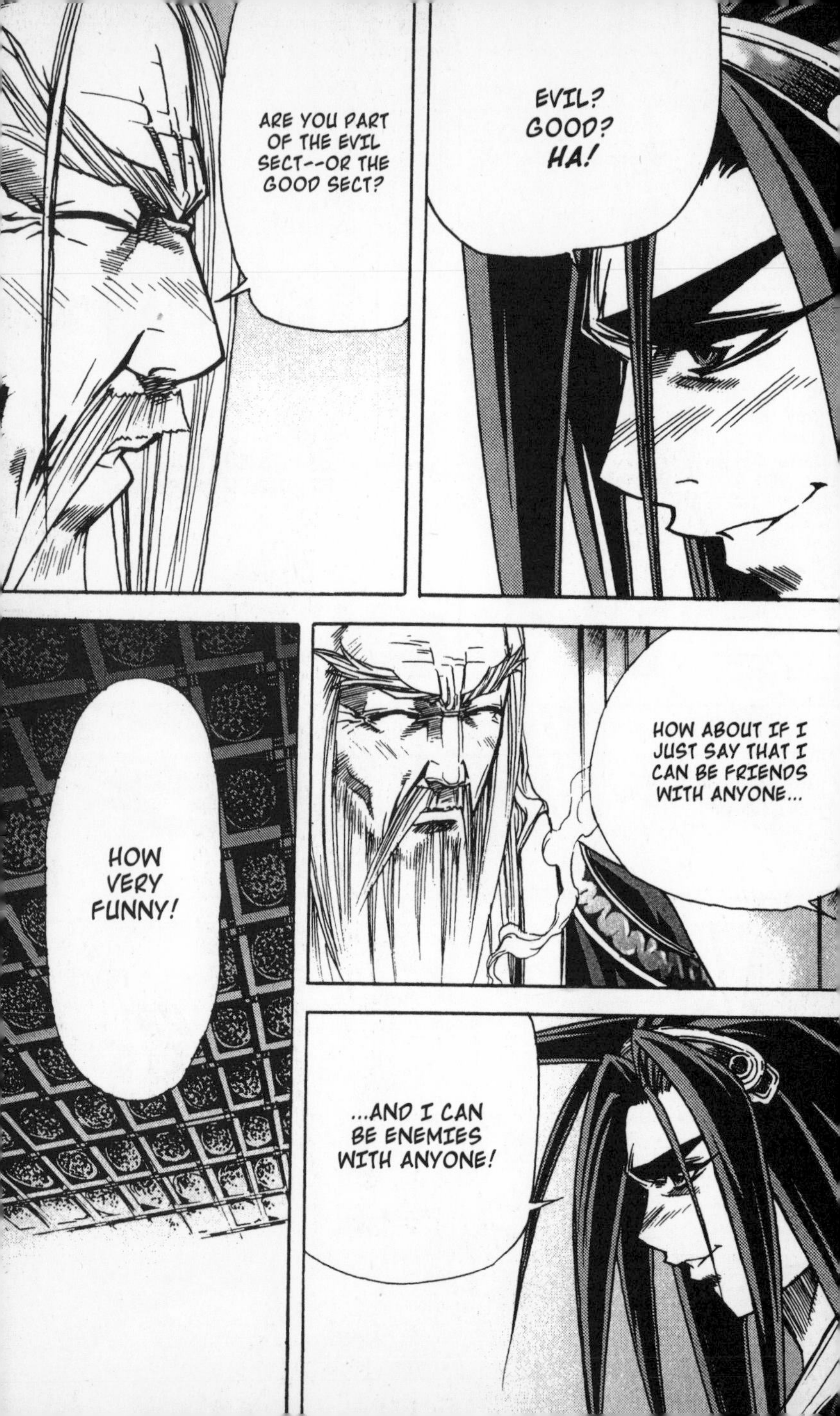
ARE YOU PART OF THE EVIL SECT--OR THE GOOD SECT?
EVIL? GOOD? HA!
HOW VERY FUNNY!
HOW ABOUT IF I JUST SAY THAT I CAN BE FRIENDS WITH ANYONE...
...AND I CAN BE ENEMIES WITH ANYONE!

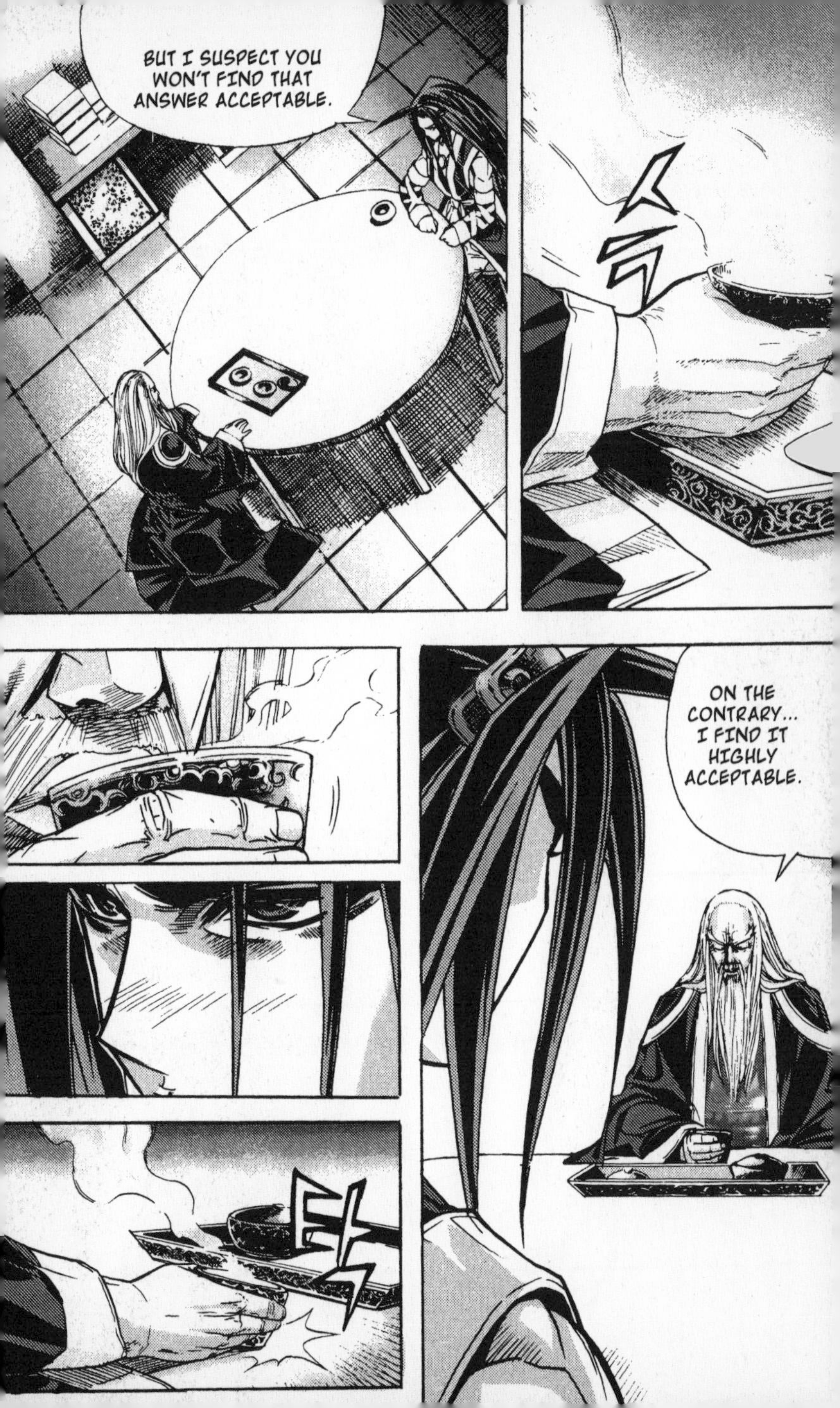
BUT I SUSPECT YOU WON'T FIND THAT ANSWER ACCEPTABLE.
ON THE CONTRARY... I FIND IT HIGHLY ACCEPTABLE.

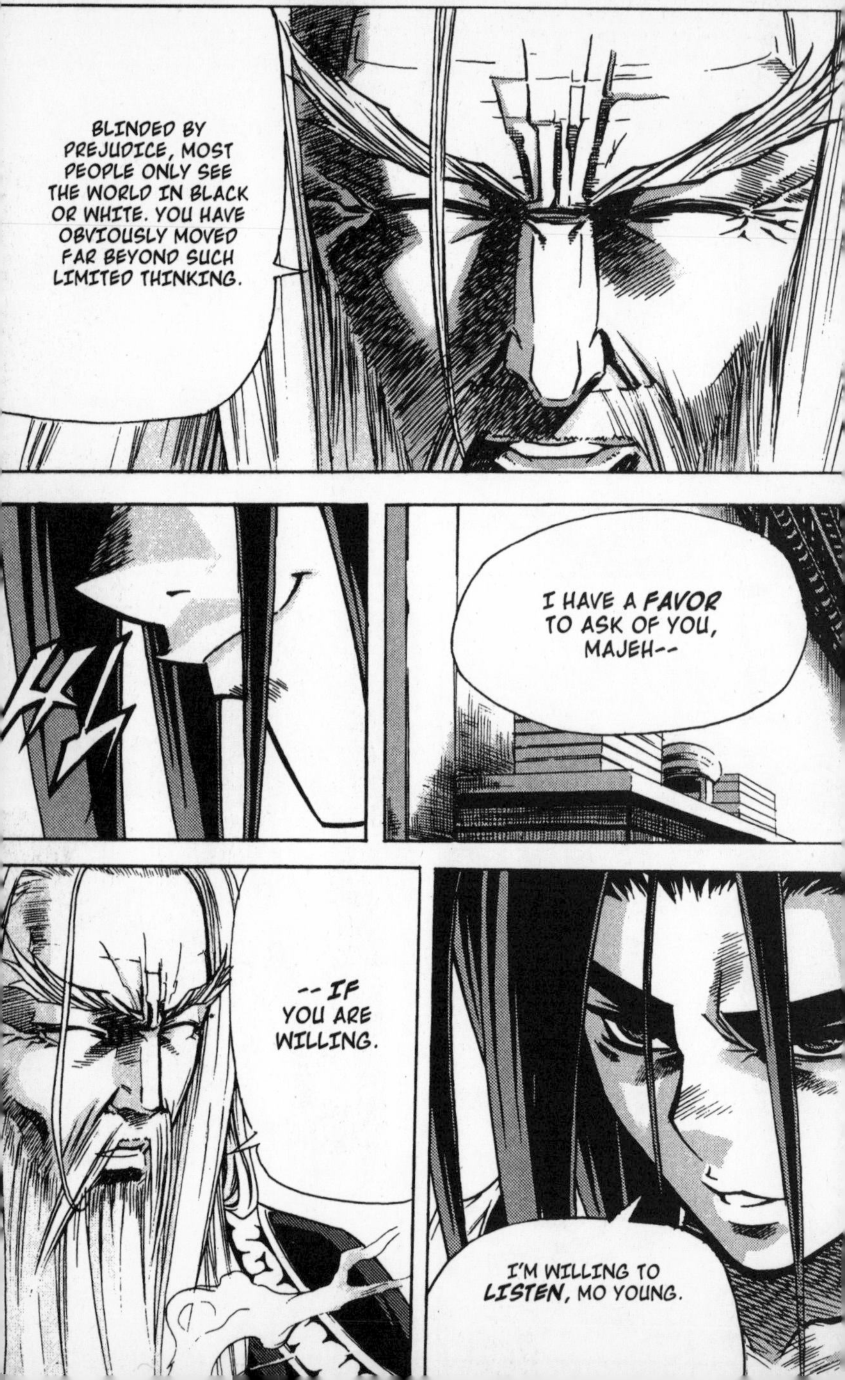
BLINDED BY PREJUDICE, MOST PEOPLE ONLY SEE THE WORLD IN BLACK OR WHITE. YOU HAVE OBVIOUSLY MOVED FAR BEYOND SUCH LIMITED THINKING.
I HAVE A *FAVOR* TO ASK OF YOU, MAJEH--
--*IF* YOU ARE WILLING.
I'M WILLING TO *LISTEN*, MO YOUNG.

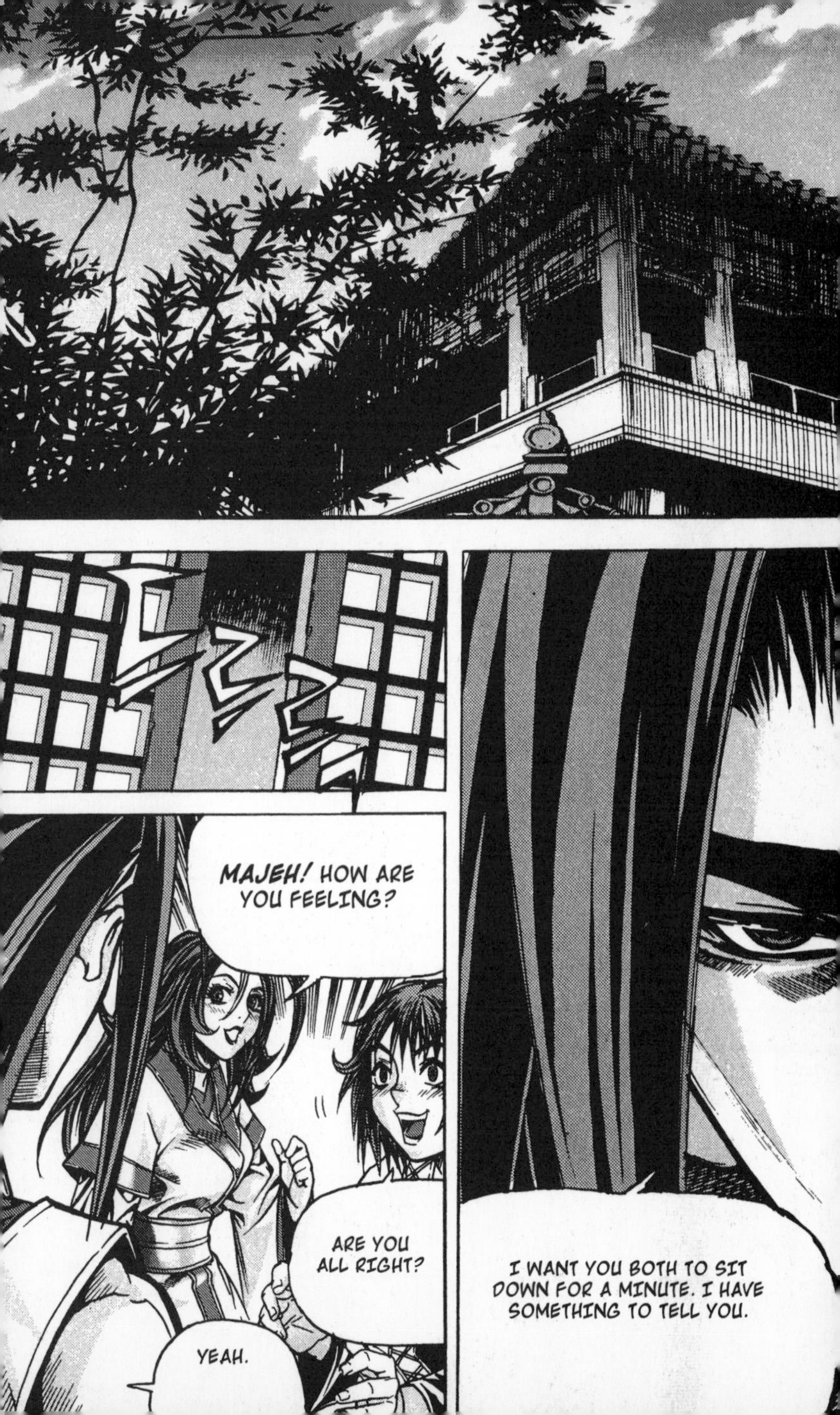
MAJEH! HOW ARE YOU FEELING?
ARE YOU ALL RIGHT?
YEAH.
I WANT YOU BOTH TO SIT DOWN FOR A MINUTE. I HAVE SOMETHING TO TELL YOU.

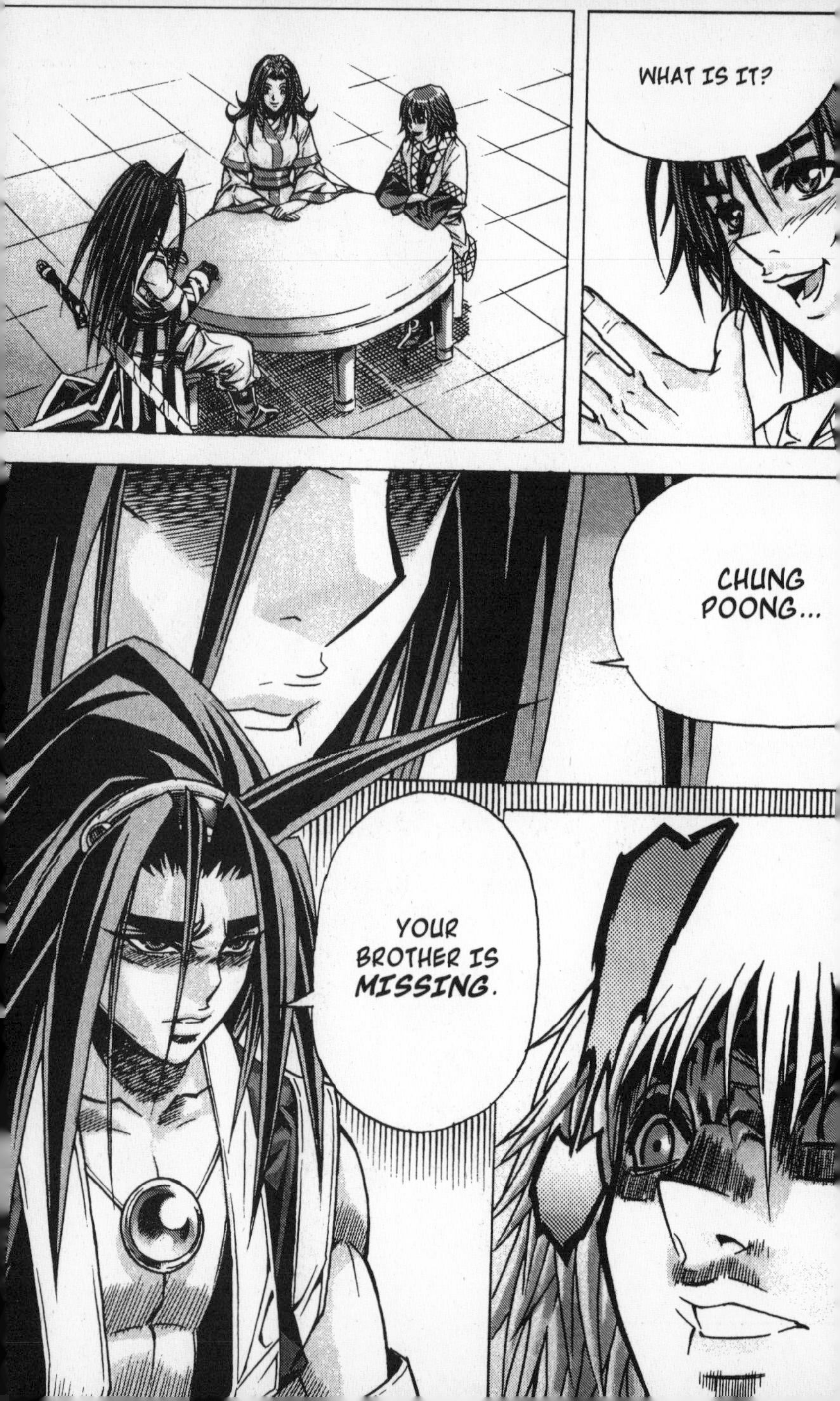
WHAT IS IT?
CHUNG POONG...
YOUR BROTHER IS MISSING.

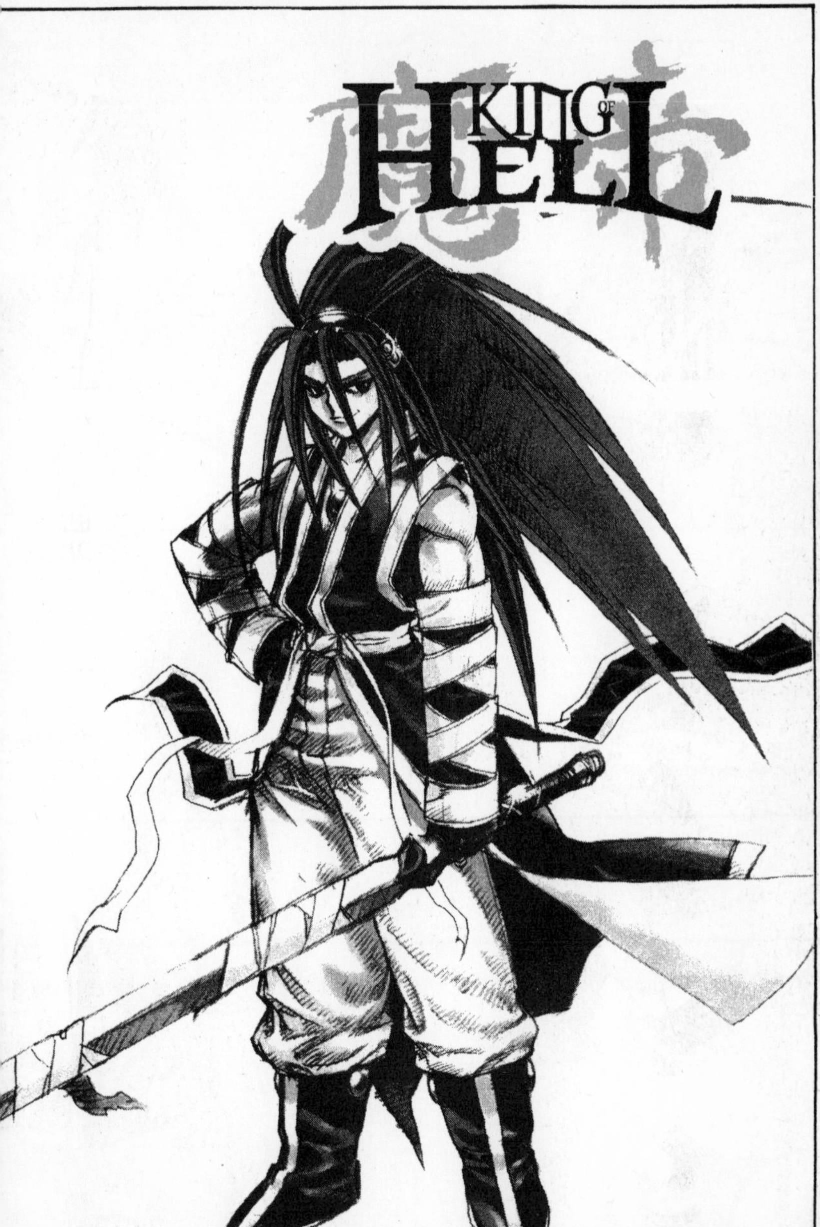
KING OF HELL

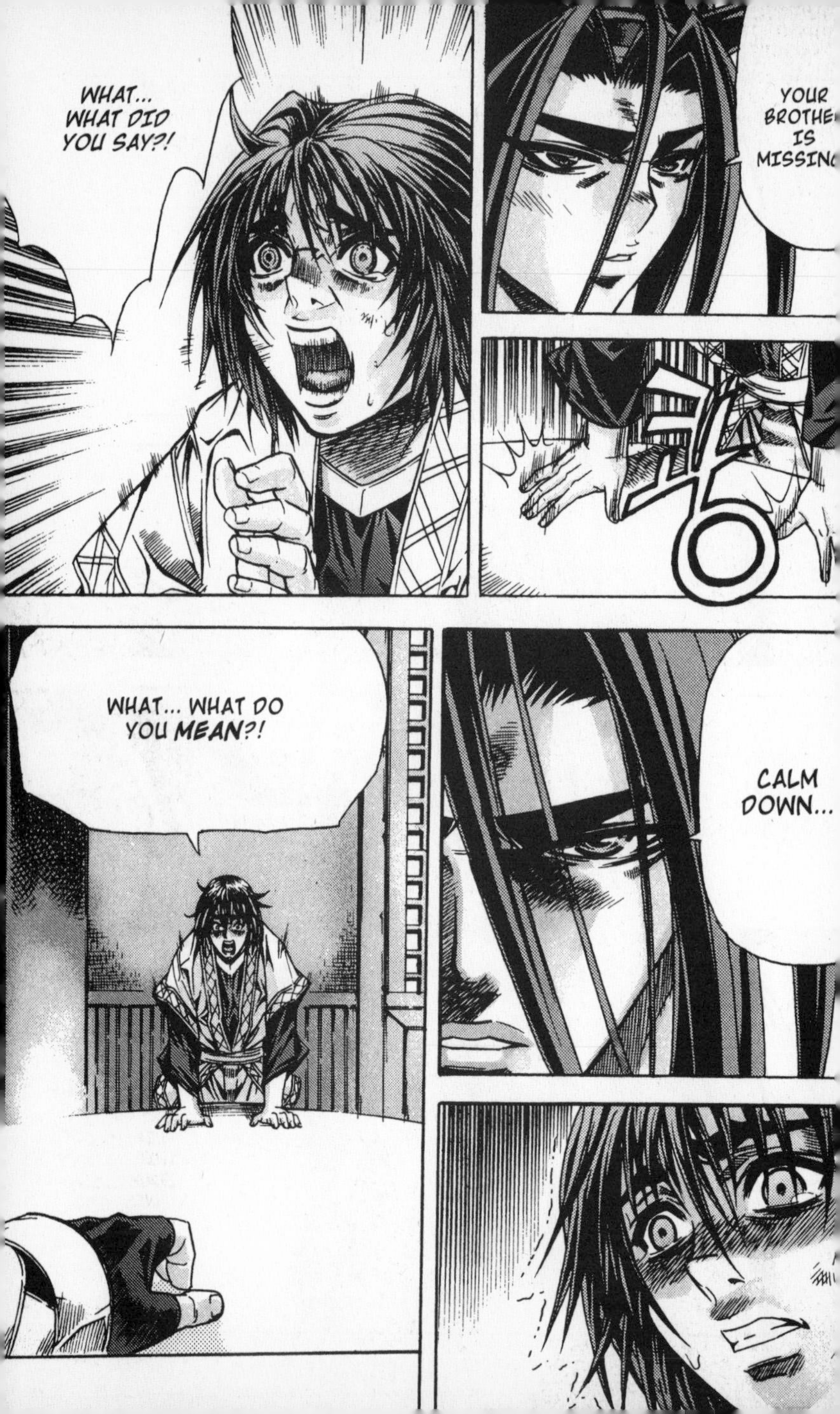
WHAT... WHAT DID YOU SAY?!
YOUR BROTHE IS MISSIN
WHAT... WHAT DO YOU **MEAN**?!
CALM DOWN...

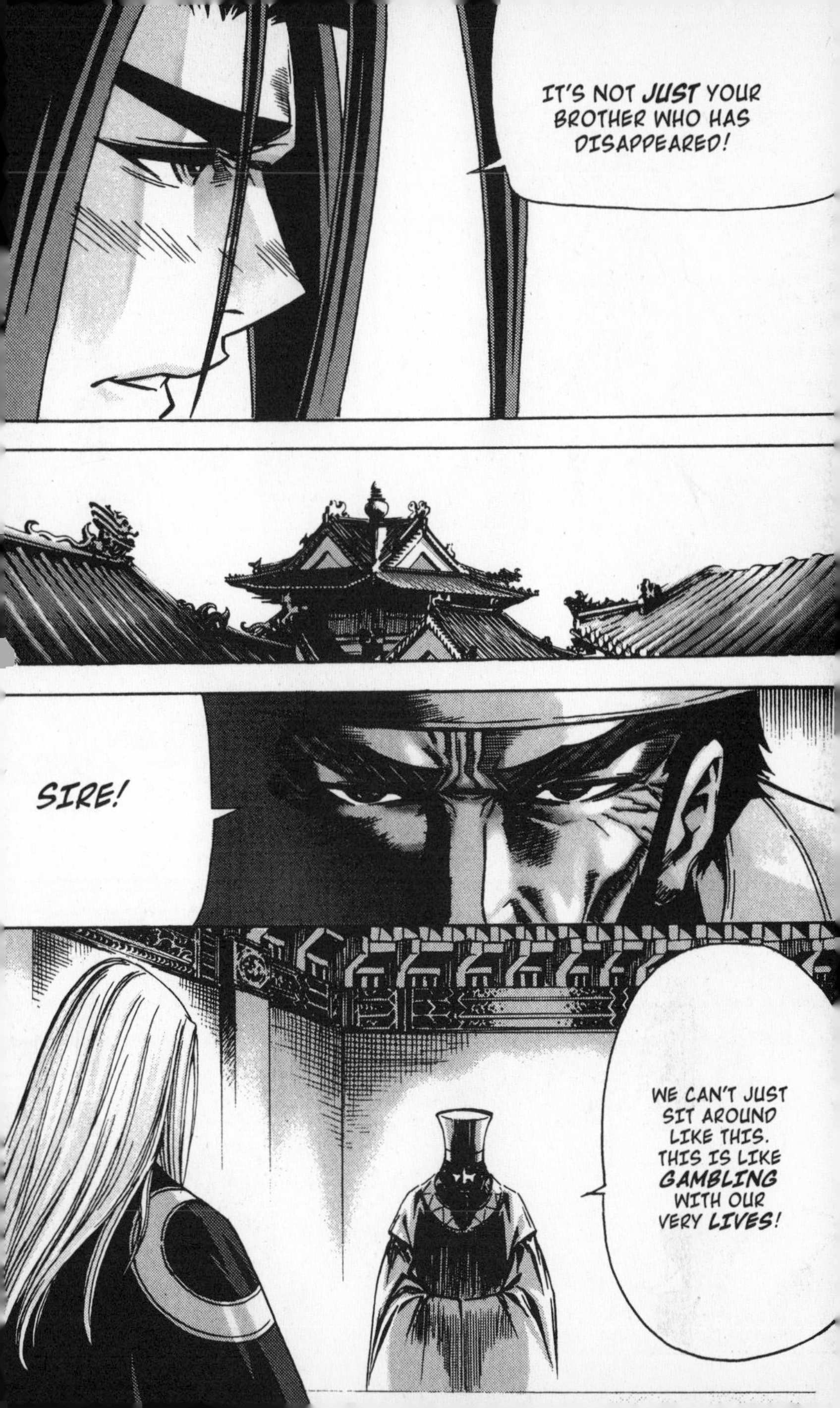
IT'S NOT JUST YOUR BROTHER WHO HAS DISAPPEARED!
SIRE!
WE CAN'T JUST SIT AROUND LIKE THIS. THIS IS LIKE GAMBLING WITH OUR VERY LIVES!

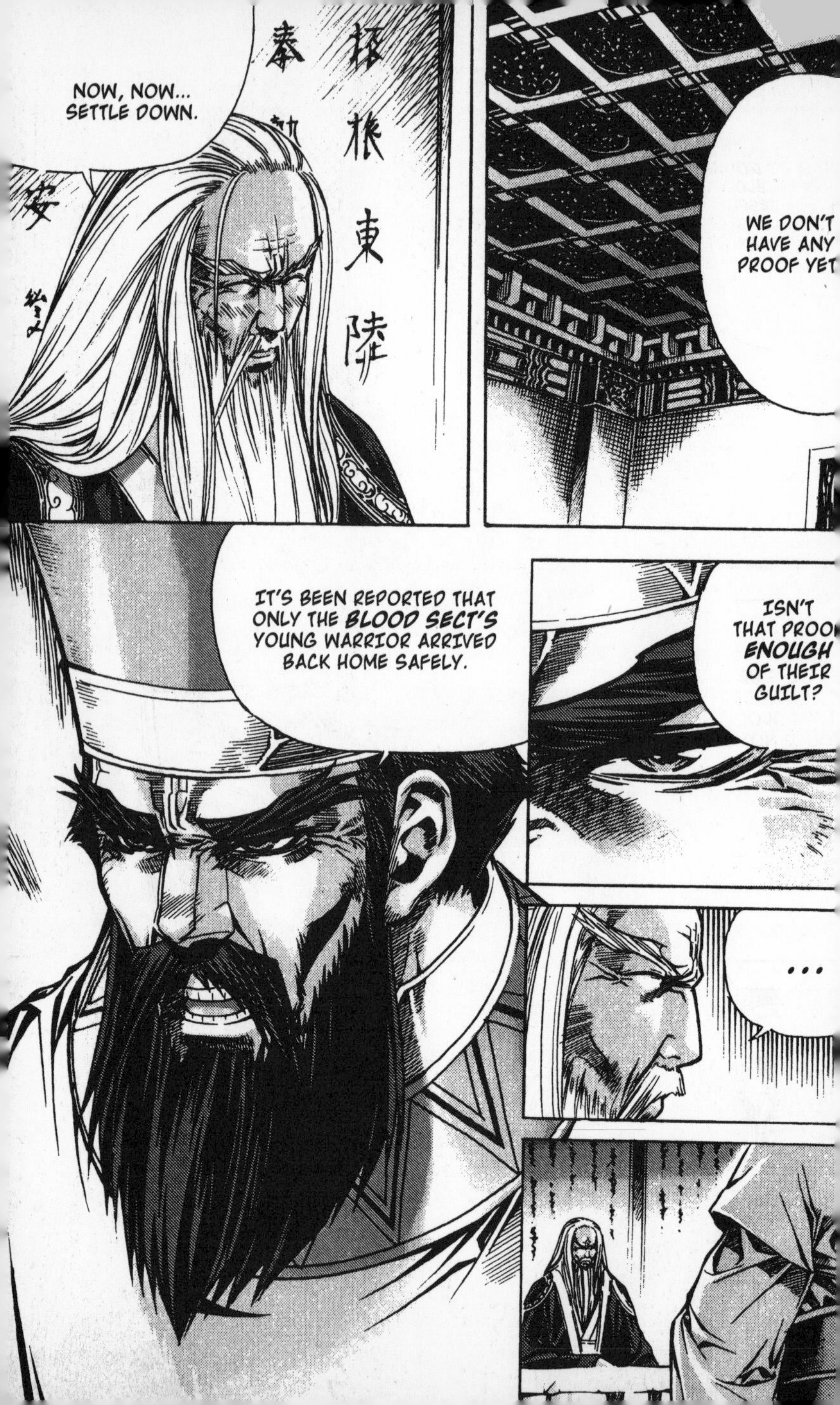
NOW, NOW... SETTLE DOWN.
WE DON'T HAVE ANY PROOF YET
IT'S BEEN REPORTED THAT ONLY THE BLOOD SECT'S YOUNG WARRIOR ARRIVED BACK HOME SAFELY.
ISN'T THAT PROO ENOUGH OF THEIR GUILT?
...

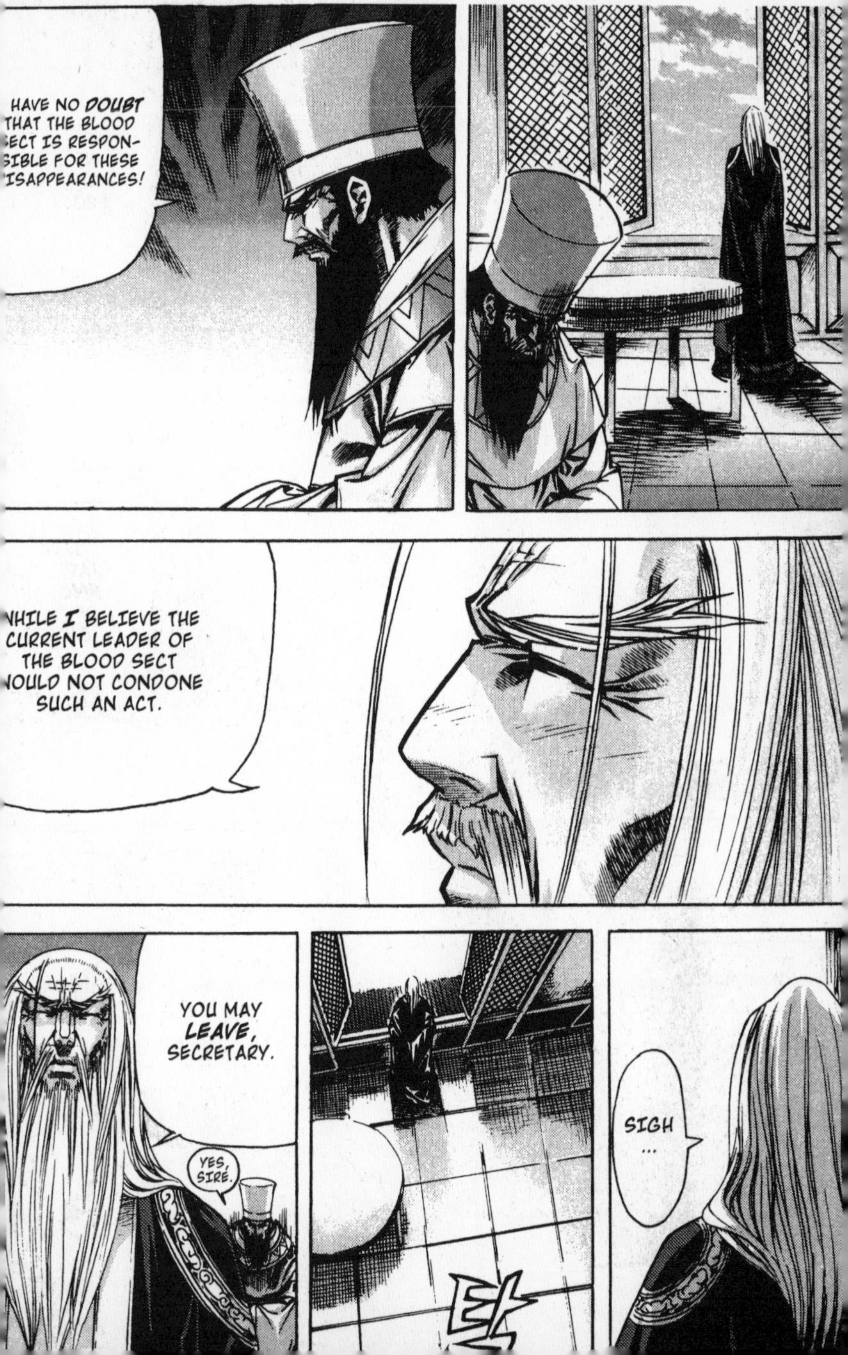
HAVE NO DOUBT THAT THE BLOOD SECT IS RESPONSIBLE FOR THESE DISAPPEARANCES!
WHILE I BELIEVE THE CURRENT LEADER OF THE BLOOD SECT WOULD NOT CONDONE SUCH AN ACT.
YOU MAY LEAVE, SECRETARY.
YES, SIRE.
SIGH ...

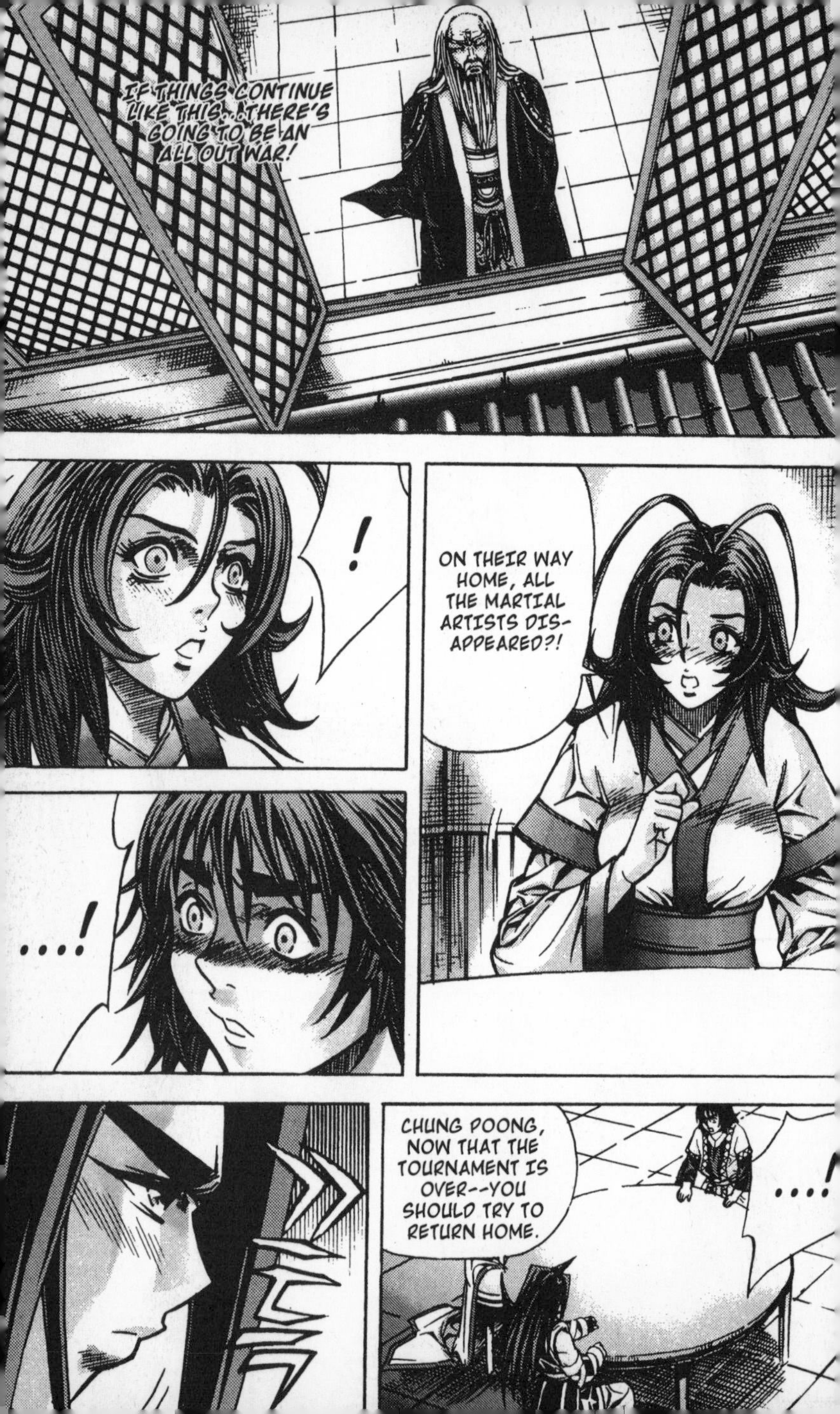

IF THINGS CONTINUE LIKE THIS... THERE'S GOING TO BE AN ALL OUT WAR!
!
ON THEIR WAY HOME, ALL THE MARTIAL ARTISTS DIS-APPEARED?!
....!
CHUNG POONG, NOW THAT THE TOURNAMENT IS OVER--YOU SHOULD TRY TO RETURN HOME.
....

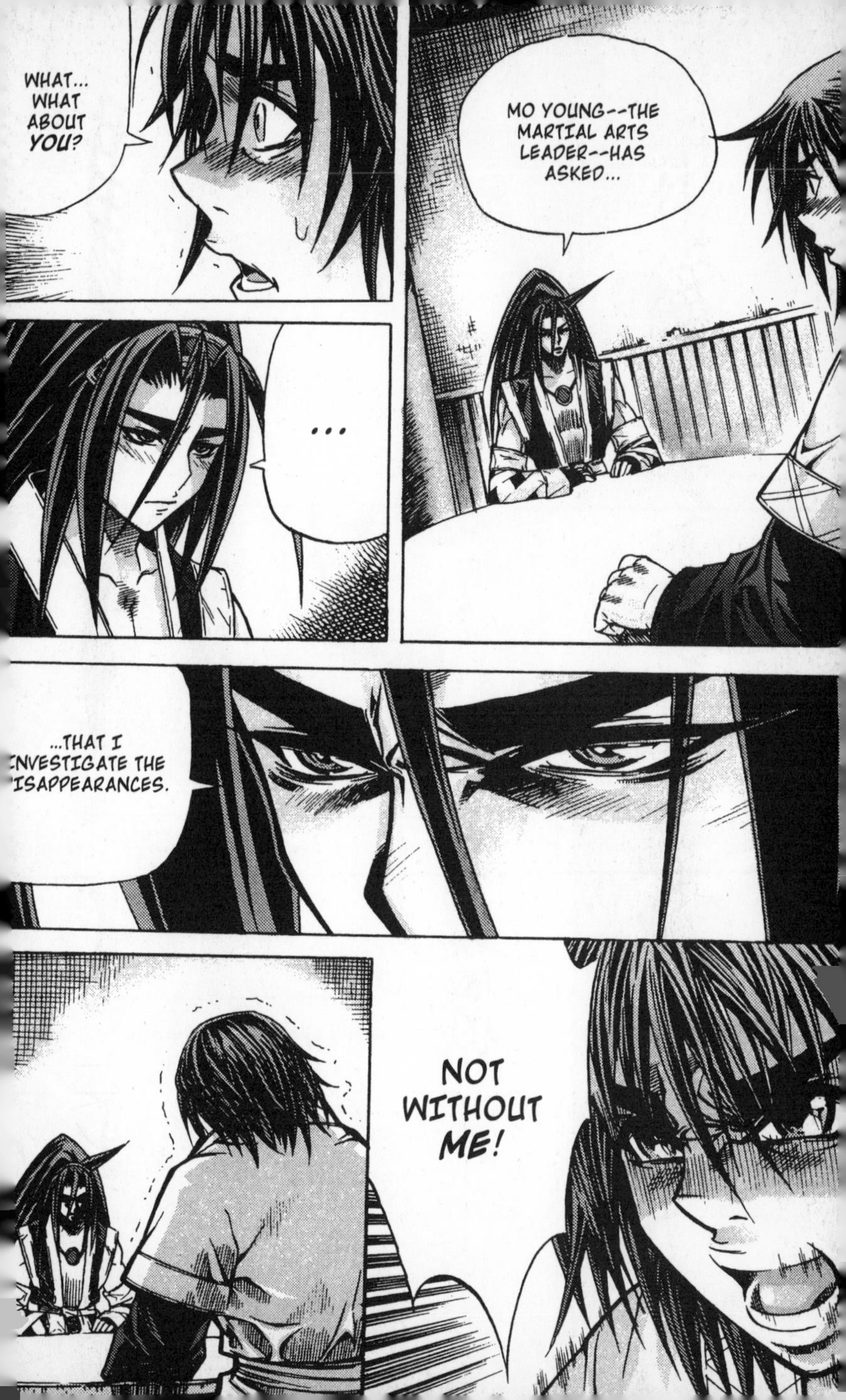
WHAT... WHAT ABOUT YOU?
...
MO YOUNG--THE MARTIAL ARTS LEADER--HAS ASKED...
...THAT I NVESTIGATE THE ISAPPEARANCES.
NOT WITHOUT ME!

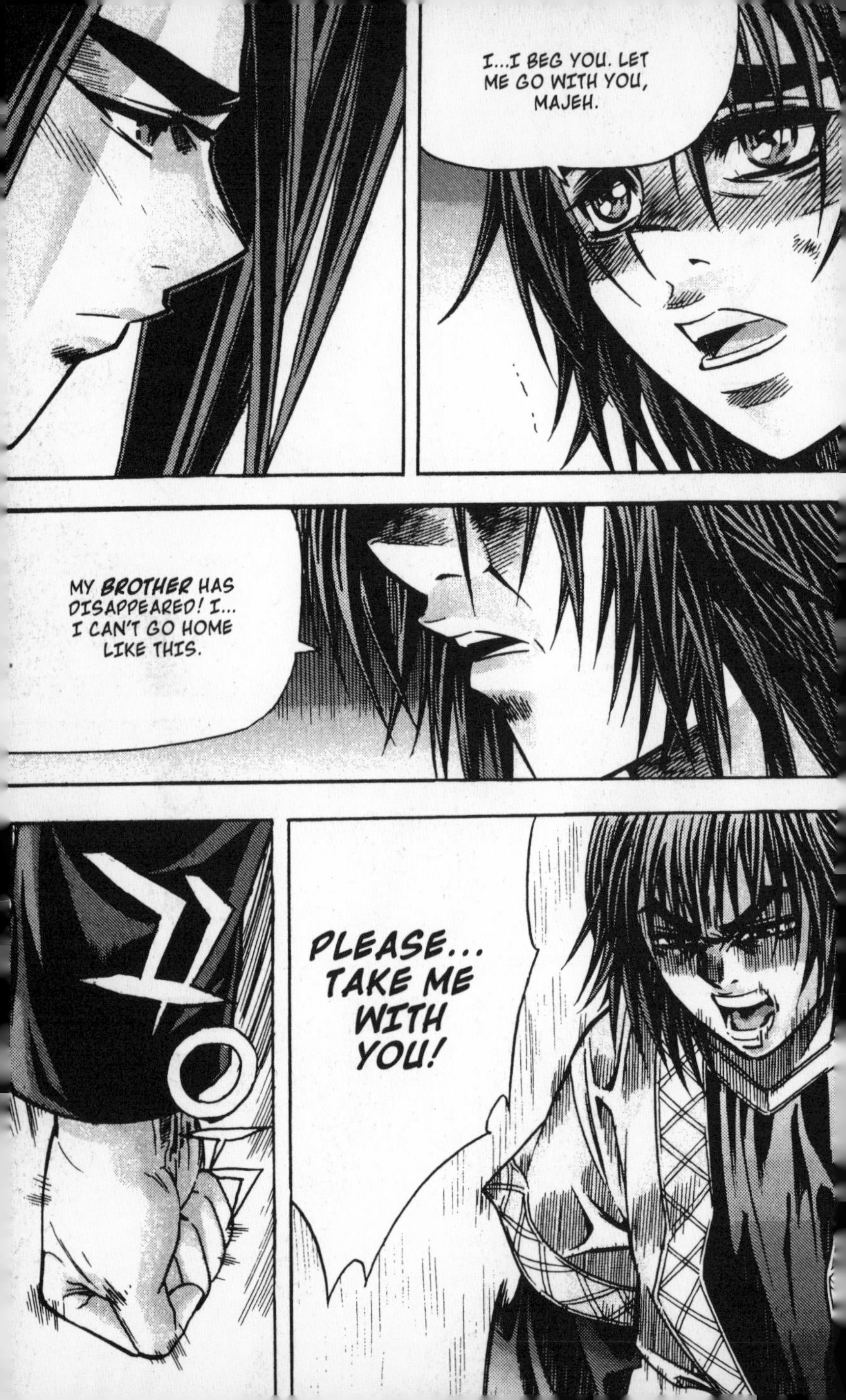
I...I BEG YOU. LET ME GO WITH YOU, MAJEH.
MY BROTHER HAS DISAPPEARED! I... I CAN'T GO HOME LIKE THIS.
PLEASE... TAKE ME WITH YOU!

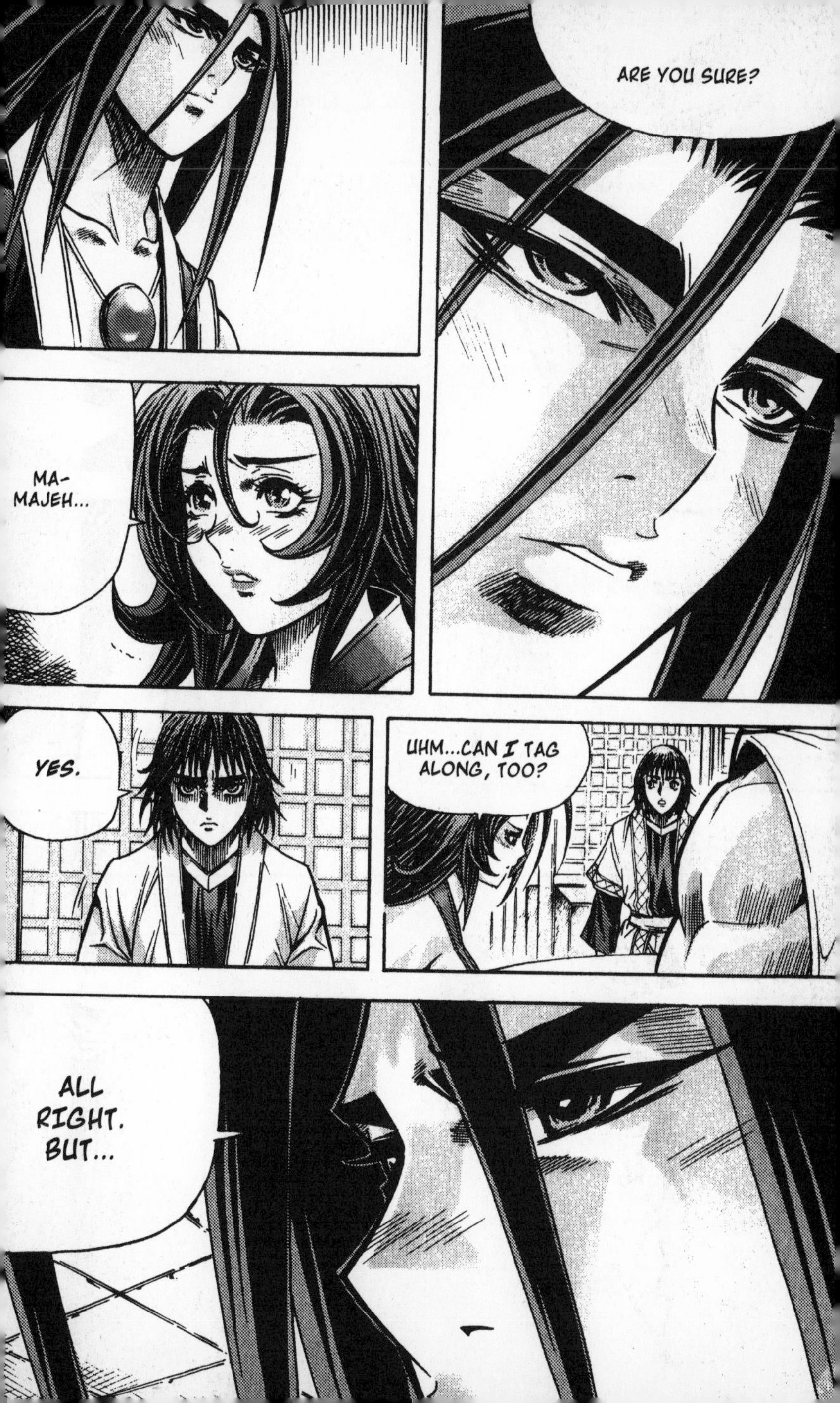
MA-
MAJEH...
ARE YOU SURE?
YES.
UHM...CAN I TAG ALONG, TOO?
ALL RIGHT. BUT...

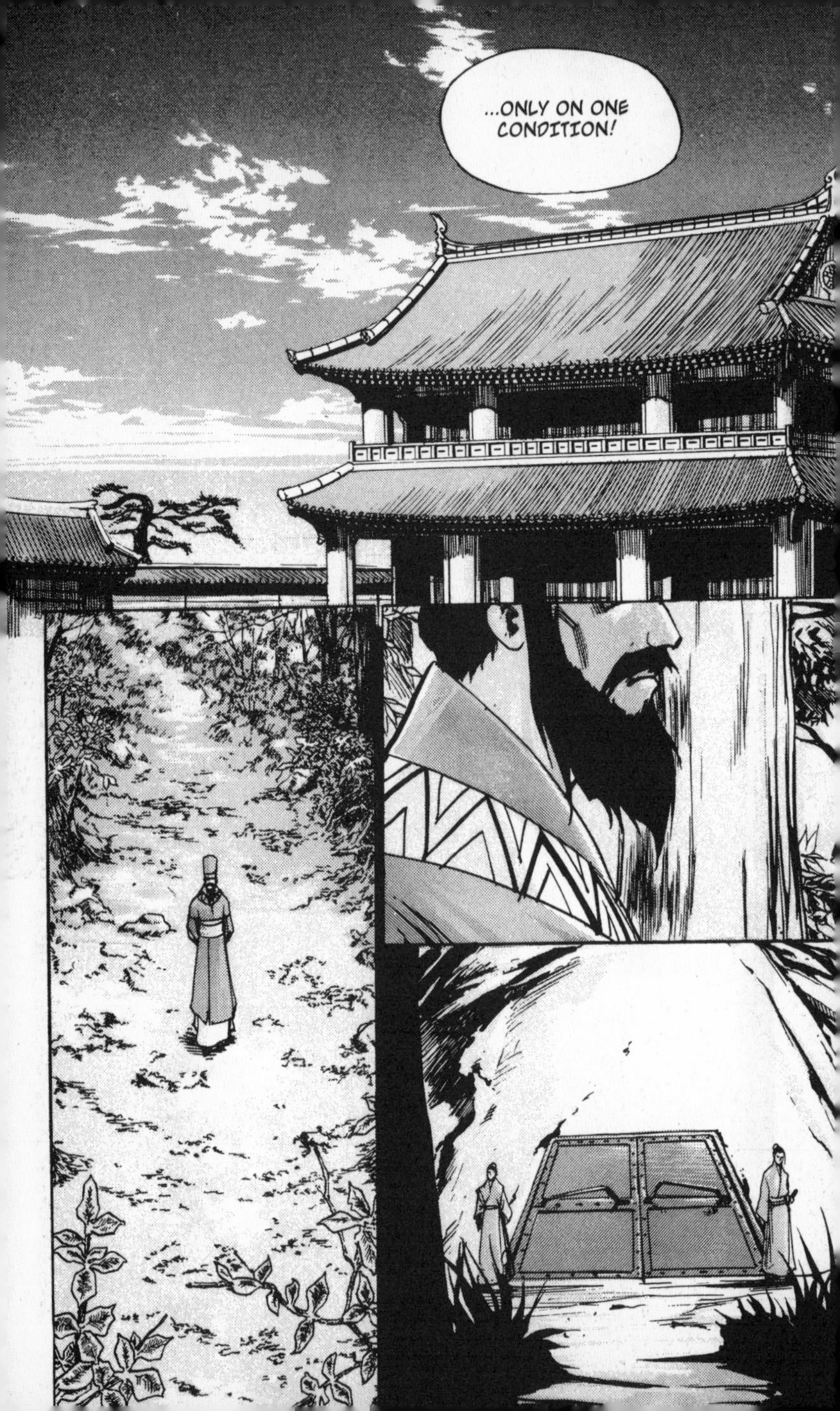
...ONLY ON ONE CONDITION!

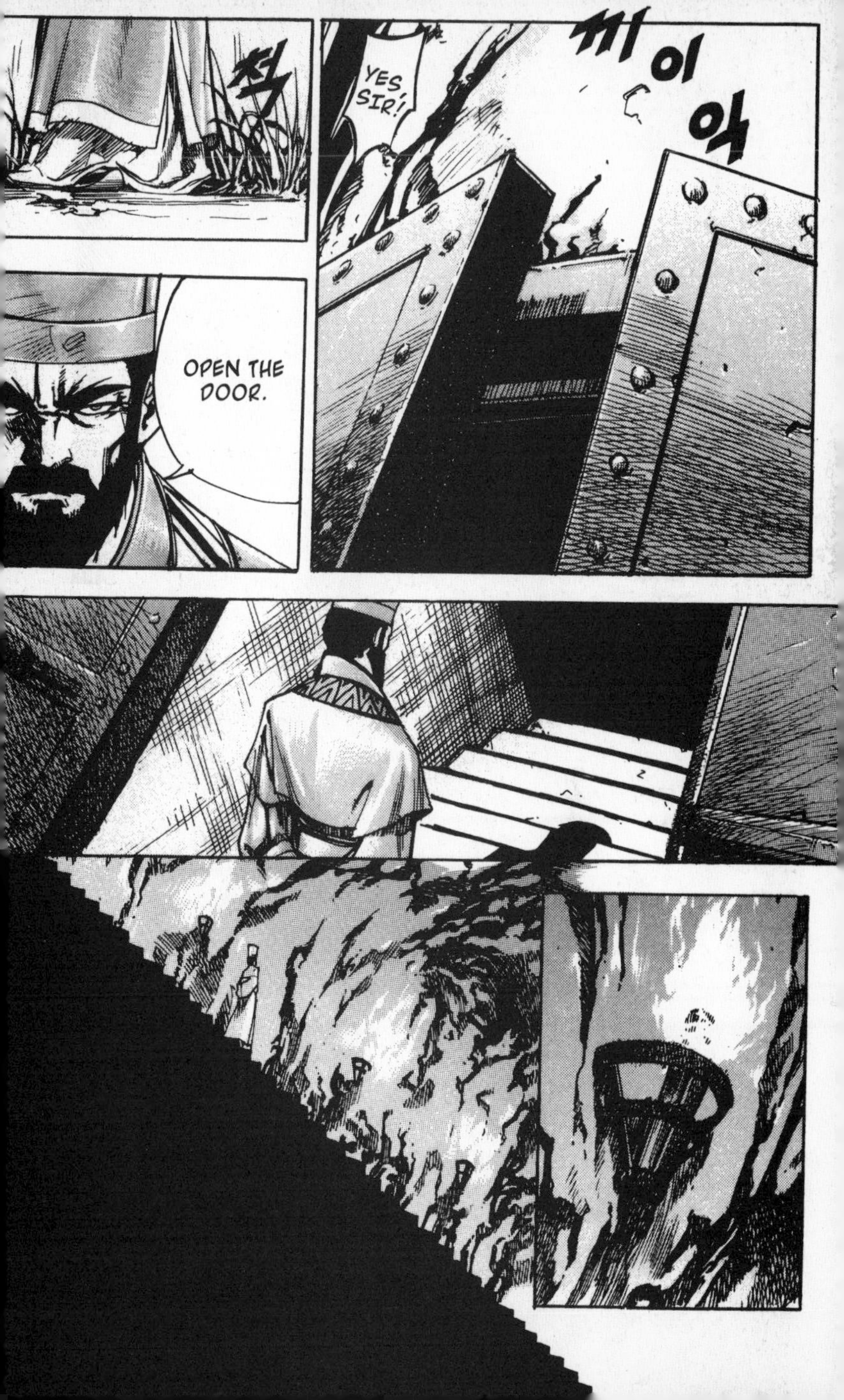
척
OPEN THE DOOR.
YES SIR!
끼이아

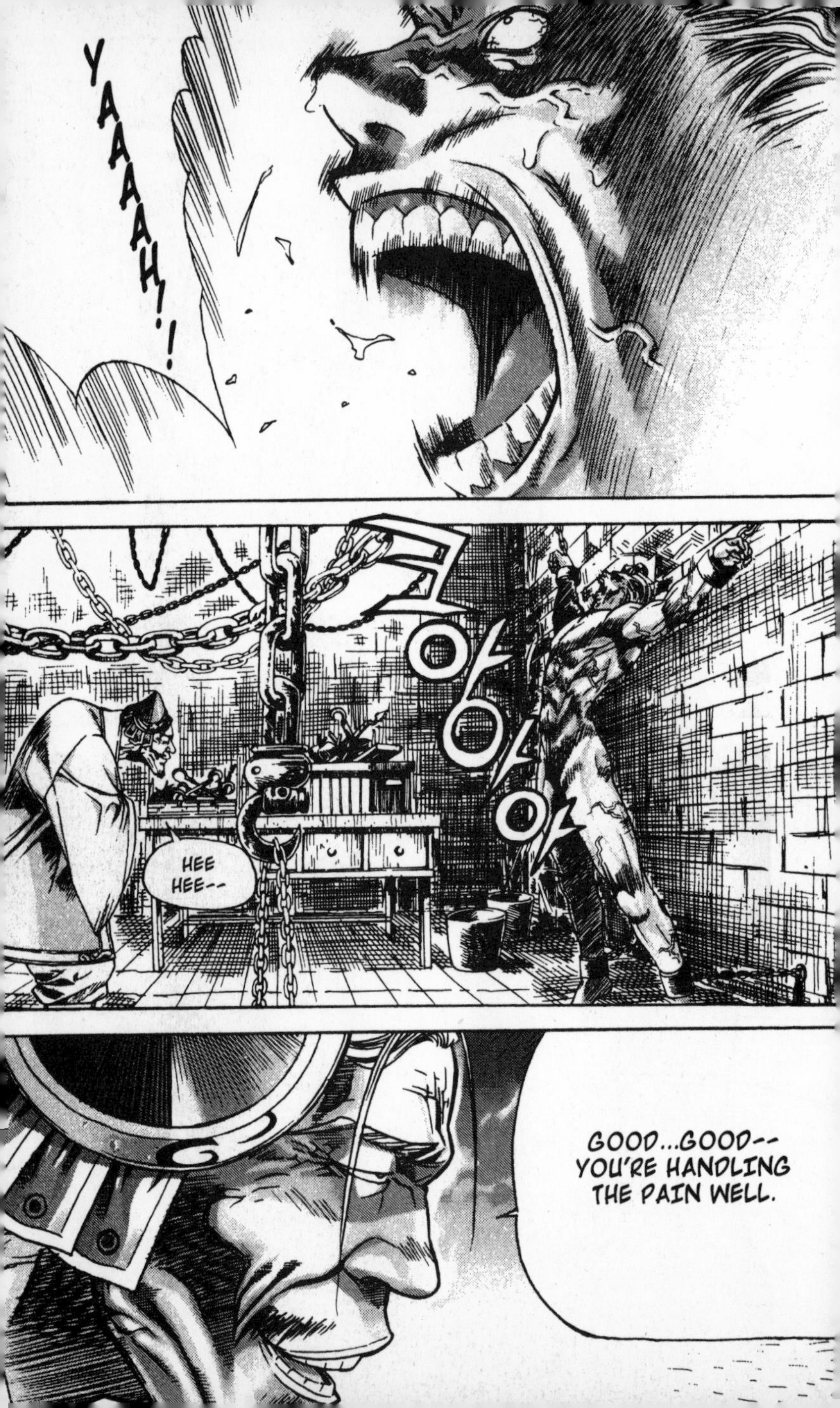
YAAAAH!!
HEE HEE--
GOOD...GOOD-- YOU'RE HANDLING THE PAIN WELL.

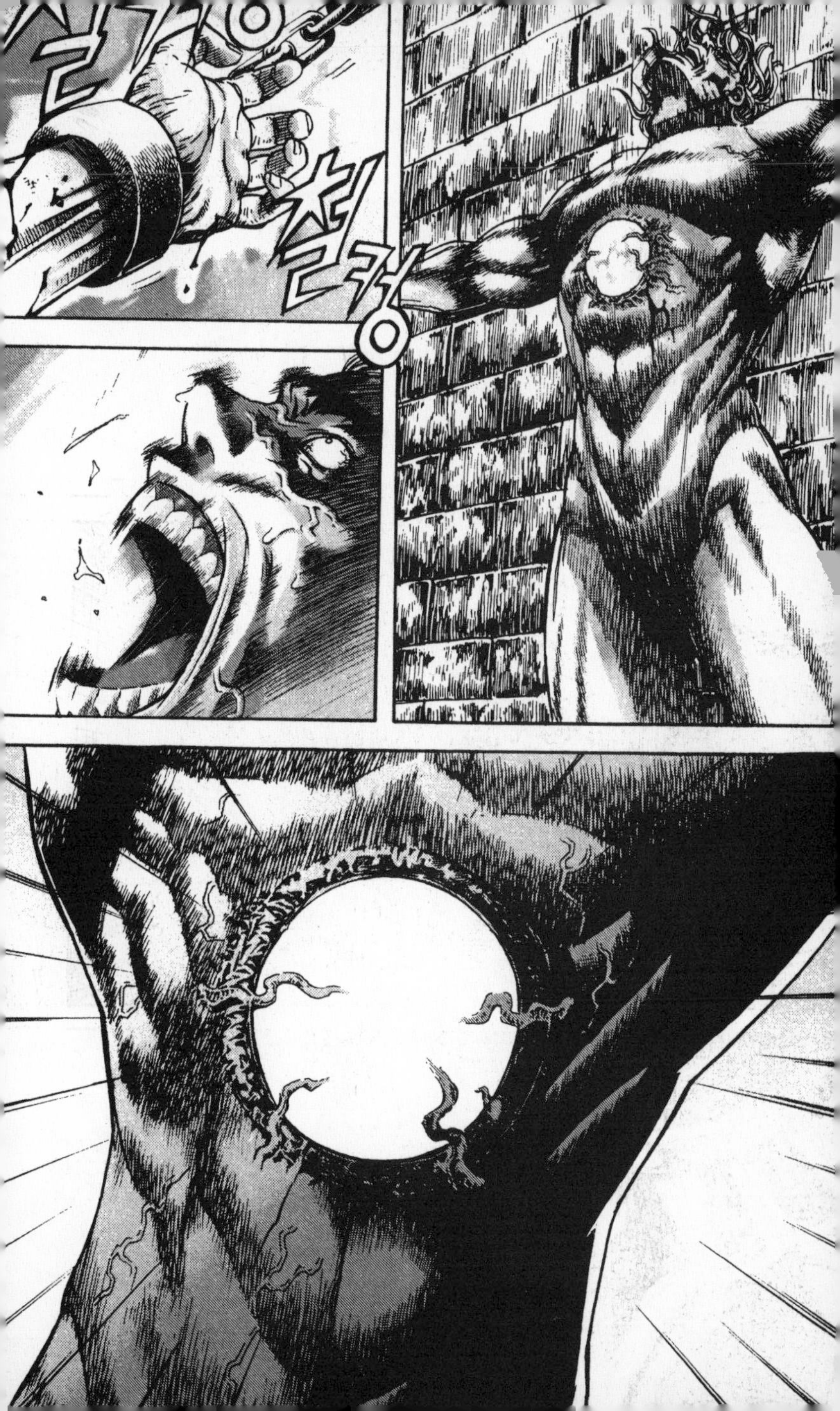
철컹

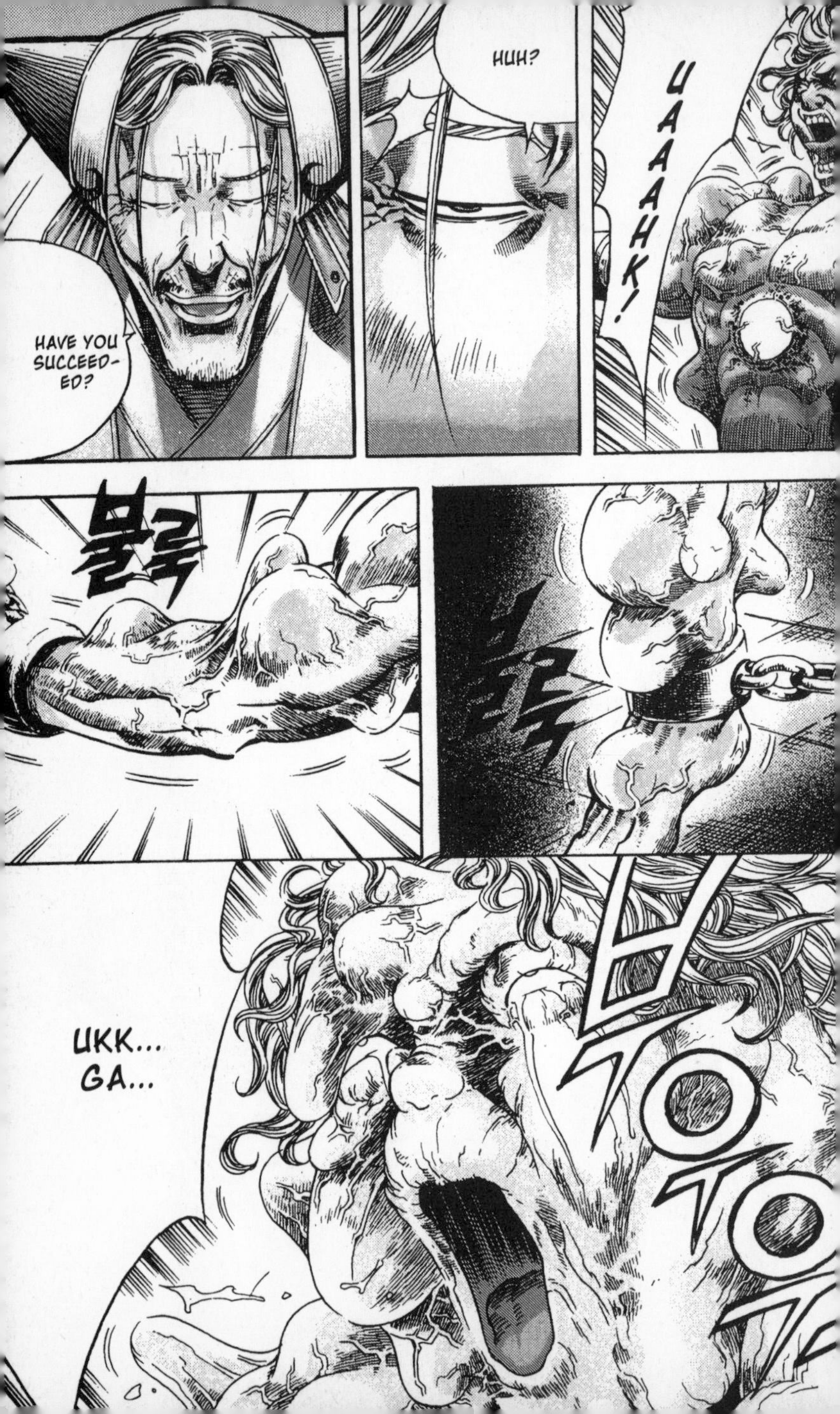
HAVE YOU SUCCEED-ED?
HUH?
UAAAAHK!
불룩
UKK... GA...

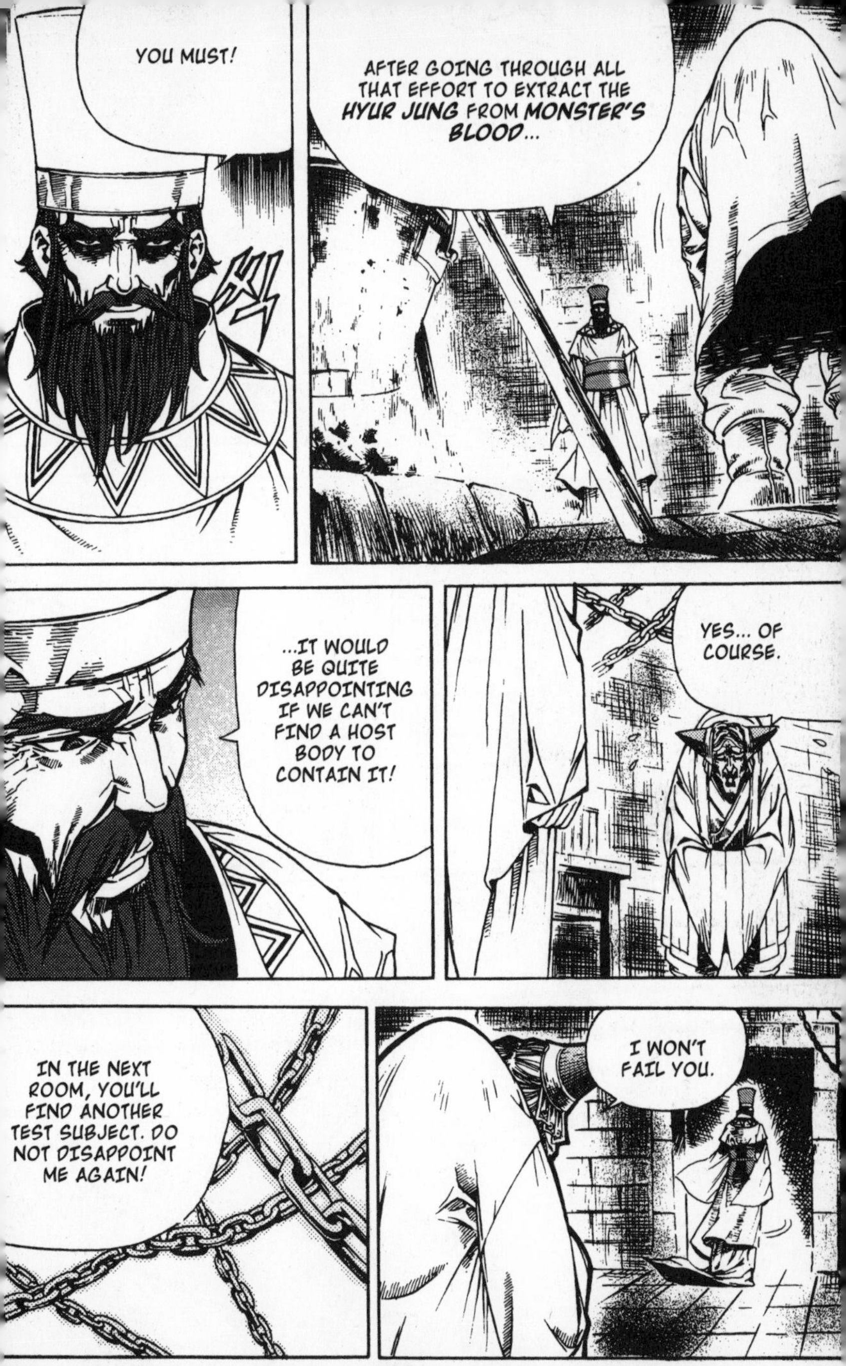
YOU MUST!
AFTER GOING THROUGH ALL THAT EFFORT TO EXTRACT THE HYUR JUNG FROM MONSTER'S BLOOD...
...IT WOULD BE QUITE DISAPPOINTING IF WE CAN'T FIND A HOST BODY TO CONTAIN IT!
YES... OF COURSE.
IN THE NEXT ROOM, YOU'LL FIND ANOTHER TEST SUBJECT. DO NOT DISAPPOINT ME AGAIN!
I WON'T FAIL YOU.

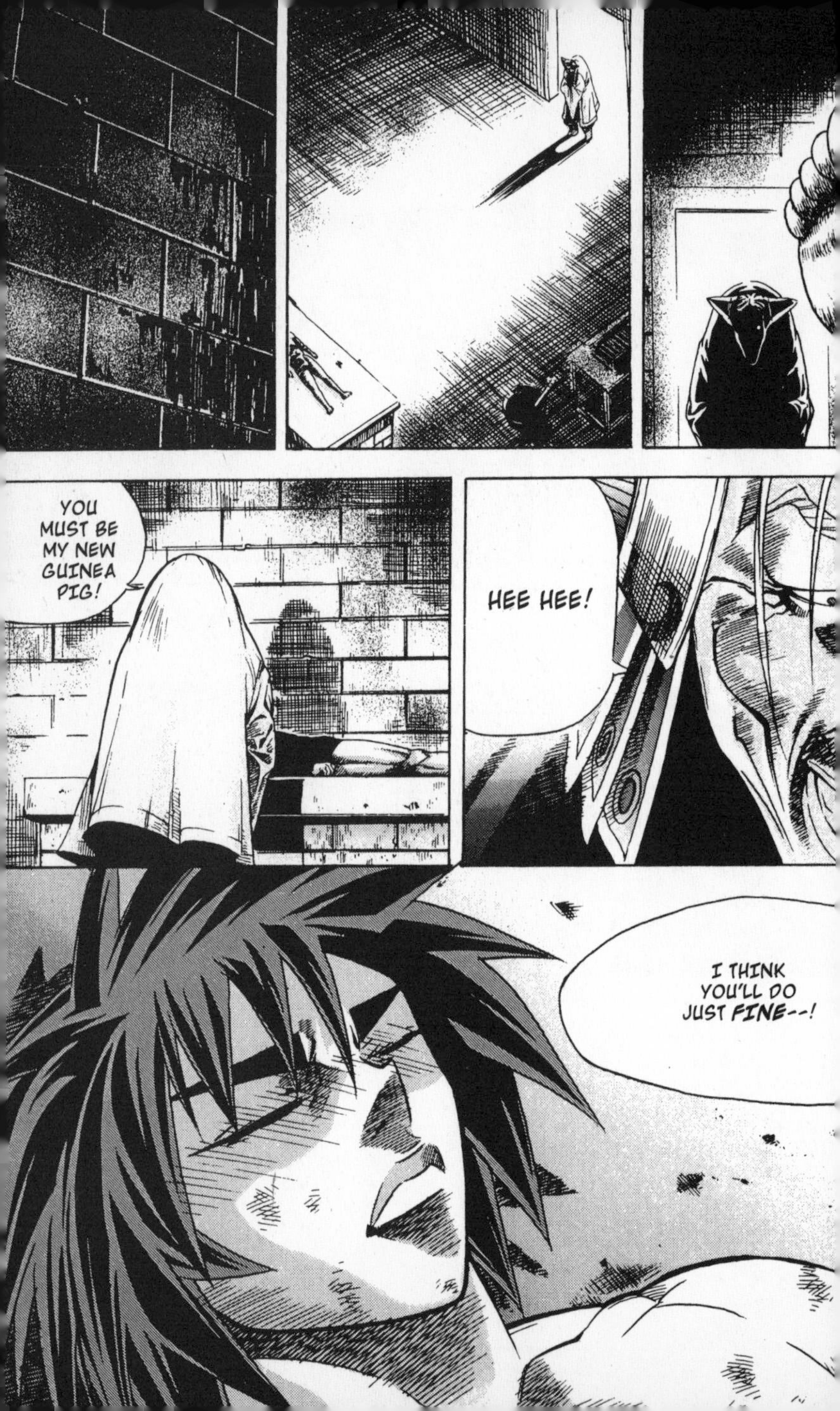
YOU MUST BE MY NEW GUINEA PIG!
HEE HEE!
I THINK YOU'LL DO JUST *FINE*--!

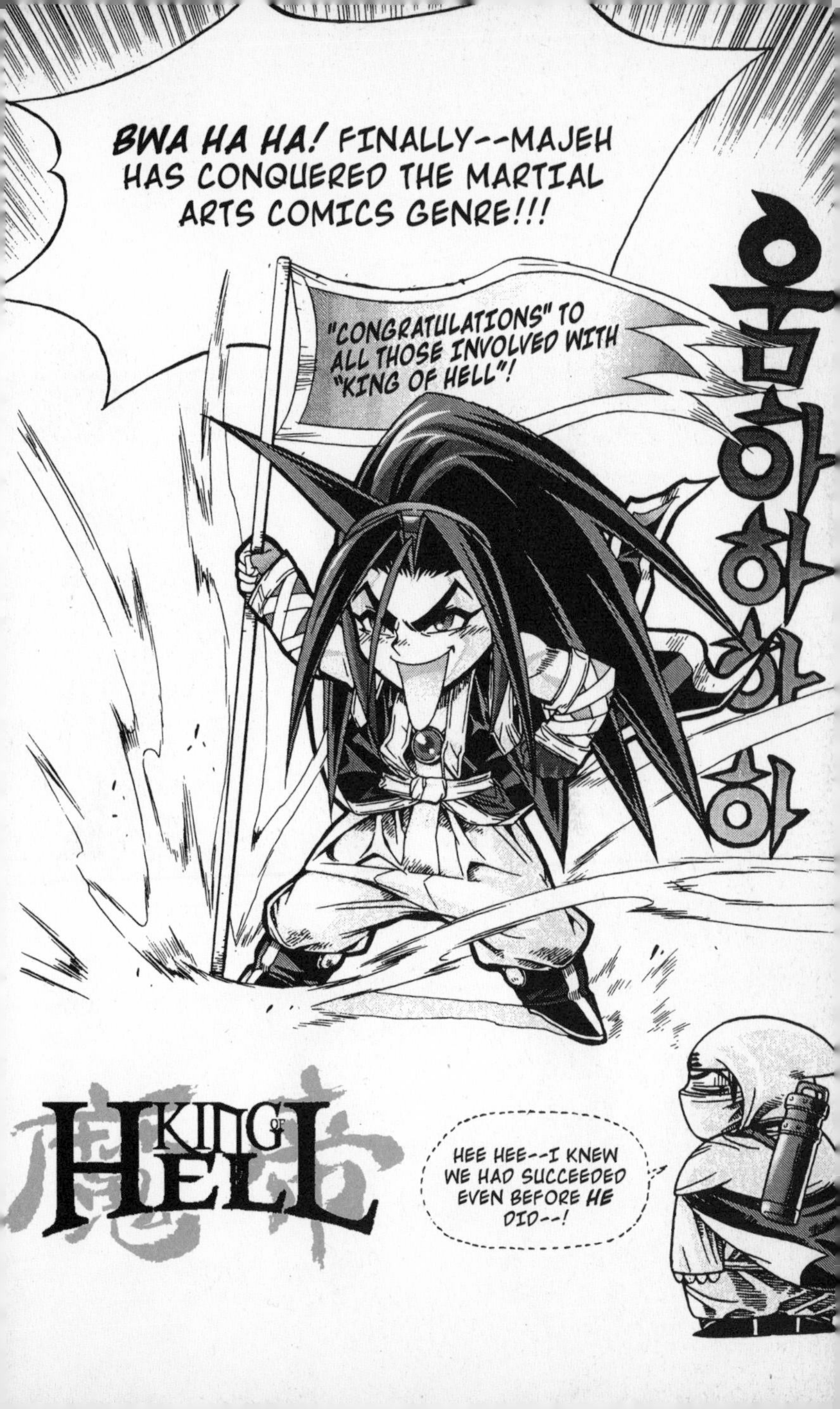
BWA HA HA! FINALLY--MAJEH HAS CONQUERED THE MARTIAL ARTS COMICS GENRE!!!
"CONGRATULATIONS" TO ALL THOSE INVOLVED WITH "KING OF HELL"!
웃하하하하
KING OF HELL
HEE HEE--I KNEW WE HAD SUCCEEDED EVEN BEFORE HE DID--!

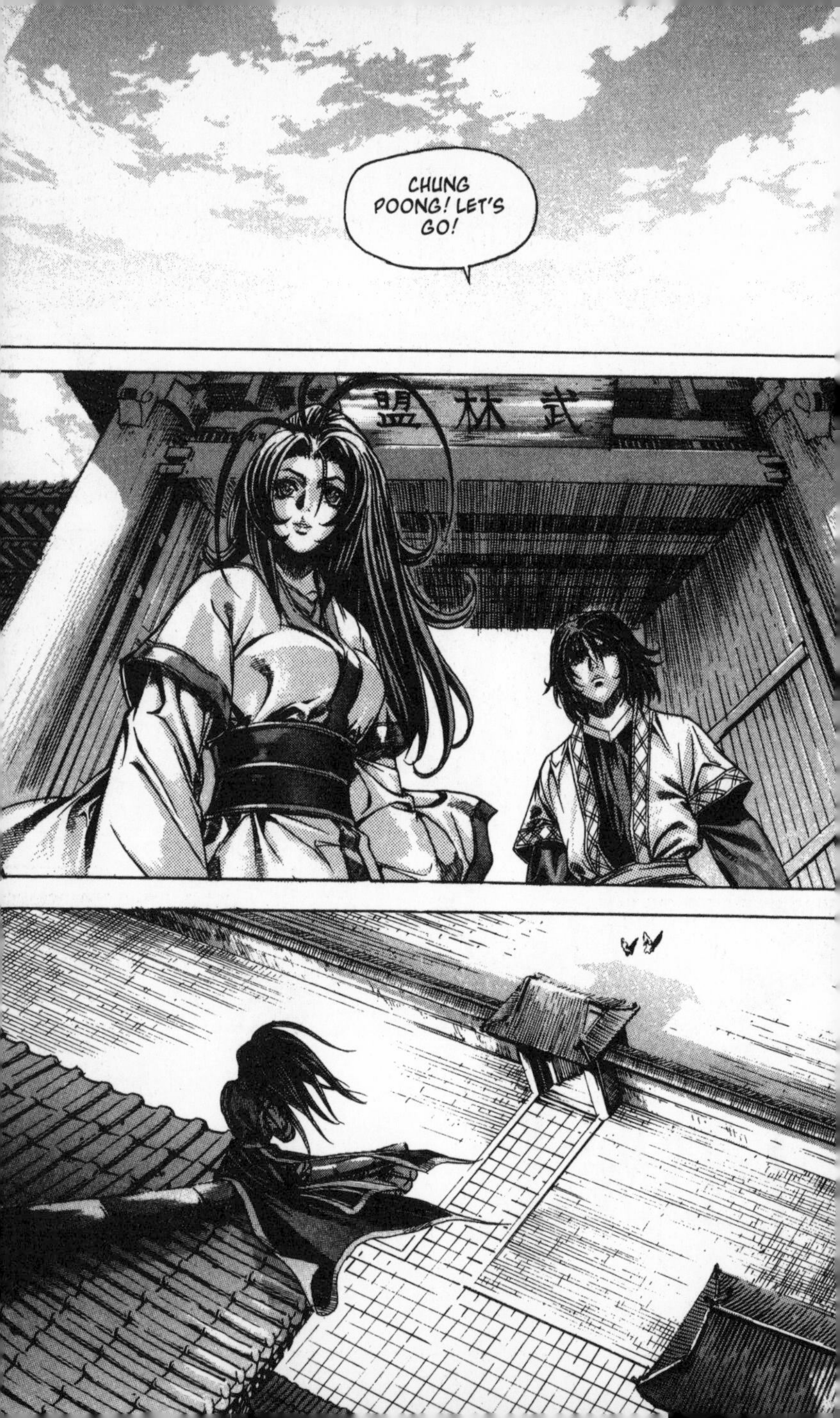
CHUNG POONG! LET'S GO!
武林盟

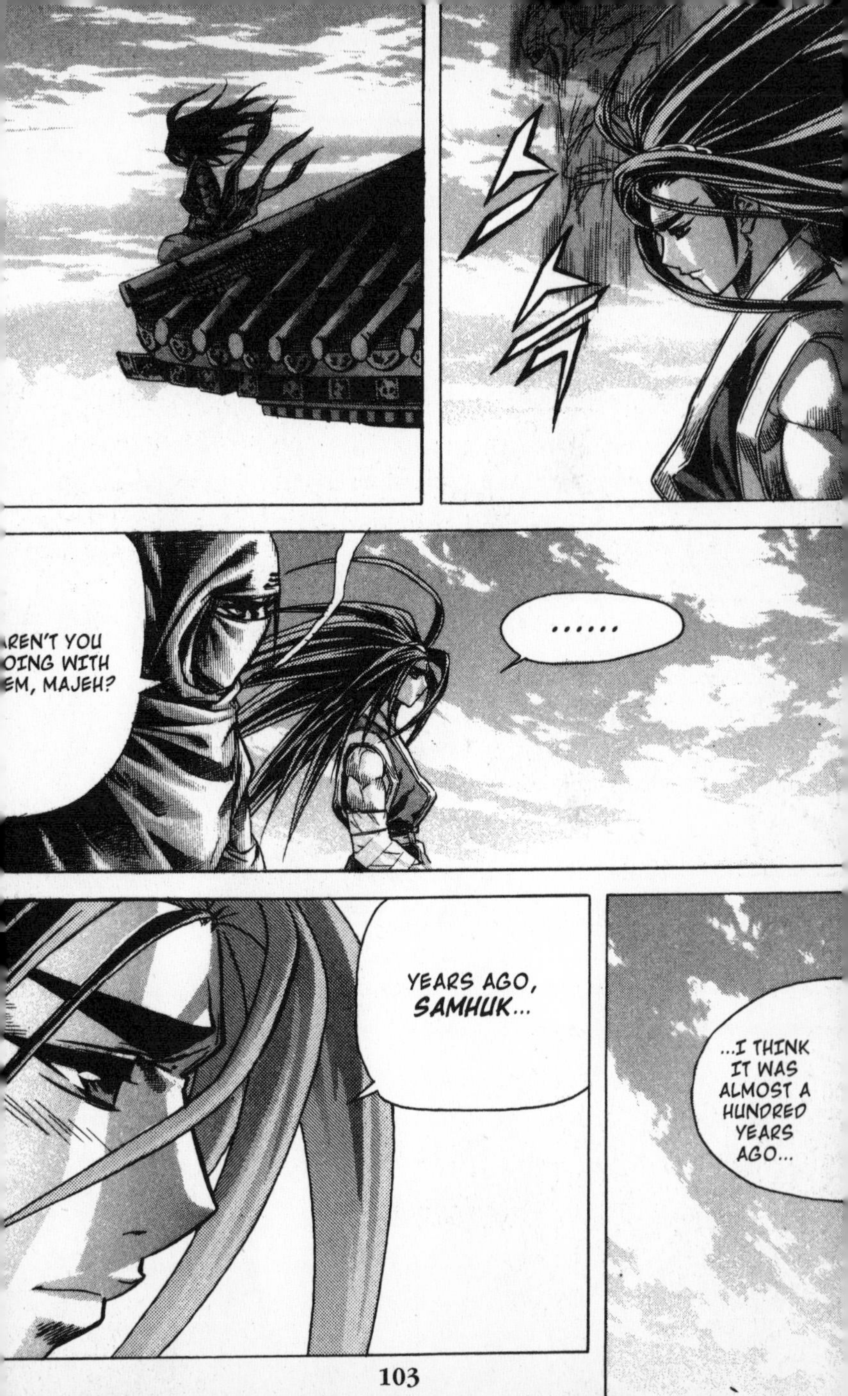

ʀEN'T YOU
OING WITH
EM, MAJEH?
......
YEARS AGO,
SAMHUK...
...I THINK
IT WAS
ALMOST A
HUNDRED
YEARS
AGO...

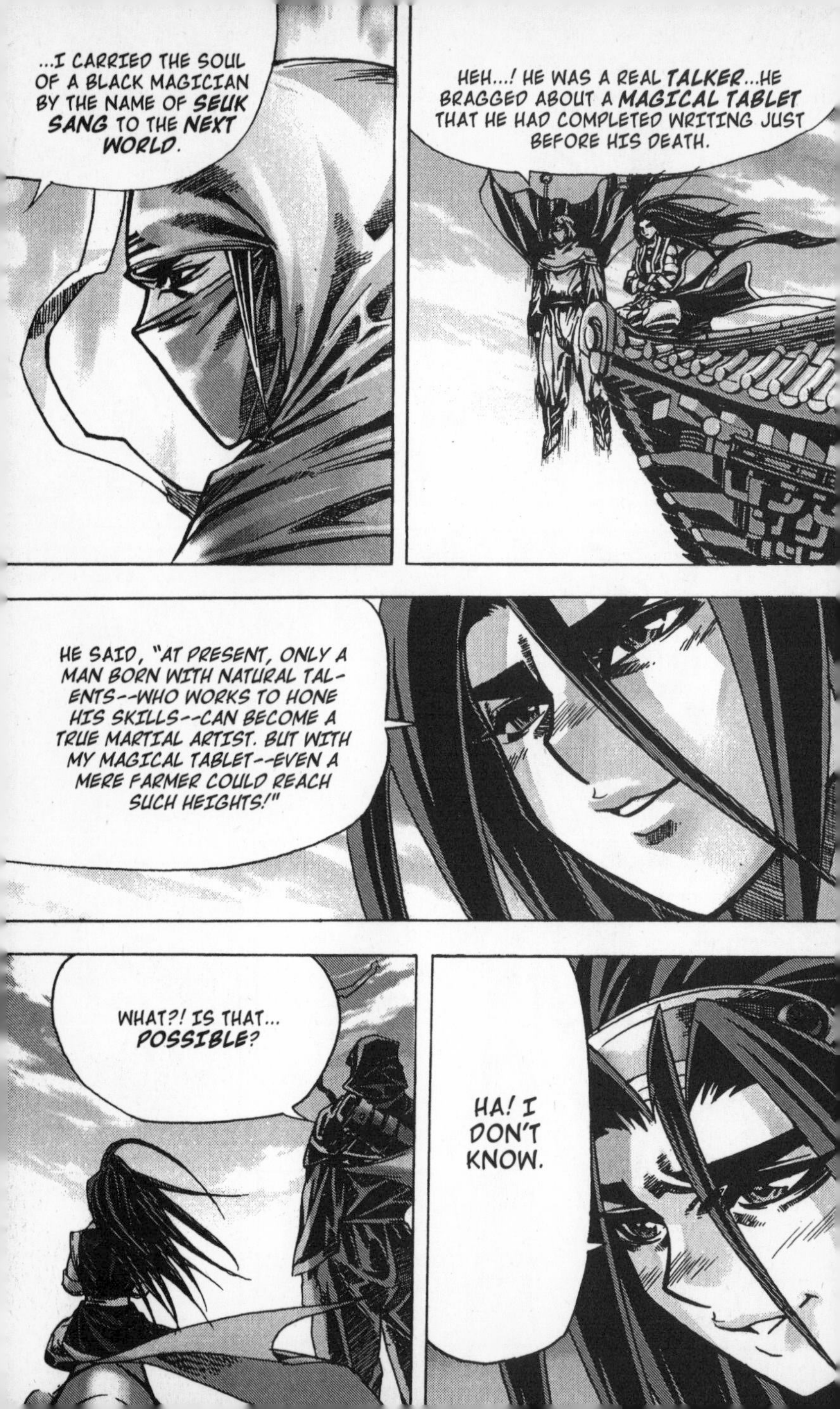
...I CARRIED THE SOUL OF A BLACK MAGICIAN BY THE NAME OF **SEUK SANG** TO THE **NEXT WORLD**.
HEH...! HE WAS A REAL **TALKER**...HE BRAGGED ABOUT A **MAGICAL TABLET** THAT HE HAD COMPLETED WRITING JUST BEFORE HIS DEATH.
HE SAID, "AT PRESENT, ONLY A MAN BORN WITH NATURAL TAL-ENTS--WHO WORKS TO HONE HIS SKILLS--CAN BECOME A TRUE MARTIAL ARTIST. BUT WITH MY MAGICAL TABLET--EVEN A MERE FARMER COULD REACH SUCH HEIGHTS!"
WHAT?! IS THAT... **POSSIBLE**?
HA! I DON'T KNOW.

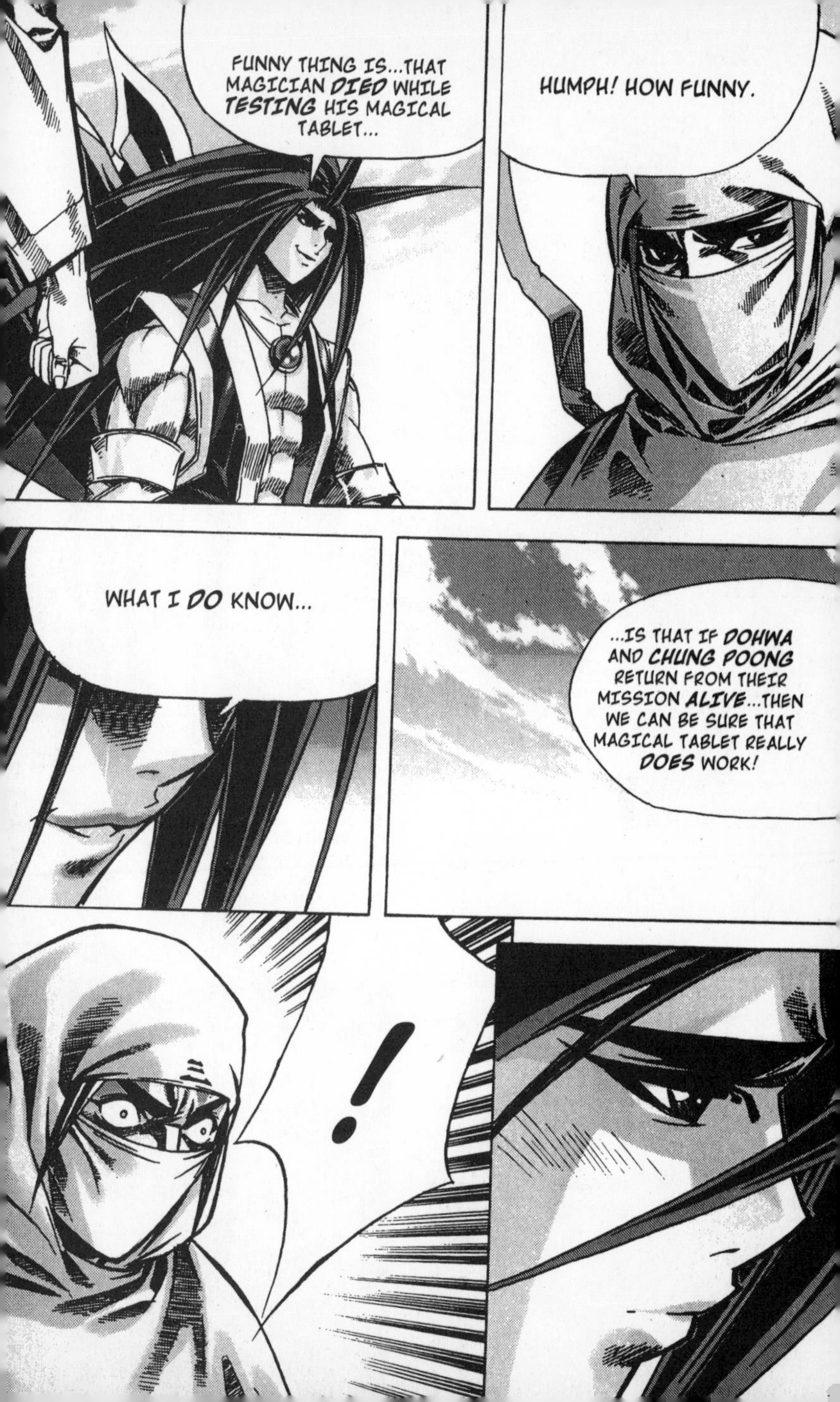
FUNNY THING IS...THAT MAGICIAN DIED WHILE TESTING HIS MAGICAL TABLET...
HUMPH! HOW FUNNY.
WHAT I DO KNOW...
...IS THAT IF DOHWA AND CHUNG POONG RETURN FROM THEIR MISSION ALIVE...THEN WE CAN BE SURE THAT MAGICAL TABLET REALLY DOES WORK!
!

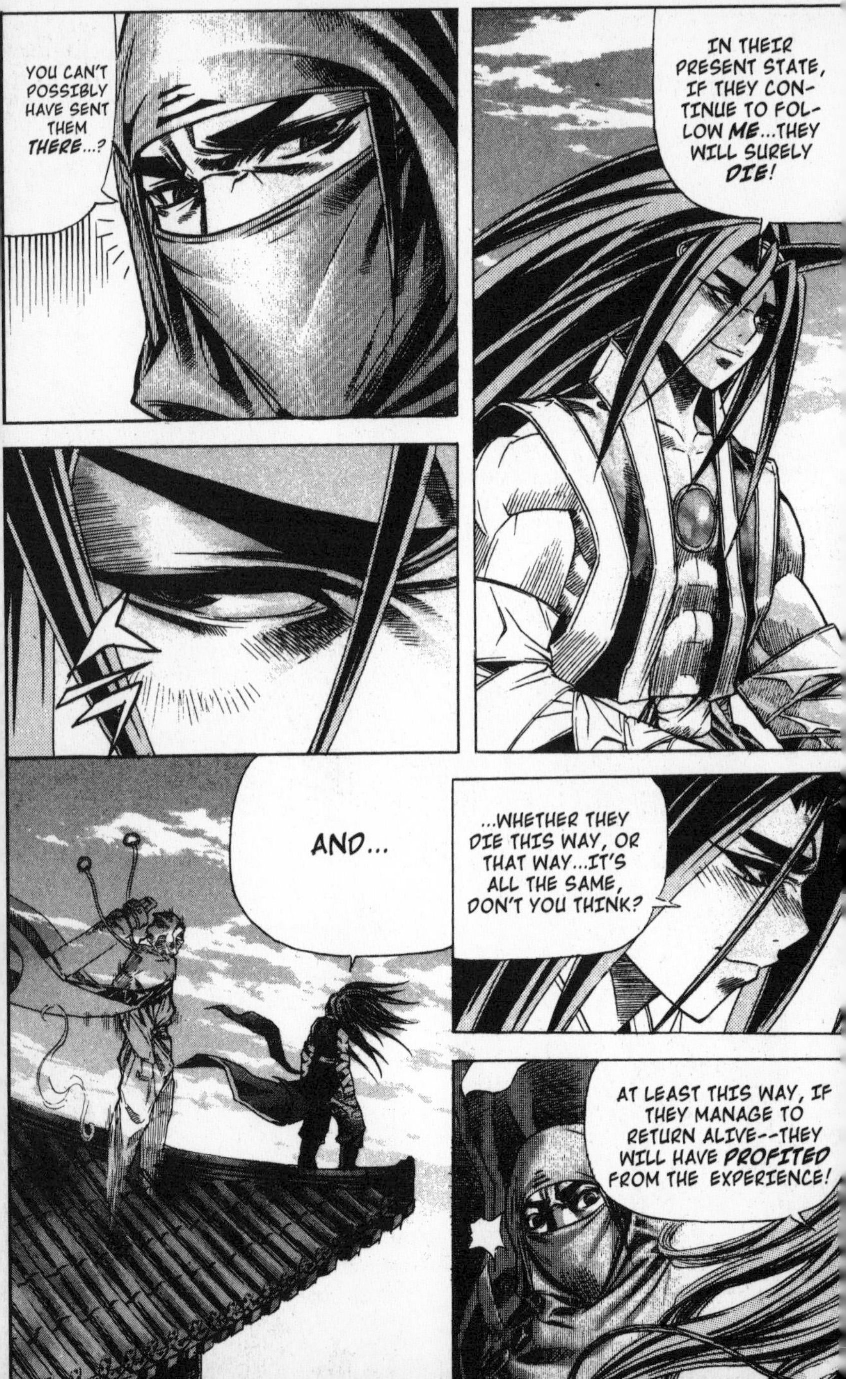
YOU CAN'T POSSIBLY HAVE SENT THEM THERE...?
IN THEIR PRESENT STATE, IF THEY CON-TINUE TO FOL-LOW ME...THEY WILL SURELY DIE!
AND...
...WHETHER THEY DIE THIS WAY, OR THAT WAY...IT'S ALL THE SAME, DON'T YOU THINK?
AT LEAST THIS WAY, IF THEY MANAGE TO RETURN ALIVE--THEY WILL HAVE PROFITED FROM THE EXPERIENCE!

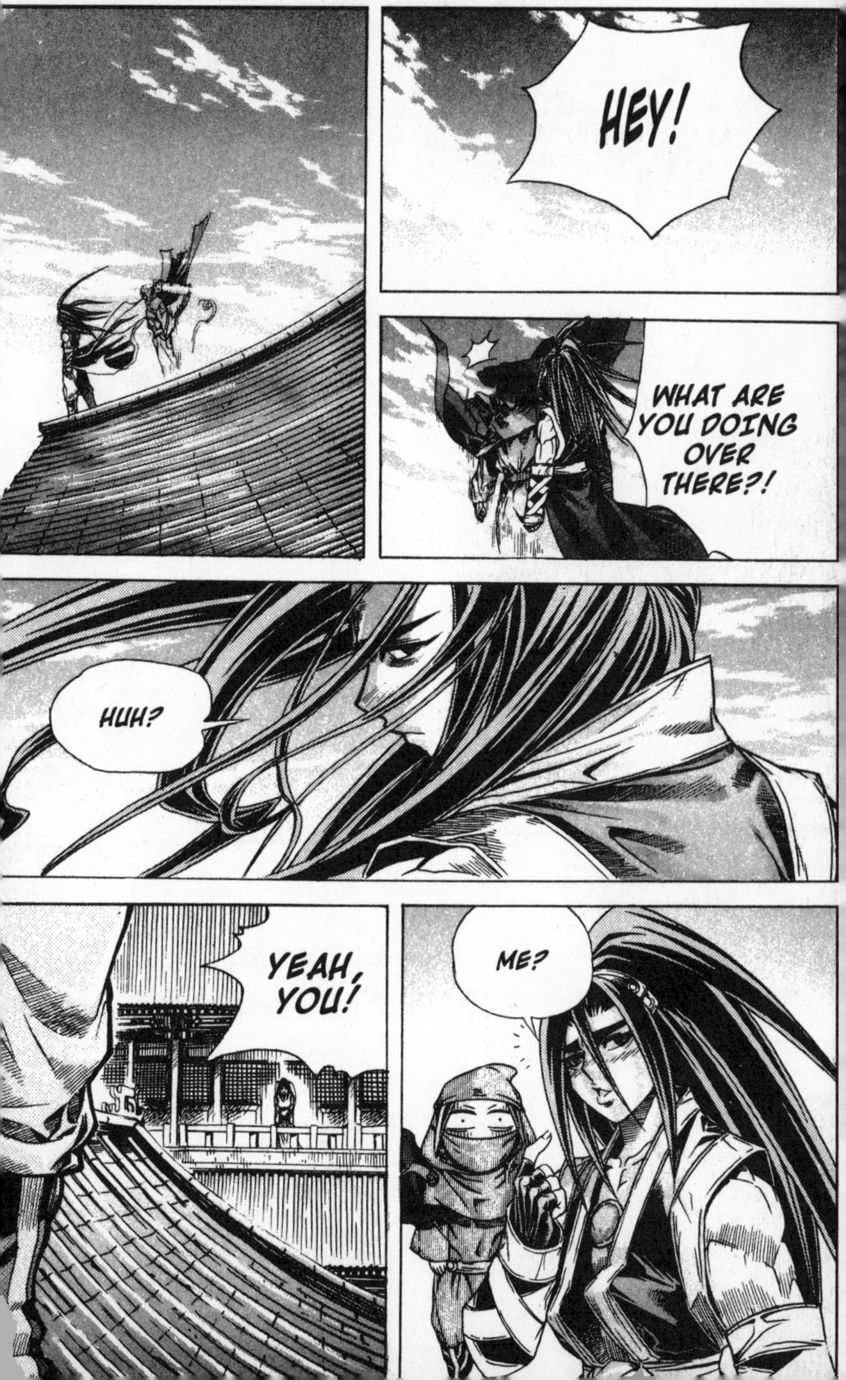
HEY!
WHAT ARE YOU DOING OVER THERE?!
HUH?
YEAH, YOU!
ME?

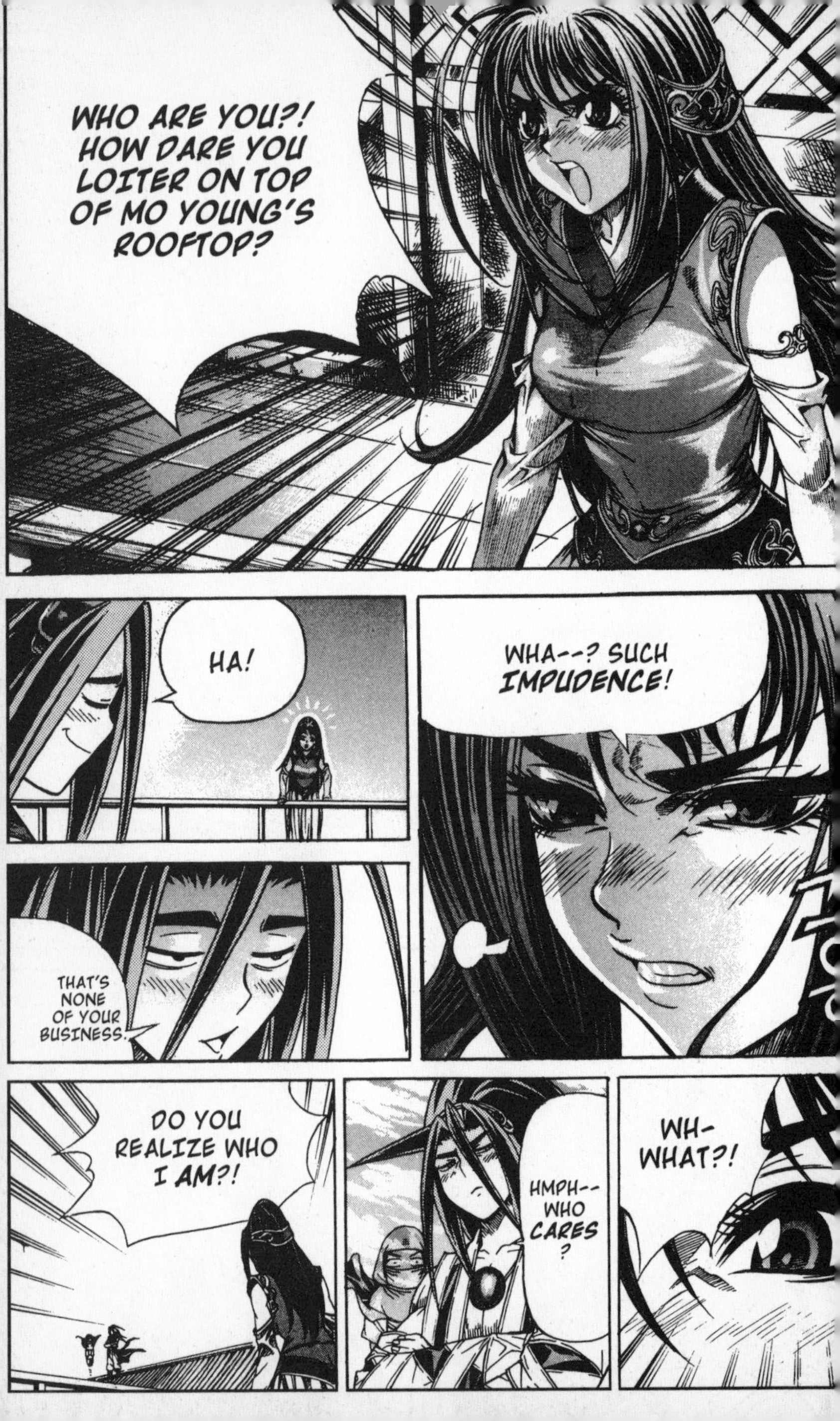
WHO ARE YOU?! HOW DARE YOU LOITER ON TOP OF MO YOUNG'S ROOFTOP?
HA!
WHA--? SUCH IMPUDENCE!
THAT'S NONE OF YOUR BUSINESS.
DO YOU REALIZE WHO I AM?!
HMPH-- WHO CARES?
WH- WHAT?!

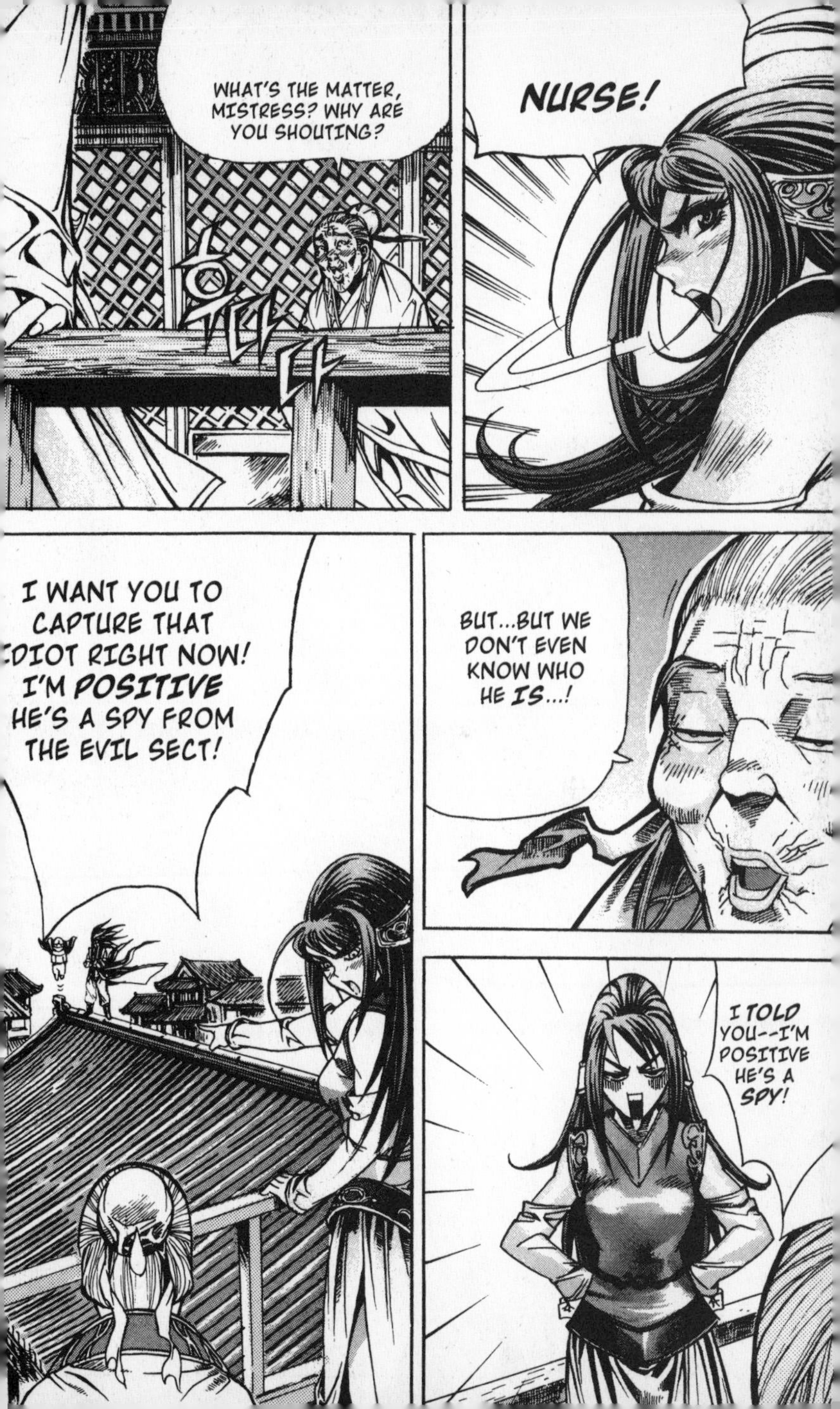
WHAT'S THE MATTER, MISTRESS? WHY ARE YOU SHOUTING?
NURSE!
I WANT YOU TO CAPTURE THAT IDIOT RIGHT NOW! I'M POSITIVE HE'S A SPY FROM THE EVIL SECT!
BUT...BUT WE DON'T EVEN KNOW WHO HE IS...!
I TOLD YOU--I'M POSITIVE HE'S A SPY!

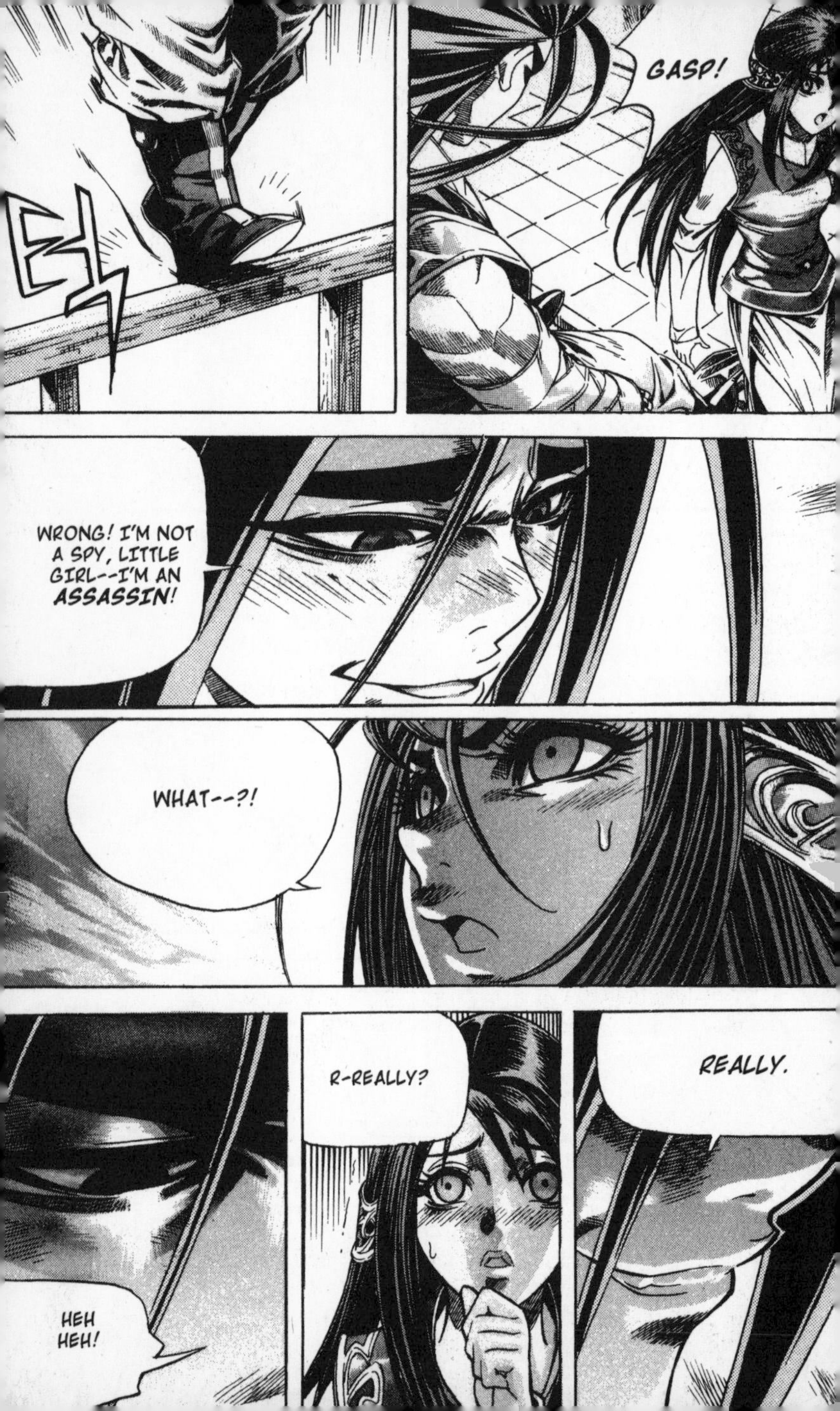
GASP!
WRONG! I'M NOT A SPY, LITTLE GIRL--I'M AN ASSASSIN!
WHAT--?!
HEH HEH!
R-REALLY?
REALLY.

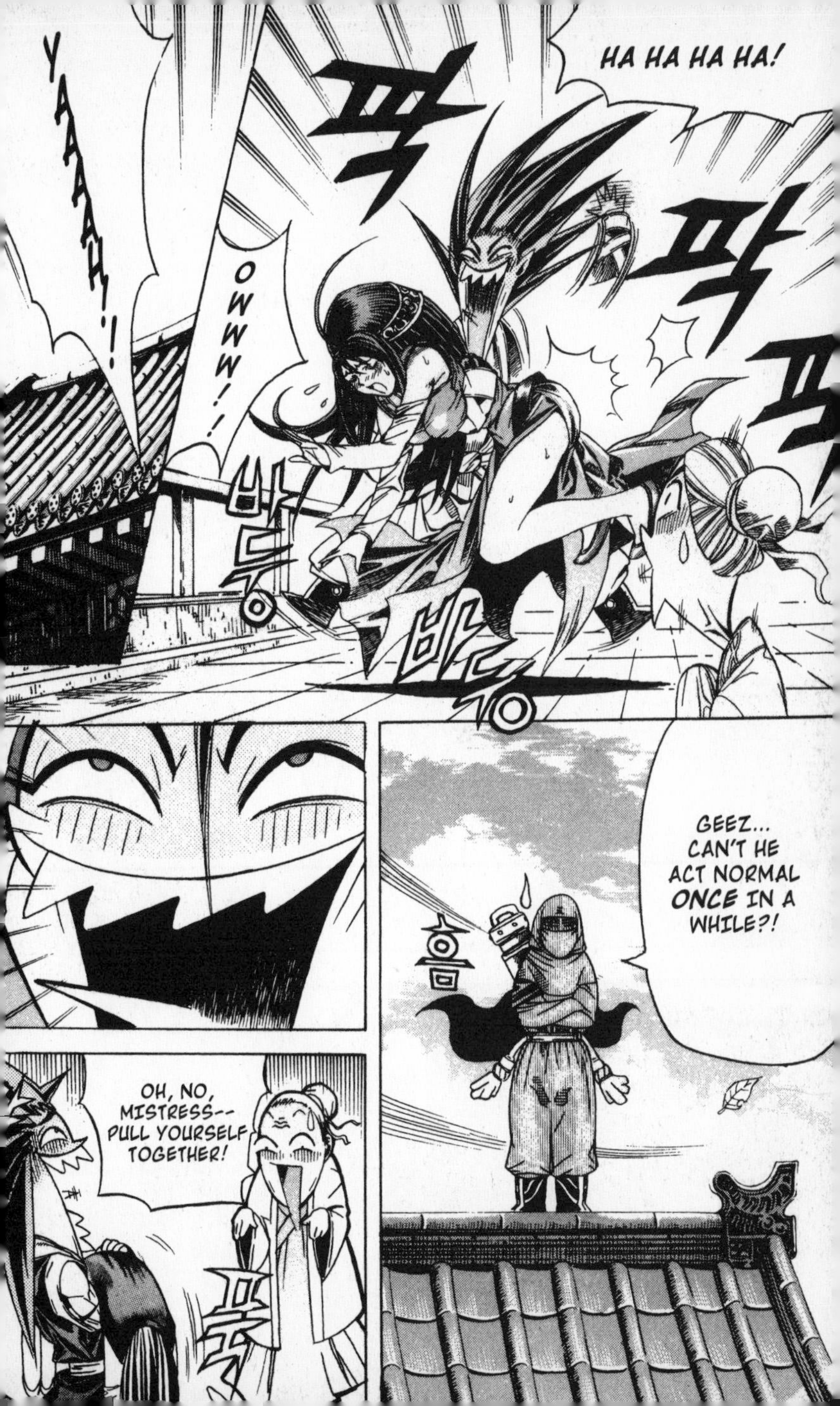
YAAAAH!!!
OWWW!!!
퍽
HA HA HA HA!
팍
퍽
OH, NO, MISTRESS-- PULL YOURSELF TOGETHER!
흠
GEEZ... CAN'T HE ACT NORMAL ONCE IN A WHILE?!

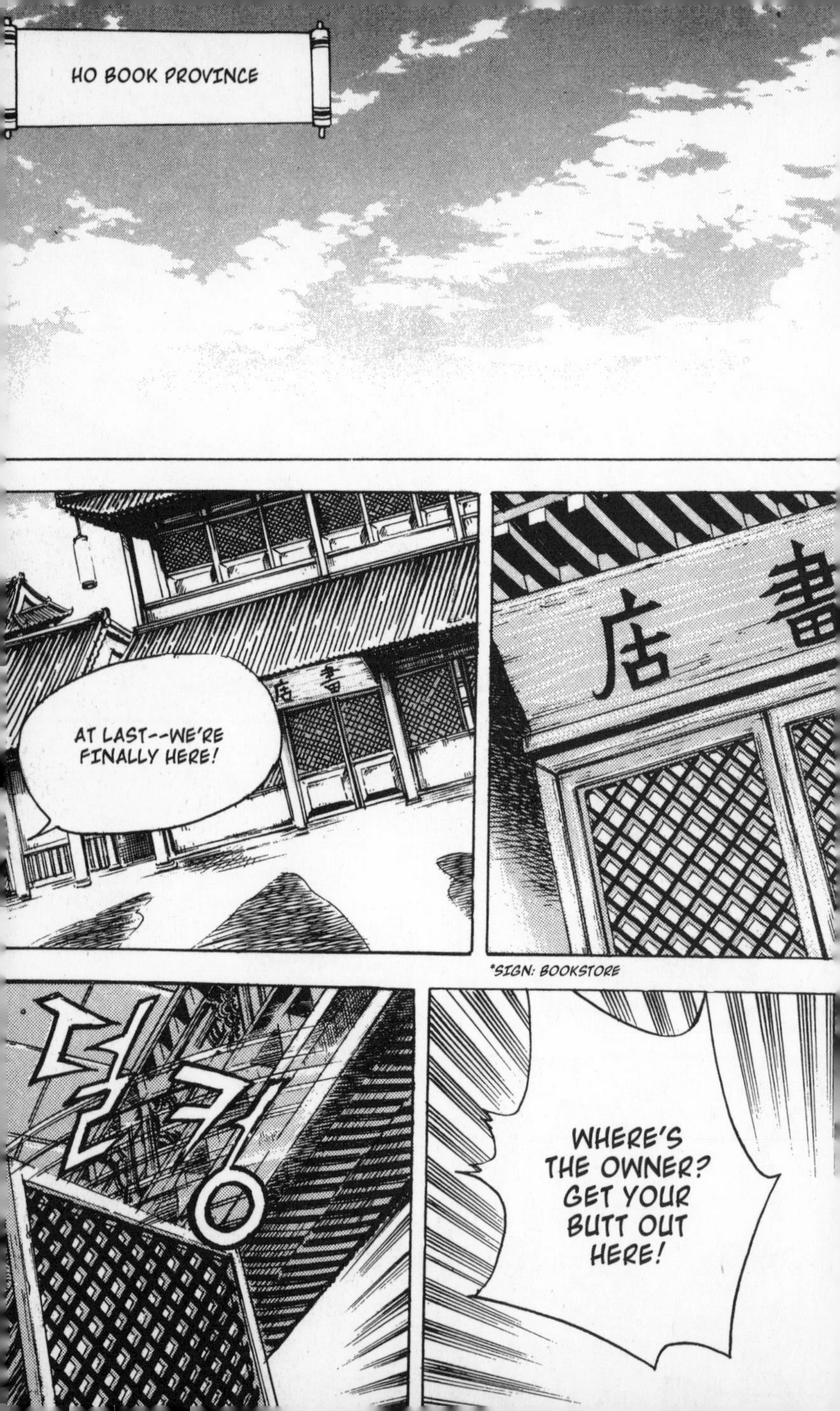
HO BOOK PROVINCE
AT LAST--WE'RE FINALLY HERE!
書店
*SIGN: BOOKSTORE
WHERE'S THE OWNER? GET YOUR BUTT OUT HERE!

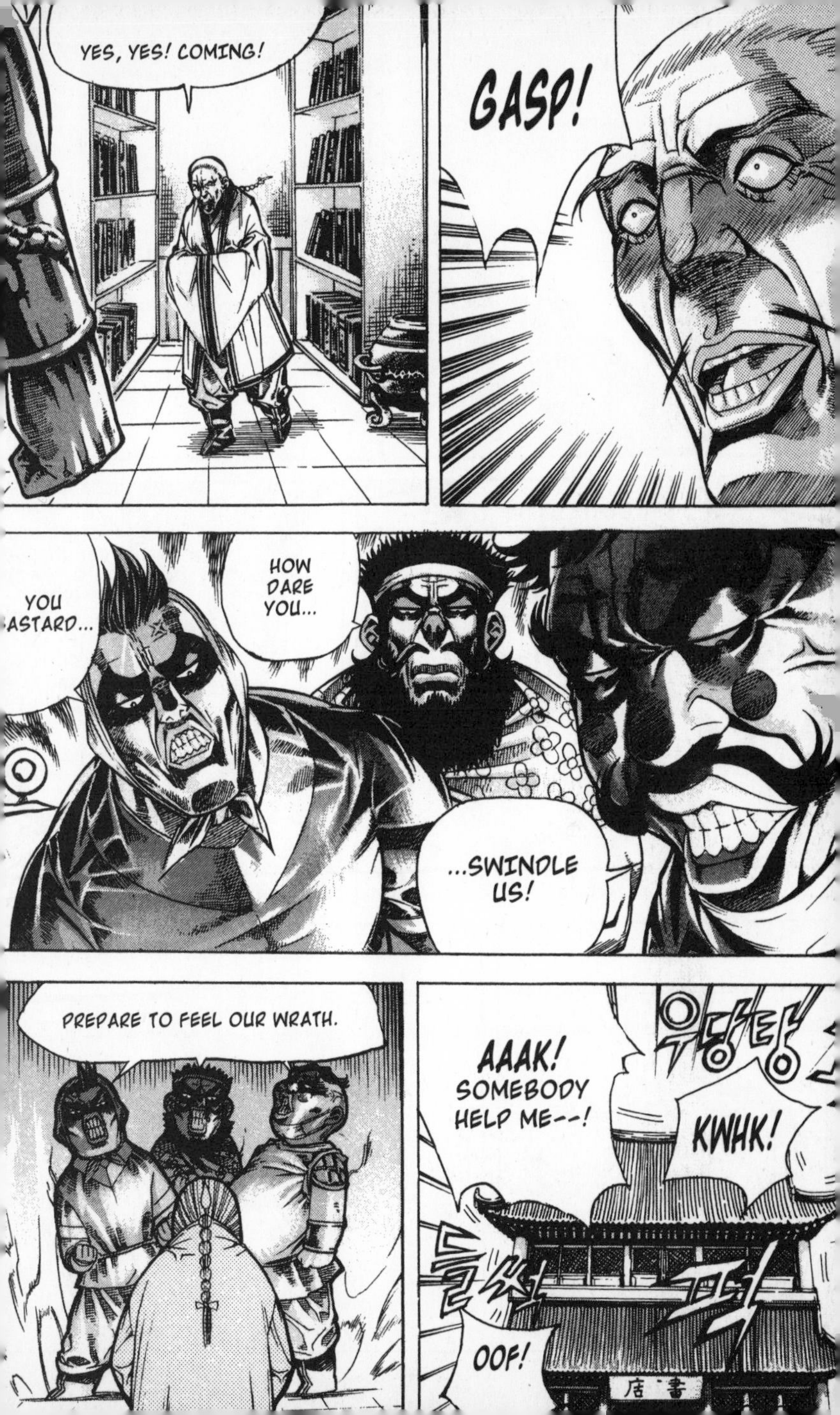

YES, YES! COMING!
GASP!
YOU ASTARD...
HOW DARE YOU...
...SWINDLE US!
PREPARE TO FEEL OUR WRATH.
AAAK! SOMEBODY HELP ME--!
KWHK!
OOF!
書店

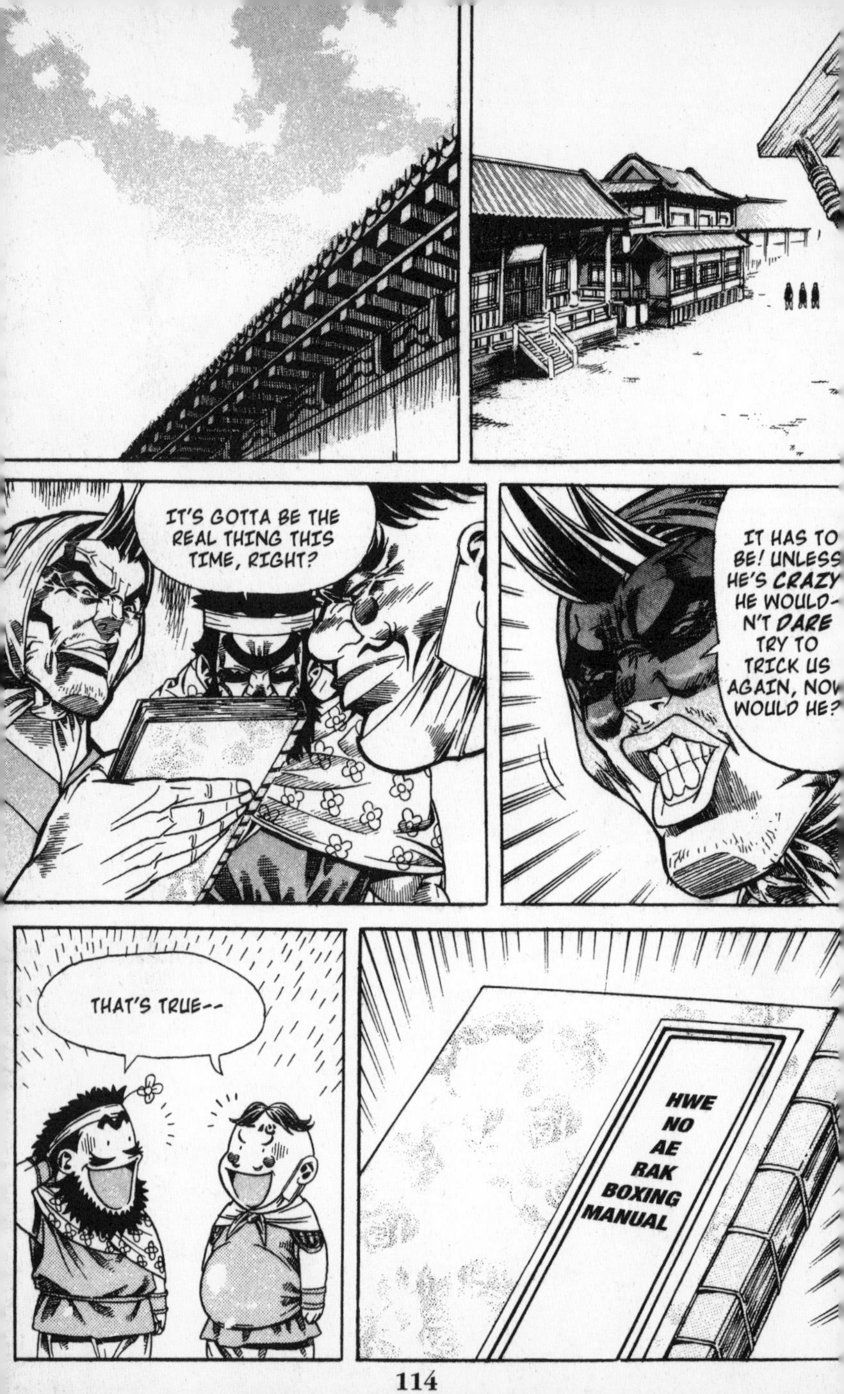
IT'S GOTTA BE THE REAL THING THIS TIME, RIGHT?
IT HAS TO BE! UNLESS HE'S *CRAZY* HE WOULDN'T *DARE* TRY TO TRICK US AGAIN, NOW WOULD HE?
THAT'S TRUE--
HWE NO AE RAK BOXING MANUAL

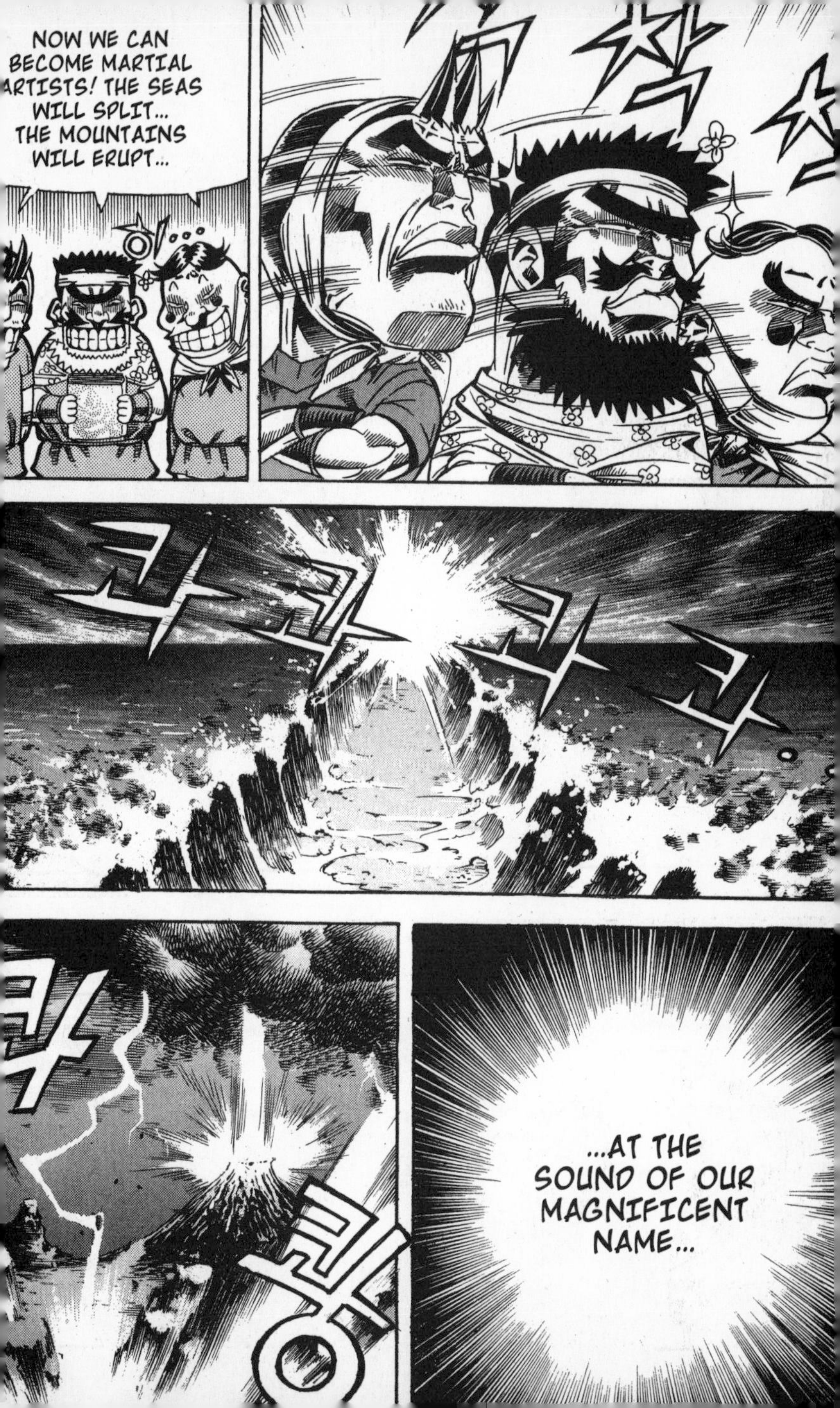
NOW WE CAN BECOME MARTIAL ARTISTS! THE SEAS WILL SPLIT... THE MOUNTAINS WILL ERUPT...
...AT THE SOUND OF OUR MAGNIFICENT NAME...

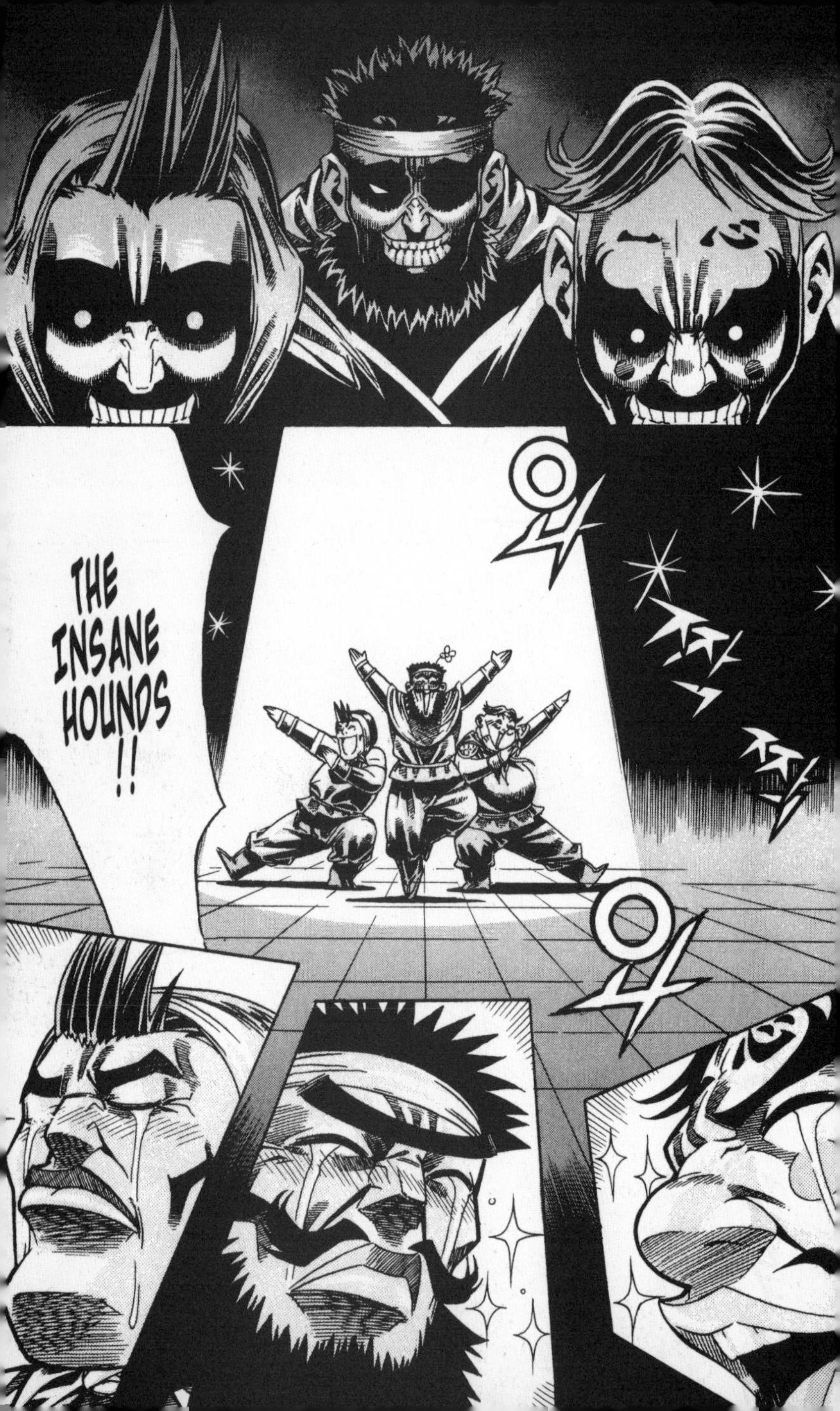
THE INSANE HOUNDS !!

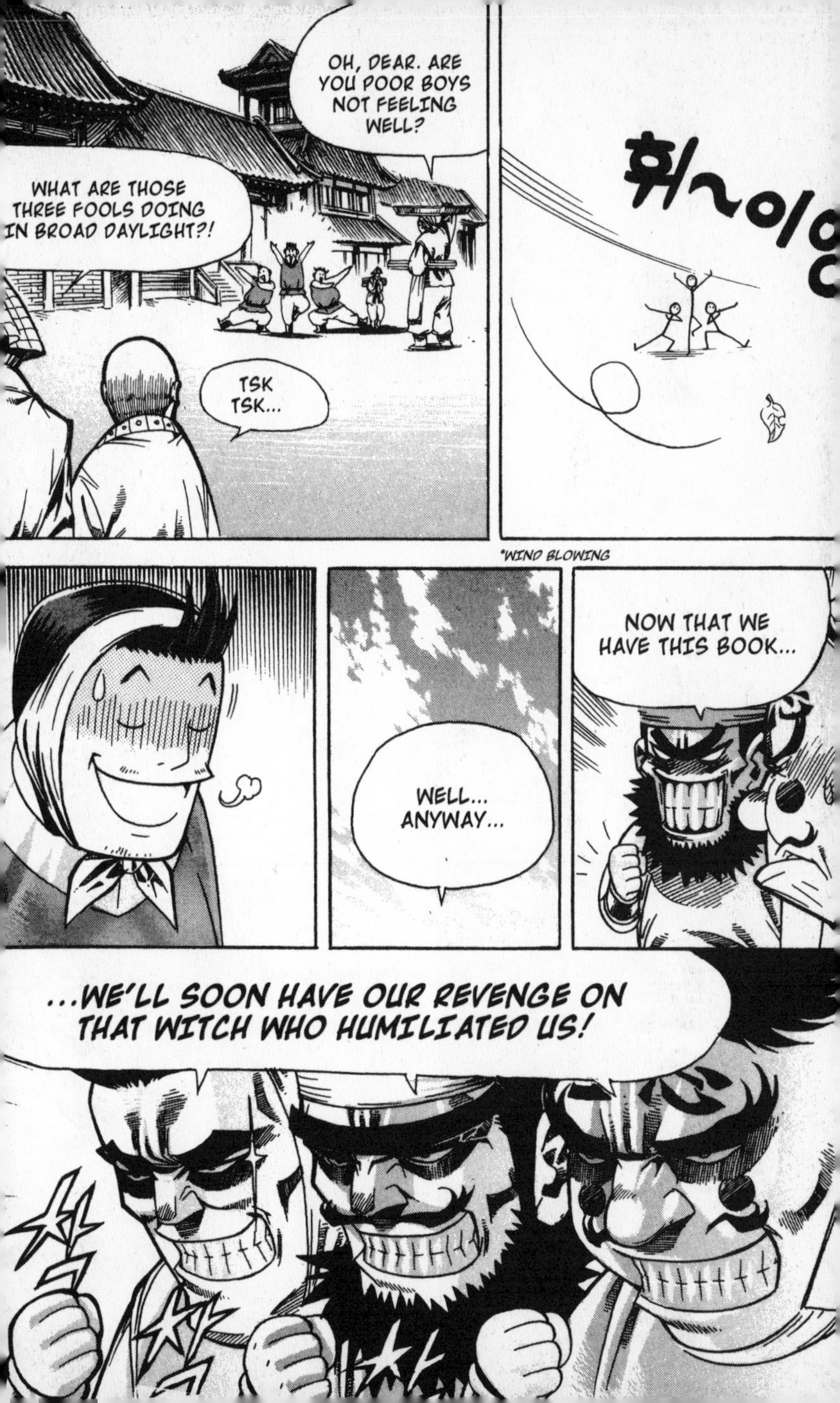
OH, DEAR. ARE YOU POOR BOYS NOT FEELING WELL?
WHAT ARE THOSE THREE FOOLS DOING IN BROAD DAYLIGHT?!
TSK TSK...
휘~이
*WIND BLOWING
WELL... ANYWAY...
NOW THAT WE HAVE THIS BOOK...
...WE'LL SOON HAVE OUR REVENGE ON THAT WITCH WHO HUMILIATED US!

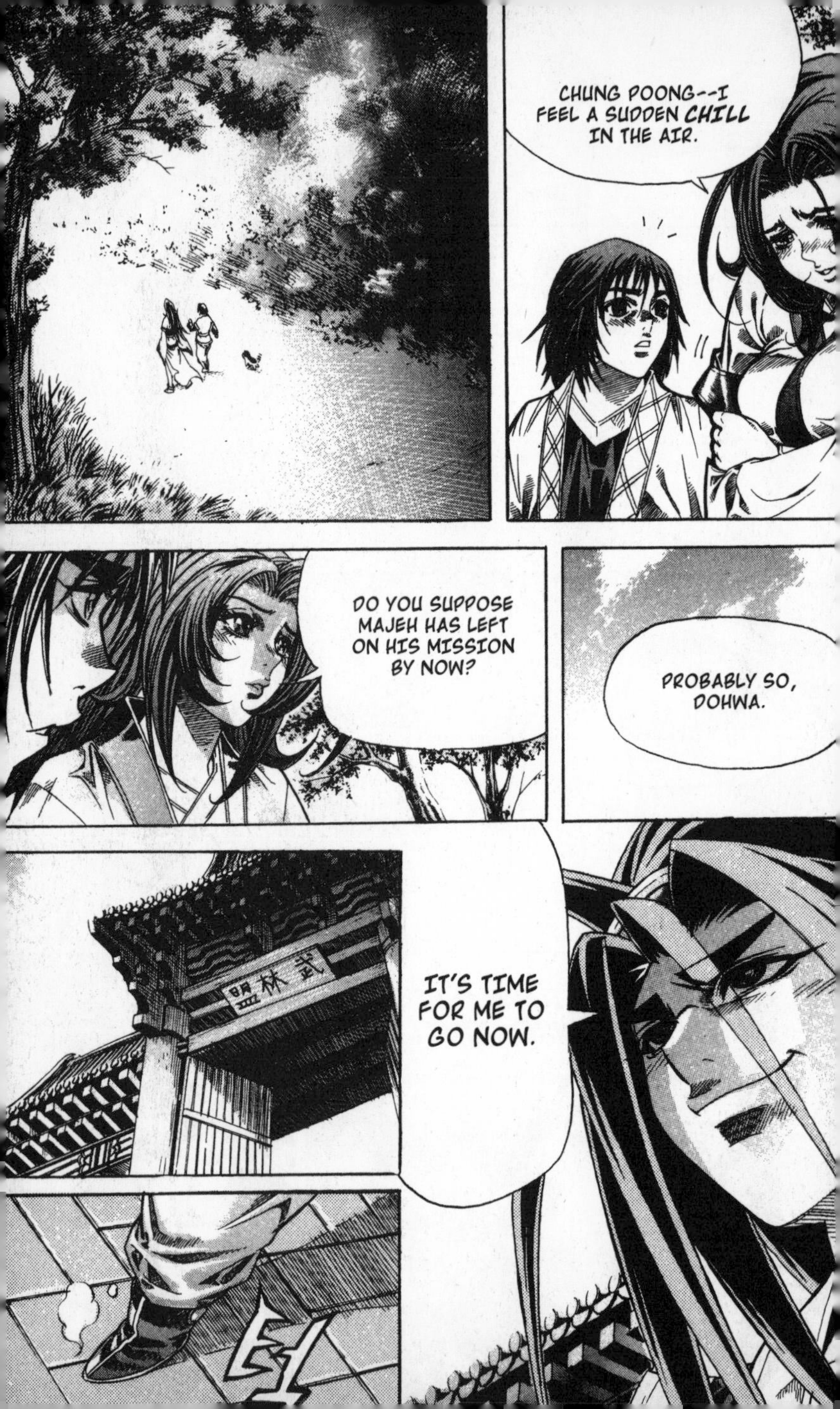
CHUNG POONG--I FEEL A SUDDEN CHILL IN THE AIR.
DO YOU SUPPOSE MAJEH HAS LEFT ON HIS MISSION BY NOW?
PROBABLY SO, DOHWA.
武林盟
IT'S TIME FOR ME TO GO NOW.

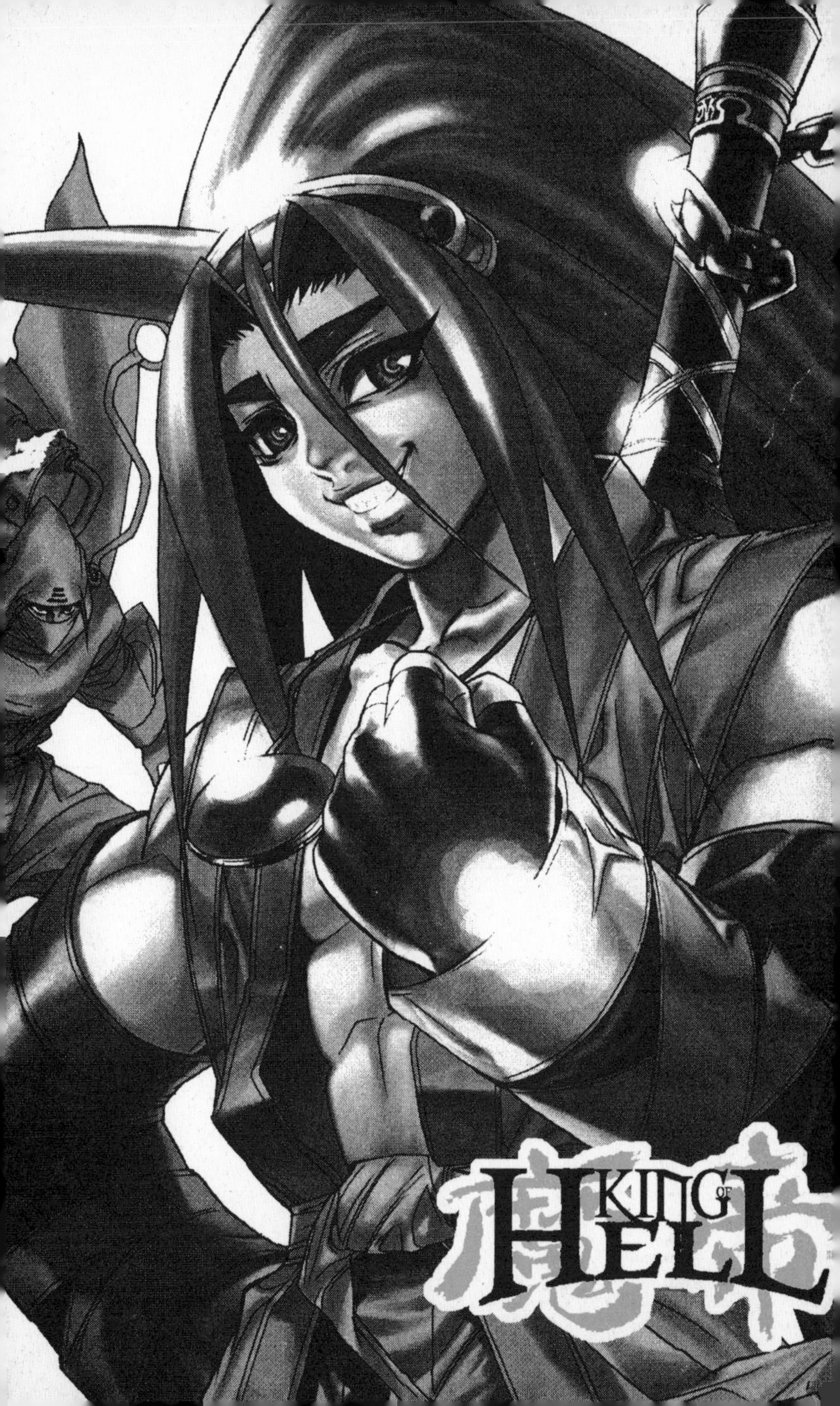
KING OF HELL

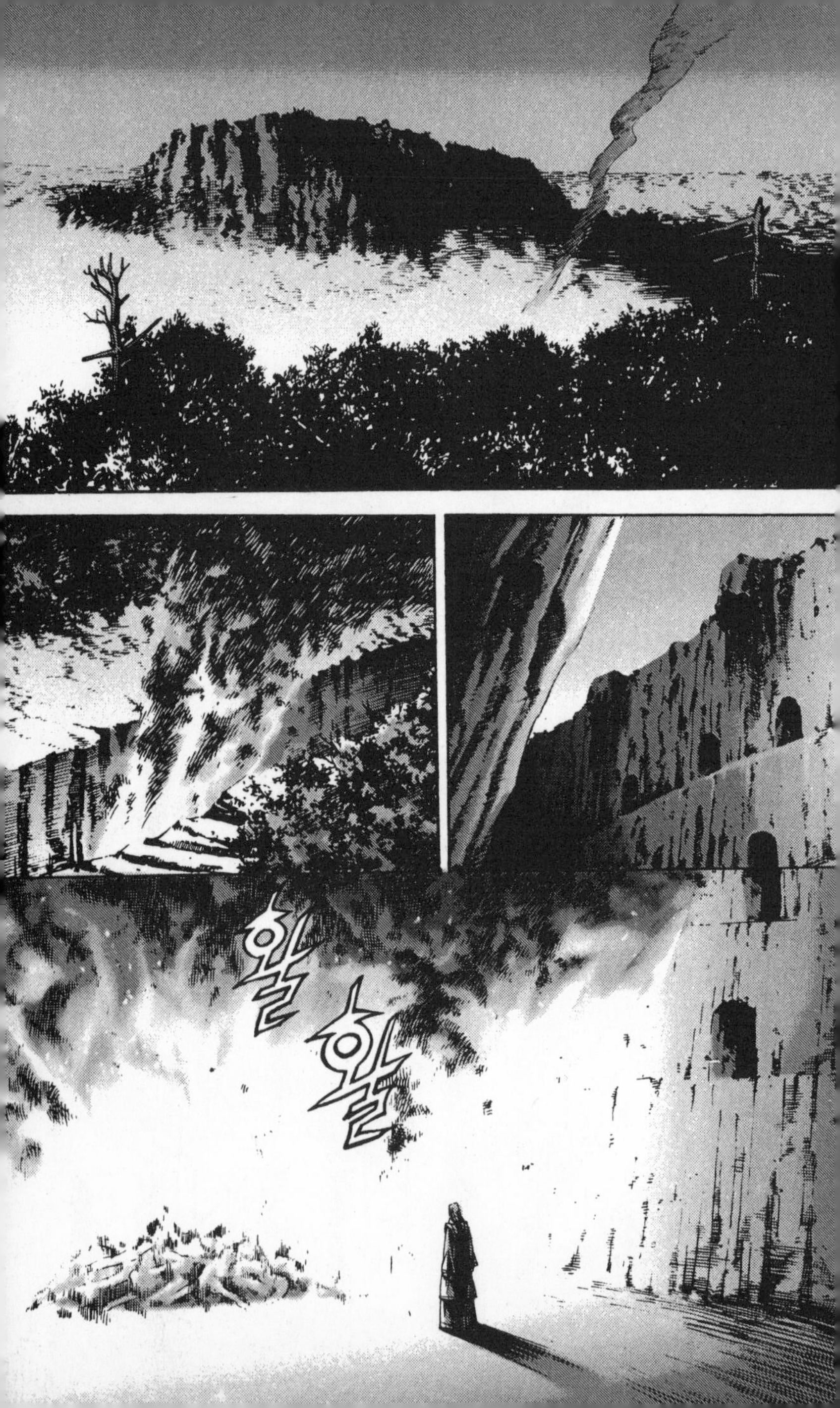
활
활

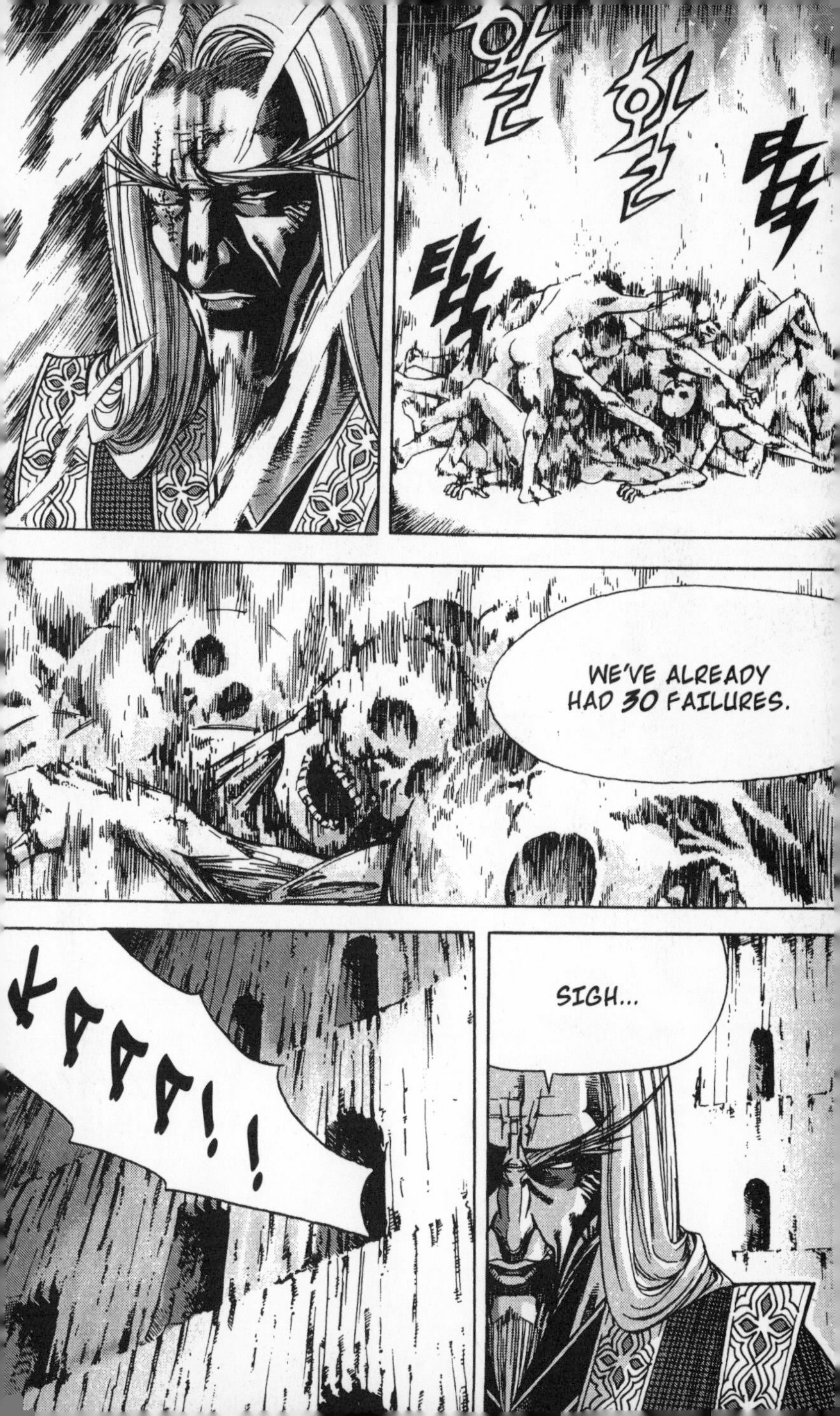
활활
탁탁
WE'VE ALREADY HAD 30 FAILURES.
KAAA!!
SIGH...

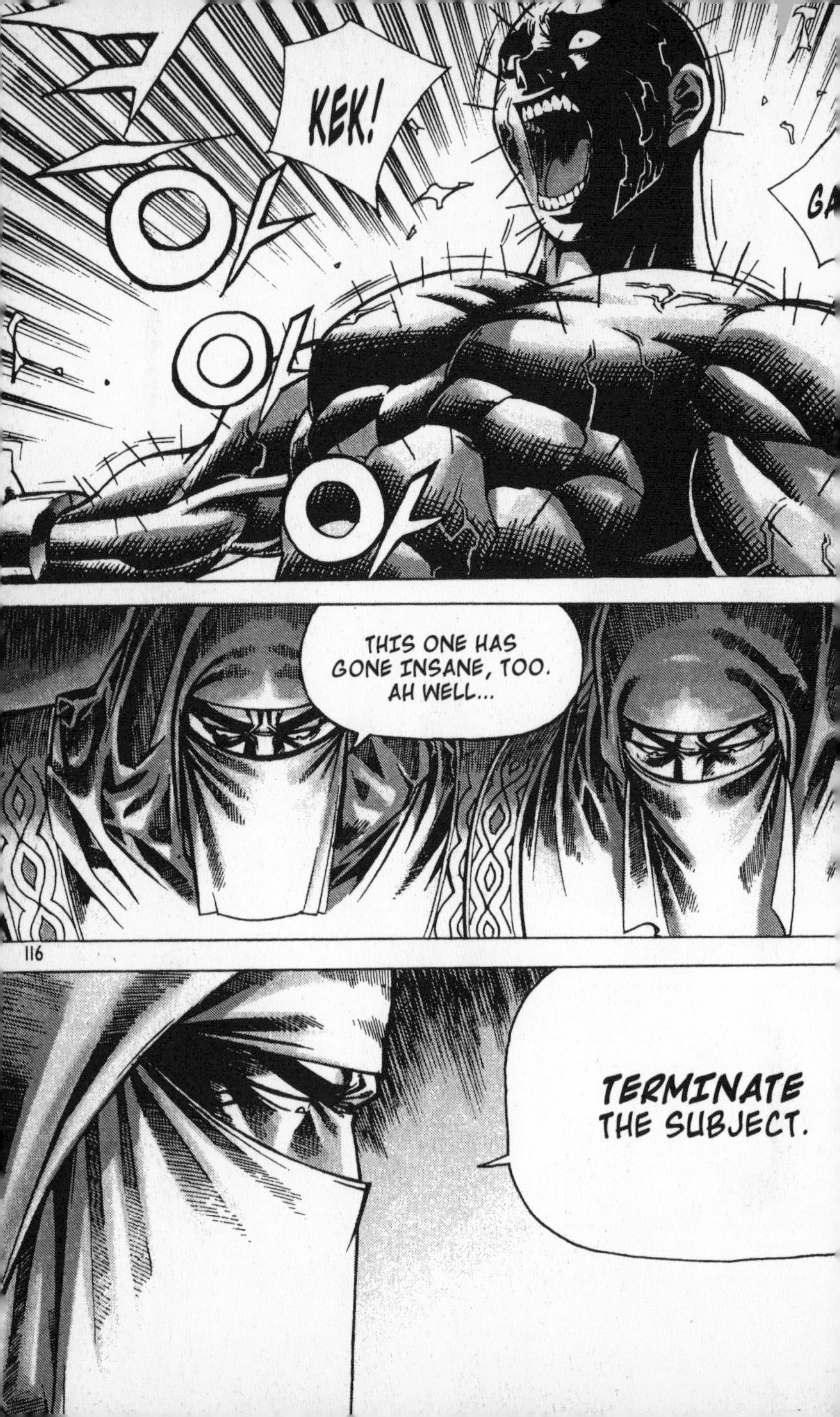
KEK!
GA
THIS ONE HAS GONE INSANE, TOO. AH WELL...
TERMINATE THE SUBJECT.

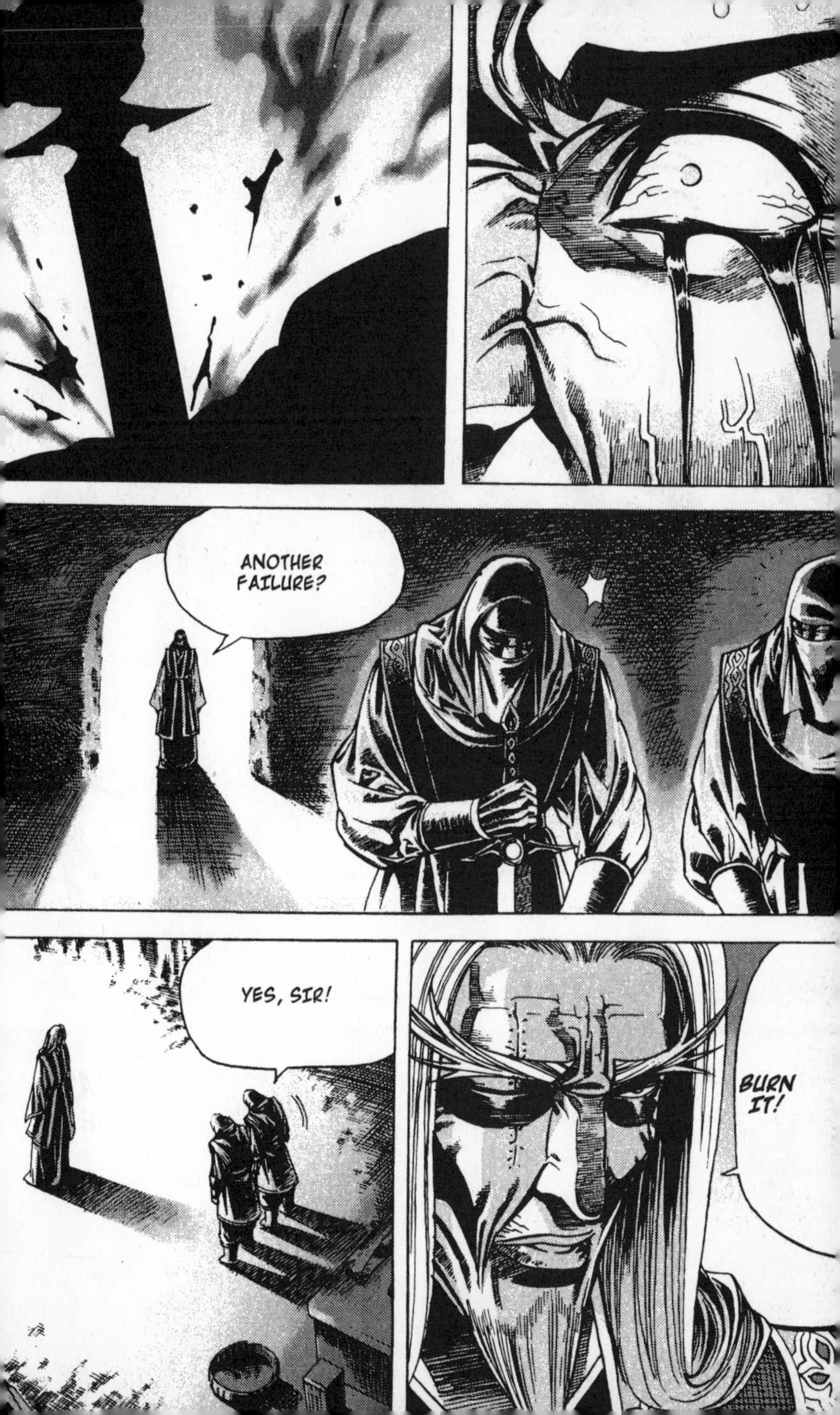
ANOTHER FAILURE?
YES, SIR!
BURN IT!

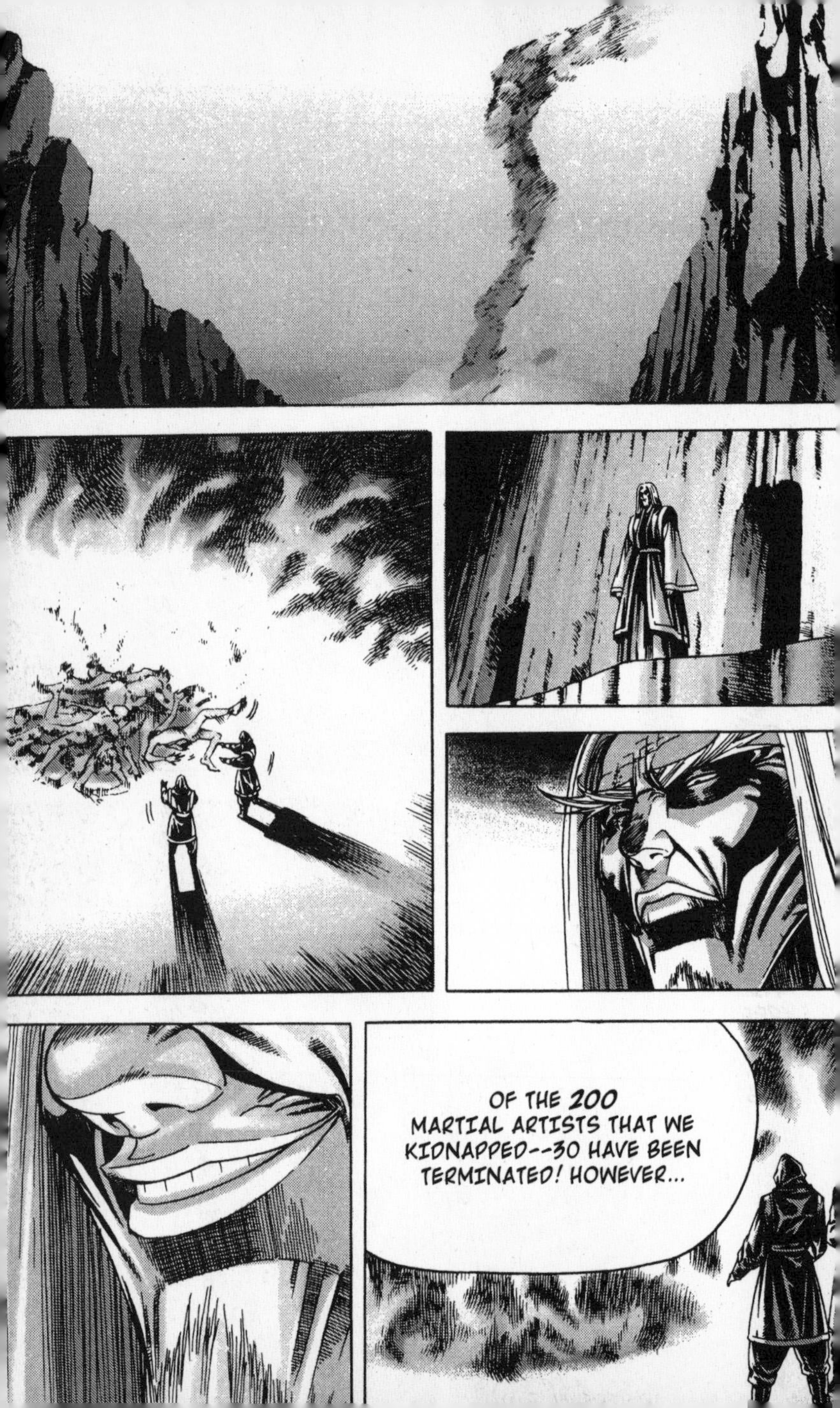
OF THE 200 MARTIAL ARTISTS THAT WE KIDNAPPED--30 HAVE BEEN TERMINATED! HOWEVER...

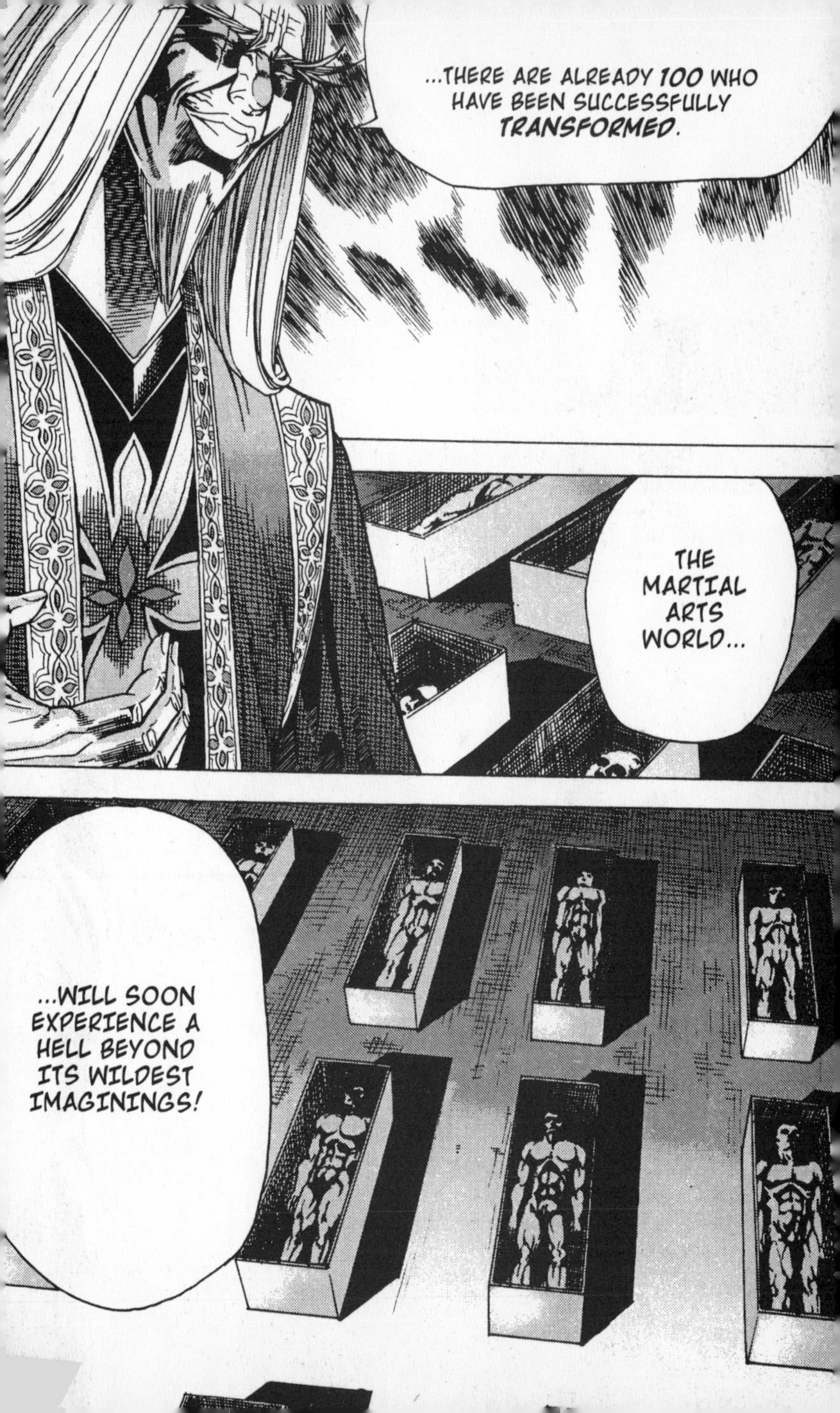
...THERE ARE ALREADY 100 WHO HAVE BEEN SUCCESSFULLY TRANSFORMED.
THE MARTIAL ARTS WORLD...
...WILL SOON EXPERIENCE A HELL BEYOND ITS WILDEST IMAGININGS!

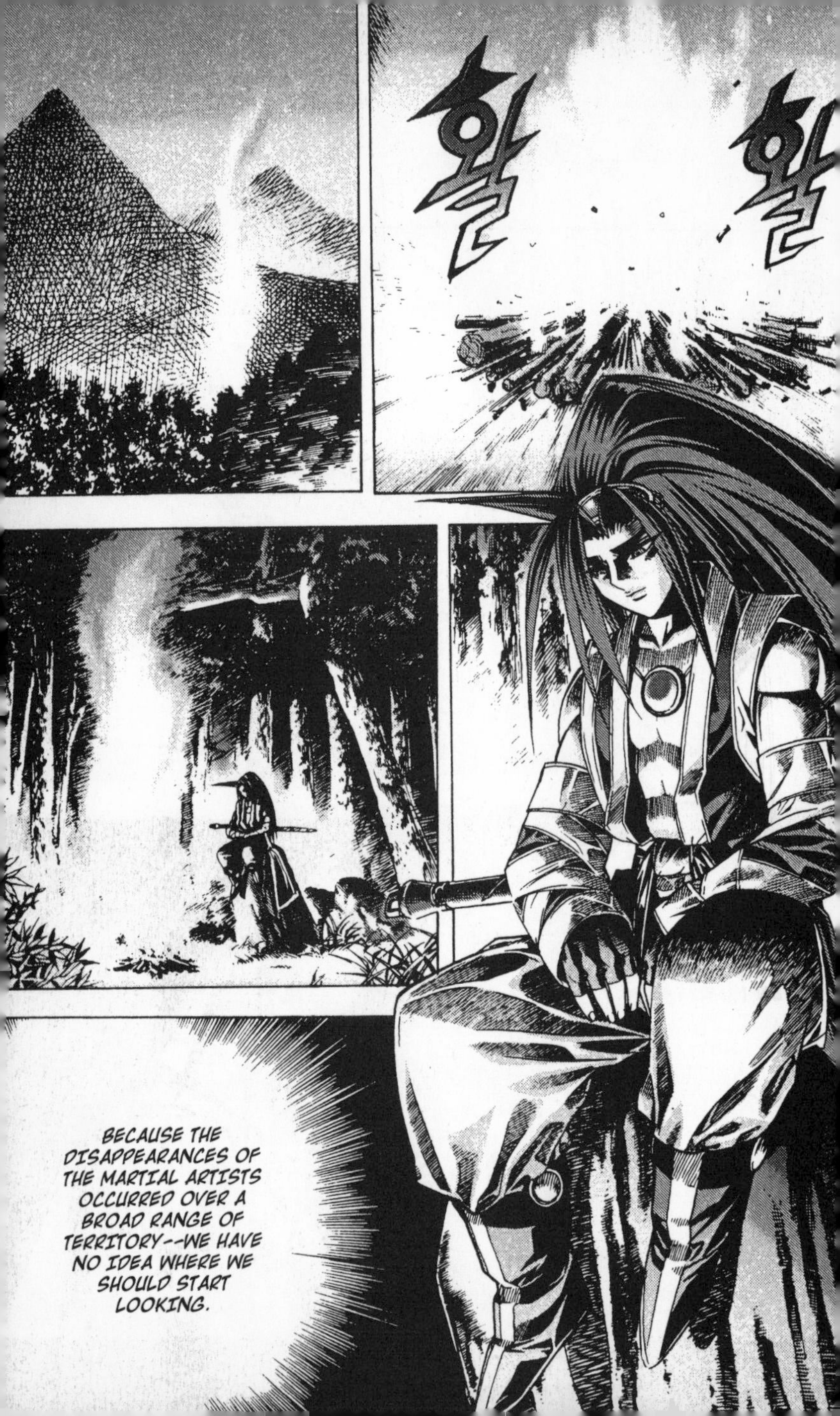

확
휙
BECAUSE THE DISAPPEARANCES OF THE MARTIAL ARTISTS OCCURRED OVER A BROAD RANGE OF TERRITORY--WE HAVE NO IDEA WHERE WE SHOULD START LOOKING.

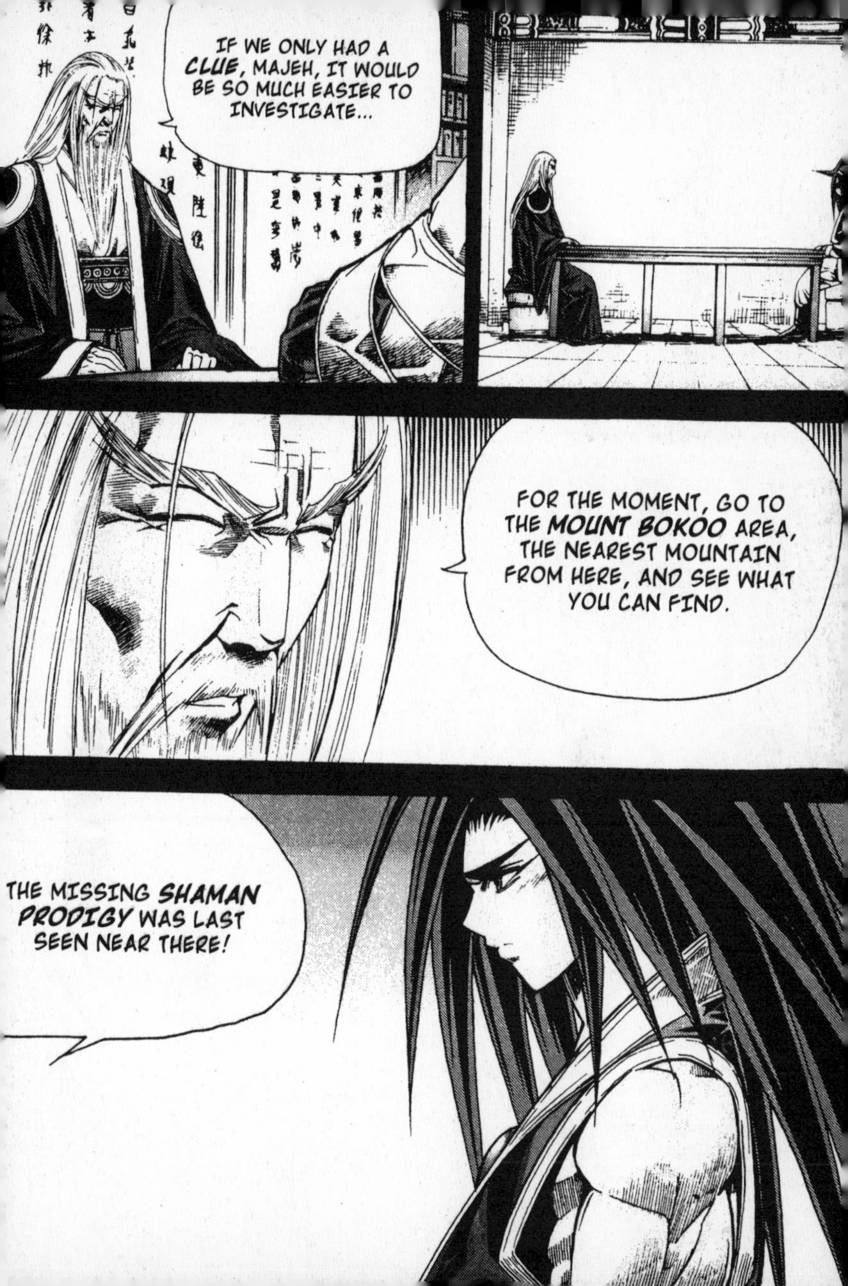
IF WE ONLY HAD A CLUE, MAJEH, IT WOULD BE SO MUCH EASIER TO INVESTIGATE...
FOR THE MOMENT, GO TO THE MOUNT BOKOO AREA, THE NEAREST MOUNTAIN FROM HERE, AND SEE WHAT YOU CAN FIND.
THE MISSING SHAMAN PRODIGY WAS LAST SEEN NEAR THERE!

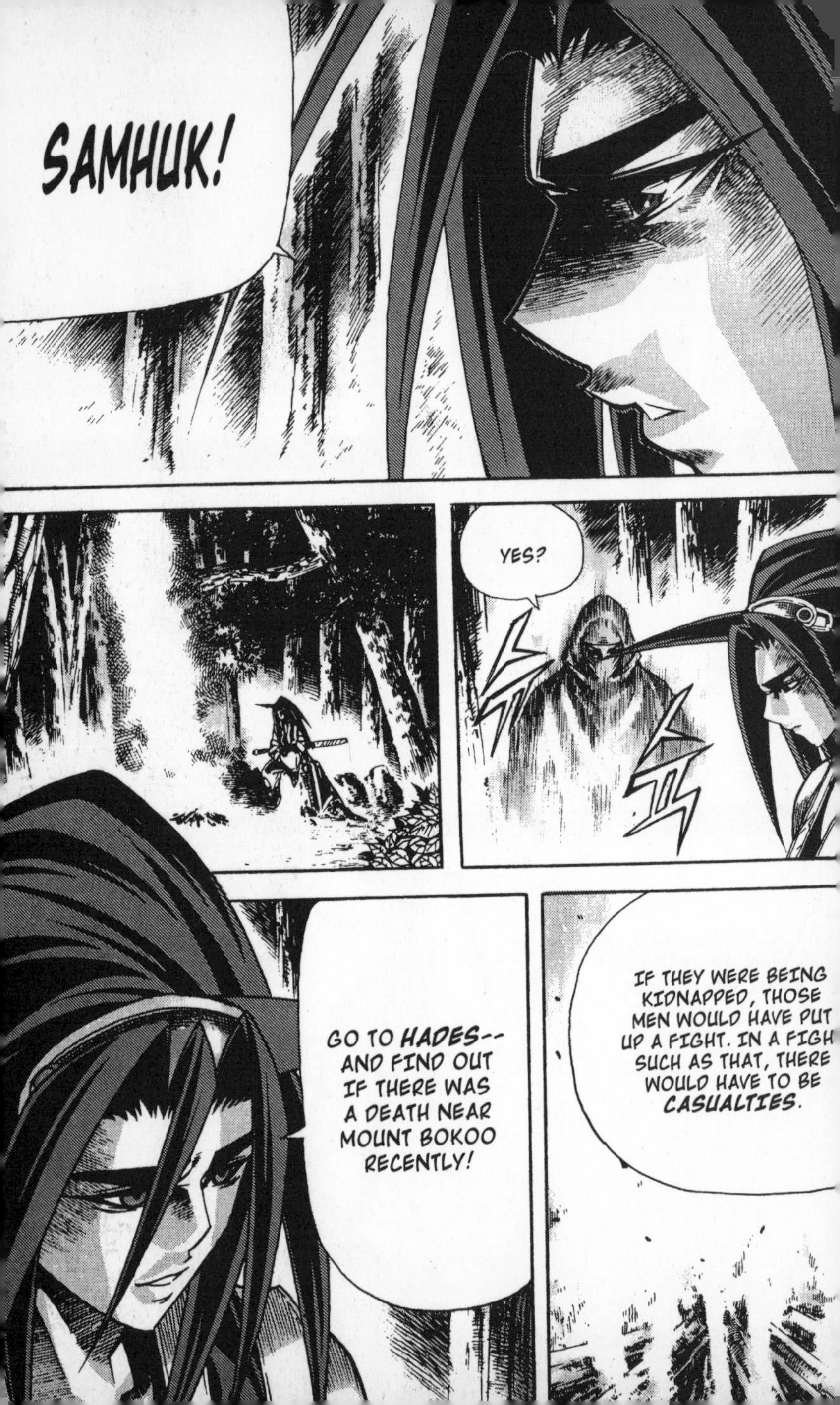
SAMHUK!
YES?
GO TO HADES--AND FIND OUT IF THERE WAS A DEATH NEAR MOUNT BOKOO RECENTLY!
IF THEY WERE BEING KIDNAPPED, THOSE MEN WOULD HAVE PUT UP A FIGHT. IN A FIGH SUCH AS THAT, THERE WOULD HAVE TO BE CASUALTIES.

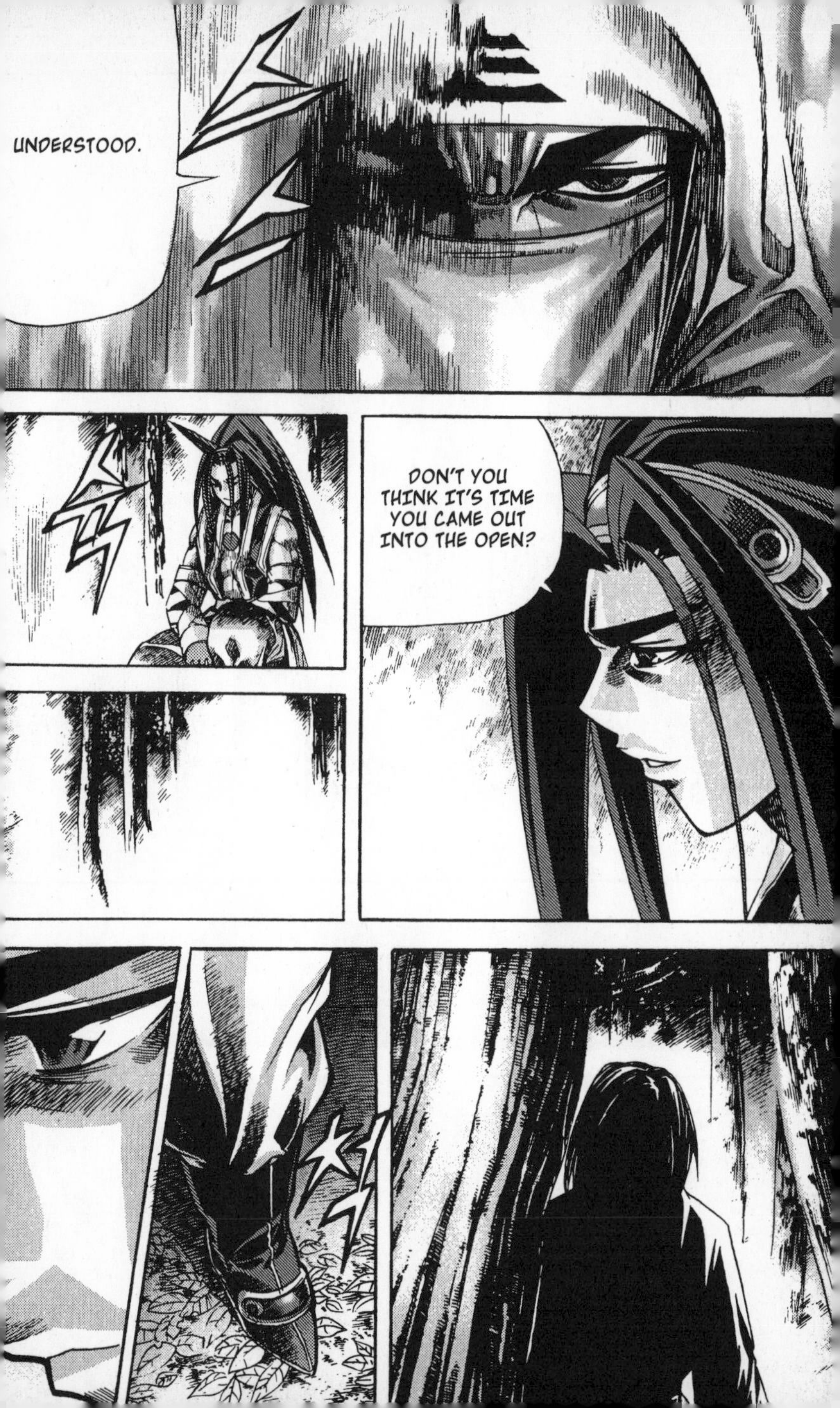
UNDERSTOOD.
DON'T YOU THINK IT'S TIME YOU CAME OUT INTO THE OPEN?

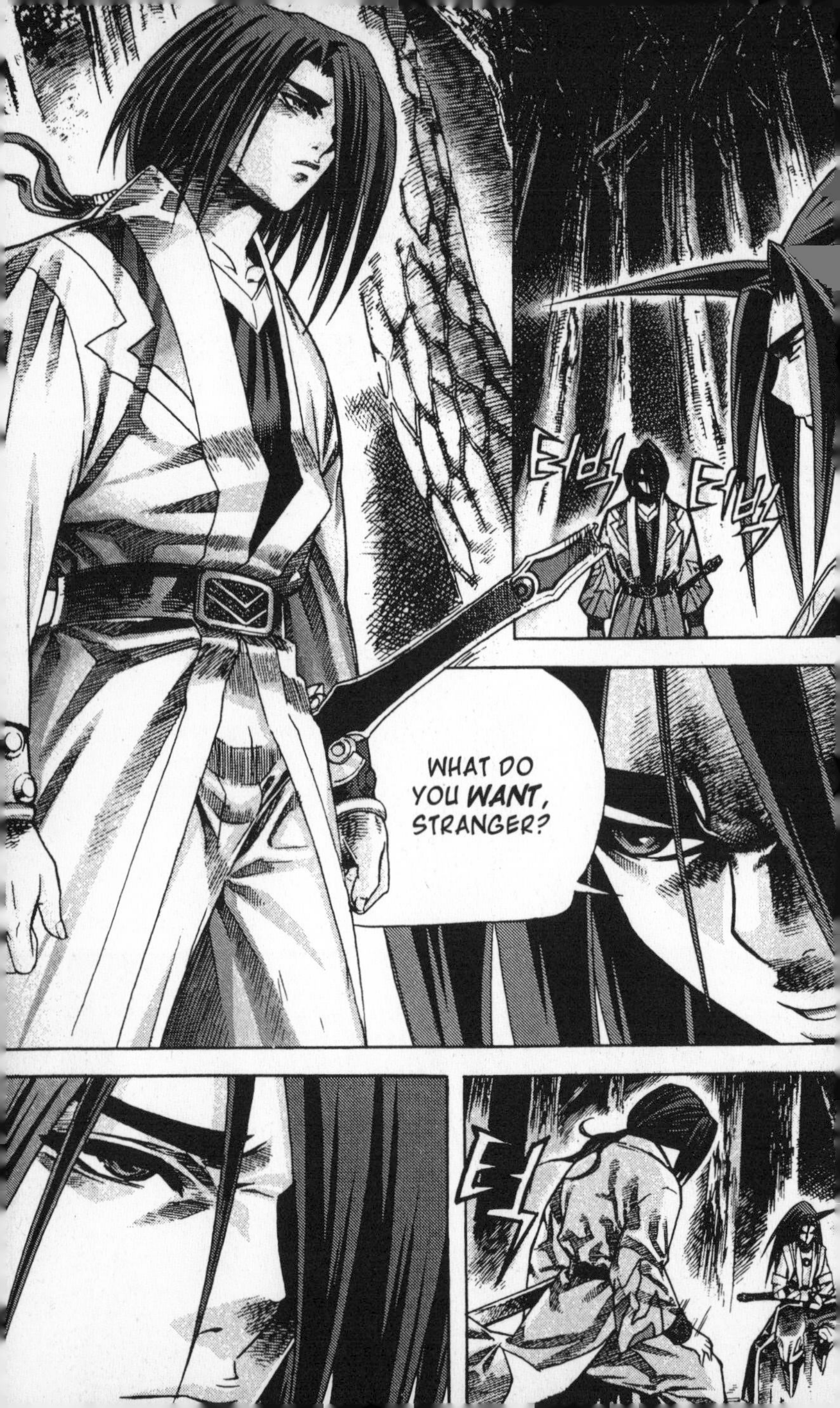
터벅
터벅
WHAT DO YOU WANT, STRANGER?

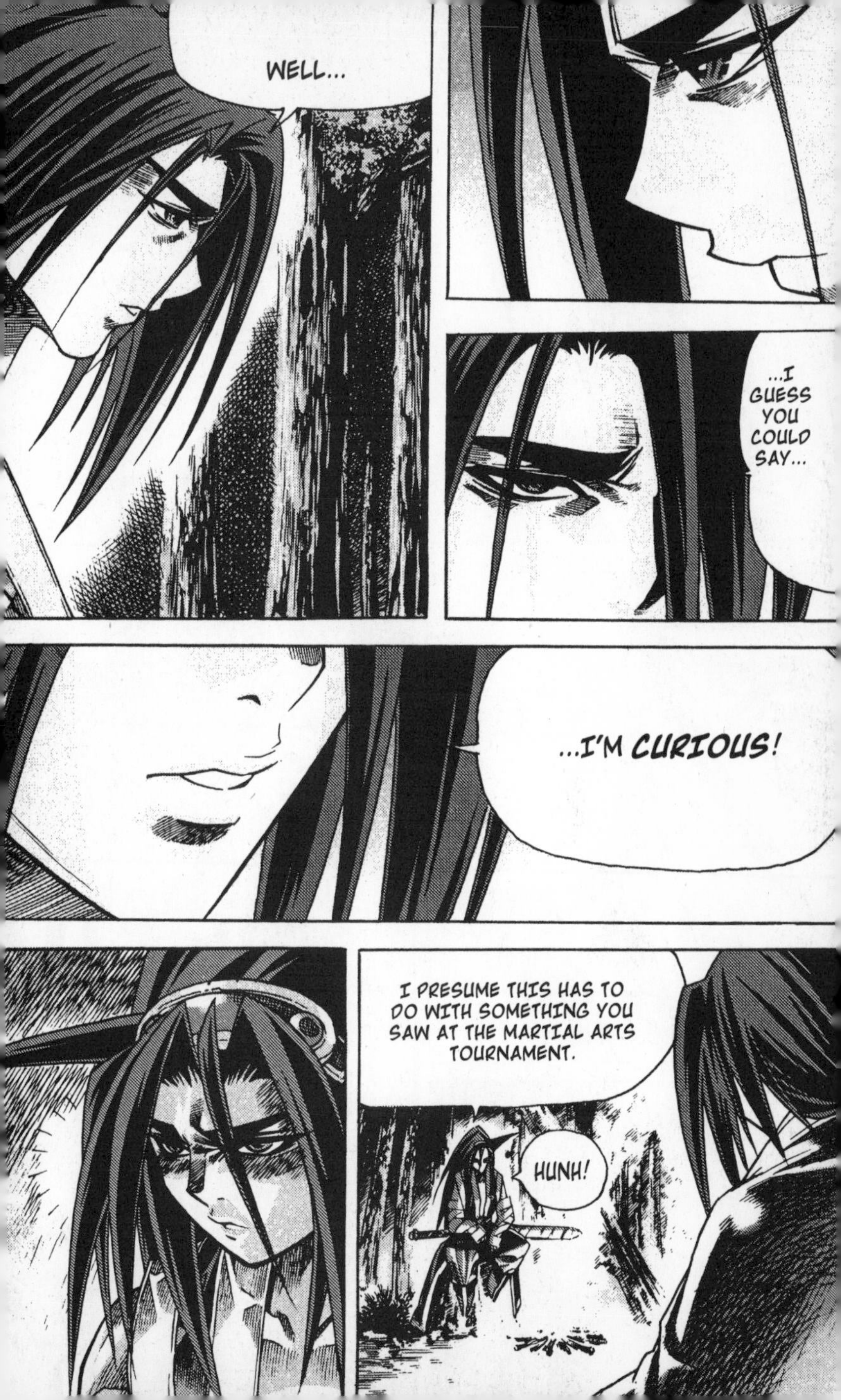
WELL...
...I GUESS YOU COULD SAY...
...I'M CURIOUS!
I PRESUME THIS HAS TO DO WITH SOMETHING YOU SAW AT THE MARTIAL ARTS TOURNAMENT.
HUNH!

THAT'S RIGHT. I HAD AN EXCELLENT VANTAGE POINT-- AND WAS ABLE TO CLEARLY SEE EVERYTHING.

AHH. SO YOU'RE HERE TO--?

PLEASE...DON'T MISUNDER-STAND.

THEN GET TO THE POINT.

AFTER SEEING WHAT I DID--I WOULDN'T BE FOOLISH ENOUGH TO FIGHT YOU!

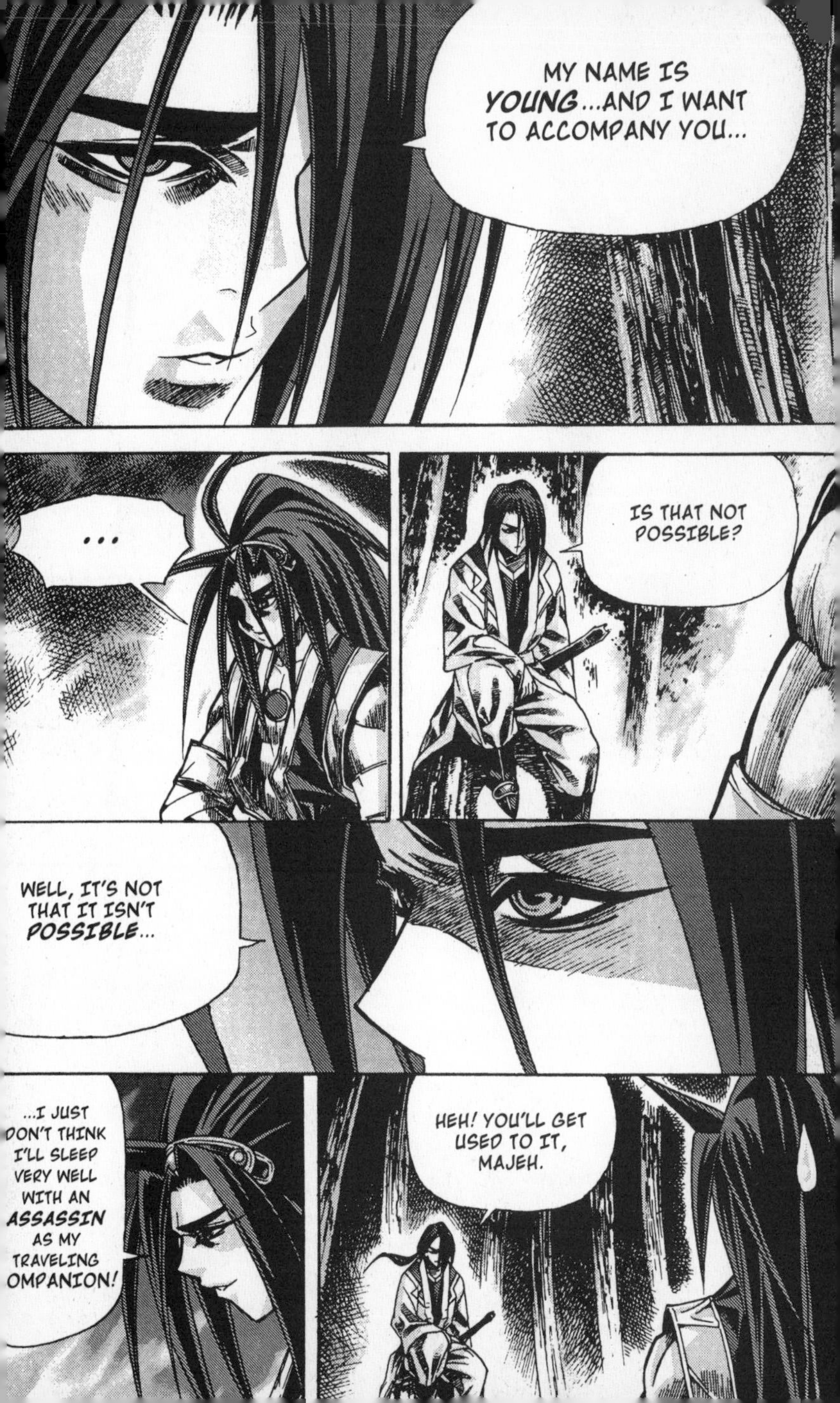
MY NAME IS YOUNG...AND I WANT TO ACCOMPANY YOU...
...
IS THAT NOT POSSIBLE?
WELL, IT'S NOT THAT IT ISN'T POSSIBLE...
...I JUST DON'T THINK I'LL SLEEP VERY WELL WITH AN ASSASSIN AS MY TRAVELING OMPANION!
HEH! YOU'LL GET USED TO IT, MAJEH.

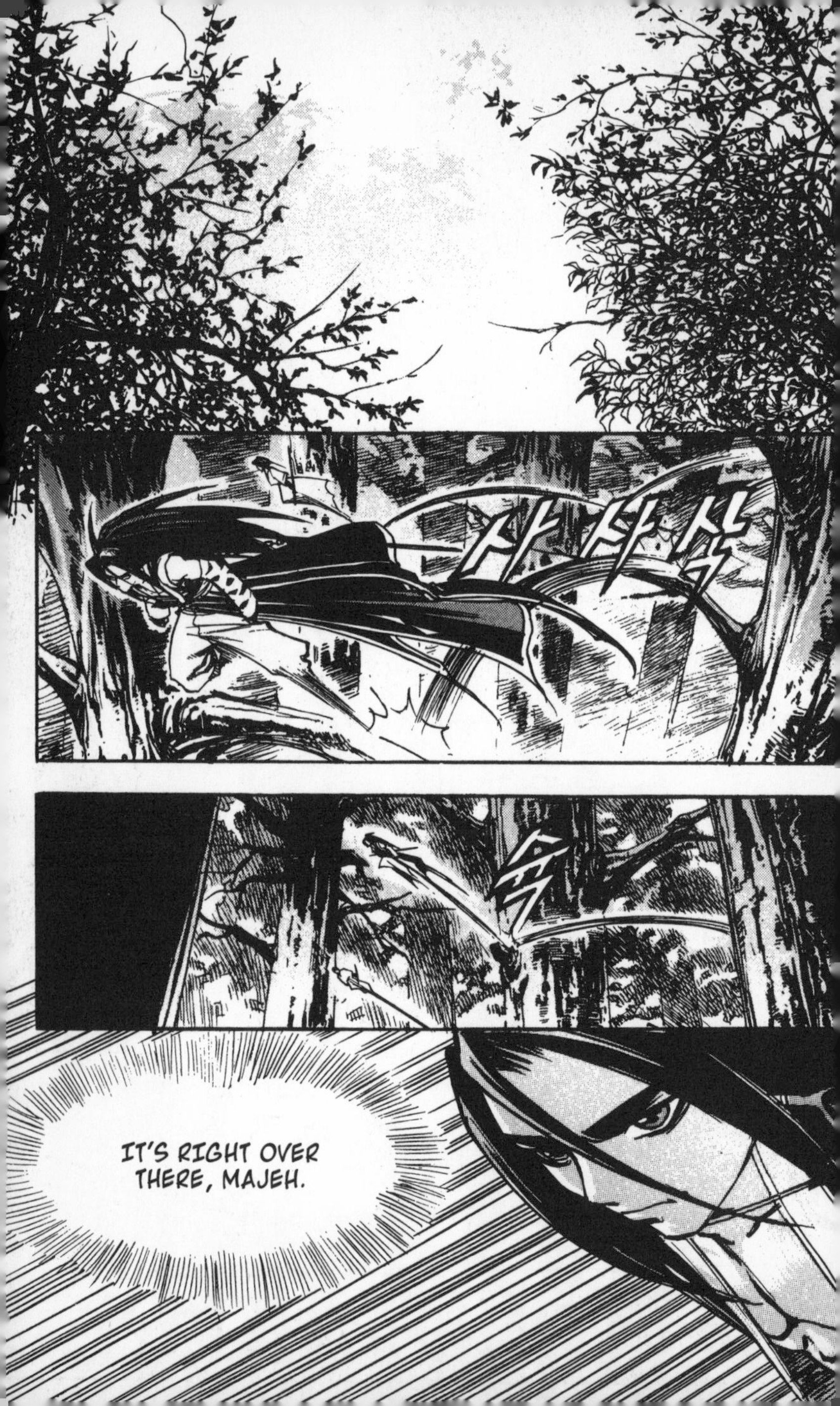
IT'S RIGHT OVER
THERE, MAJEH.

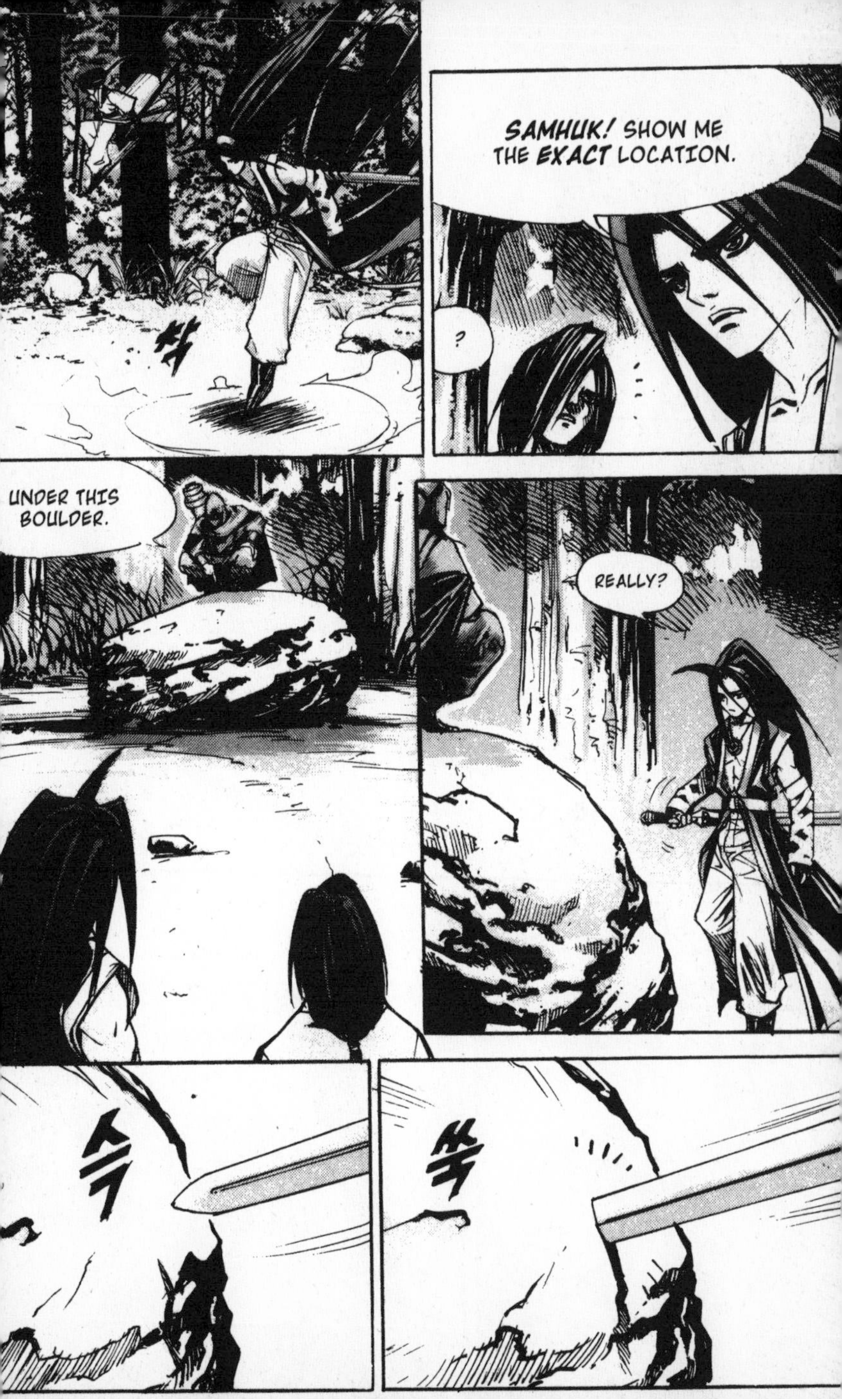

싹
SAMHUK! SHOW ME THE EXACT LOCATION.
?
...
UNDER THIS BOULDER.
REALLY?
스
쓱

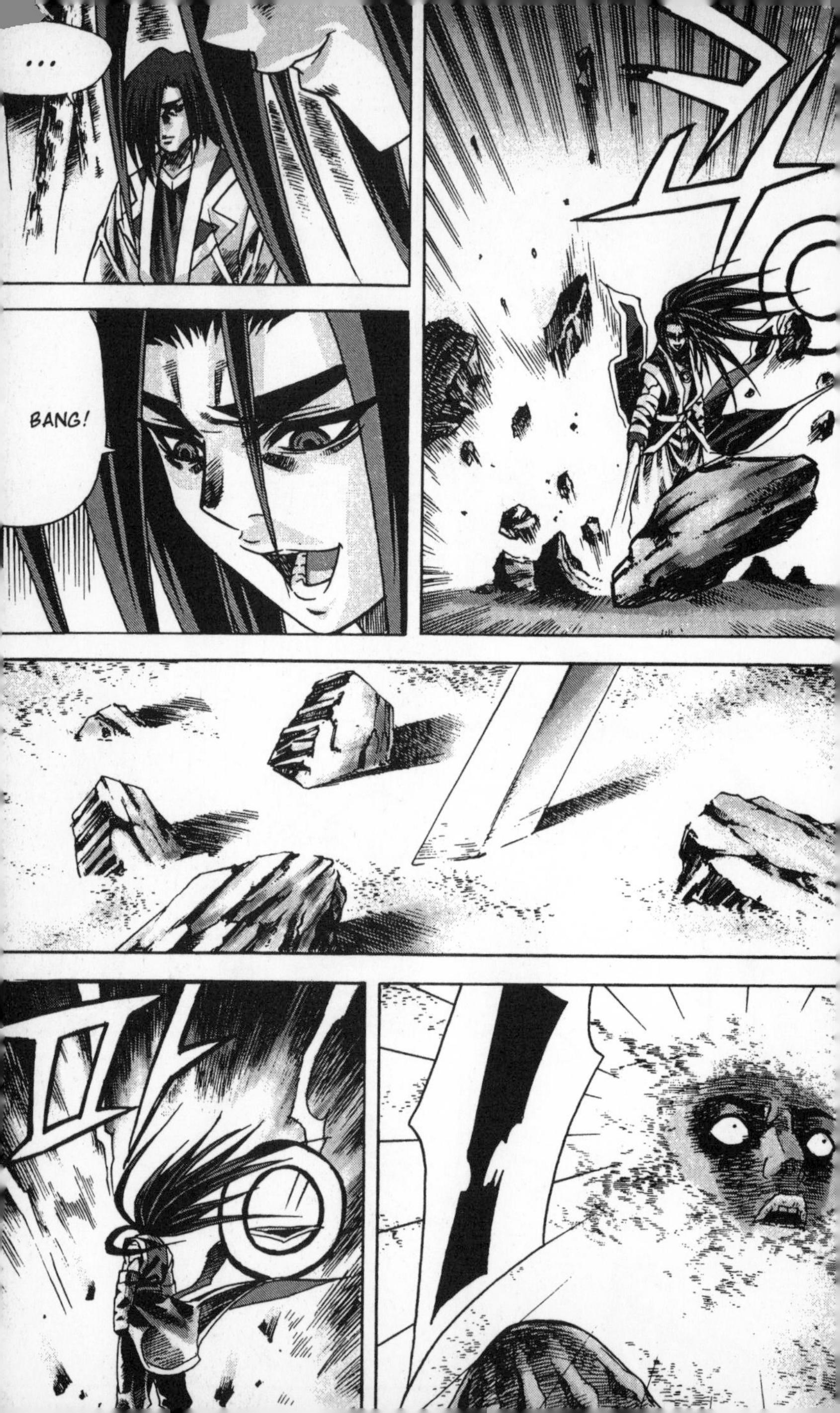
...
BANG!

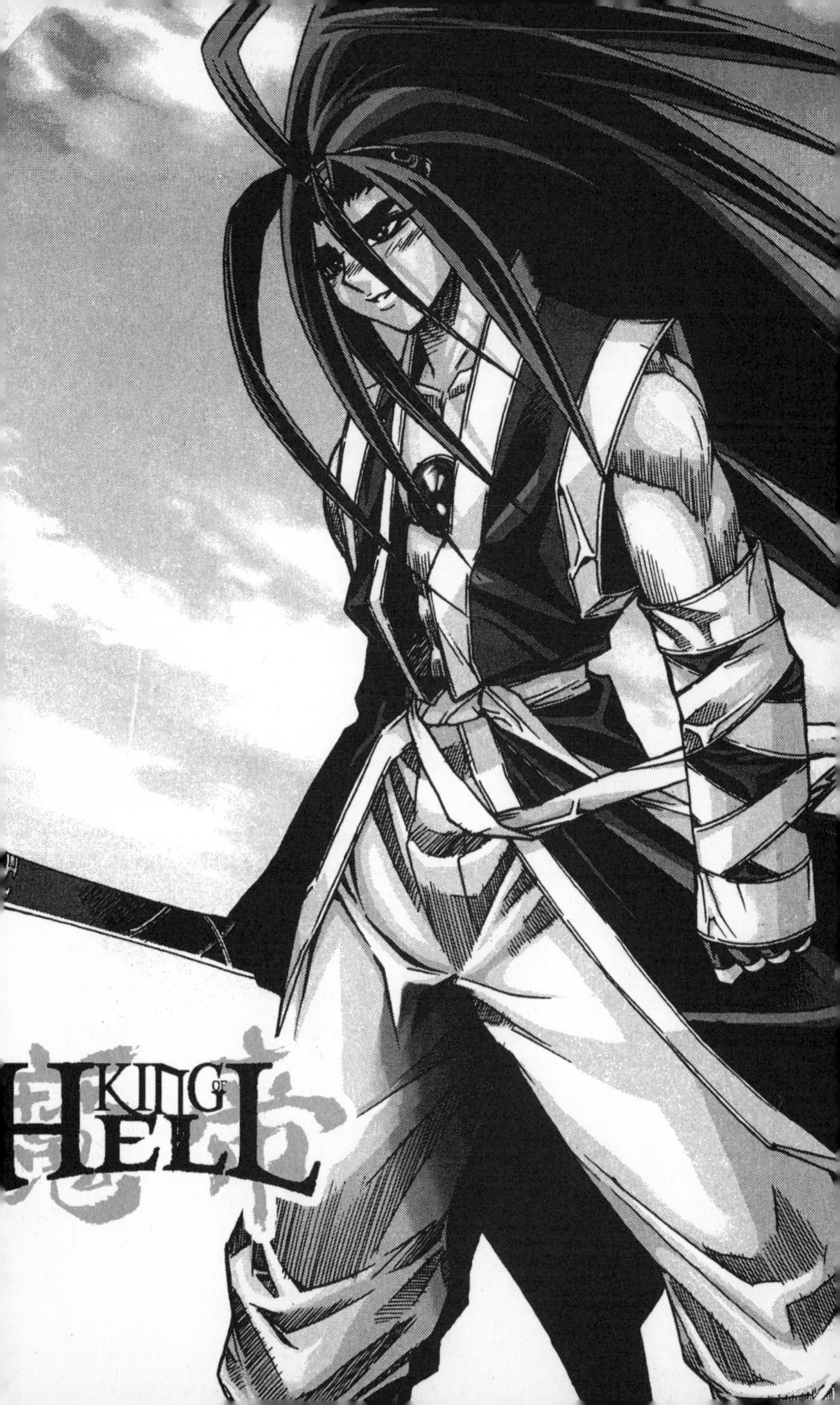
KING OF HELL

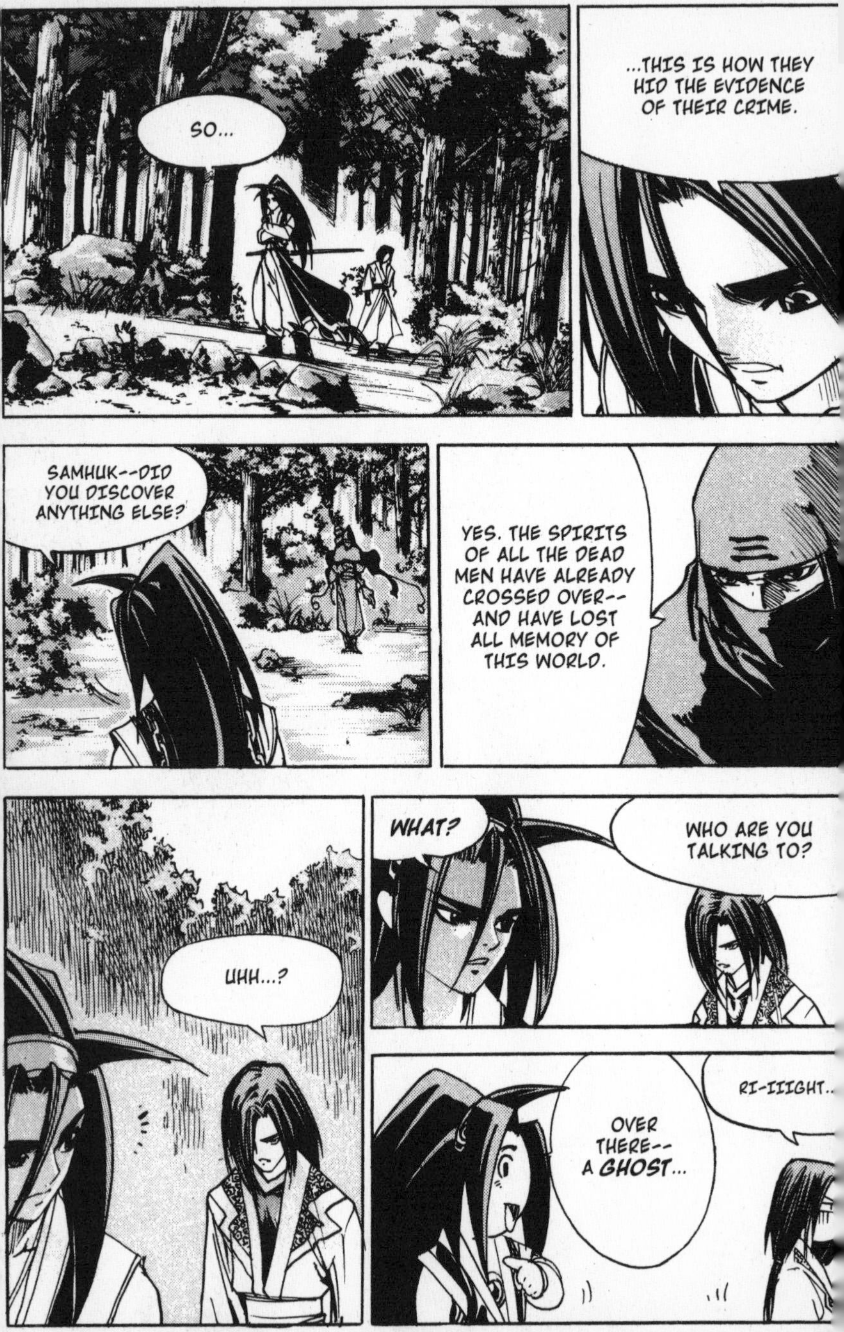
SO...
...THIS IS HOW THEY HID THE EVIDENCE OF THEIR CRIME.
SAMHUK--DID YOU DISCOVER ANYTHING ELSE?
YES. THE SPIRITS OF ALL THE DEAD MEN HAVE ALREADY CROSSED OVER--AND HAVE LOST ALL MEMORY OF THIS WORLD.
UHH...?
WHAT?
WHO ARE YOU TALKING TO?
OVER THERE--A GHOST...
RI-IIIGHT...

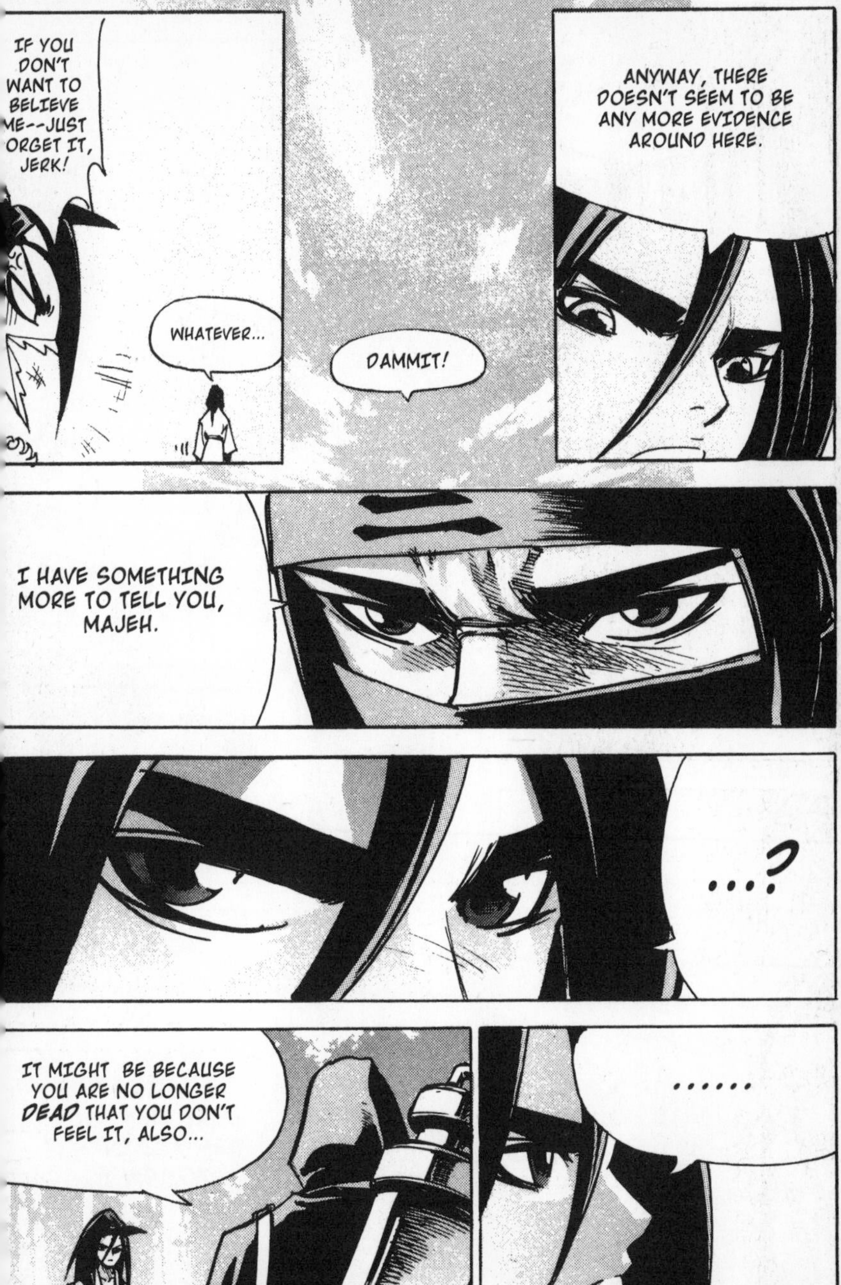
IF YOU DON'T WANT TO BELIEVE ME--JUST ORGET IT, JERK!
WHATEVER...
DAMMIT!
ANYWAY, THERE DOESN'T SEEM TO BE ANY MORE EVIDENCE AROUND HERE.
I HAVE SOMETHING MORE TO TELL YOU, MAJEH.
...?
IT MIGHT BE BECAUSE YOU ARE NO LONGER DEAD THAT YOU DON'T FEEL IT, ALSO...
......

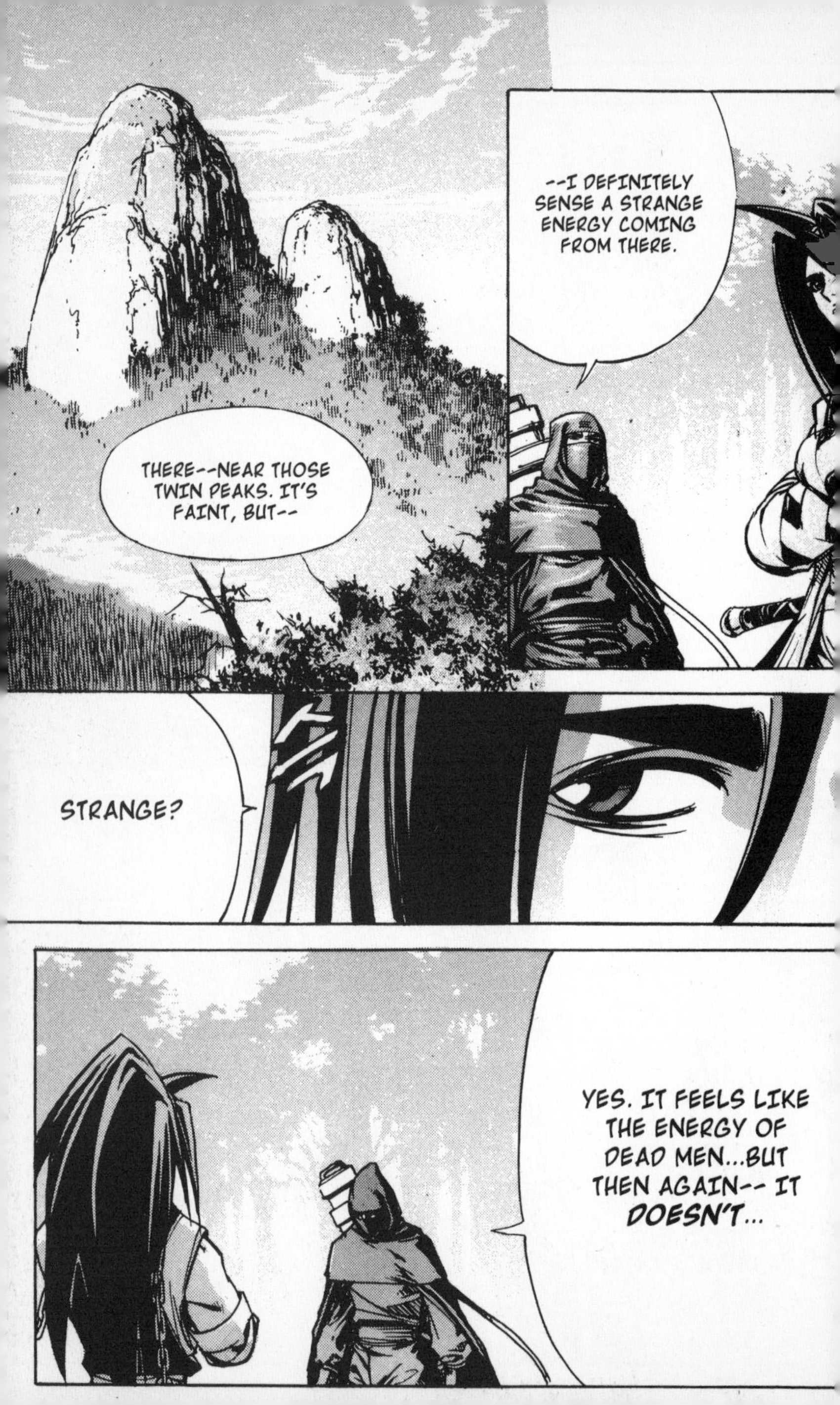
THERE--NEAR THOSE TWIN PEAKS. IT'S FAINT, BUT--
--I DEFINITELY SENSE A STRANGE ENERGY COMING FROM THERE.
STRANGE?
YES. IT FEELS LIKE THE ENERGY OF DEAD MEN...BUT THEN AGAIN-- IT *DOESN'T*...

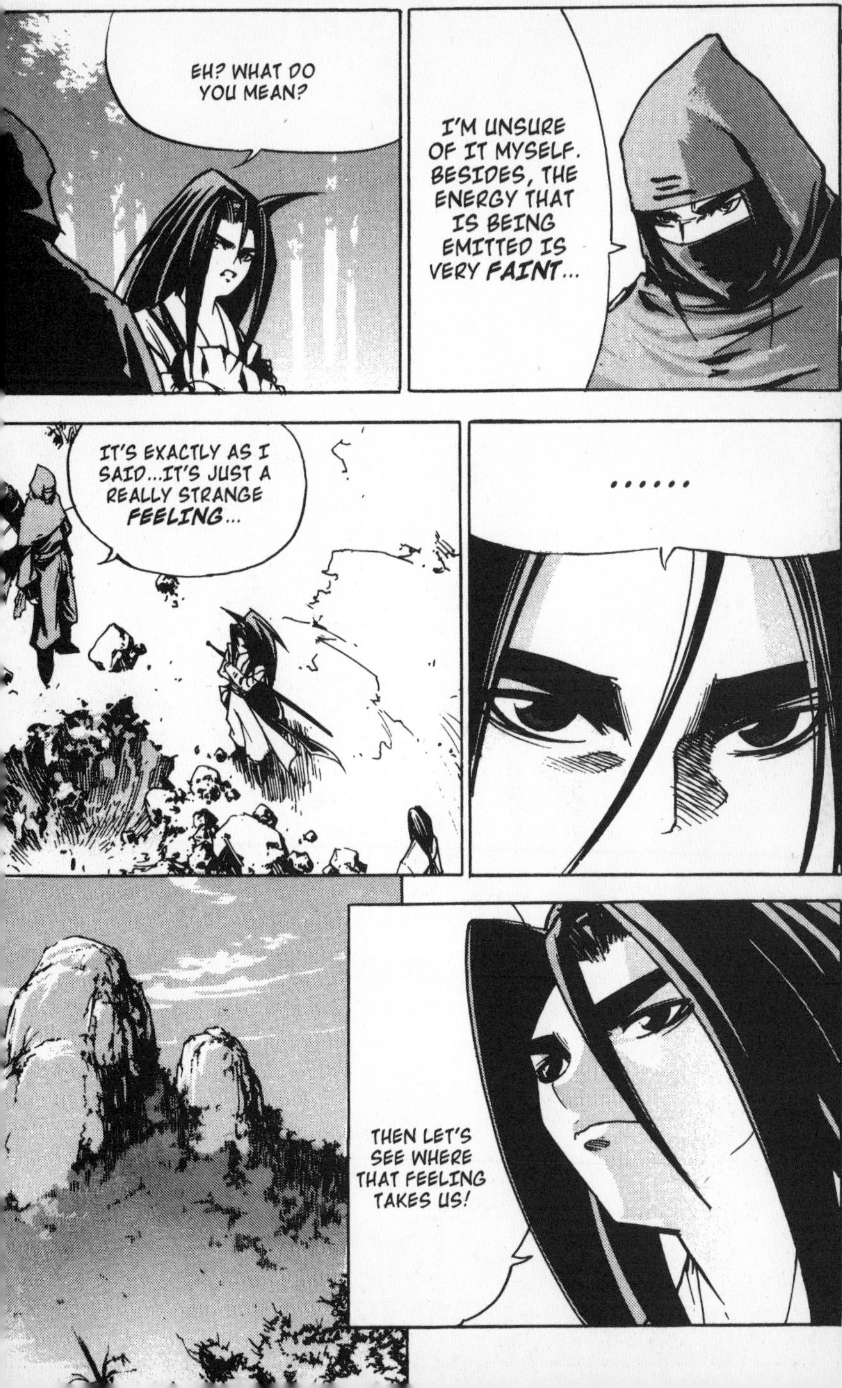
EH? WHAT DO YOU MEAN?
I'M UNSURE OF IT MYSELF. BESIDES, THE ENERGY THAT IS BEING EMITTED IS VERY FAINT...
IT'S EXACTLY AS I SAID...IT'S JUST A REALLY STRANGE FEELING...
......
THEN LET'S SEE WHERE THAT FEELING TAKES US!

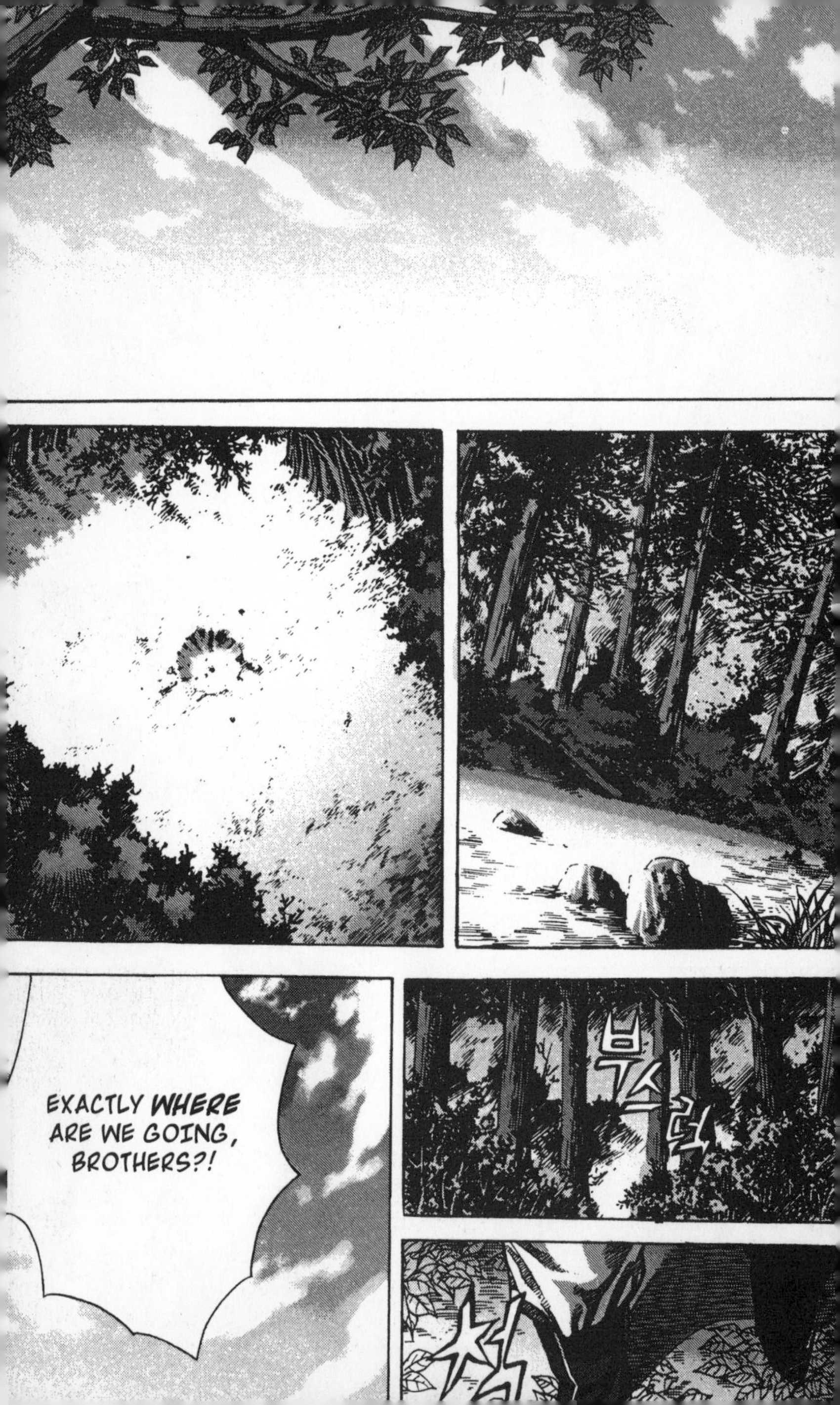
EXACTLY **WHERE** ARE WE GOING, BROTHERS?!

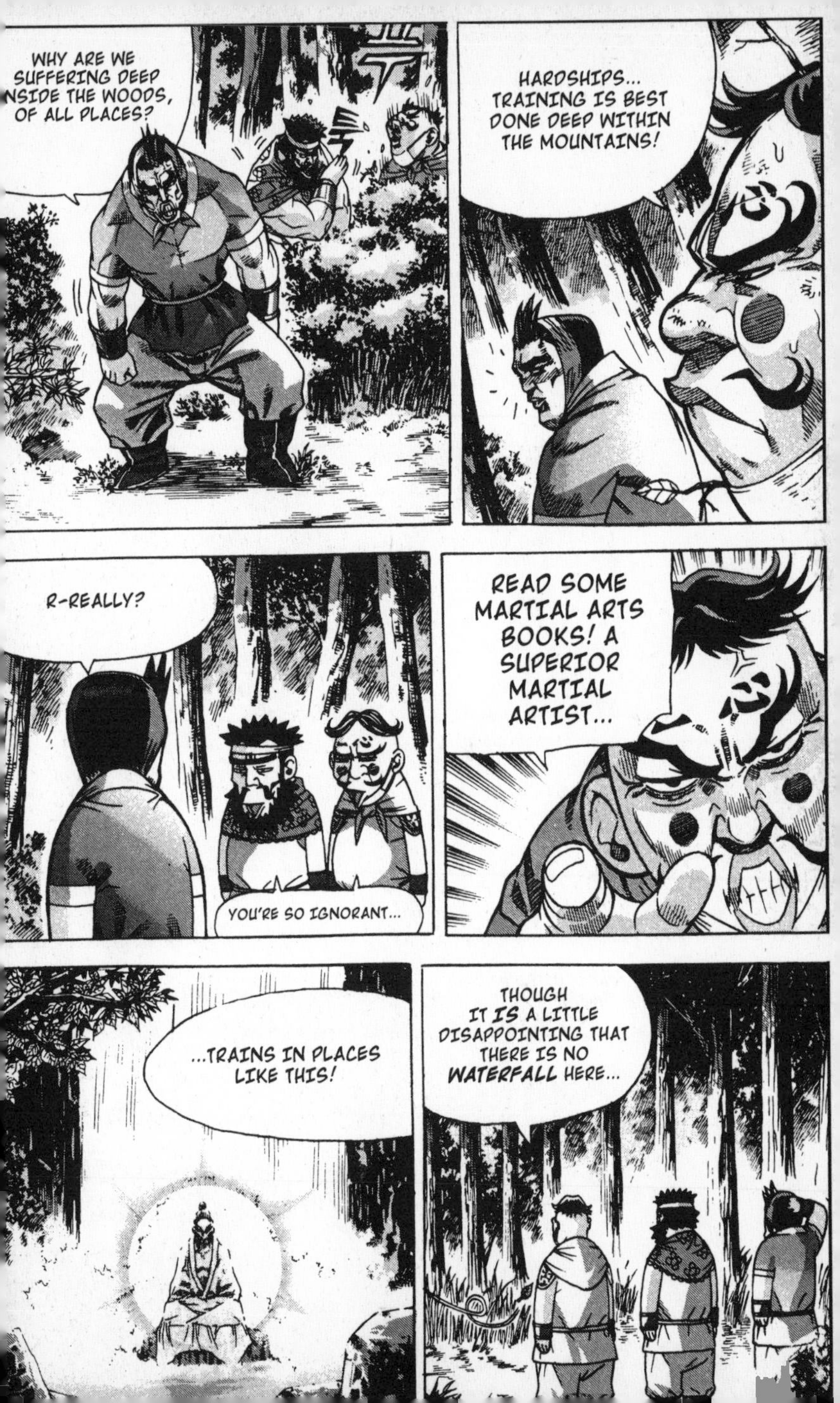
WHY ARE WE SUFFERING DEEP INSIDE THE WOODS, OF ALL PLACES?
HARDSHIPS... TRAINING IS BEST DONE DEEP WITHIN THE MOUNTAINS!
R-REALLY?
YOU'RE SO IGNORANT...
READ SOME MARTIAL ARTS BOOKS! A SUPERIOR MARTIAL ARTIST...
...TRAINS IN PLACES LIKE THIS!
THOUGH IT IS A LITTLE DISAPPOINTING THAT THERE IS NO WATERFALL HERE...

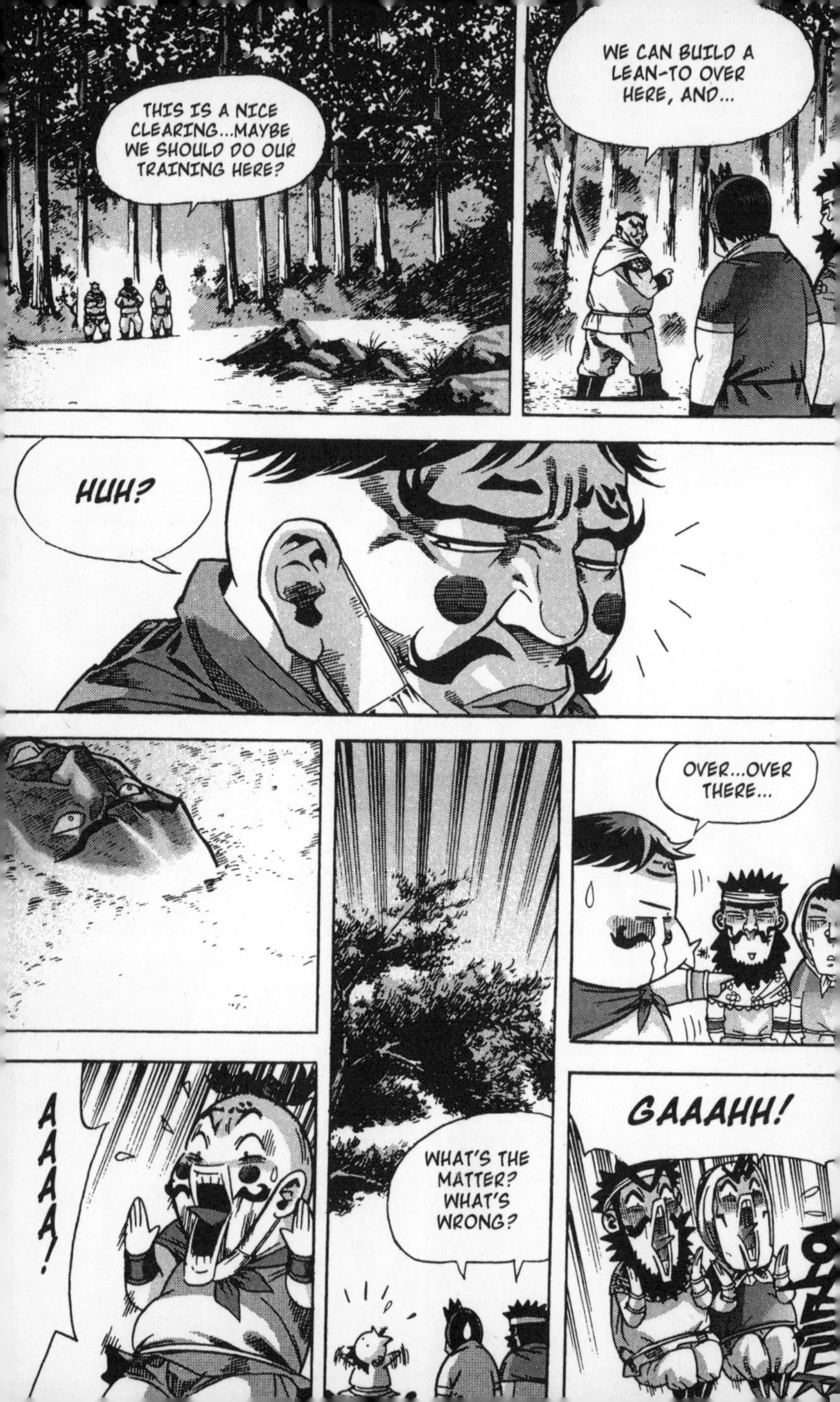
THIS IS A NICE CLEARING...MAYBE WE SHOULD DO OUR TRAINING HERE?
WE CAN BUILD A LEAN-TO OVER HERE, AND...
HUH?
AAAAA!
WHAT'S THE MATTER? WHAT'S WRONG?
OVER...OVER THERE...
GAAAHH!

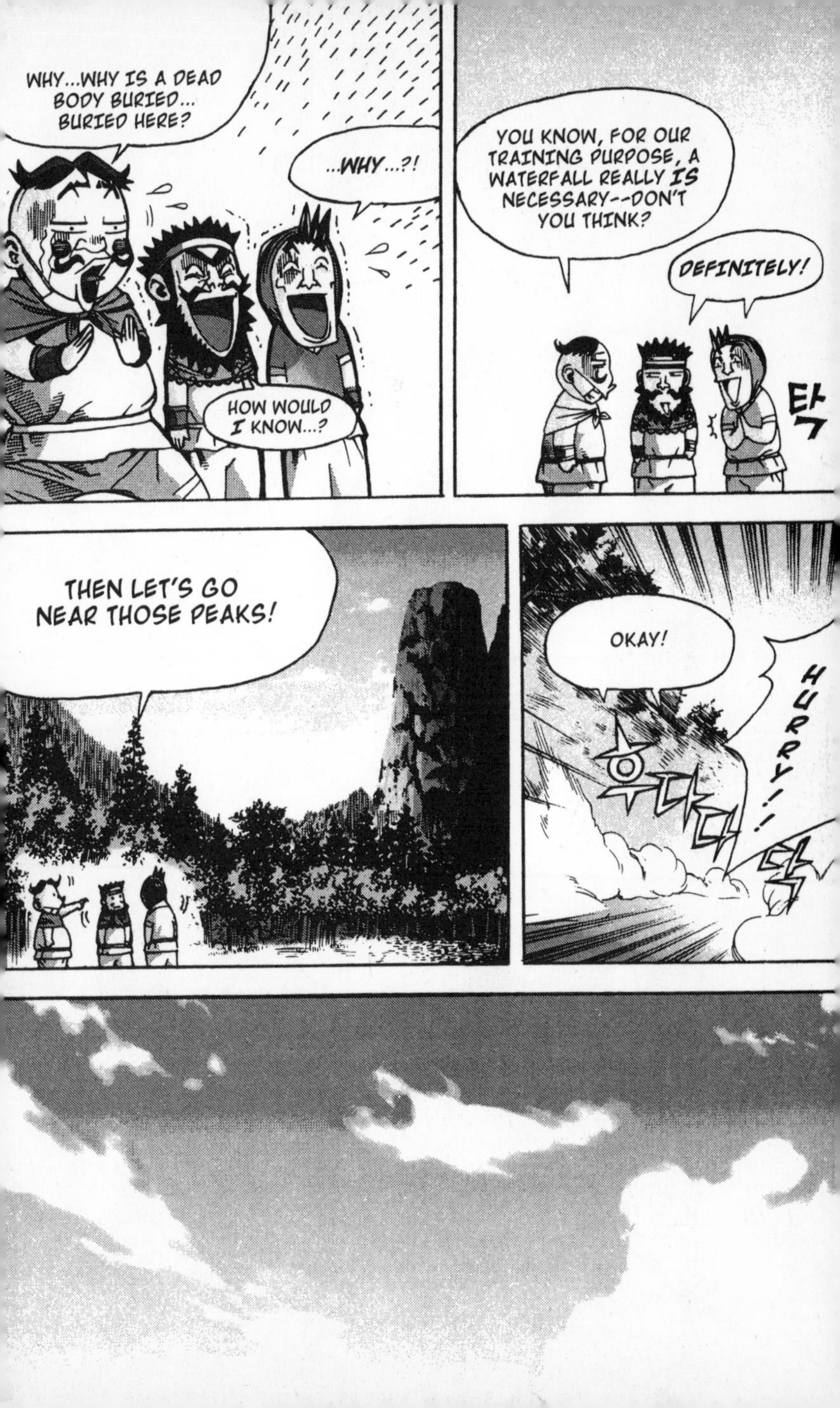
WHY...WHY IS A DEAD BODY BURIED... BURIED HERE?
...WHY...?!
HOW WOULD I KNOW...?
YOU KNOW, FOR OUR TRAINING PURPOSE, A WATERFALL REALLY IS NECESSARY--DON'T YOU THINK?
DEFINITELY!
탁
THEN LET'S GO NEAR THOSE PEAKS!
OKAY!
HURRY!!

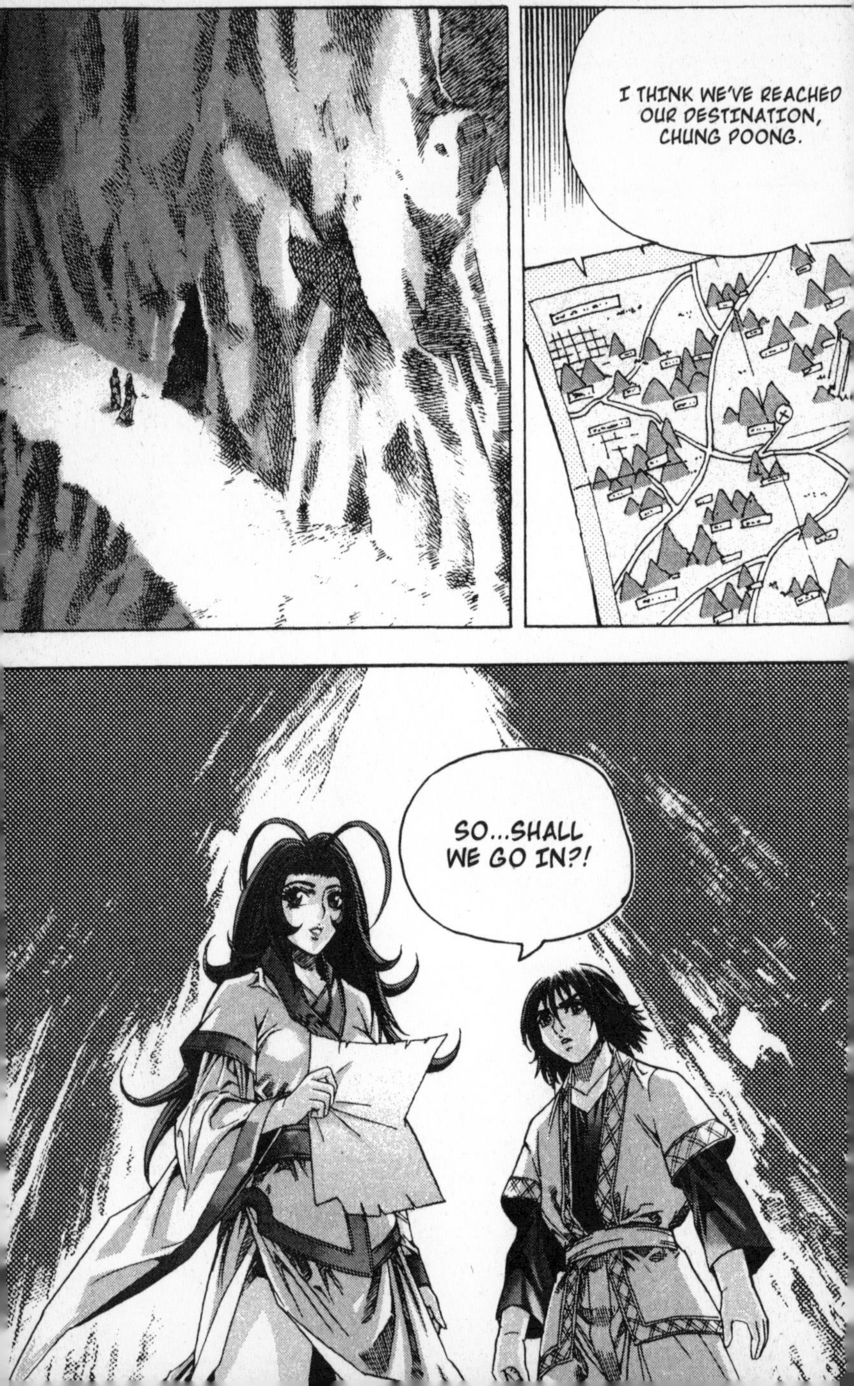
I THINK WE'VE REACHED OUR DESTINATION, CHUNG POONG.
SO...SHALL WE GO IN?!

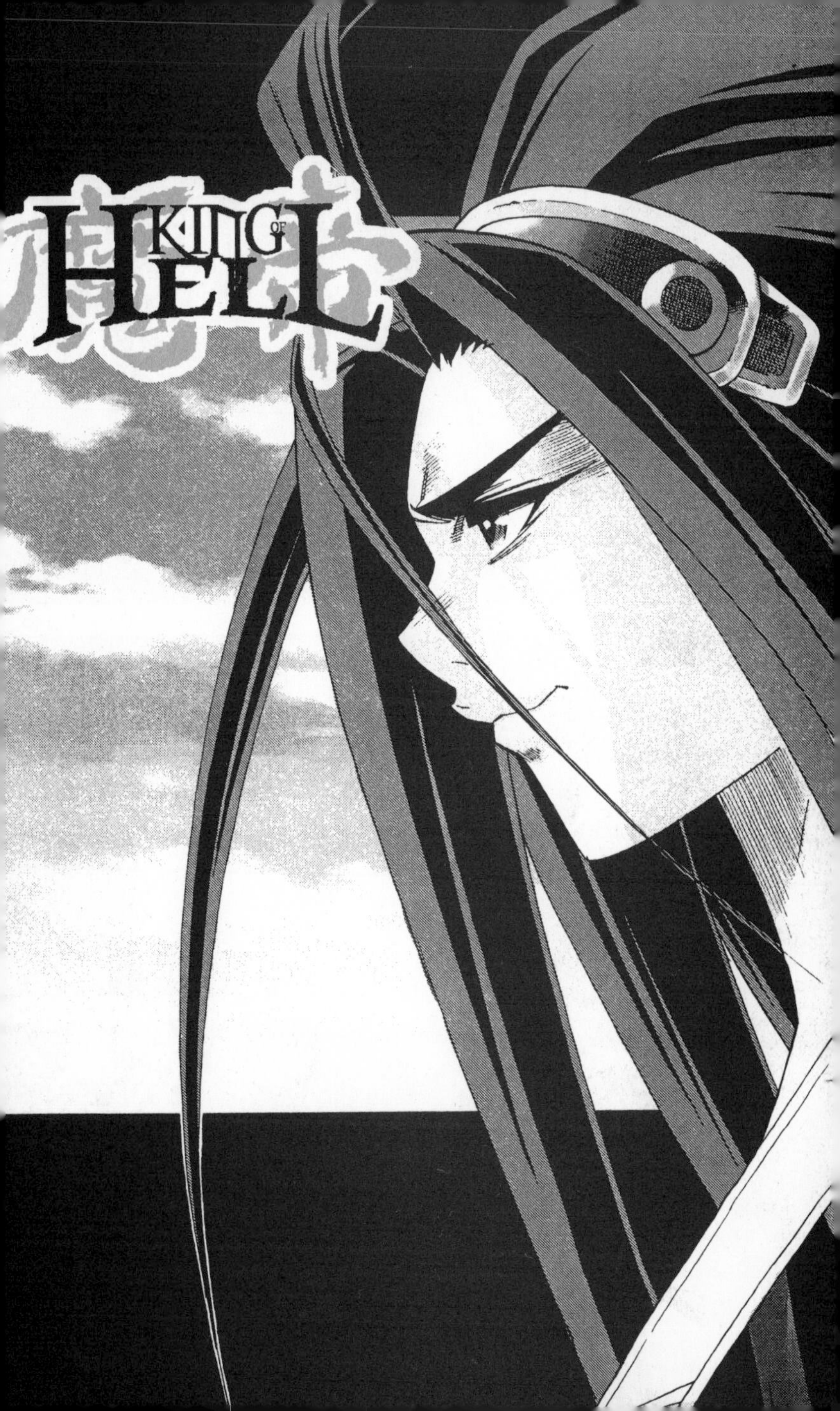
KING OF HELL

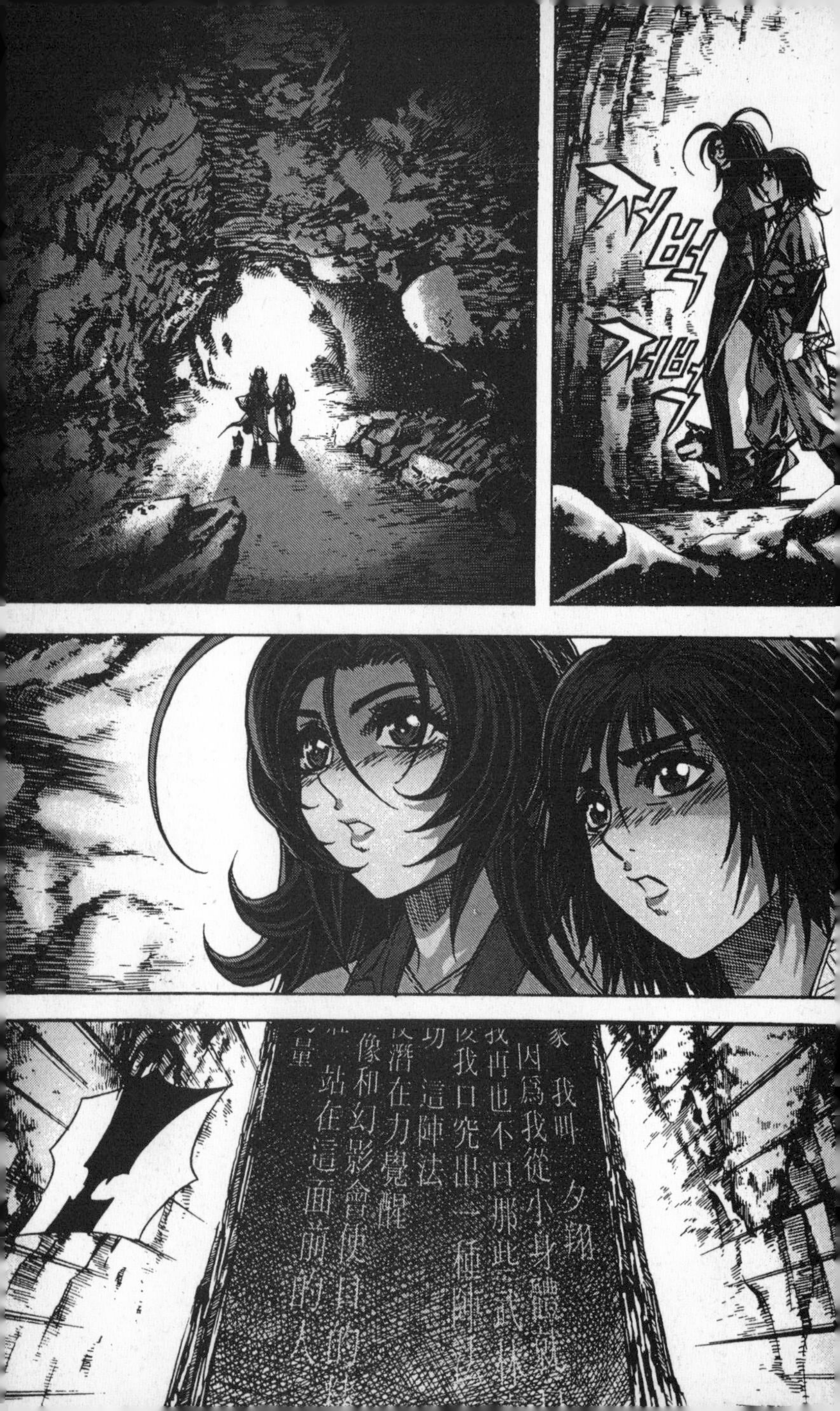

저벅
저벅
家
我叫夕翔
因爲我從小身體
再也不日那此武
我口究出一種陣
功這陣法
潛在力覺醒
像和幻影會使自
站在這面前的人的
量

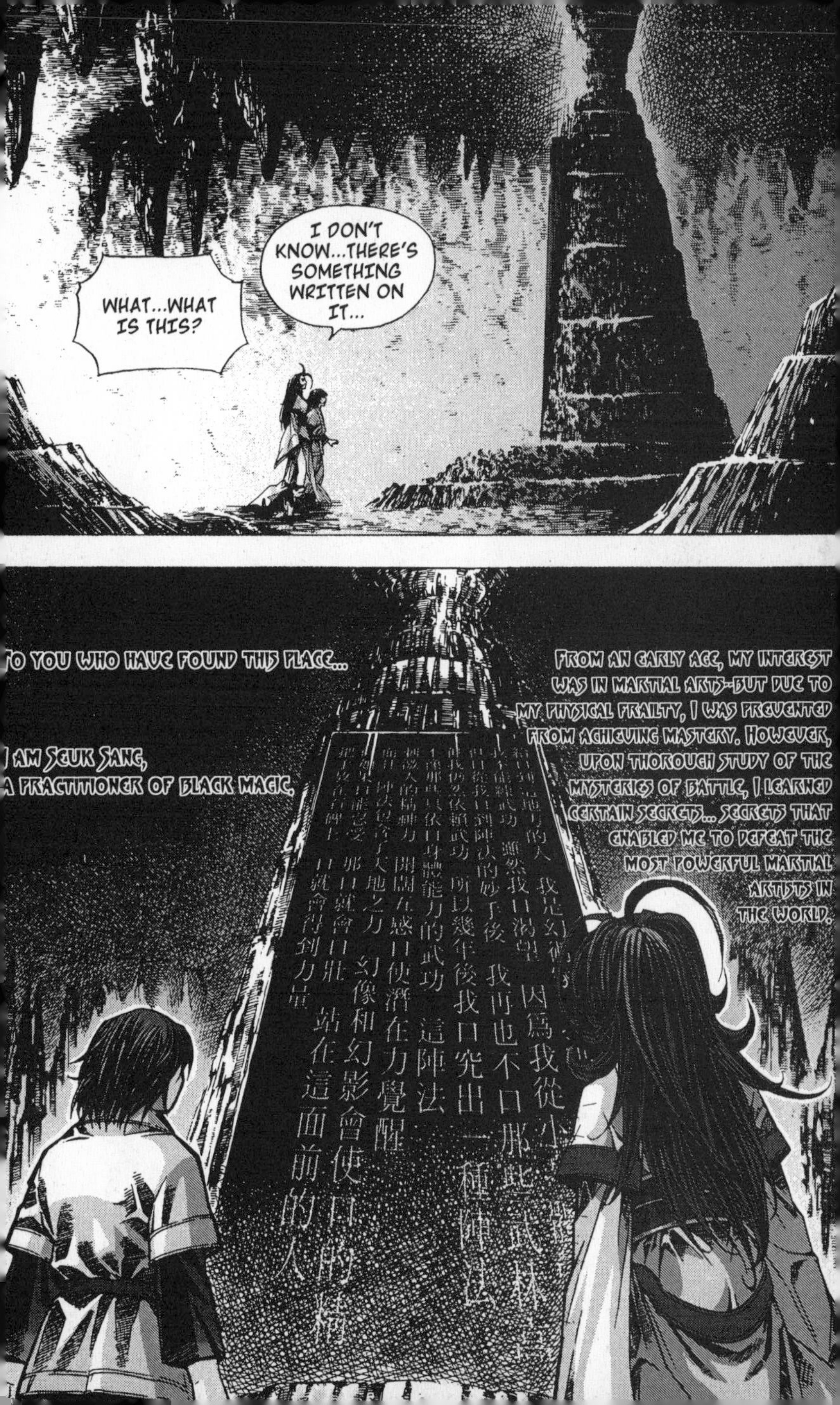
WHAT...WHAT IS THIS?
I DON'T KNOW...THERE'S SOMETHING WRITTEN ON IT...
TO YOU WHO HAVE FOUND THIS PLACE...
I AM SEUK SANG, A PRACTITIONER OF BLACK MAGIC.
FROM AN EARLY AGE, MY INTEREST WAS IN MARTIAL ARTS--BUT DUE TO MY PHYSICAL FRAILTY, I WAS PREVENTED FROM ACHIEVING MASTERY. HOWEVER, UPON THOROUGH STUDY OF THE MYSTERIES OF BATTLE, I LEARNED CERTAIN SECRETS... SECRETS THAT ENABLED ME TO DEFEAT THE MOST POWERFUL MARTIAL ARTISTS IN THE WORLD.

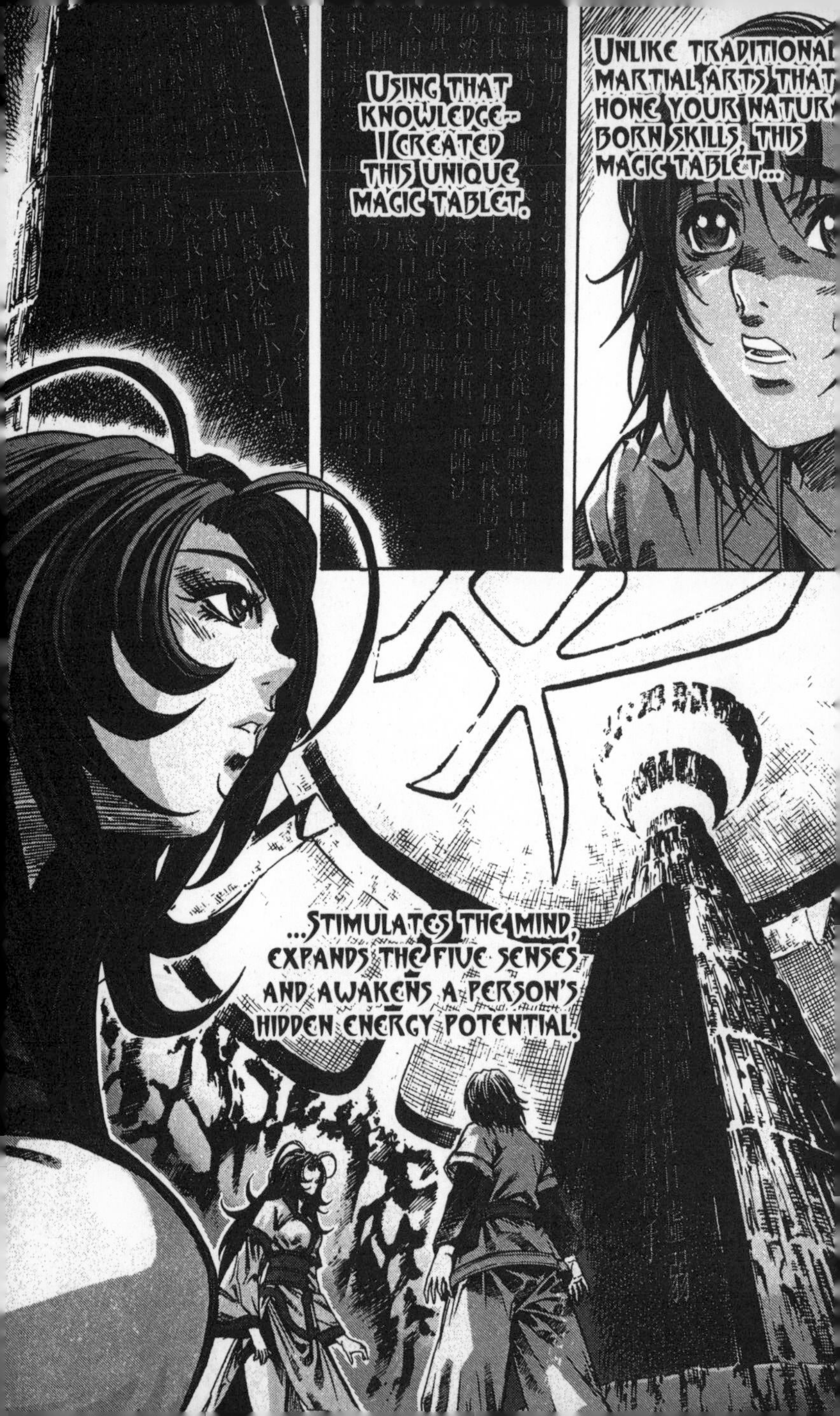
USING THAT KNOWLEDGE-- I CREATED THIS UNIQUE MAGIC TABLET.
UNLIKE TRADITIONAL MARTIAL ARTS THAT HONE YOUR NATUR BORN SKILLS, THIS MAGIC TABLET...
...STIMULATES THE MIND, EXPANDS THE FIVE SENSES AND AWAKENS A PERSON'S HIDDEN ENERGY POTENTIAL.

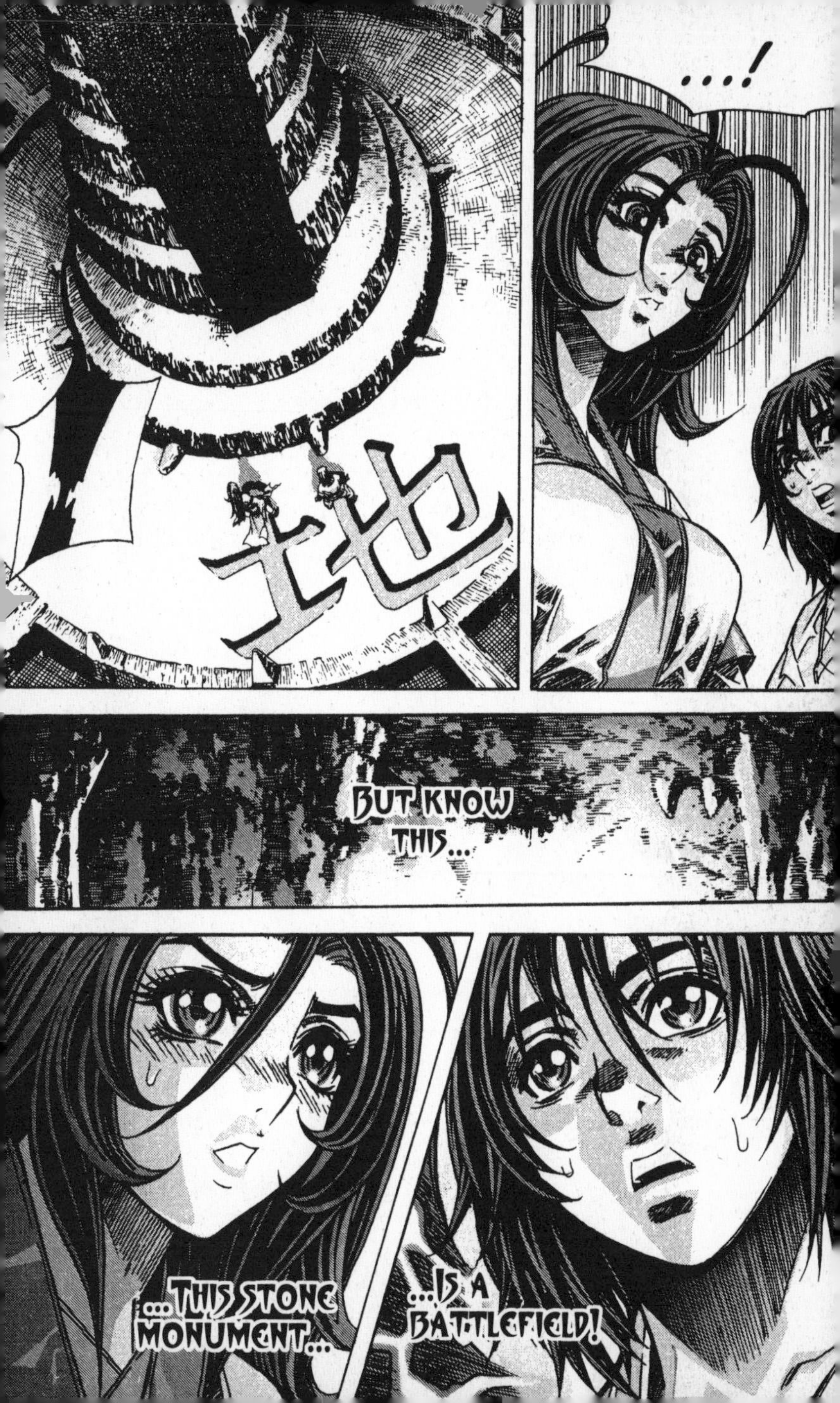
地
...!
BUT KNOW THIS...
...THIS STONE MONUMENT...
...IS A BATTLEFIELD!

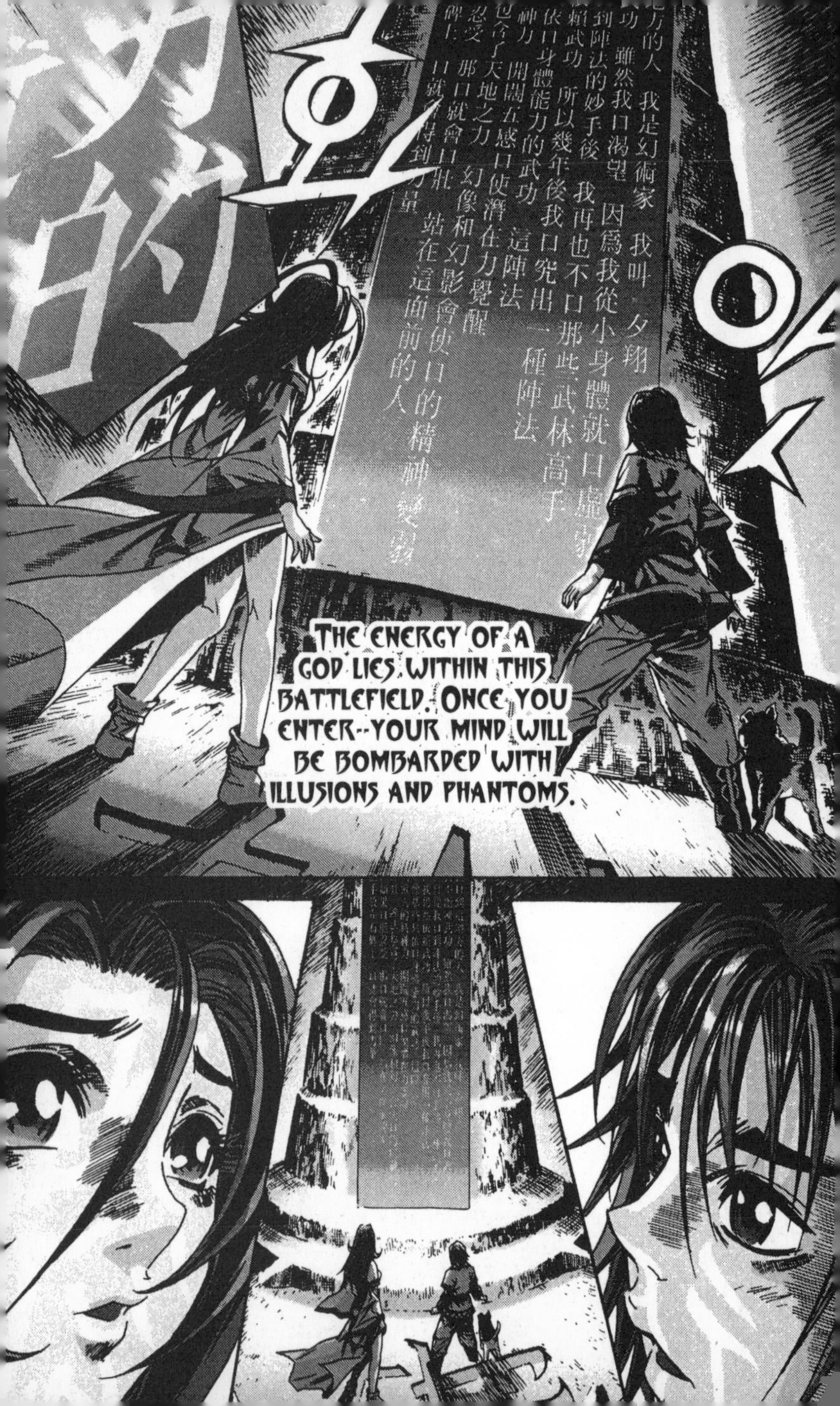

方的人 我是幻術家 我叫 夕翔
功 雖然我口渴望 因為我從小身體就口虛弱
到陣法的妙手後 我再也不口那些武林高手
賴武功 所以幾年後我口究出一種陣法
依口身體能力的武功 這陣法
神力 開闊五感口使濟在力覺醒
包含了天地之力 幻像和幻影會使口的精神變弱
忍受 那口就會口壯 站在這面前的人
碑上 口就會得到力量
THE ENERGY OF A GOD LIES WITHIN THIS BATTLEFIELD. ONCE YOU ENTER--YOUR MIND WILL BE BOMBARDED WITH ILLUSIONS AND PHANTOMS.

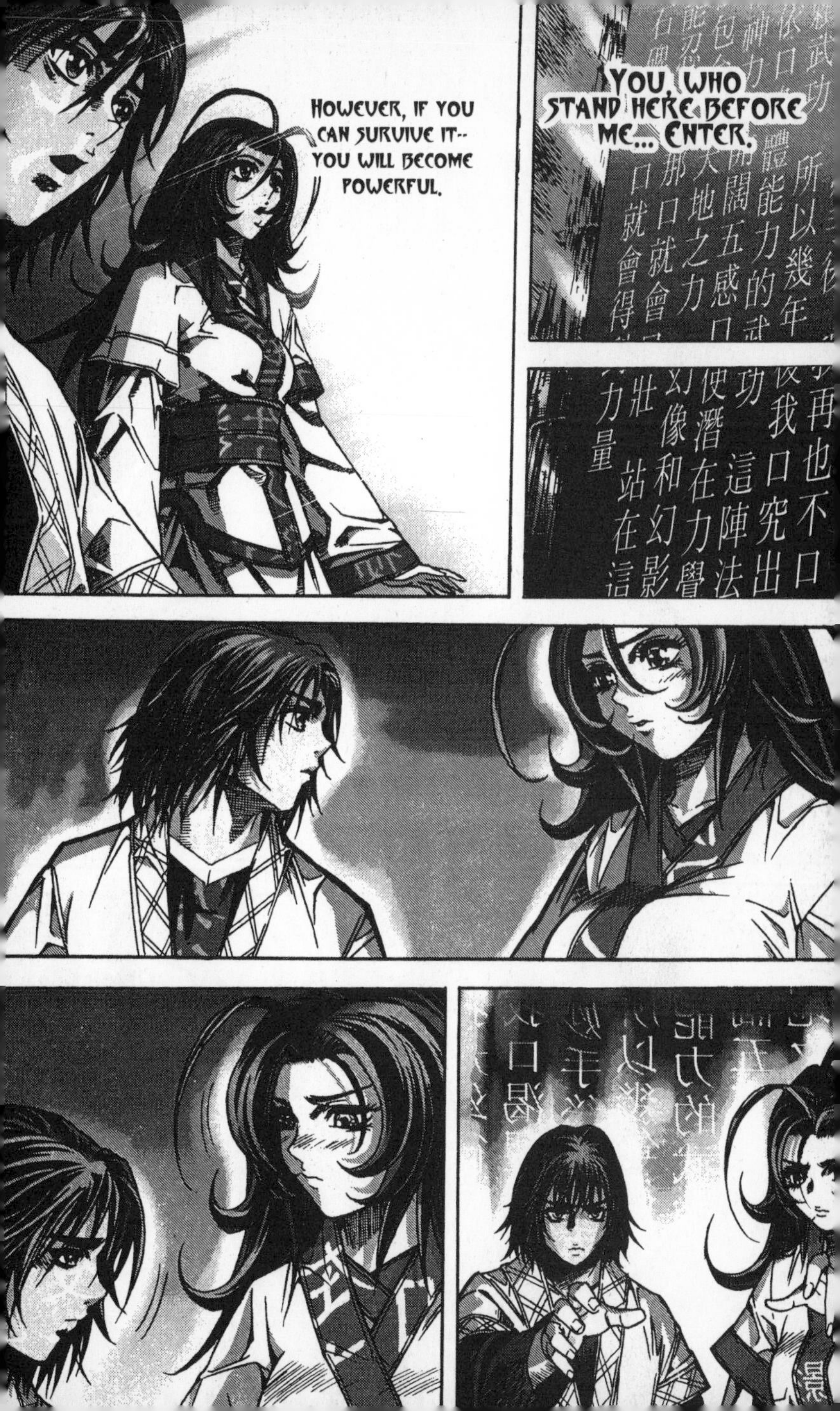
However, if you can survive it-- you will become powerful.
You, who stand here before me... Enter.

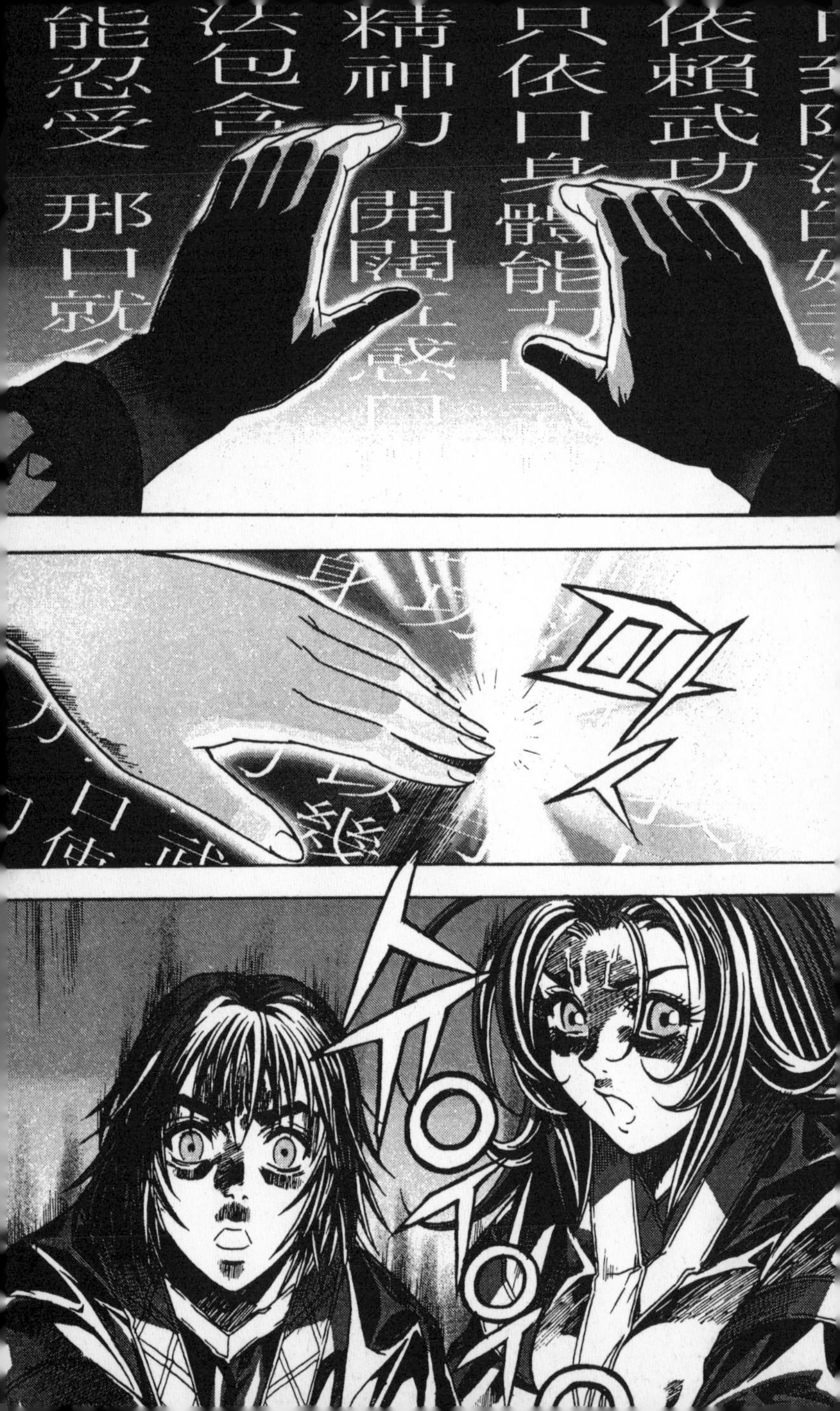

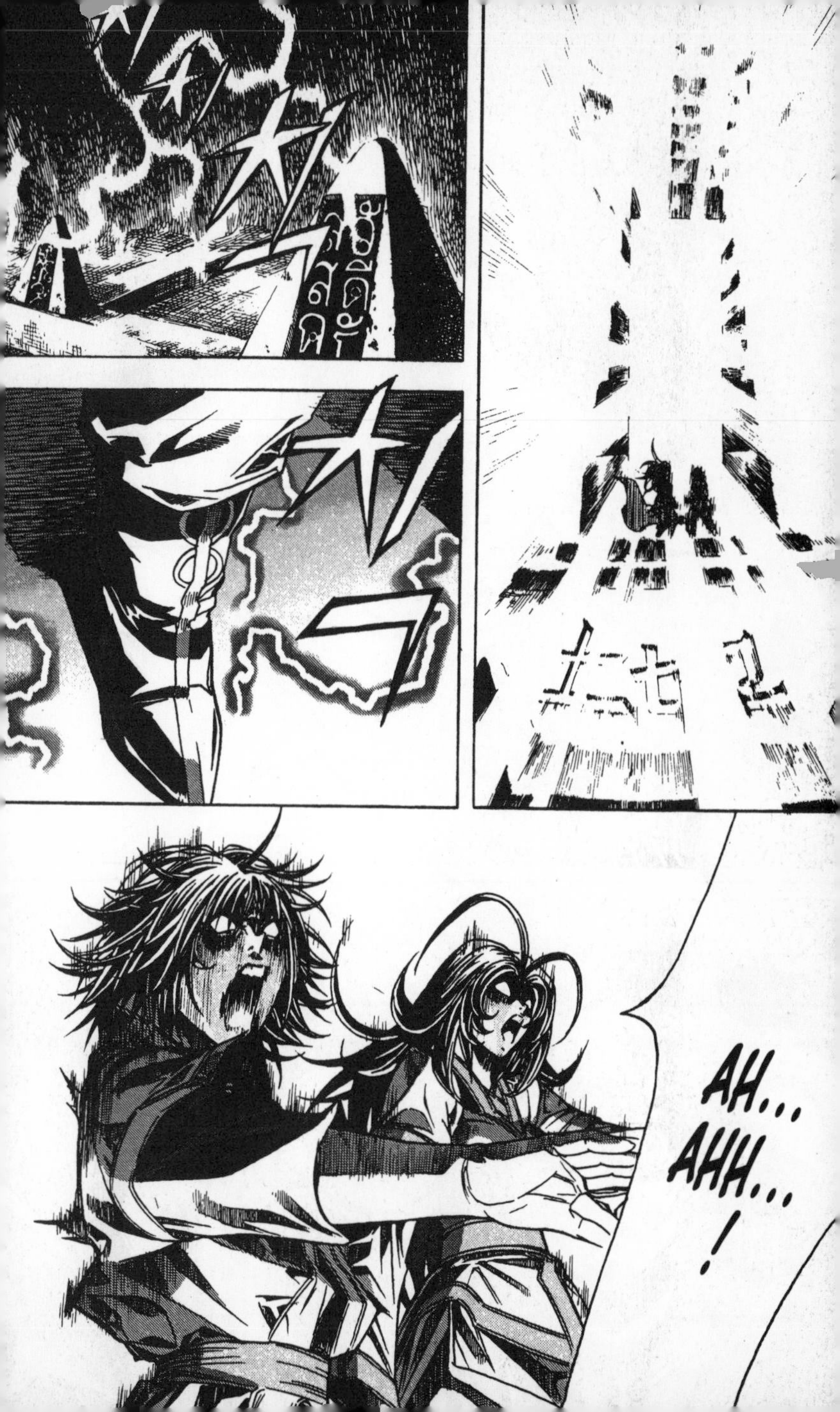
AH... AHH... !

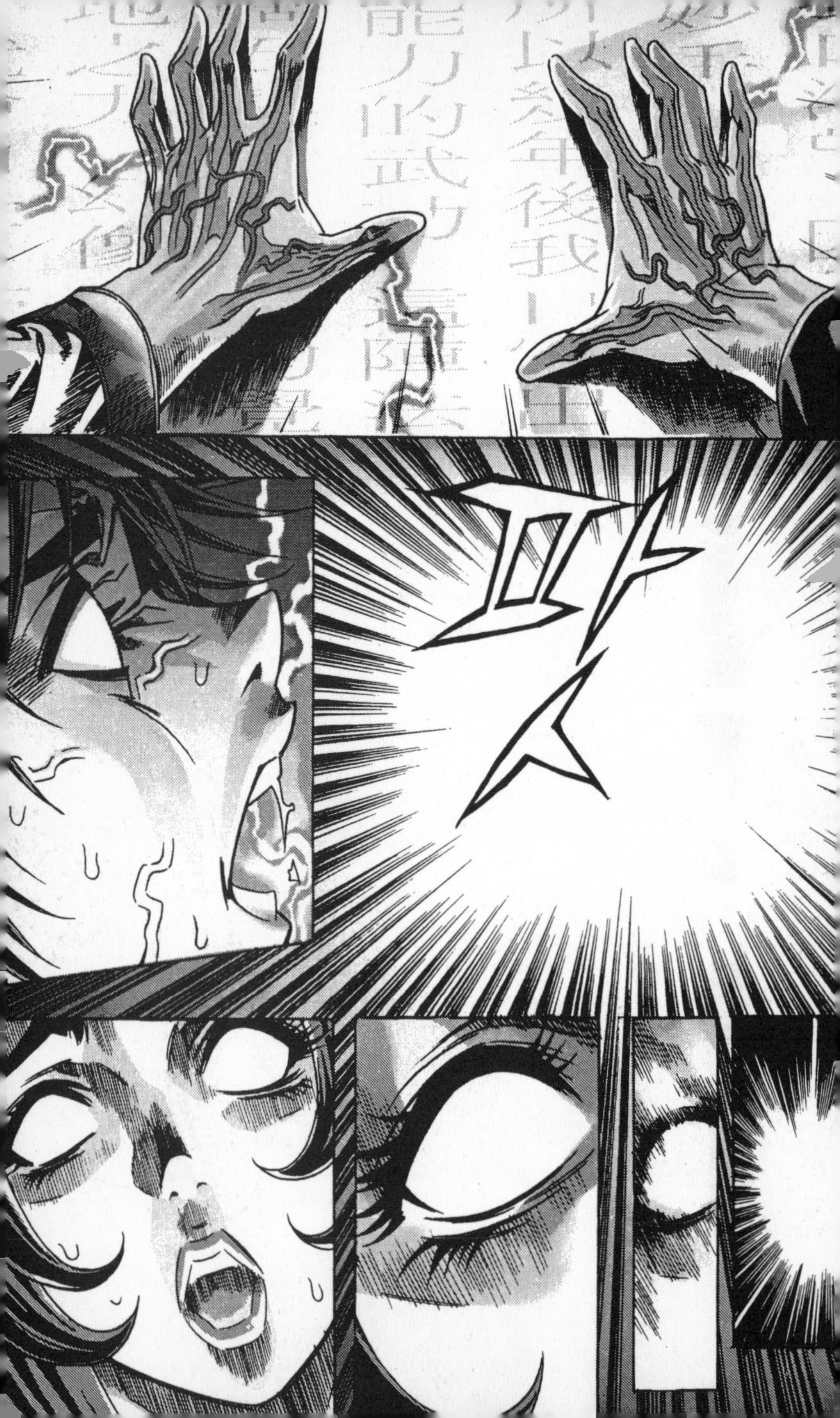

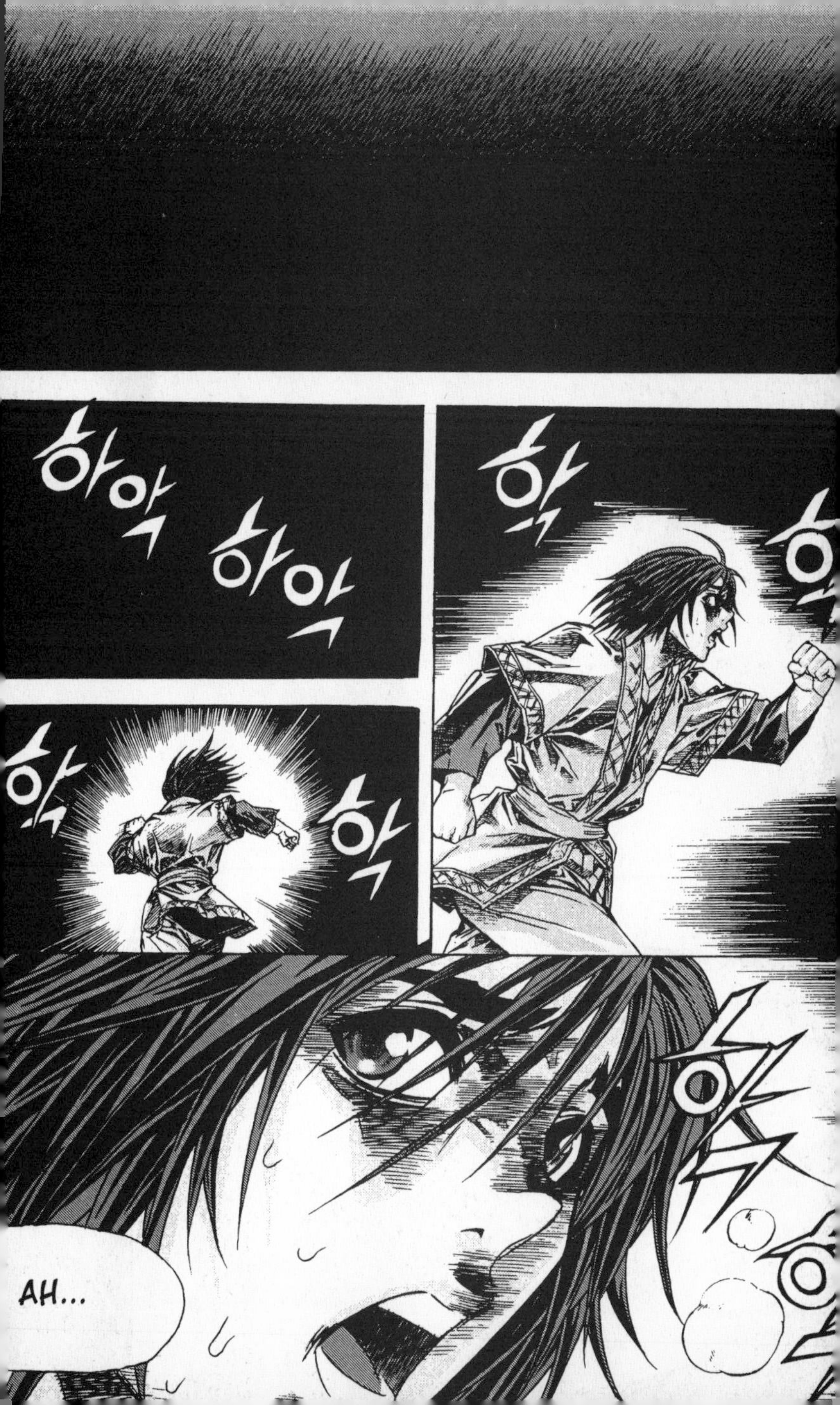
하악
하악
학
학
학
학
학
학
AH...

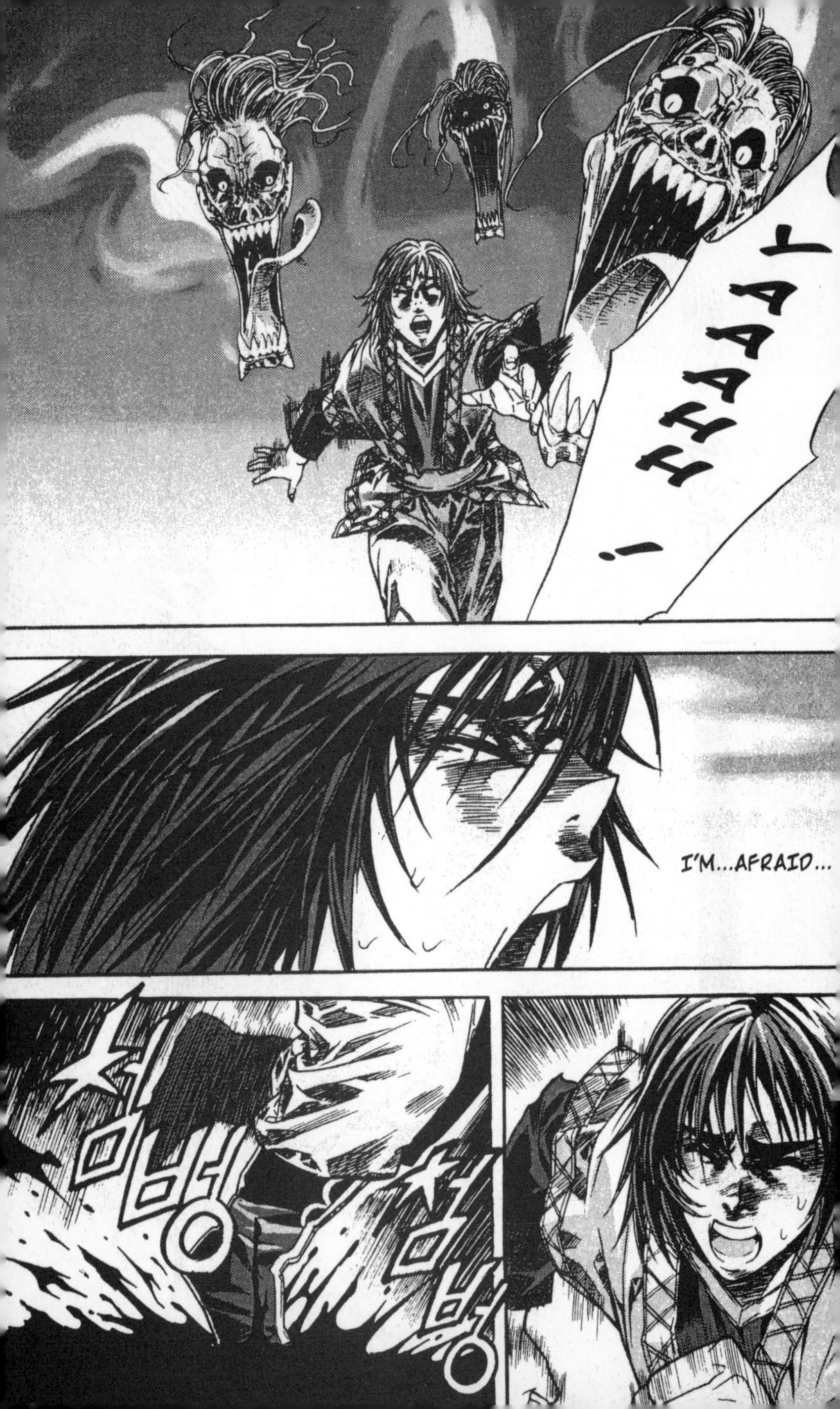
YAAAHH!
I'M...AFRAID...

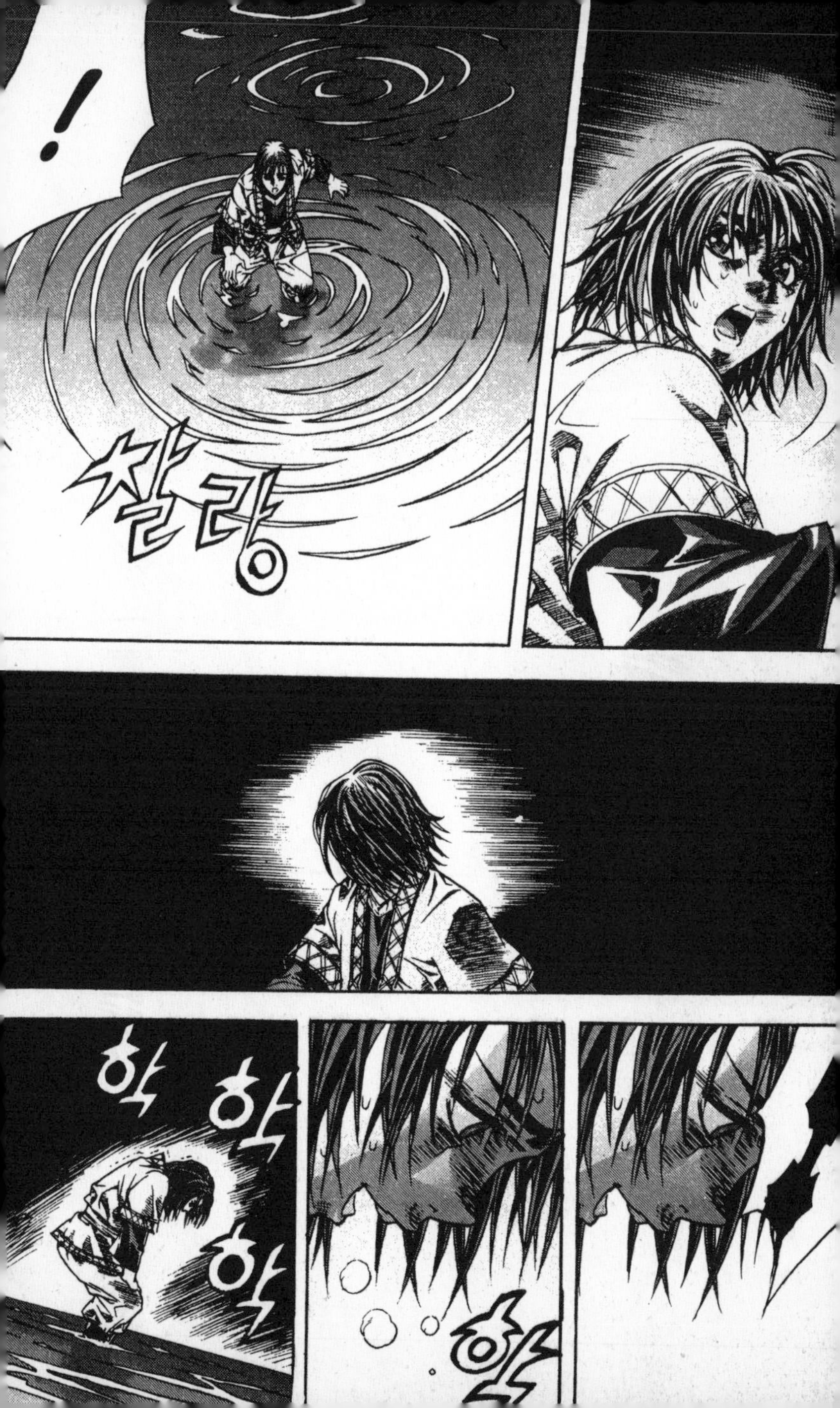
!
찰랑
학 학
학
학

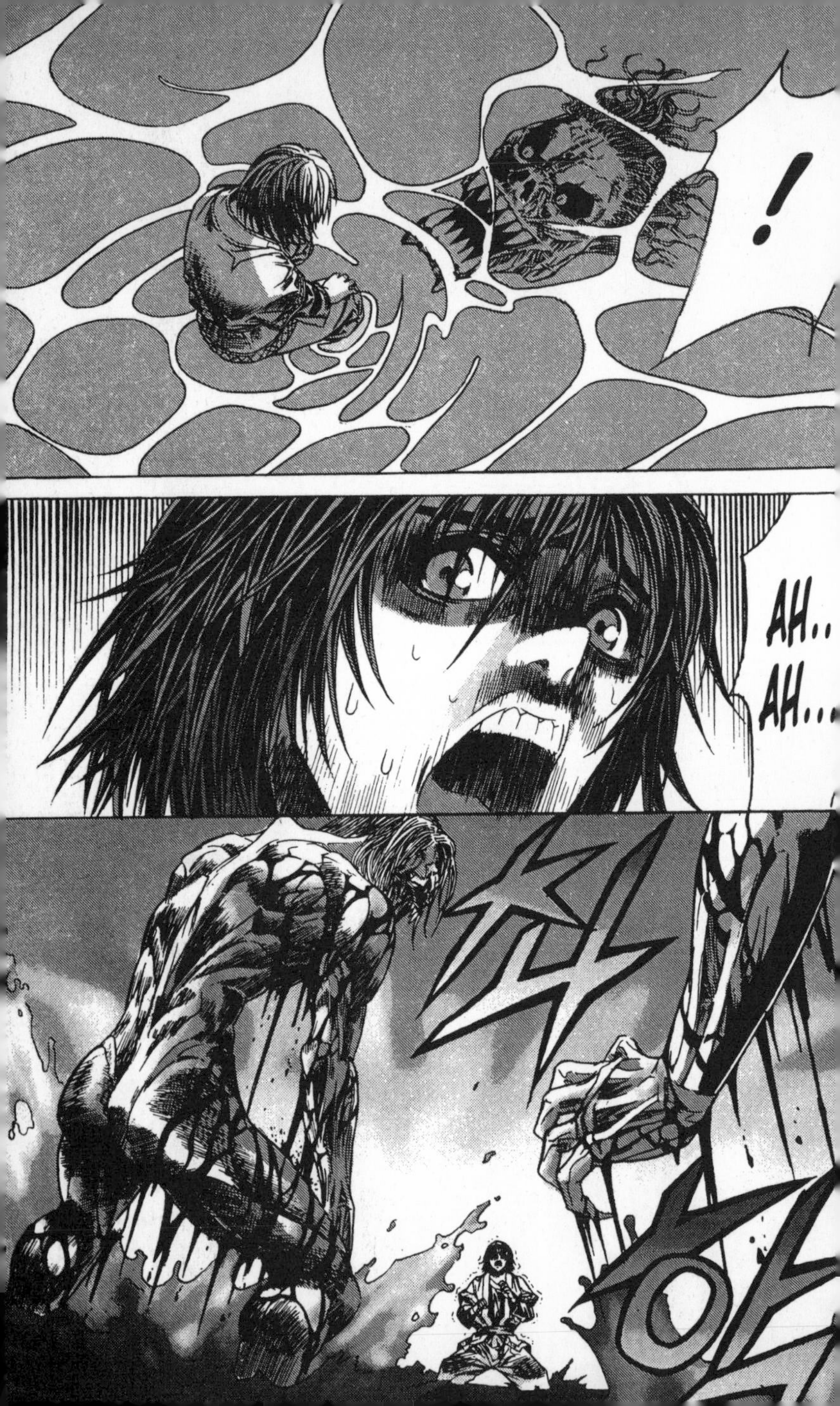
!
AH...
AH...

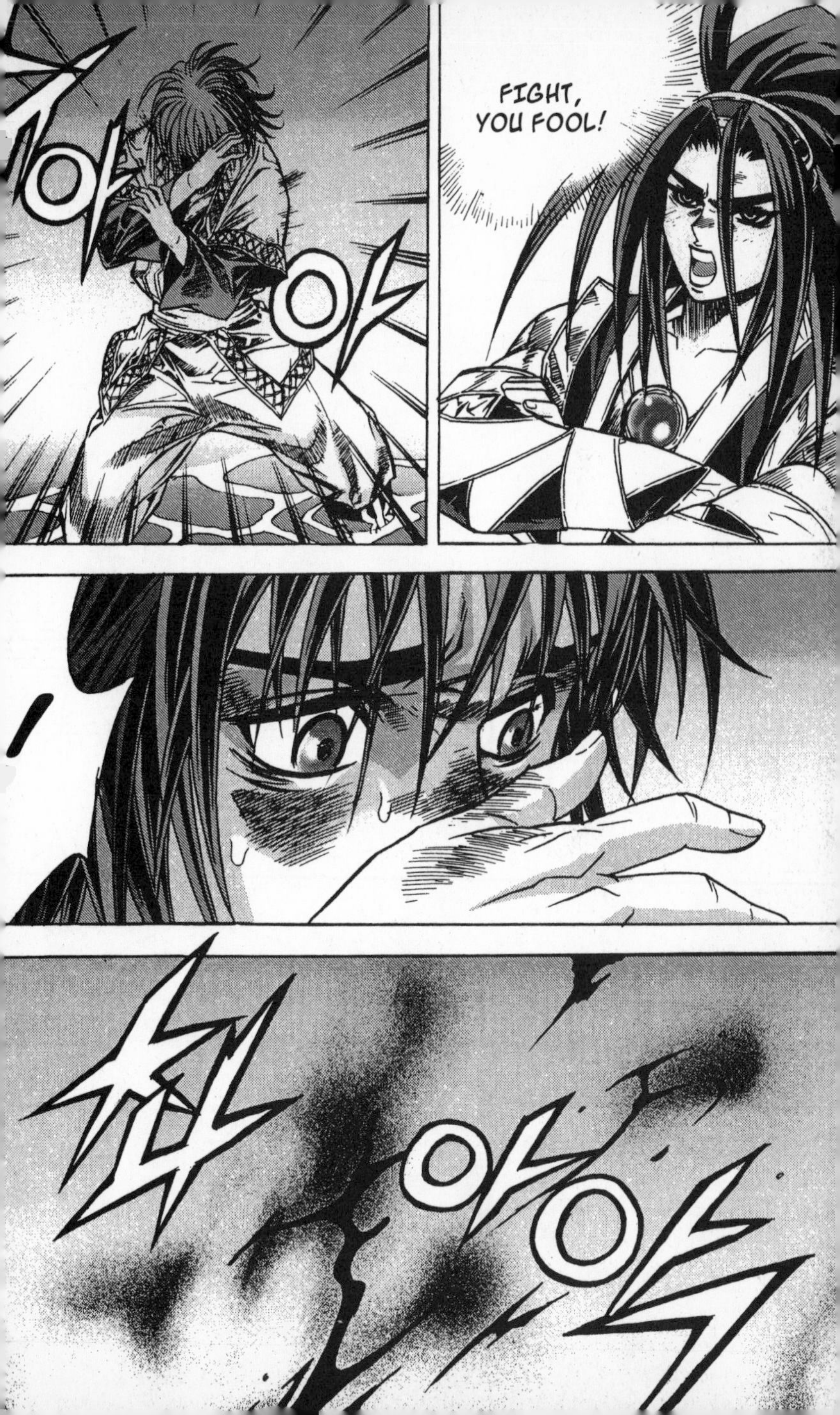
FIGHT, YOU FOOL!

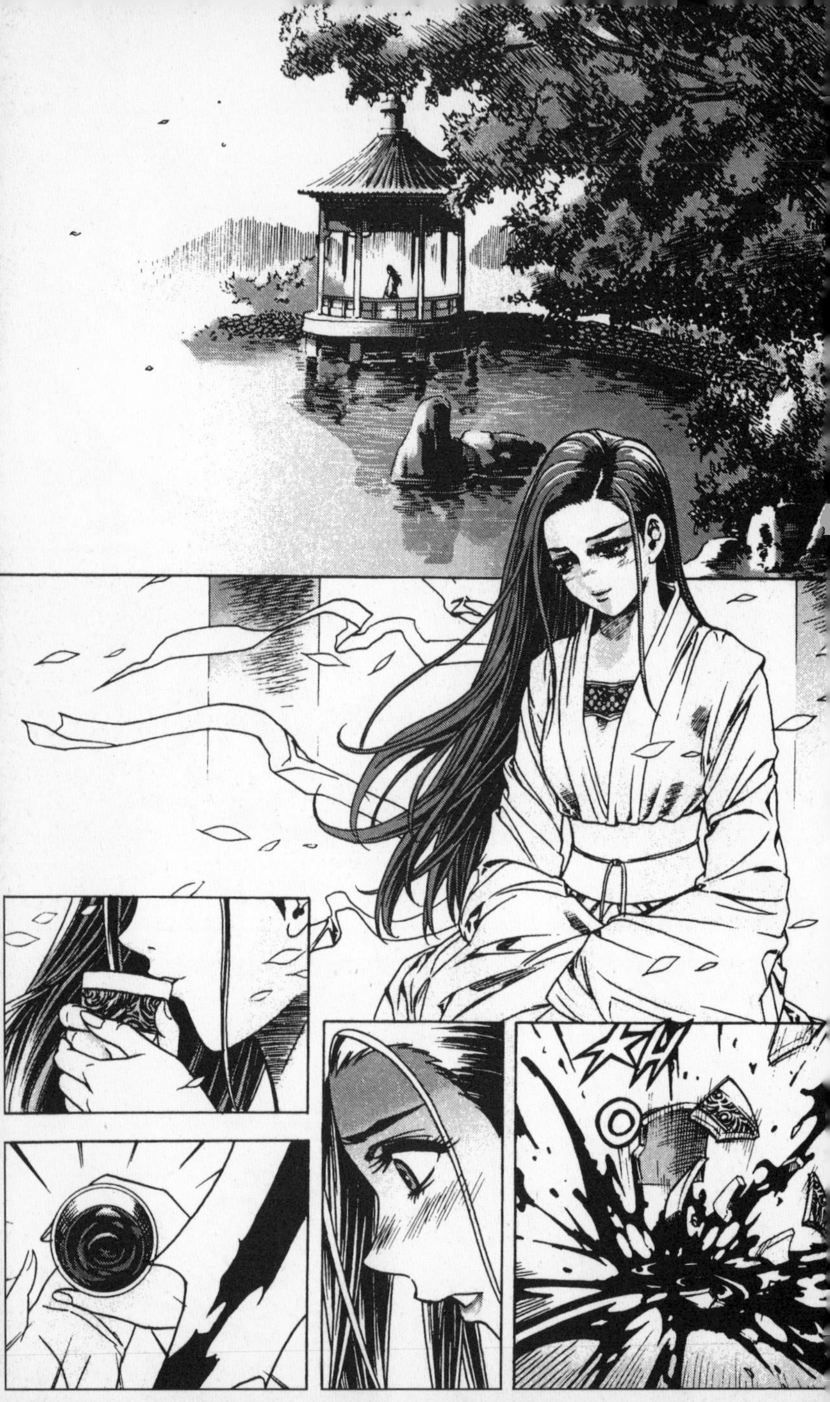

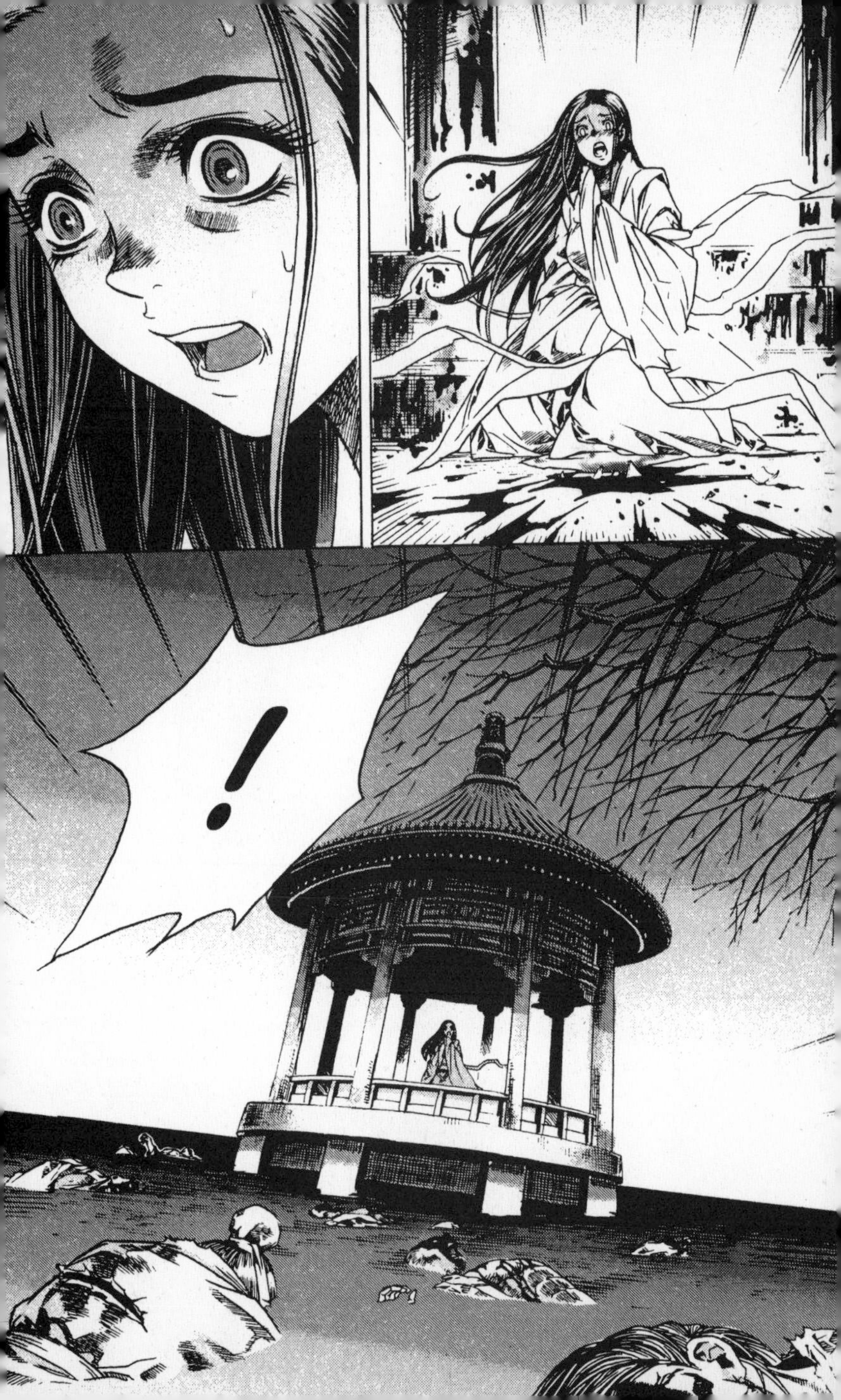
!

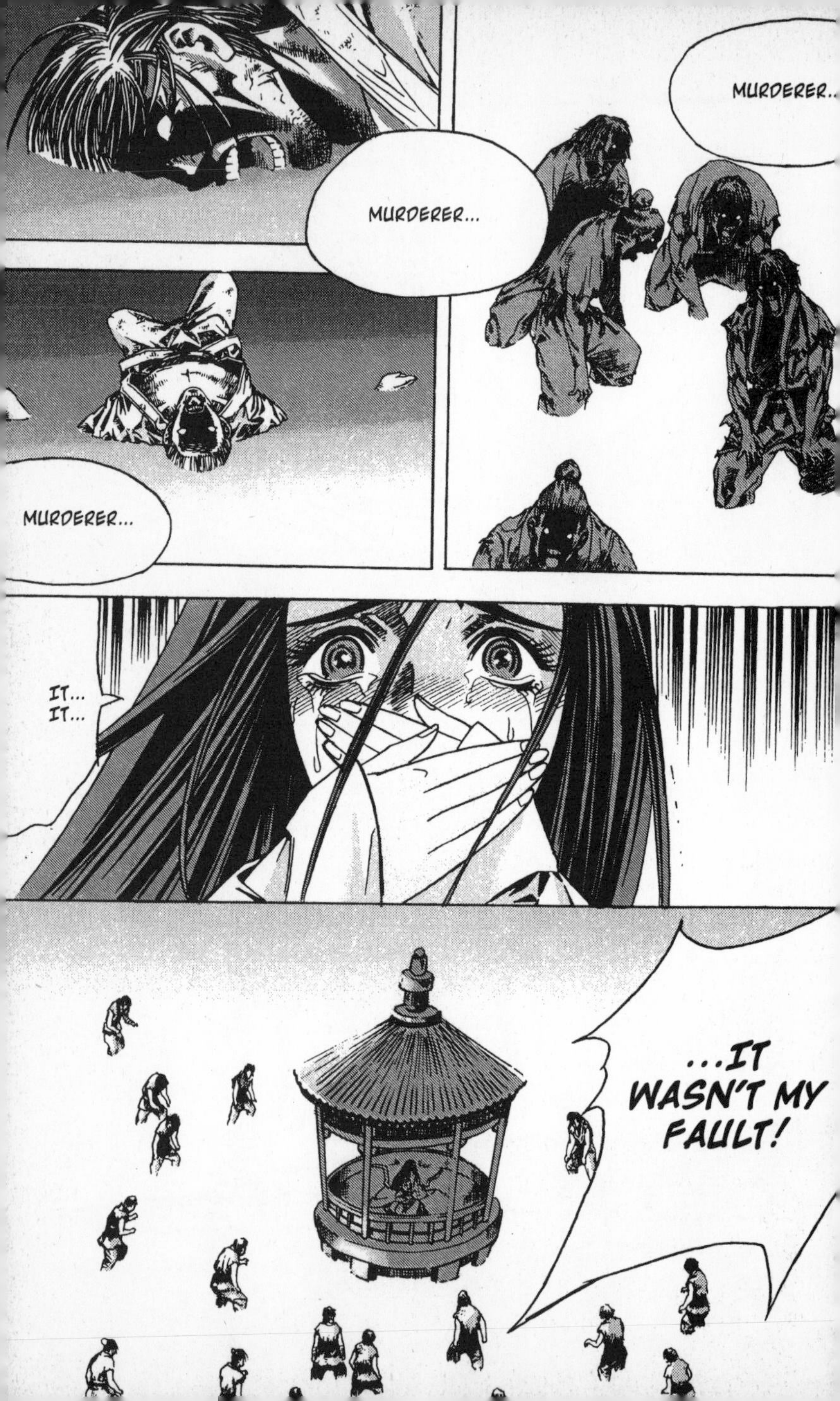
MURDERER...
MURDERER...
MURDERER...
IT... IT...
...IT WASN'T MY FAULT!

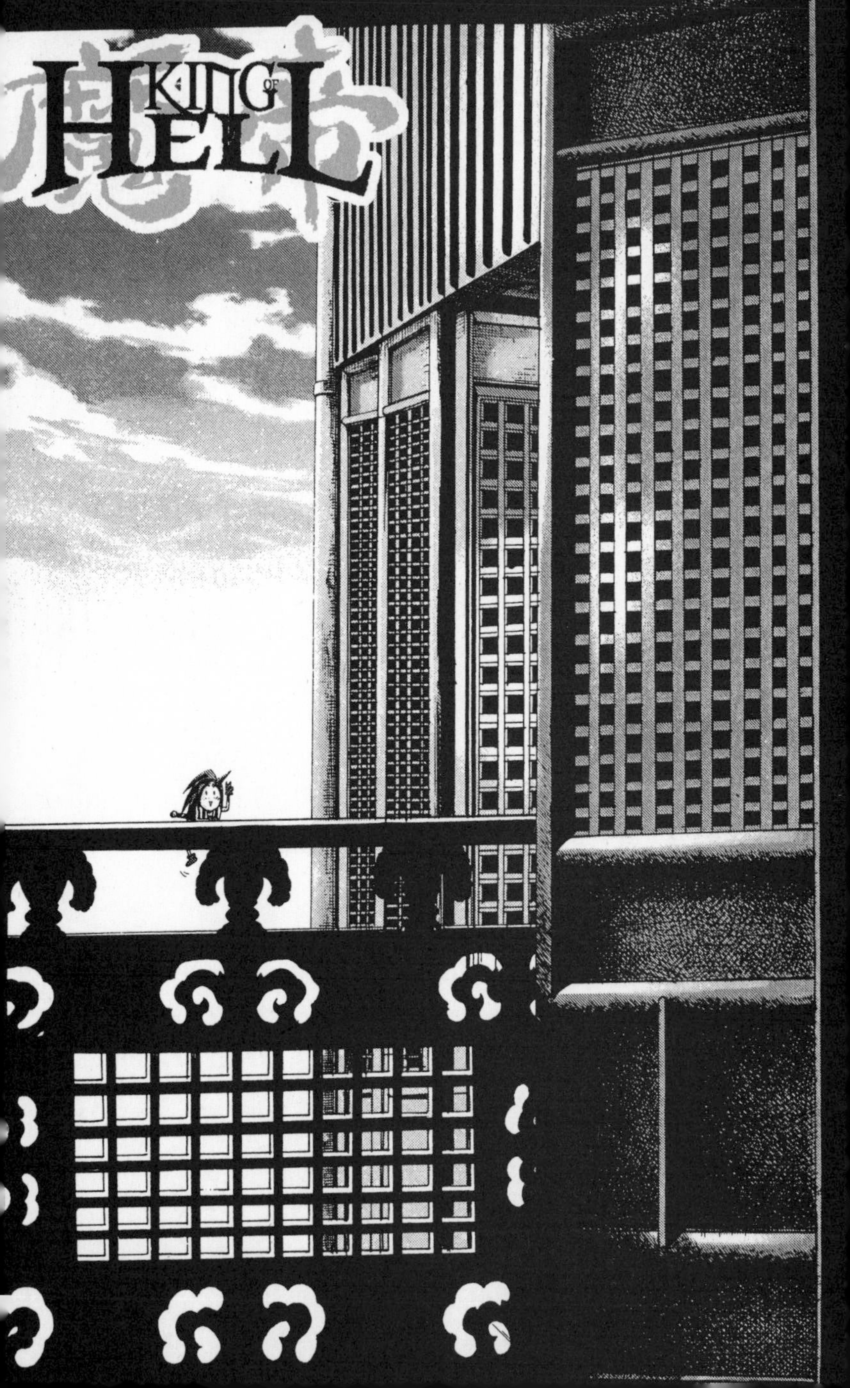
KING OF HELL

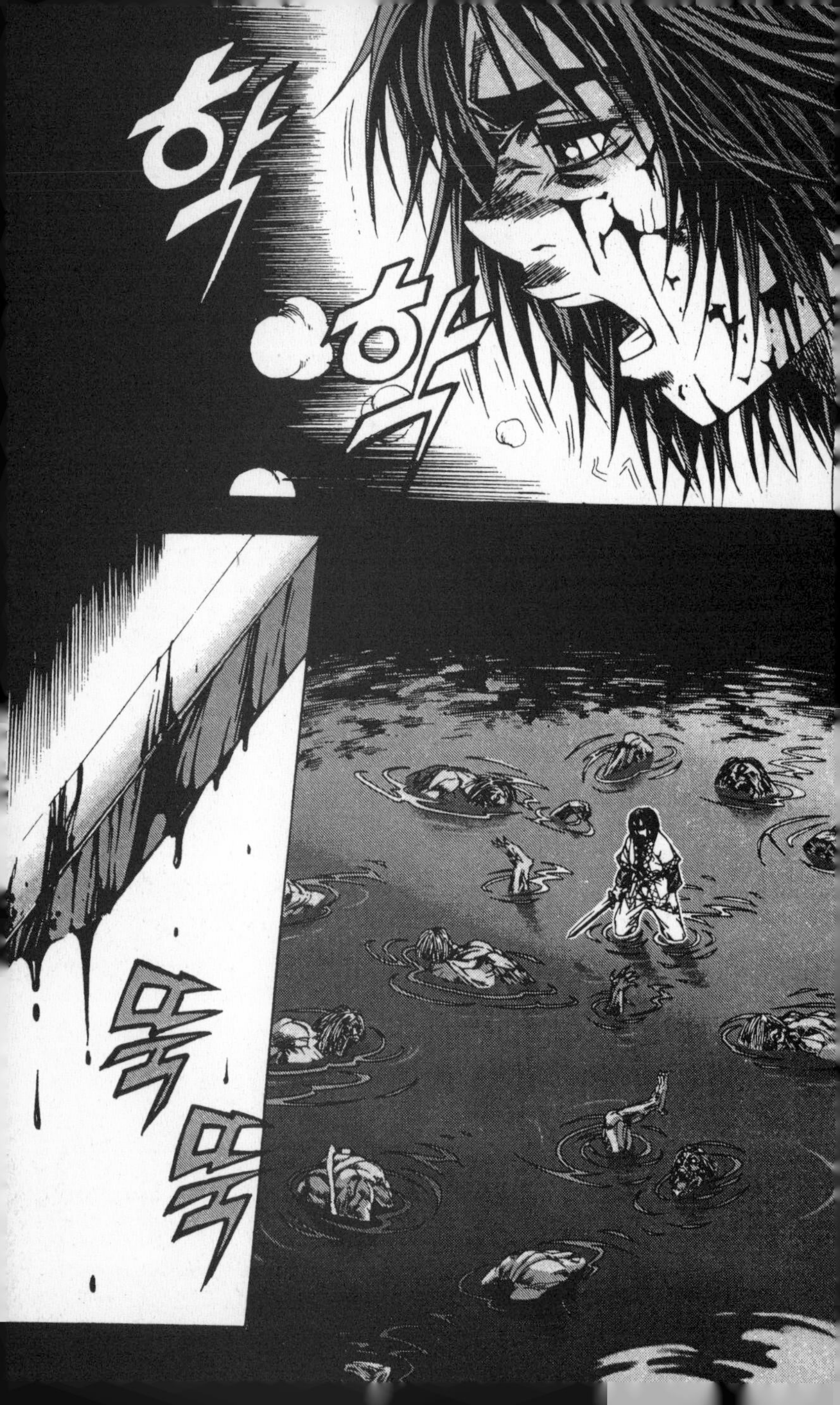
학
학
뚝
뚝

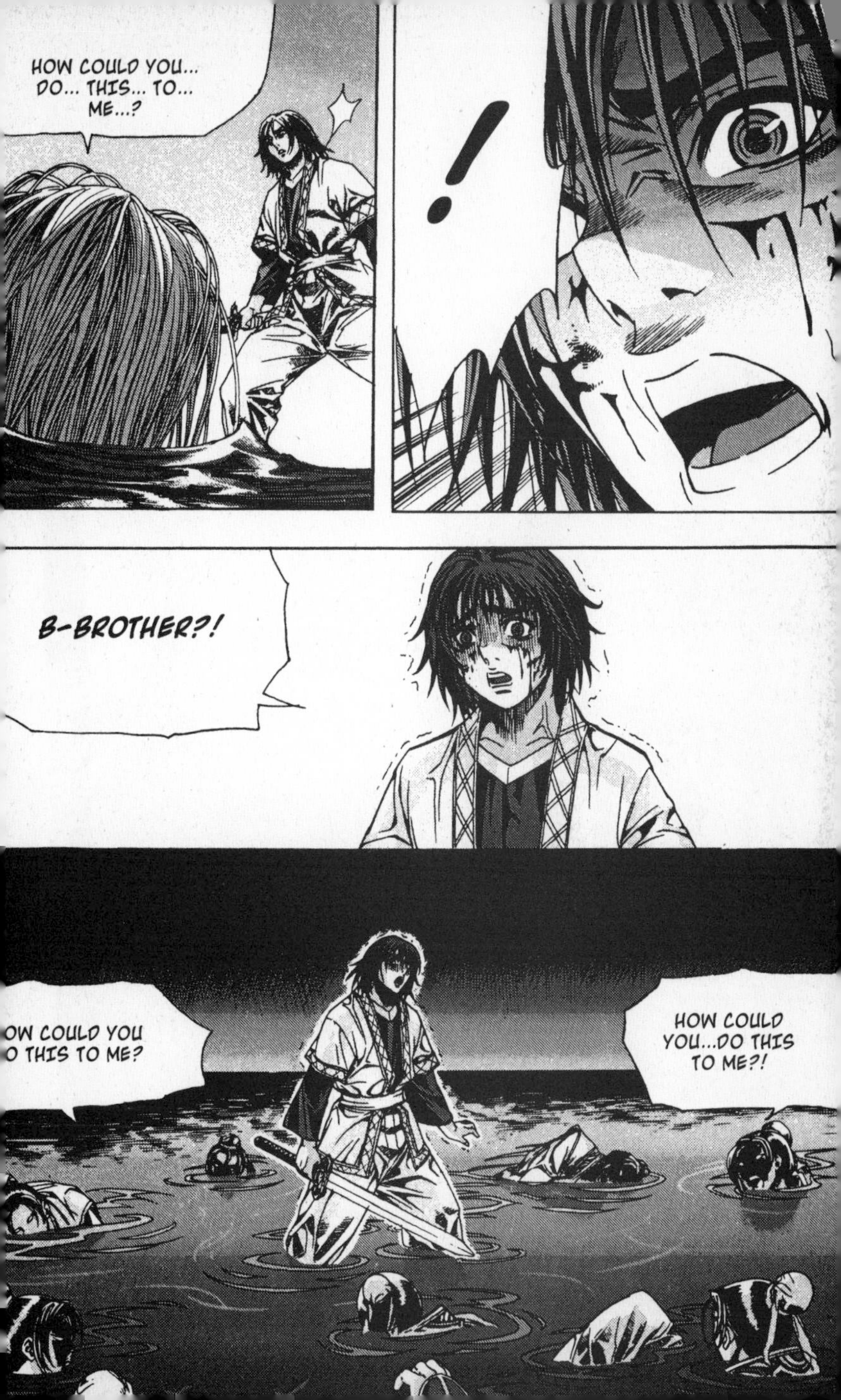
HOW COULD YOU... DO... THIS... TO... ME...?
!
B-BROTHER?!
OW COULD YOU O THIS TO ME?
HOW COULD YOU...DO THIS TO ME?!

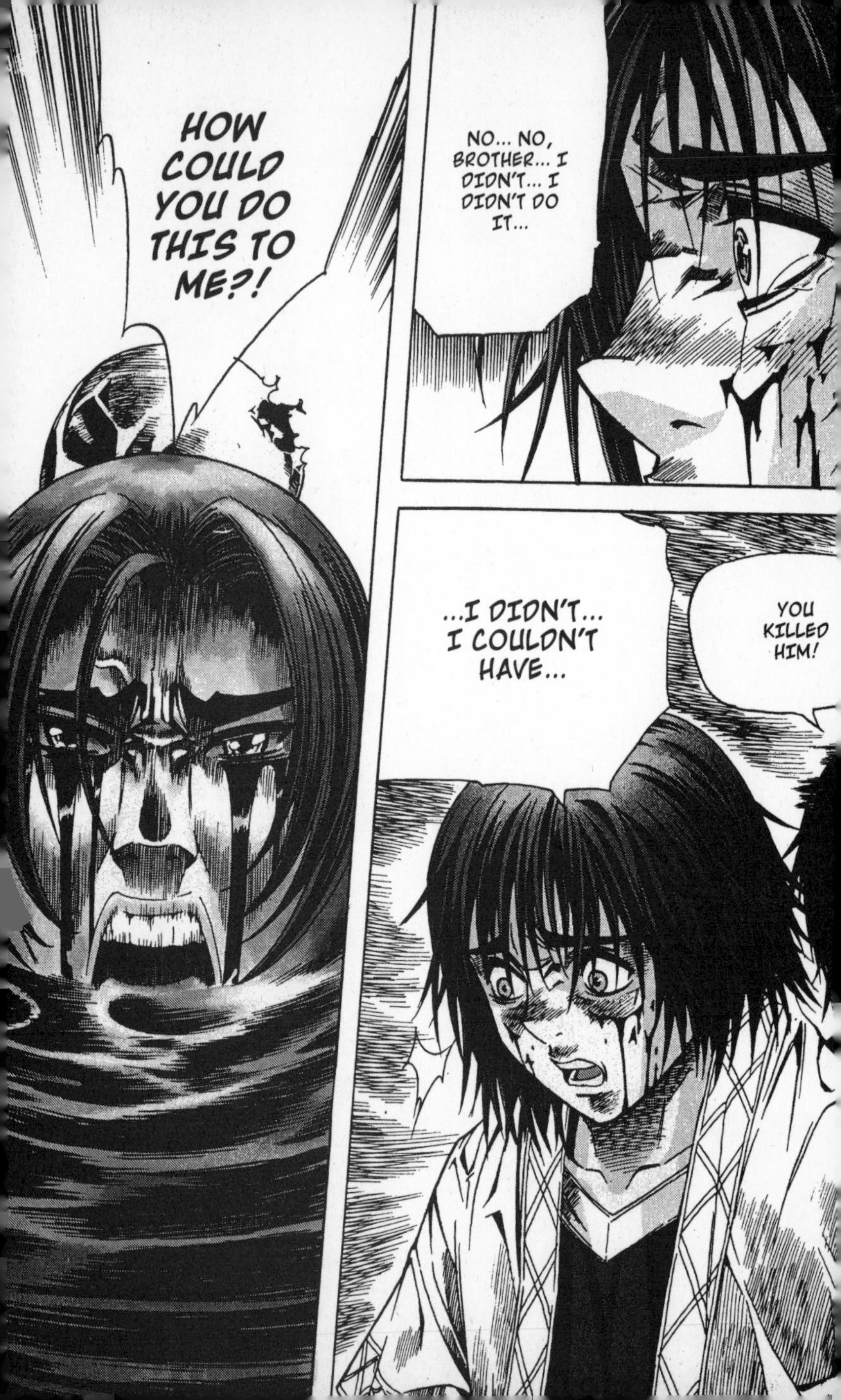
HOW COULD YOU DO THIS TO ME?!
NO... NO, BROTHER... I DIDN'T... I DIDN'T DO IT...
...I DIDN'T... I COULDN'T HAVE...
YOU KILLED HIM!

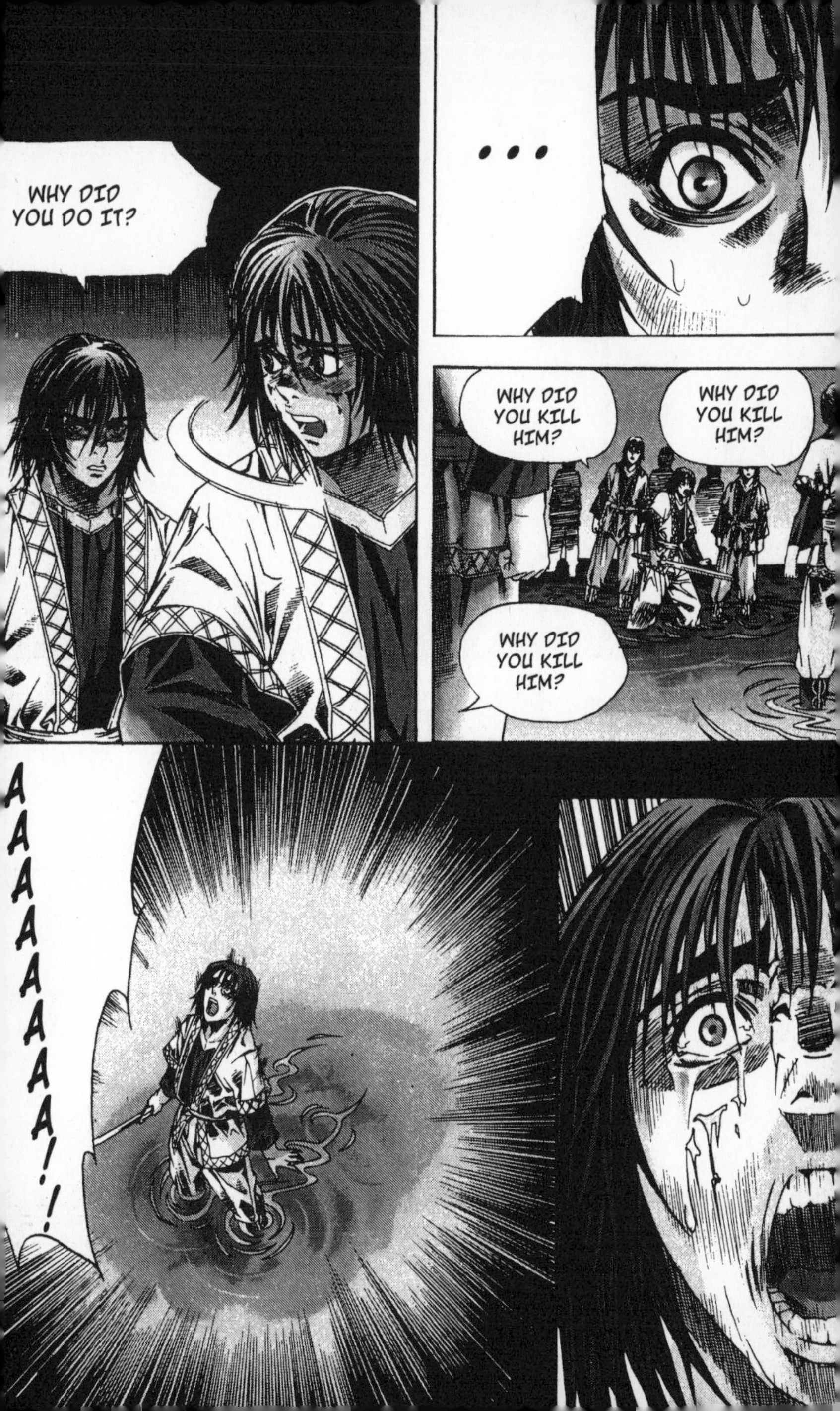
WHY DID YOU DO IT?
...
WHY DID YOU KILL HIM?
WHY DID YOU KILL HIM?
WHY DID YOU KILL HIM?
AAAAAAAA!!

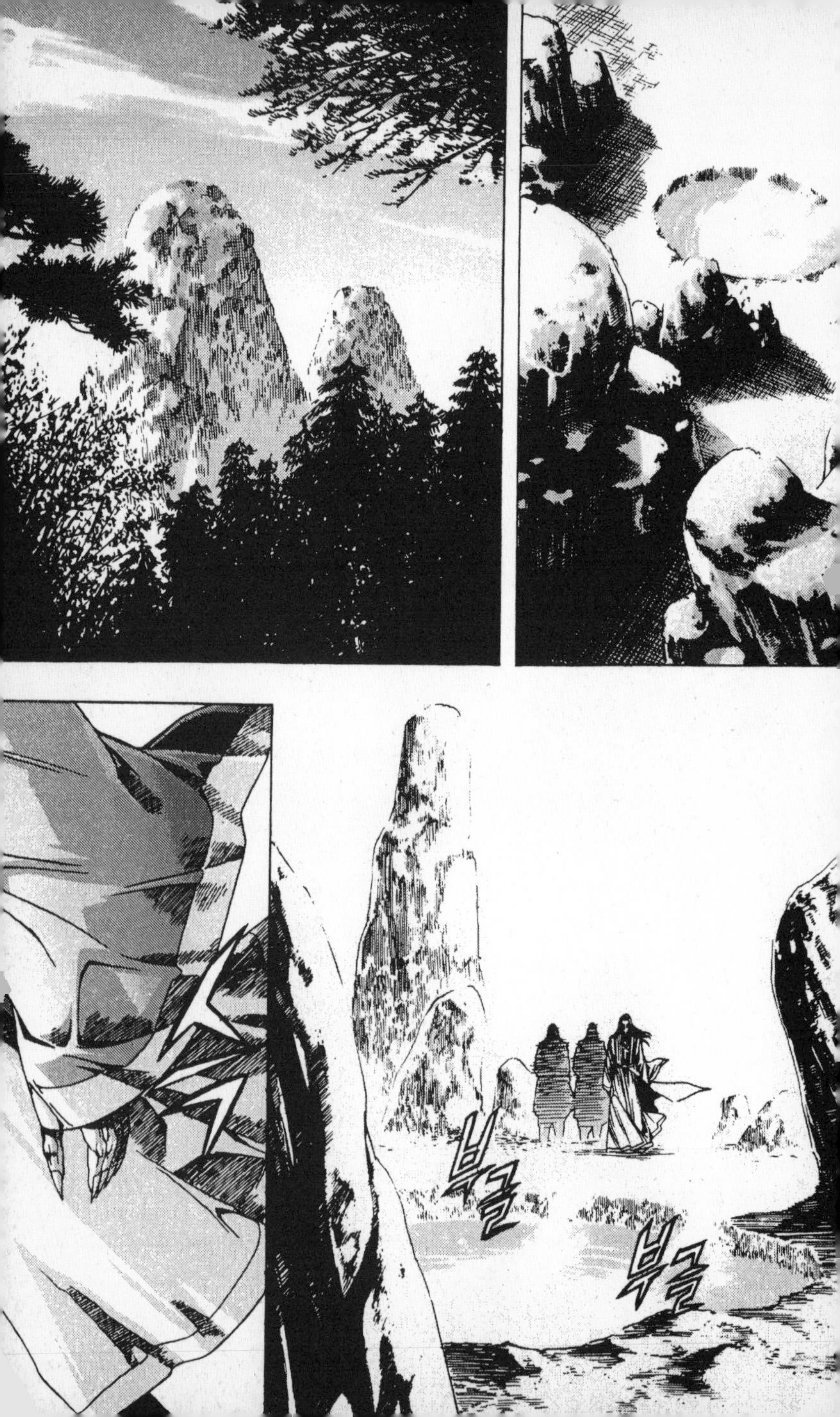

부글
부글

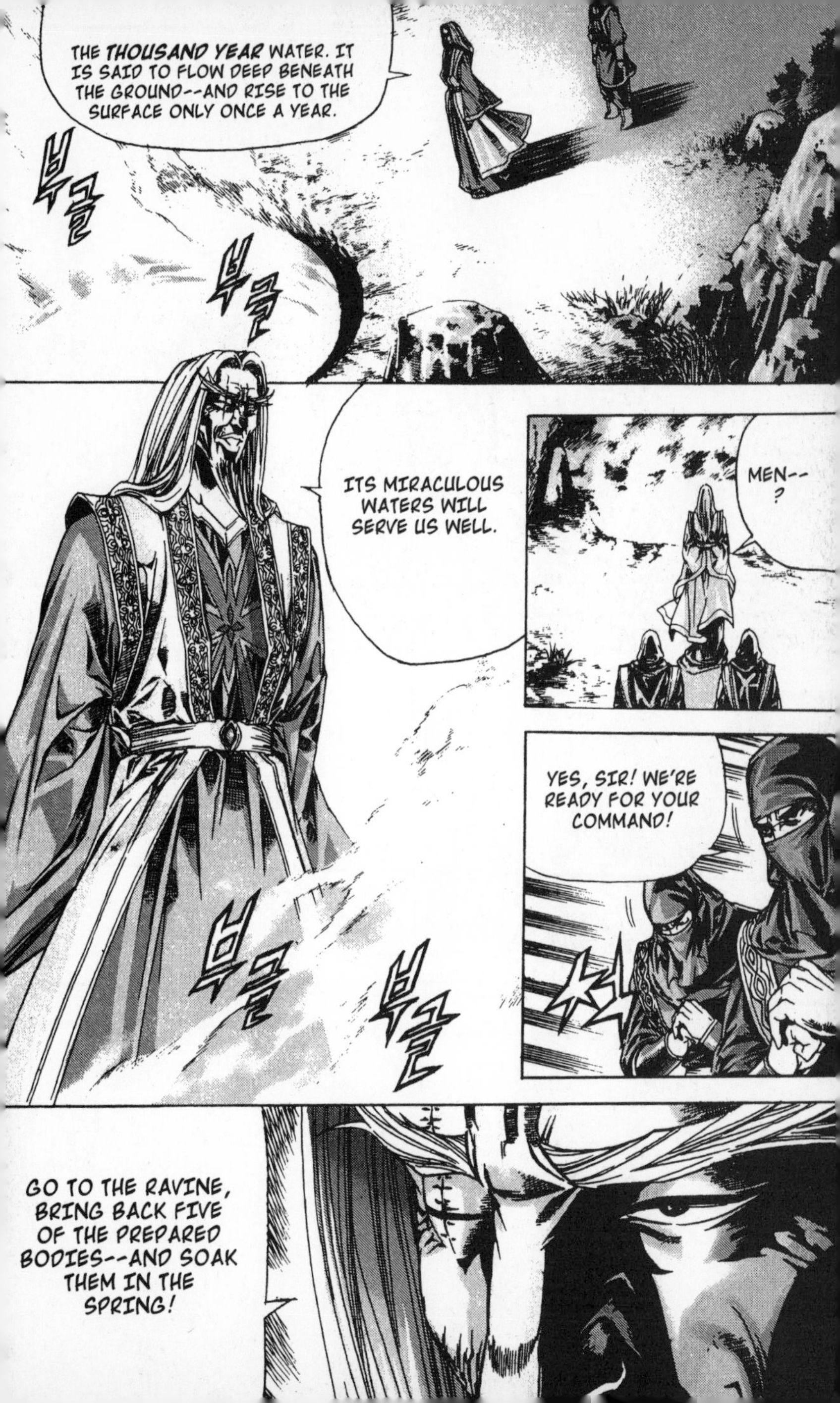
THE ***THOUSAND YEAR*** WATER. IT IS SAID TO FLOW DEEP BENEATH THE GROUND--AND RISE TO THE SURFACE ONLY ONCE A YEAR.
부글
부글
ITS MIRACULOUS WATERS WILL SERVE US WELL.
부글
보글
MEN--?
YES, SIR! WE'RE READY FOR YOUR COMMAND!
GO TO THE RAVINE, BRING BACK FIVE OF THE PREPARED BODIES--AND SOAK THEM IN THE SPRING!

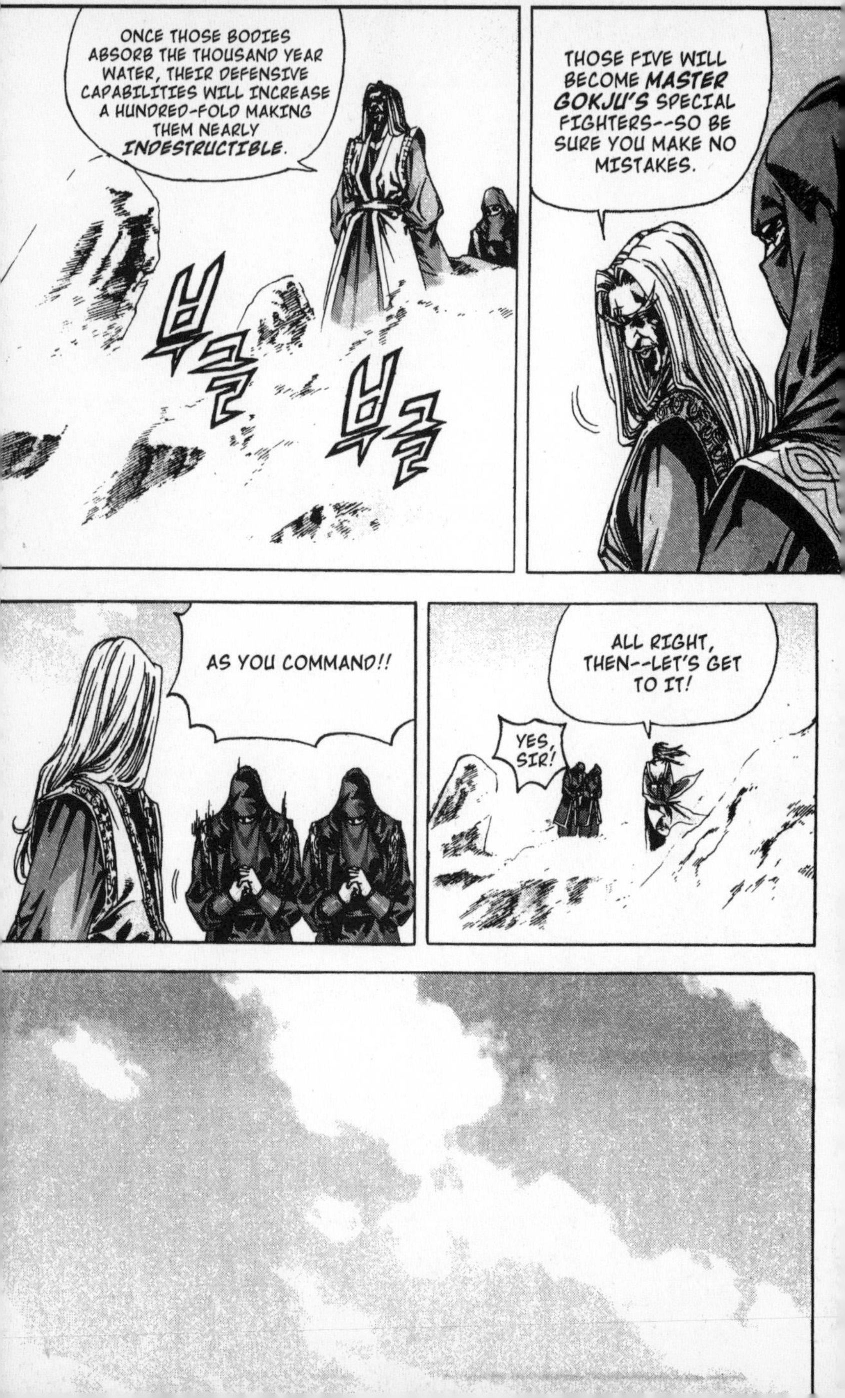

ONCE THOSE BODIES ABSORB THE THOUSAND YEAR WATER, THEIR DEFENSIVE CAPABILITIES WILL INCREASE A HUNDRED-FOLD MAKING THEM NEARLY INDESTRUCTIBLE.
부글
부글
THOSE FIVE WILL BECOME MASTER GOKJU'S SPECIAL FIGHTERS--SO BE SURE YOU MAKE NO MISTAKES.
AS YOU COMMAND!!
ALL RIGHT, THEN--LET'S GET TO IT!
YES, SIR!

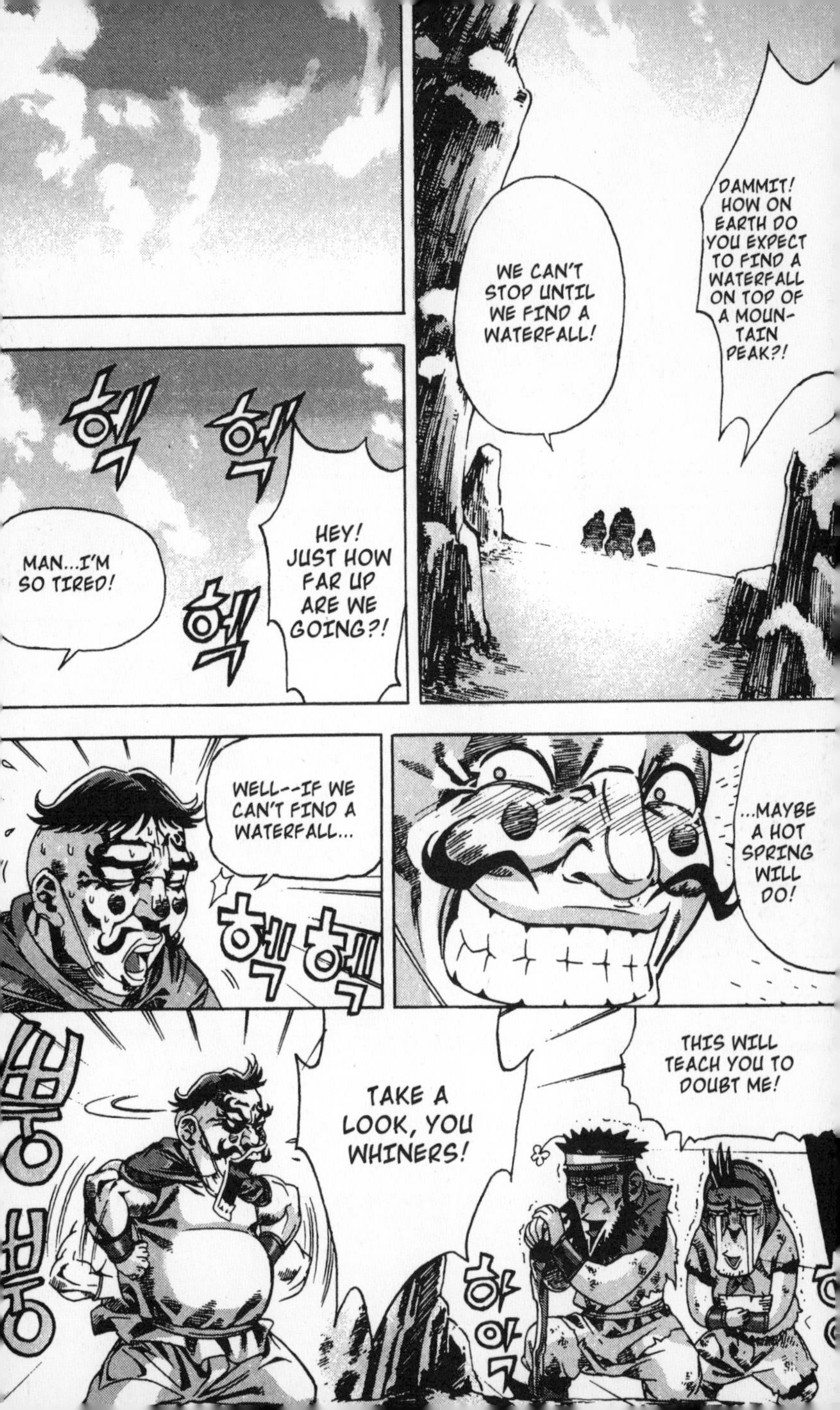
헥
헥
MAN...I'M SO TIRED!
헥
HEY! JUST HOW FAR UP ARE WE GOING?!
WE CAN'T STOP UNTIL WE FIND A WATERFALL!
DAMMIT! HOW ON EARTH DO YOU EXPECT TO FIND A WATERFALL ON TOP OF A MOUN-TAIN PEAK?!
WELL--IF WE CAN'T FIND A WATERFALL...
...MAYBE A HOT SPRING WILL DO!
TAKE A LOOK, YOU WHINERS!
THIS WILL TEACH YOU TO DOUBT ME!

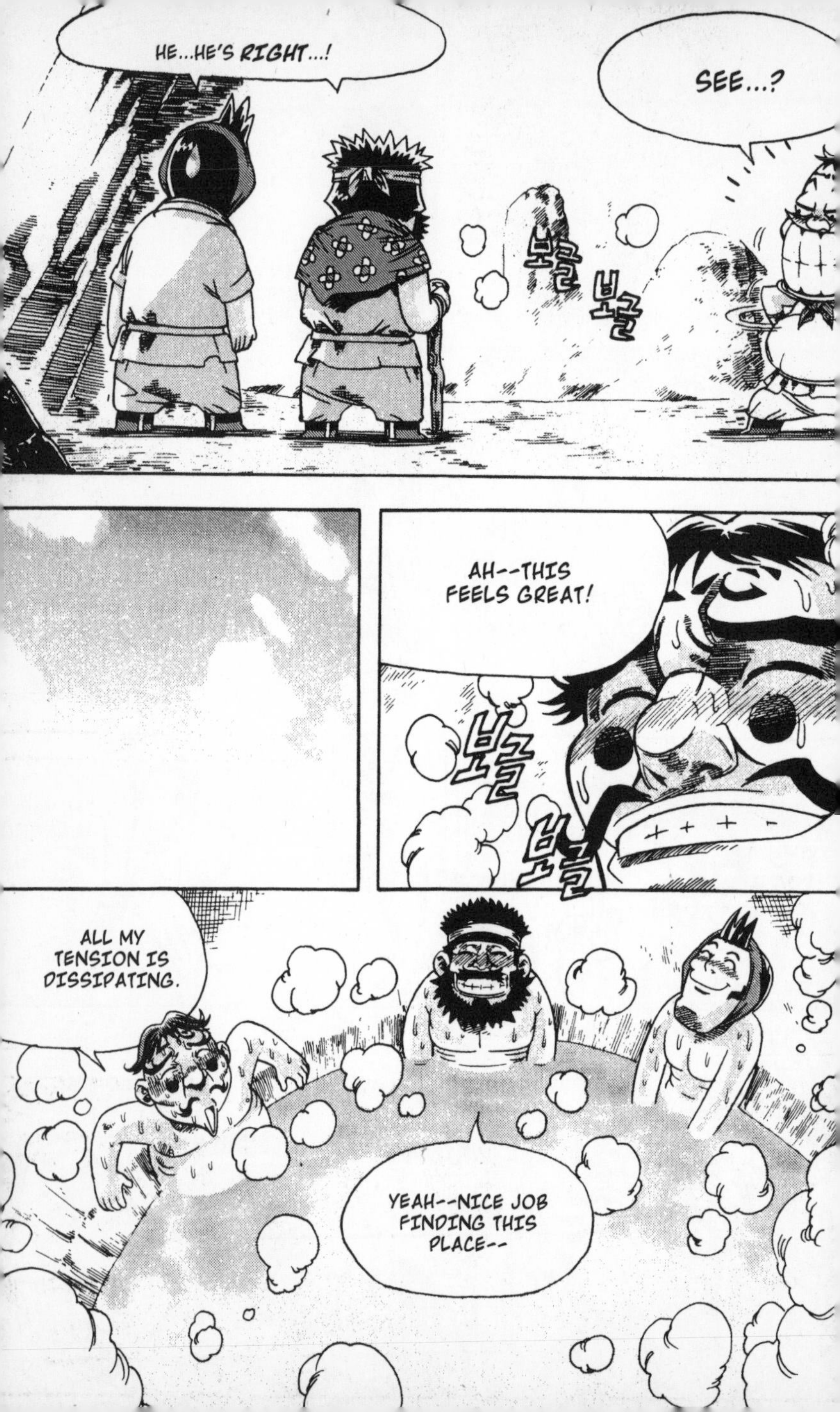
HE...HE'S **RIGHT**...!
SEE...?
보글 보글
AH--THIS FEELS GREAT!
보글 보글
ALL MY TENSION IS DISSIPATING.
YEAH--NICE JOB FINDING THIS PLACE--

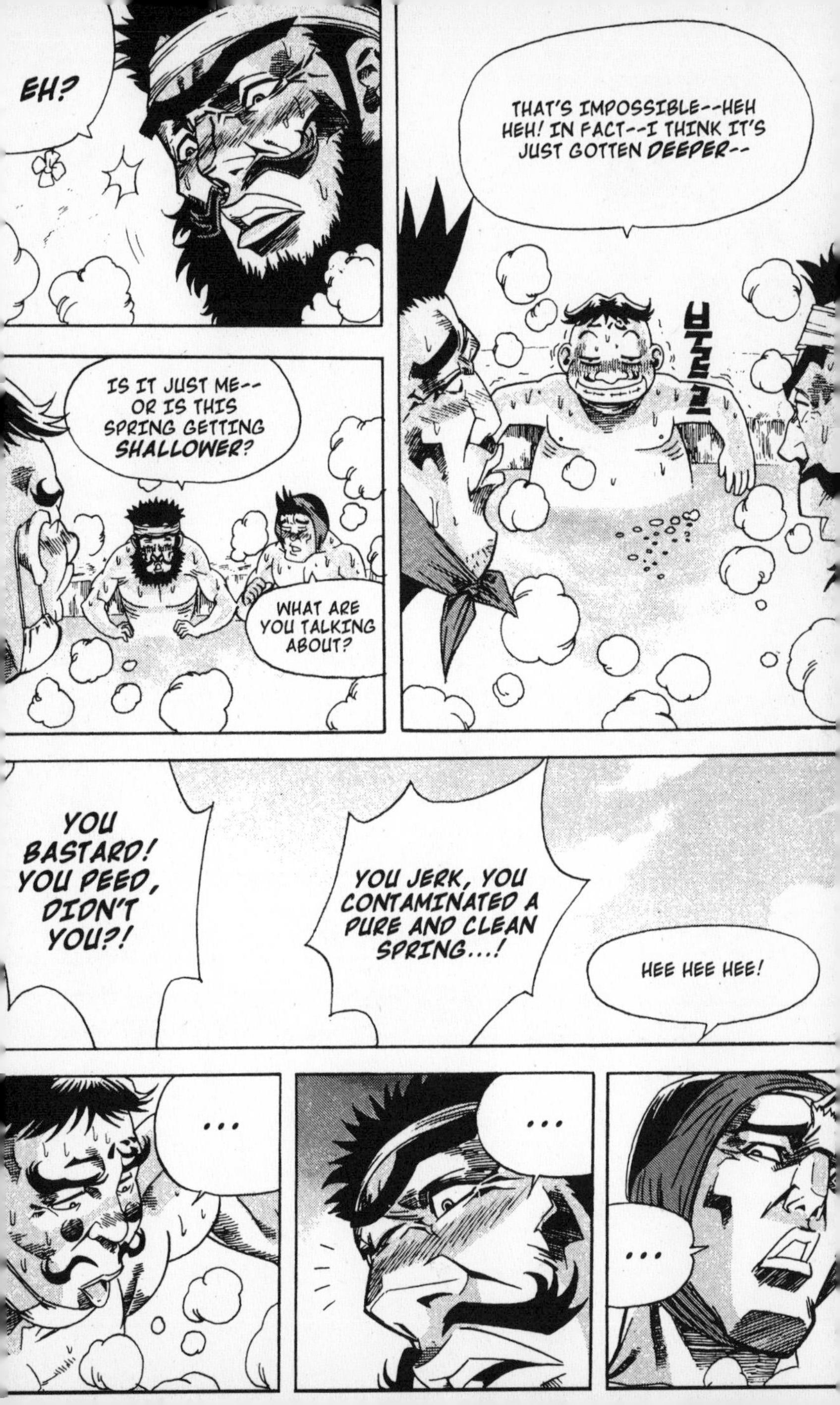
EH?
THAT'S IMPOSSIBLE--HEH HEH! IN FACT--I THINK IT'S JUST GOTTEN DEEPER--
IS IT JUST ME--OR IS THIS SPRING GETTING SHALLOWER?
WHAT ARE YOU TALKING ABOUT?
YOU BASTARD! YOU PEED, DIDN'T YOU?!
YOU JERK, YOU CONTAMINATED A PURE AND CLEAN SPRING...!
HEE HEE HEE!
...
...
...

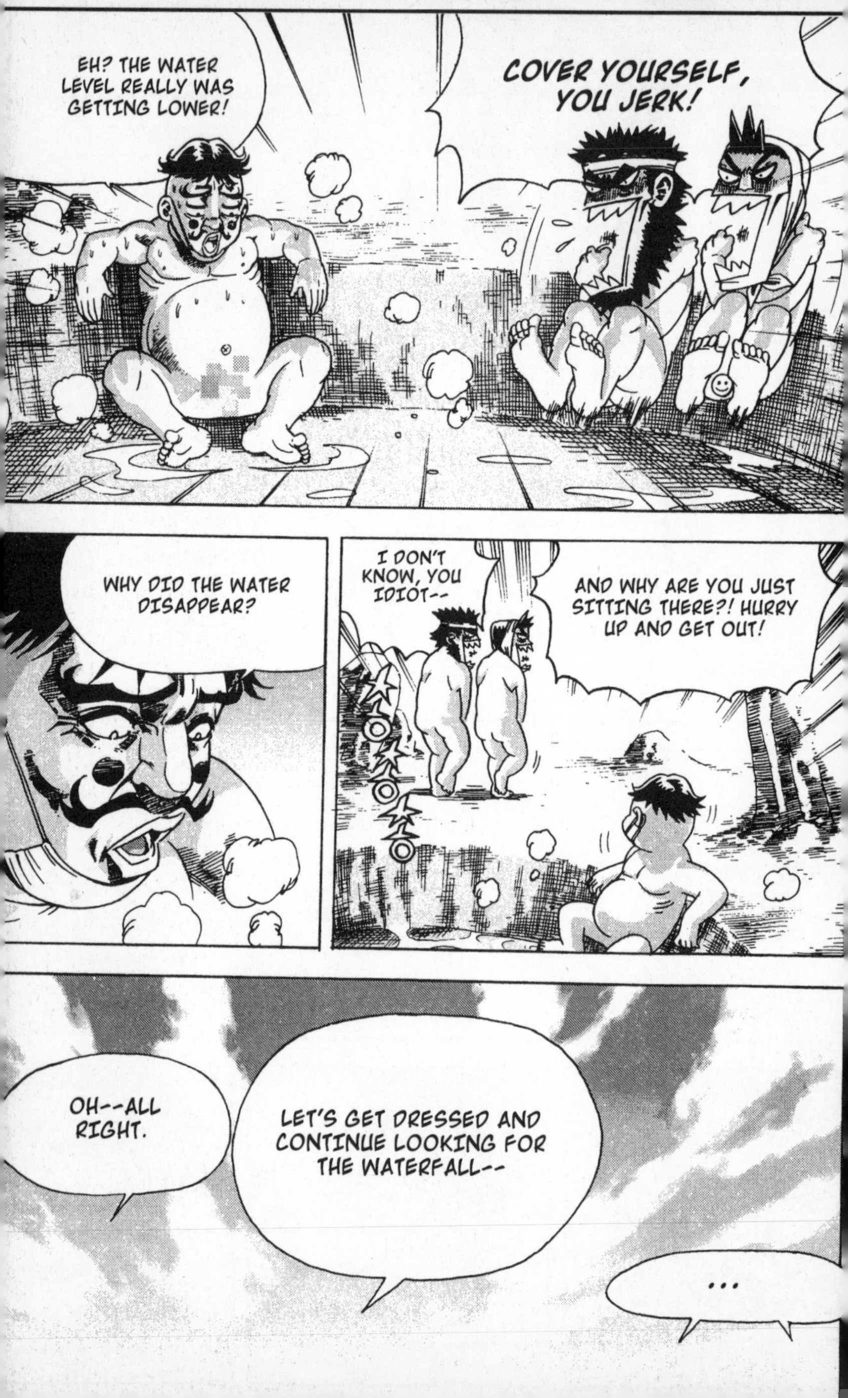
EH? THE WATER LEVEL REALLY WAS GETTING LOWER!
COVER YOURSELF, YOU JERK!
WHY DID THE WATER DISAPPEAR?
I DON'T KNOW, YOU IDIOT--
AND WHY ARE YOU JUST SITTING THERE?! HURRY UP AND GET OUT!
OH--ALL RIGHT.
LET'S GET DRESSED AND CONTINUE LOOKING FOR THE WATERFALL--
...

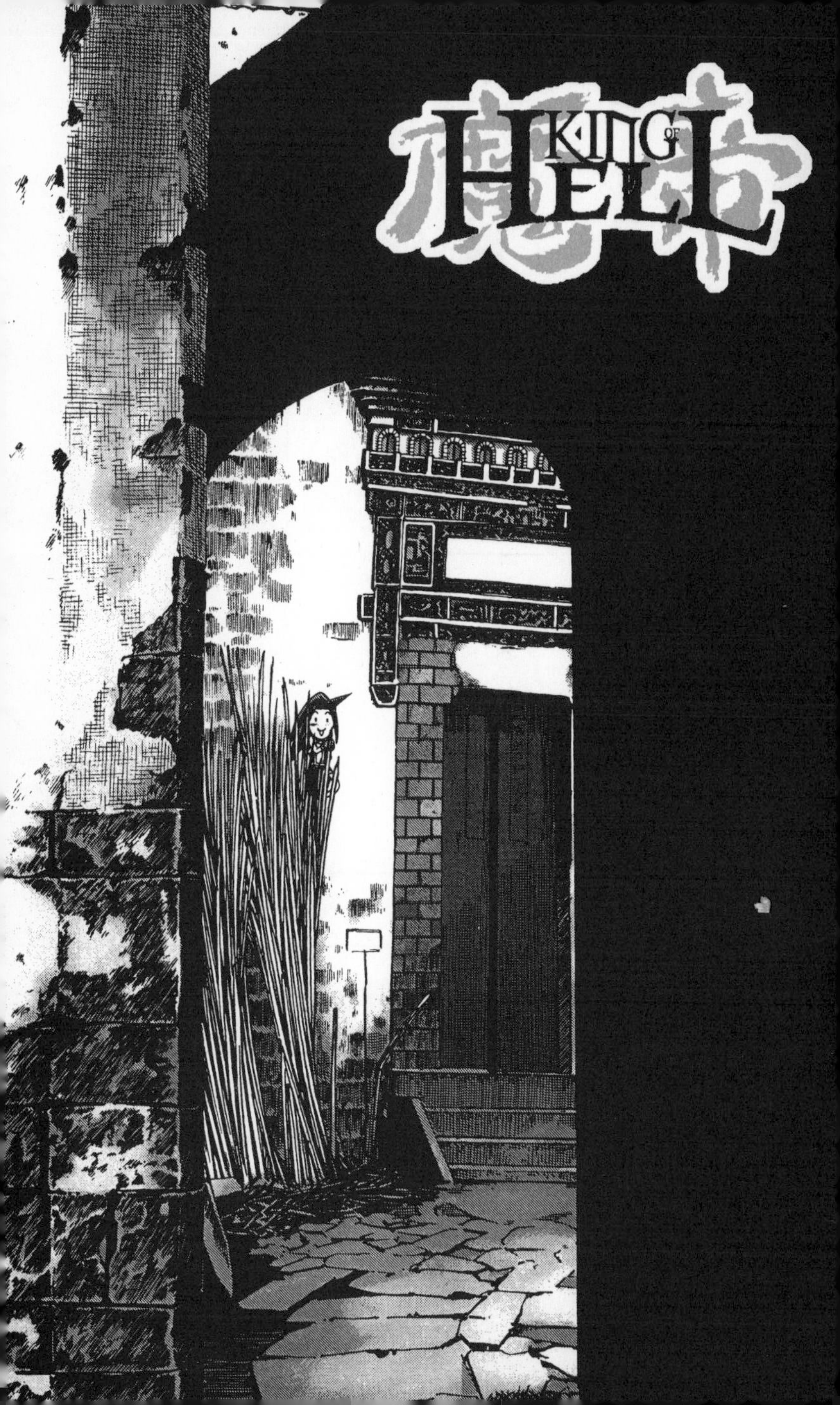
KING OF HELL

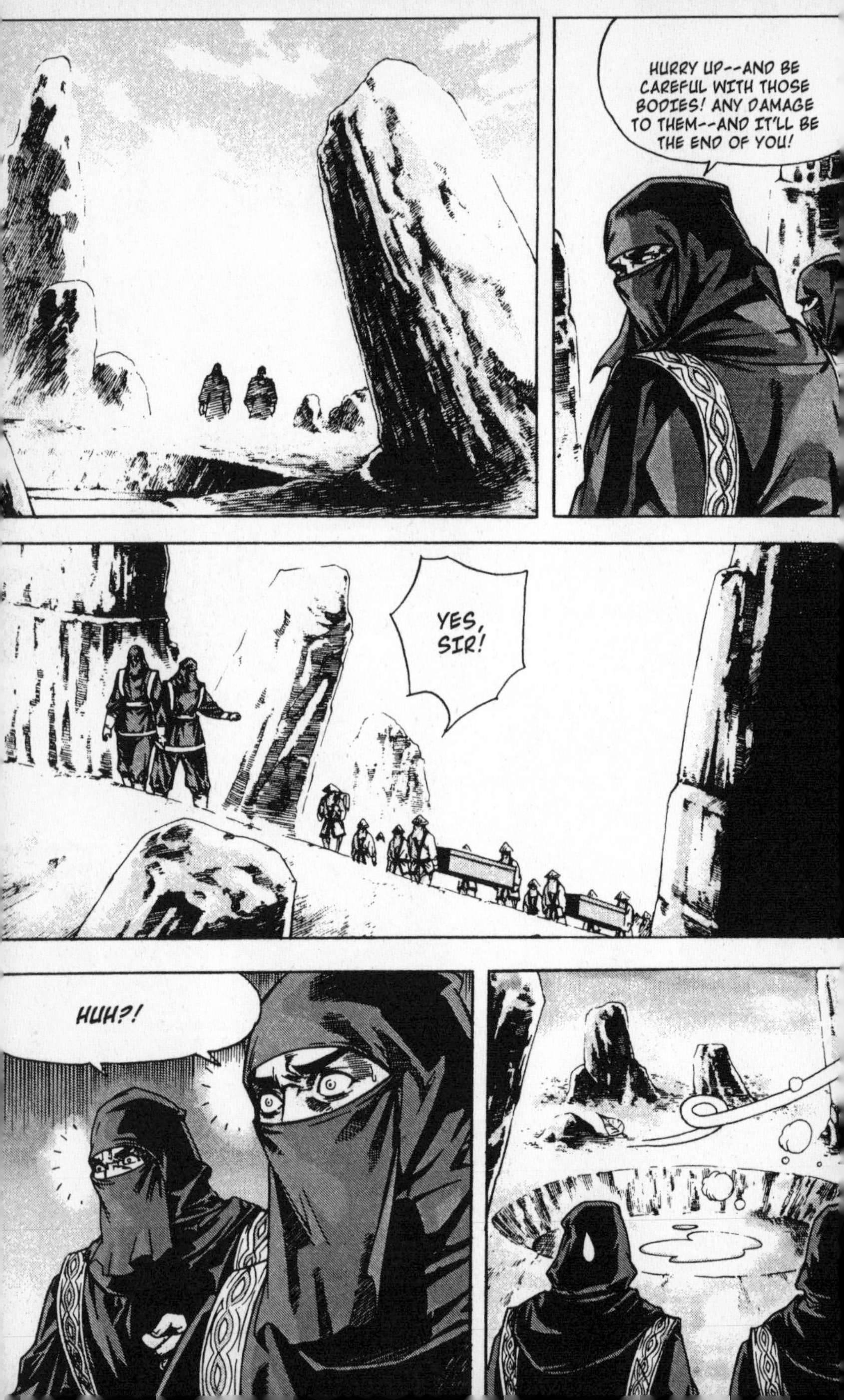
HURRY UP--AND BE CAREFUL WITH THOSE BODIES! ANY DAMAGE TO THEM--AND IT'LL BE THE END OF YOU!
YES, SIR!
HUH?!

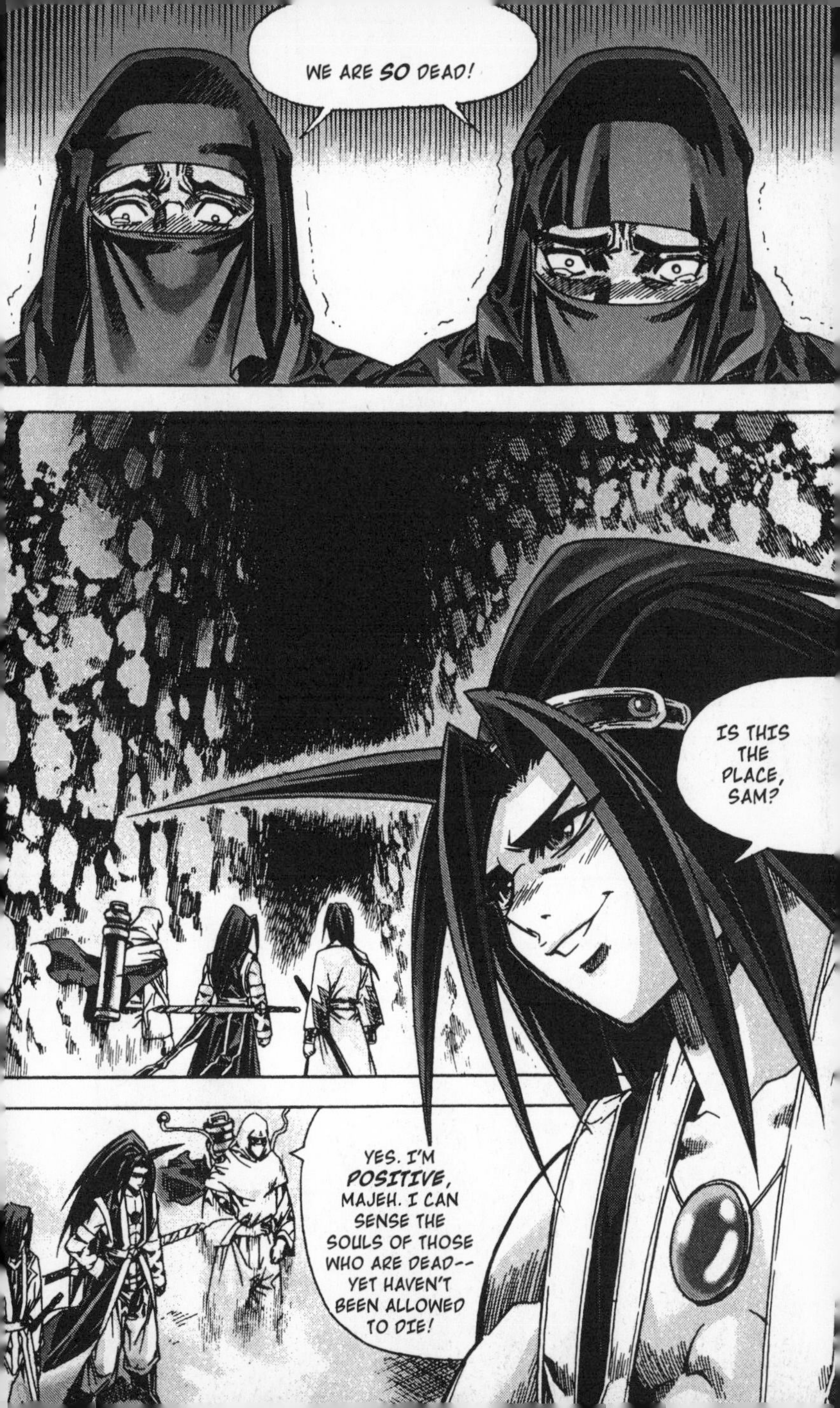
WE ARE SO DEAD!
IS THIS THE PLACE, SAM?
YES. I'M POSITIVE, MAJEH. I CAN SENSE THE SOULS OF THOSE WHO ARE DEAD--YET HAVEN'T BEEN ALLOWED TO DIE!

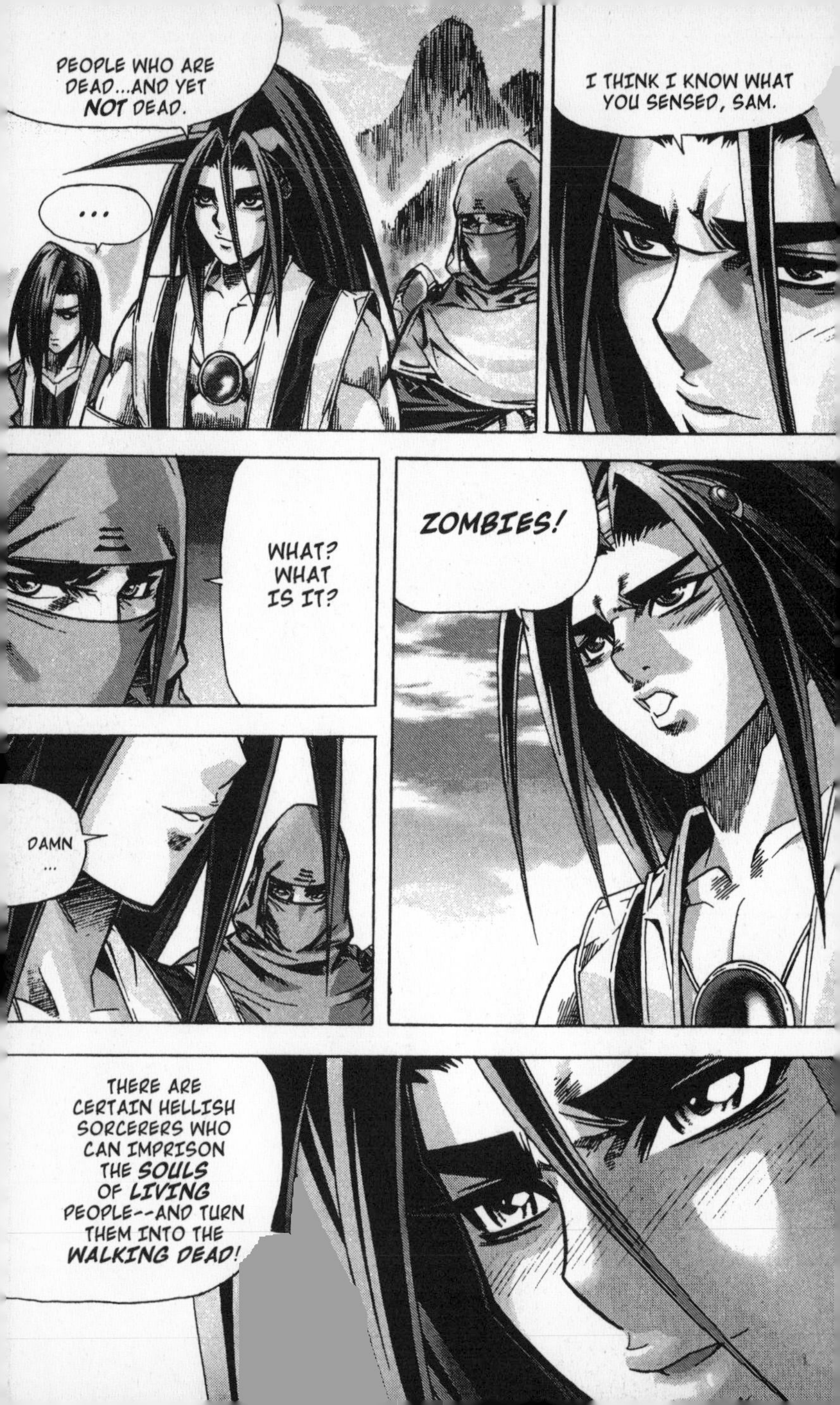

PEOPLE WHO ARE DEAD...AND YET NOT DEAD.
...
I THINK I KNOW WHAT YOU SENSED, SAM.
WHAT? WHAT IS IT?
ZOMBIES!
DAMN ...
THERE ARE CERTAIN HELLISH SORCERERS WHO CAN IMPRISON THE SOULS OF LIVING PEOPLE--AND TURN THEM INTO THE WALKING DEAD!

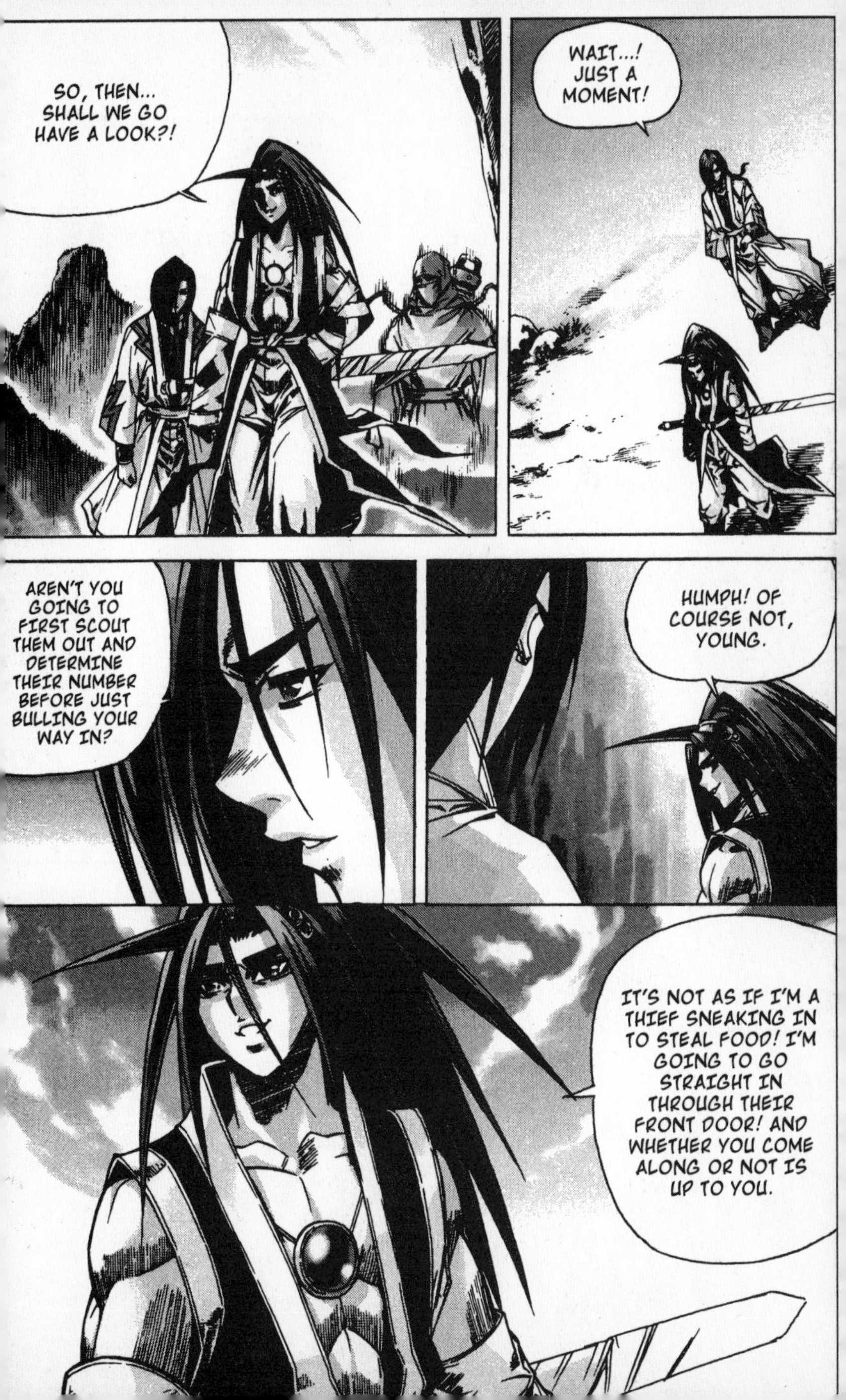

SO, THEN... SHALL WE GO HAVE A LOOK?!
WAIT...! JUST A MOMENT!
AREN'T YOU GOING TO FIRST SCOUT THEM OUT AND DETERMINE THEIR NUMBER BEFORE JUST BULLING YOUR WAY IN?
HUMPH! OF COURSE NOT, YOUNG.
IT'S NOT AS IF I'M A THIEF SNEAKING IN TO STEAL FOOD! I'M GOING TO GO STRAIGHT IN THROUGH THEIR FRONT DOOR! AND WHETHER YOU COME ALONG OR NOT IS UP TO YOU.

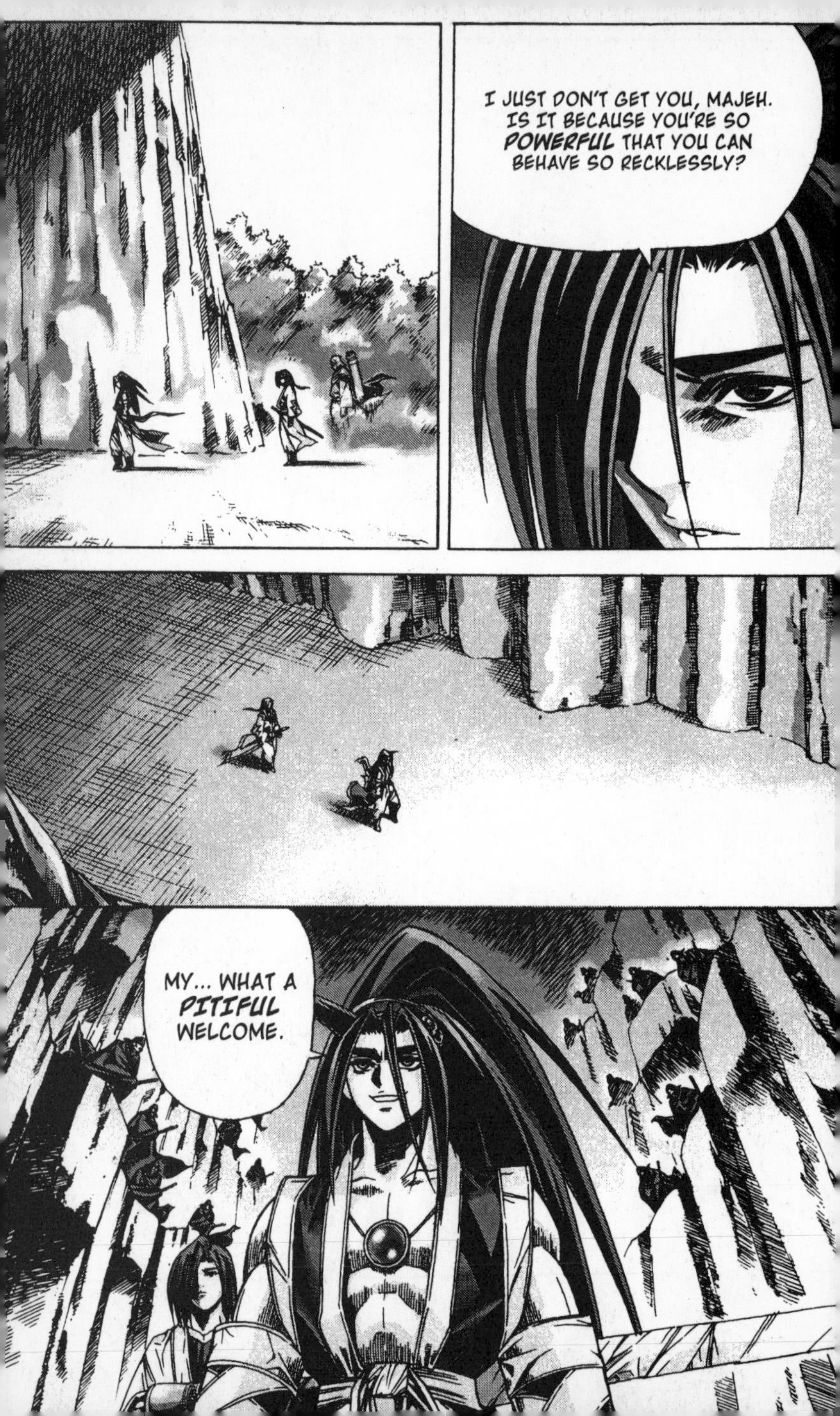
I JUST DON'T GET YOU, MAJEH. IS IT BECAUSE YOU'RE SO POWERFUL THAT YOU CAN BEHAVE SO RECKLESSLY?
MY... WHAT A PITIFUL WELCOME.

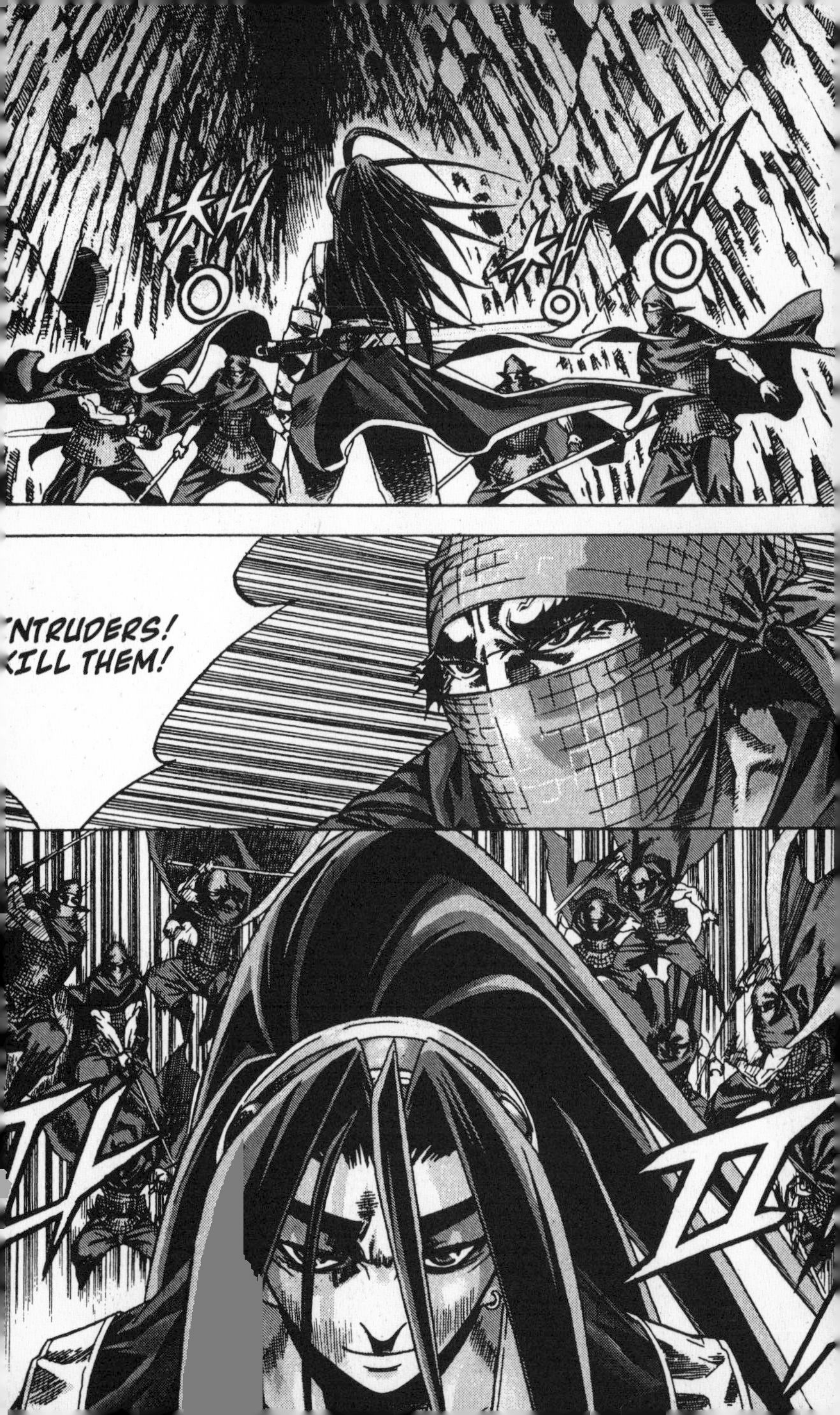
NTRUDERS!
ILL THEM!

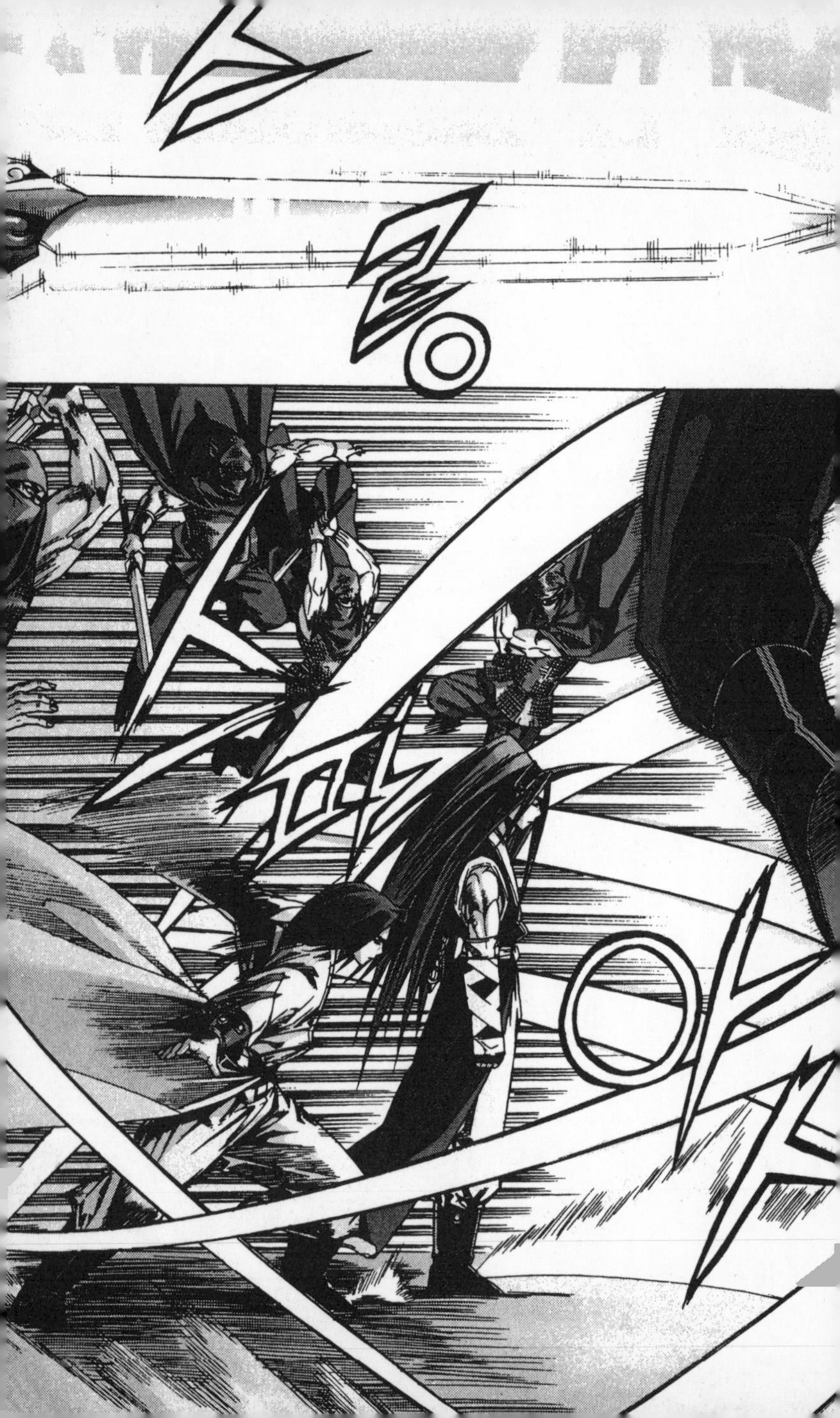

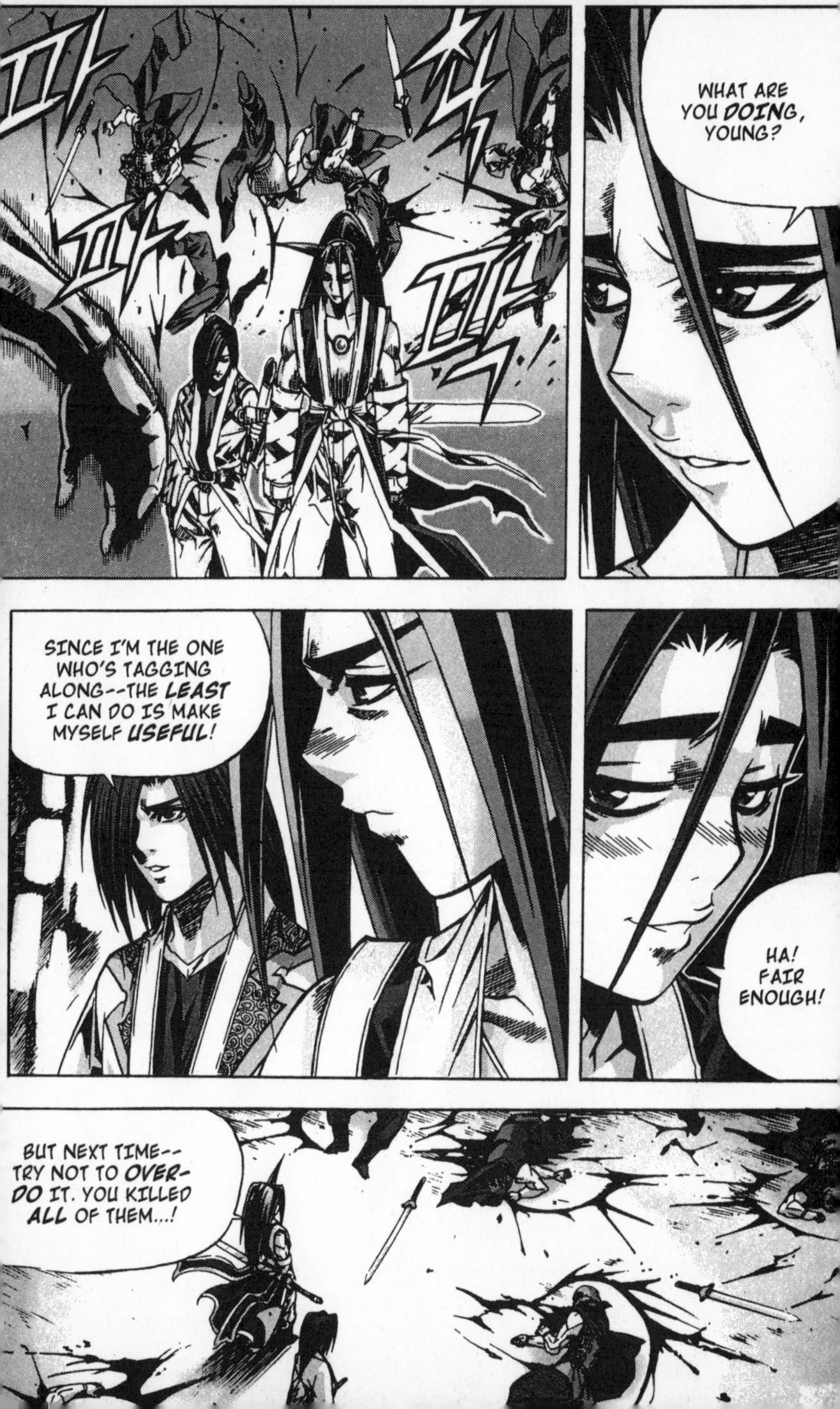
WHAT ARE YOU DOING, YOUNG?
SINCE I'M THE ONE WHO'S TAGGING ALONG--THE LEAST I CAN DO IS MAKE MYSELF USEFUL!
HA! FAIR ENOUGH!
BUT NEXT TIME--TRY NOT TO OVER-DO IT. YOU KILLED ALL OF THEM...!

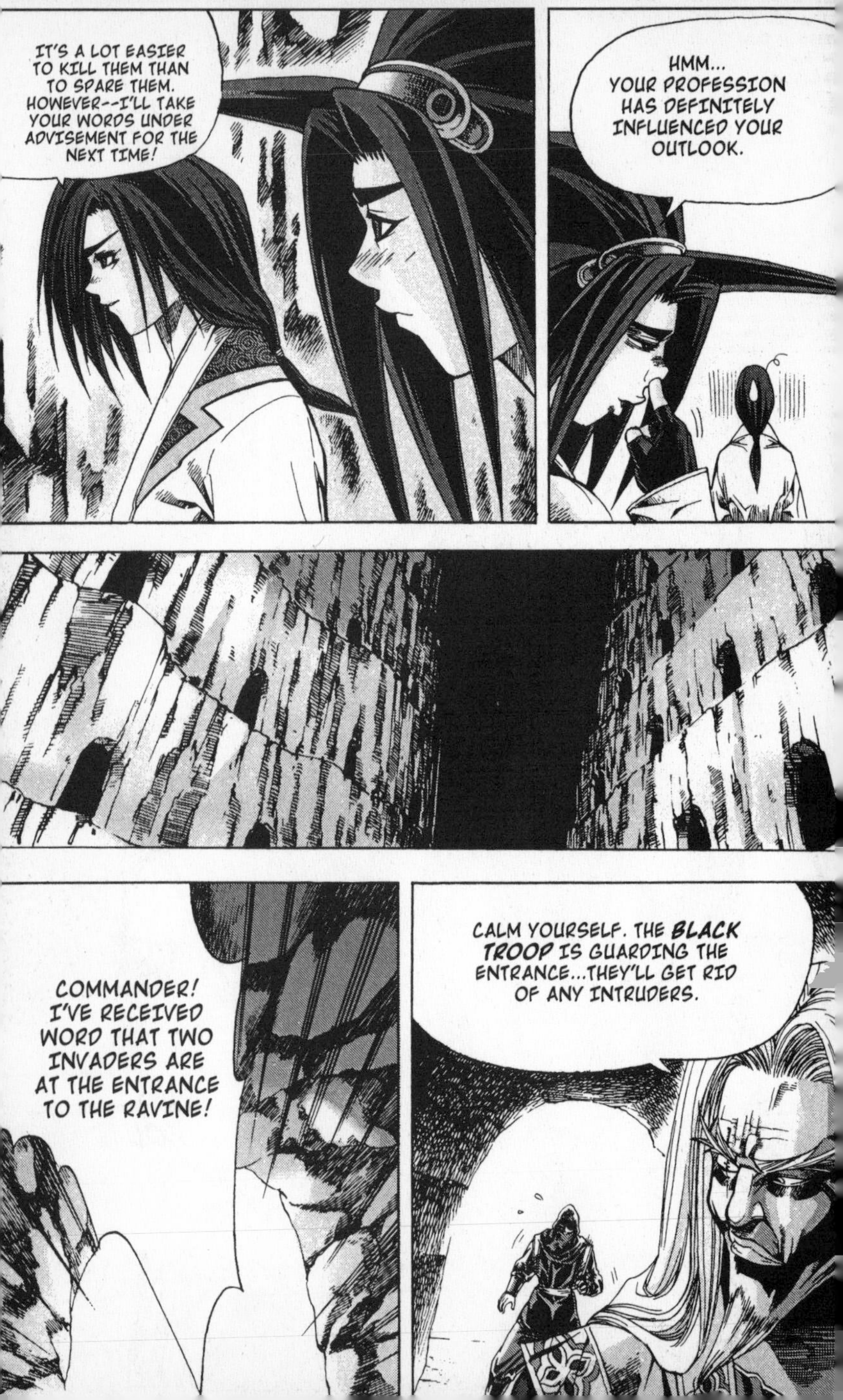
IT'S A LOT EASIER TO KILL THEM THAN TO SPARE THEM. HOWEVER--I'LL TAKE YOUR WORDS UNDER ADVISEMENT FOR THE NEXT TIME!
HMM... YOUR PROFESSION HAS DEFINITELY INFLUENCED YOUR OUTLOOK.
COMMANDER! I'VE RECEIVED WORD THAT TWO INVADERS ARE AT THE ENTRANCE TO THE RAVINE!
CALM YOURSELF. THE BLACK TROOP IS GUARDING THE ENTRANCE...THEY'LL GET RID OF ANY INTRUDERS.

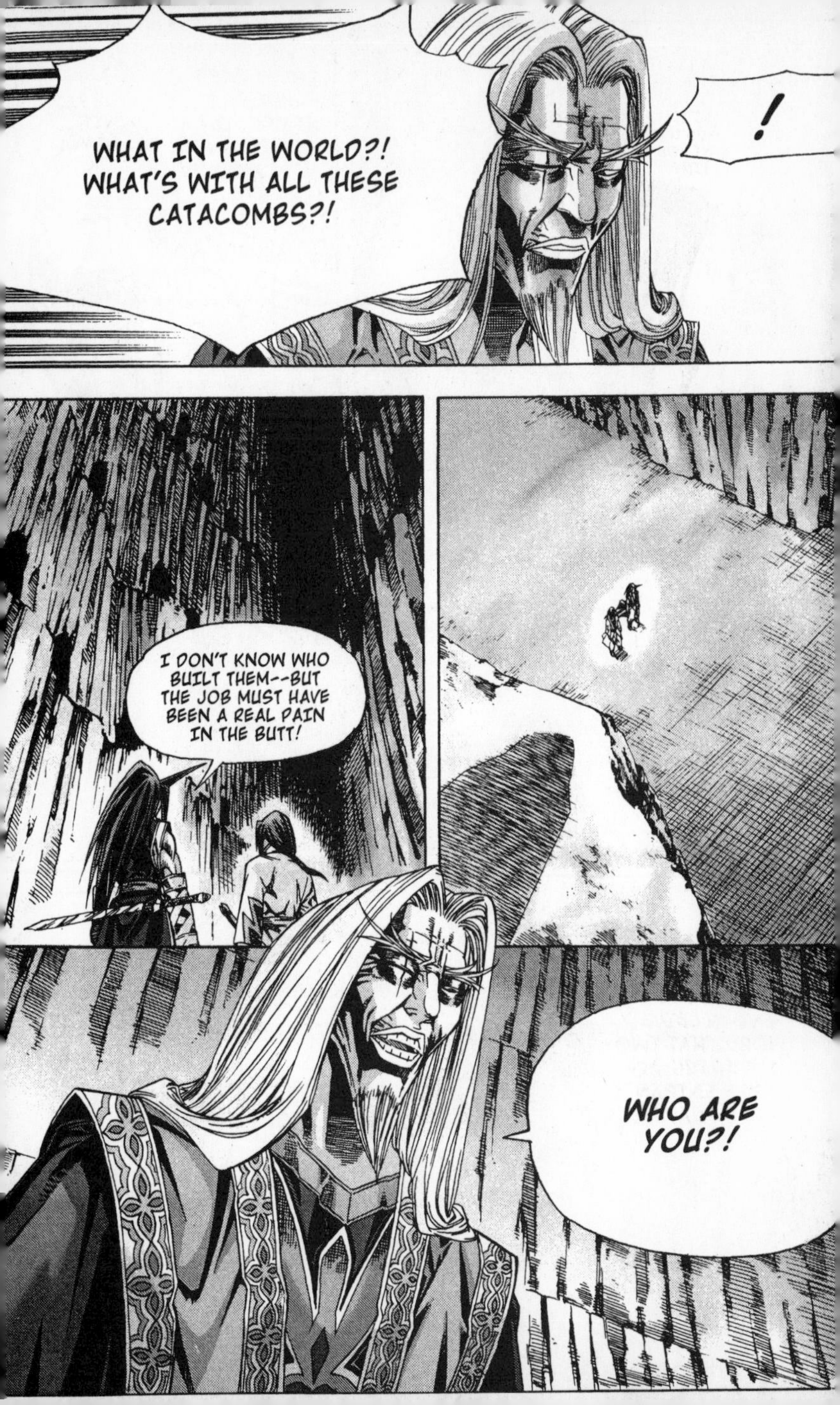
WHAT IN THE WORLD?! WHAT'S WITH ALL THESE CATACOMBS?!
!
I DON'T KNOW WHO BUILT THEM--BUT THE JOB MUST HAVE BEEN A REAL PAIN IN THE BUTT!
WHO ARE YOU?!

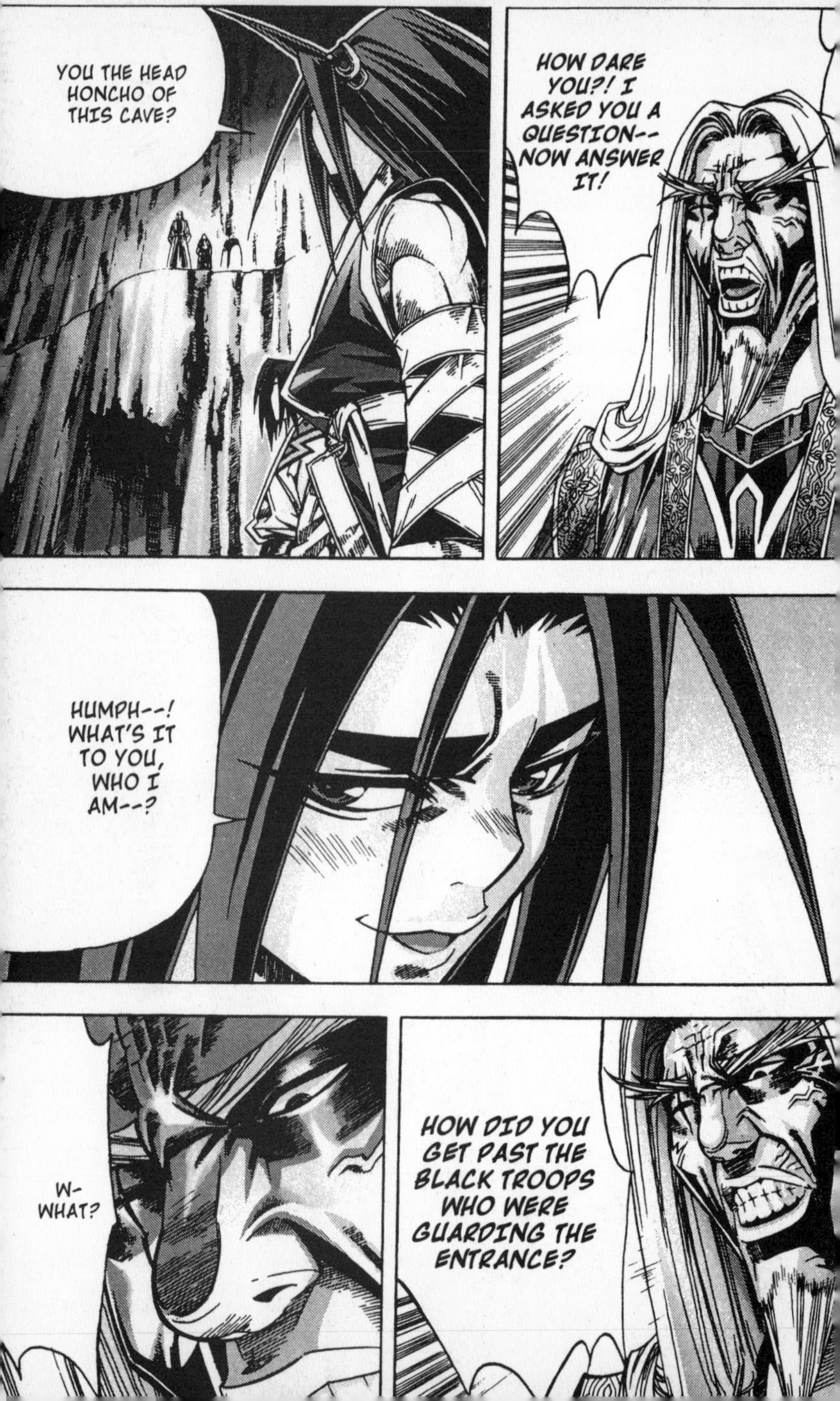
YOU THE HEAD HONCHO OF THIS CAVE?
HOW DARE YOU?! I ASKED YOU A QUESTION-- NOW ANSWER IT!
HUMPH--! WHAT'S IT TO YOU, WHO I AM--?
W- WHAT?
HOW DID YOU GET PAST THE BLACK TROOPS WHO WERE GUARDING THE ENTRANCE?

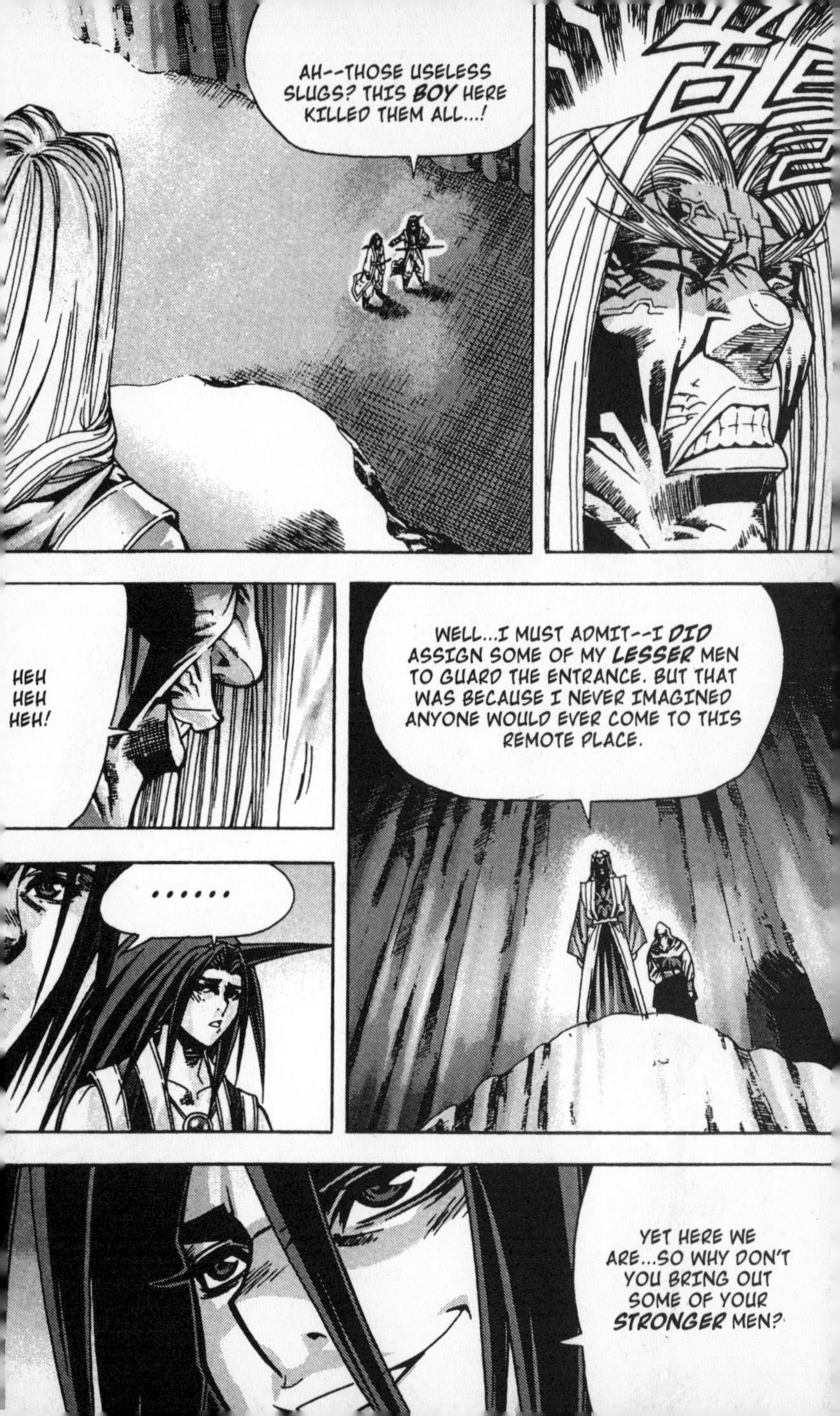
AH--THOSE USELESS SLUGS? THIS *BOY* HERE KILLED THEM ALL...!
HEH HEH HEH!
......
WELL...I MUST ADMIT--I *DID* ASSIGN SOME OF MY *LESSER* MEN TO GUARD THE ENTRANCE. BUT THAT WAS BECAUSE I NEVER IMAGINED ANYONE WOULD EVER COME TO THIS REMOTE PLACE.
YET HERE WE ARE...SO WHY DON'T YOU BRING OUT SOME OF YOUR *STRONGER* MEN?

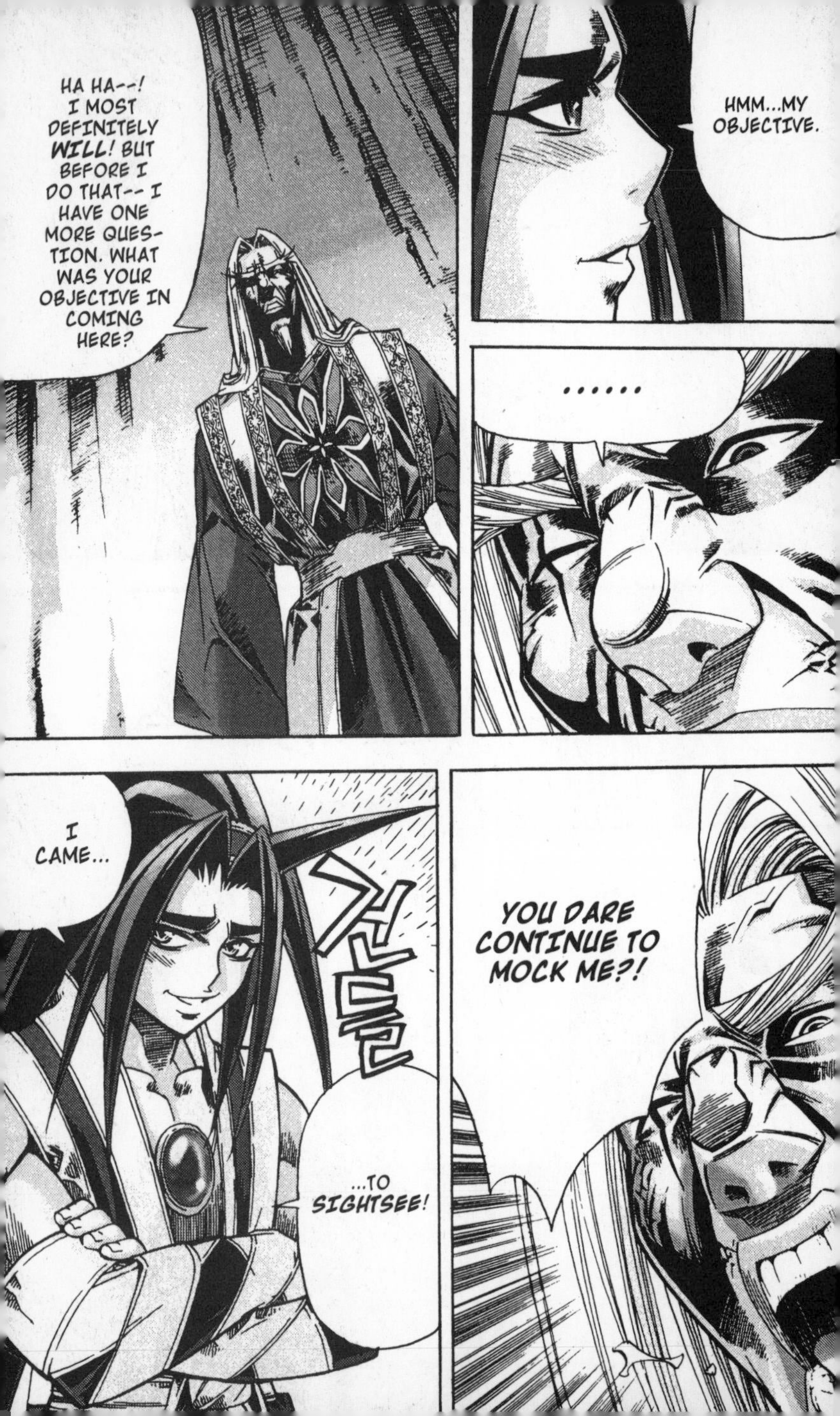
HA HA--! I MOST DEFINITELY **WILL**! BUT BEFORE I DO THAT-- I HAVE ONE MORE QUES-TION. WHAT WAS YOUR OBJECTIVE IN COMING HERE?
HMM...MY OBJECTIVE.
......
I CAME...
...TO SIGHTSEE!
YOU DARE CONTINUE TO MOCK ME?!

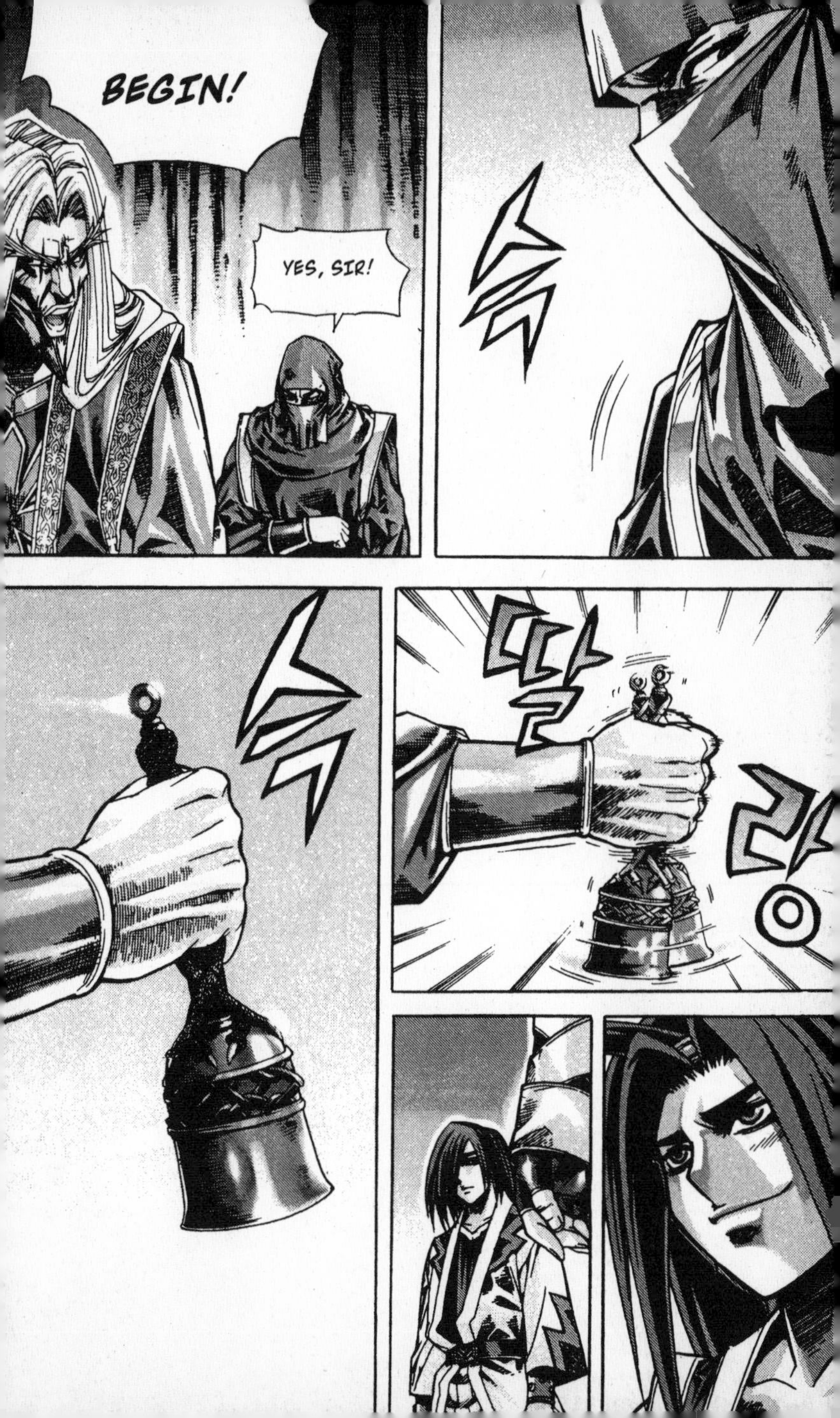
BEGIN!
YES, SIR!

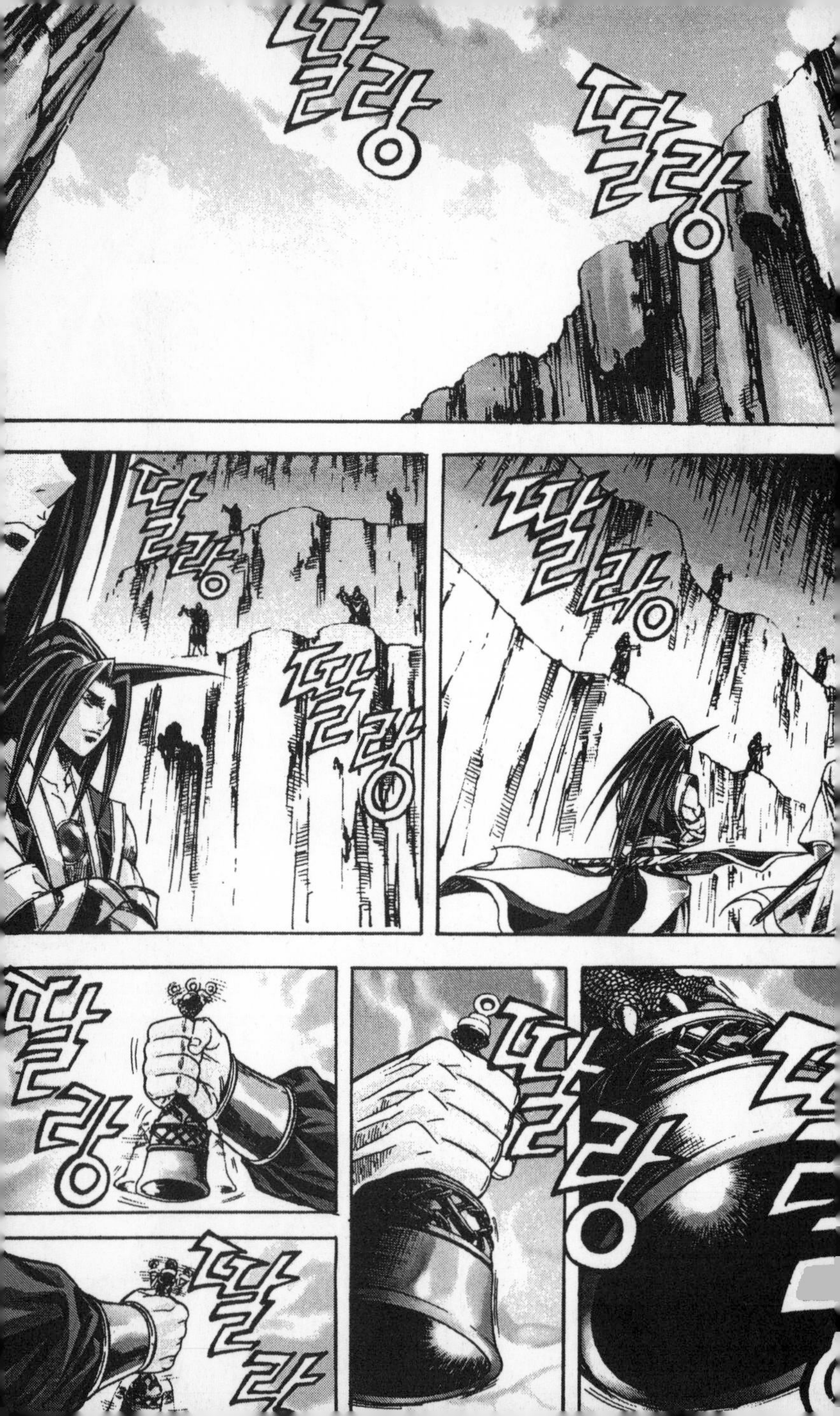
딸랑
딸랑
딸랑
딸랑
딸랑
딸랑
딸랑
딸랑
딸랑

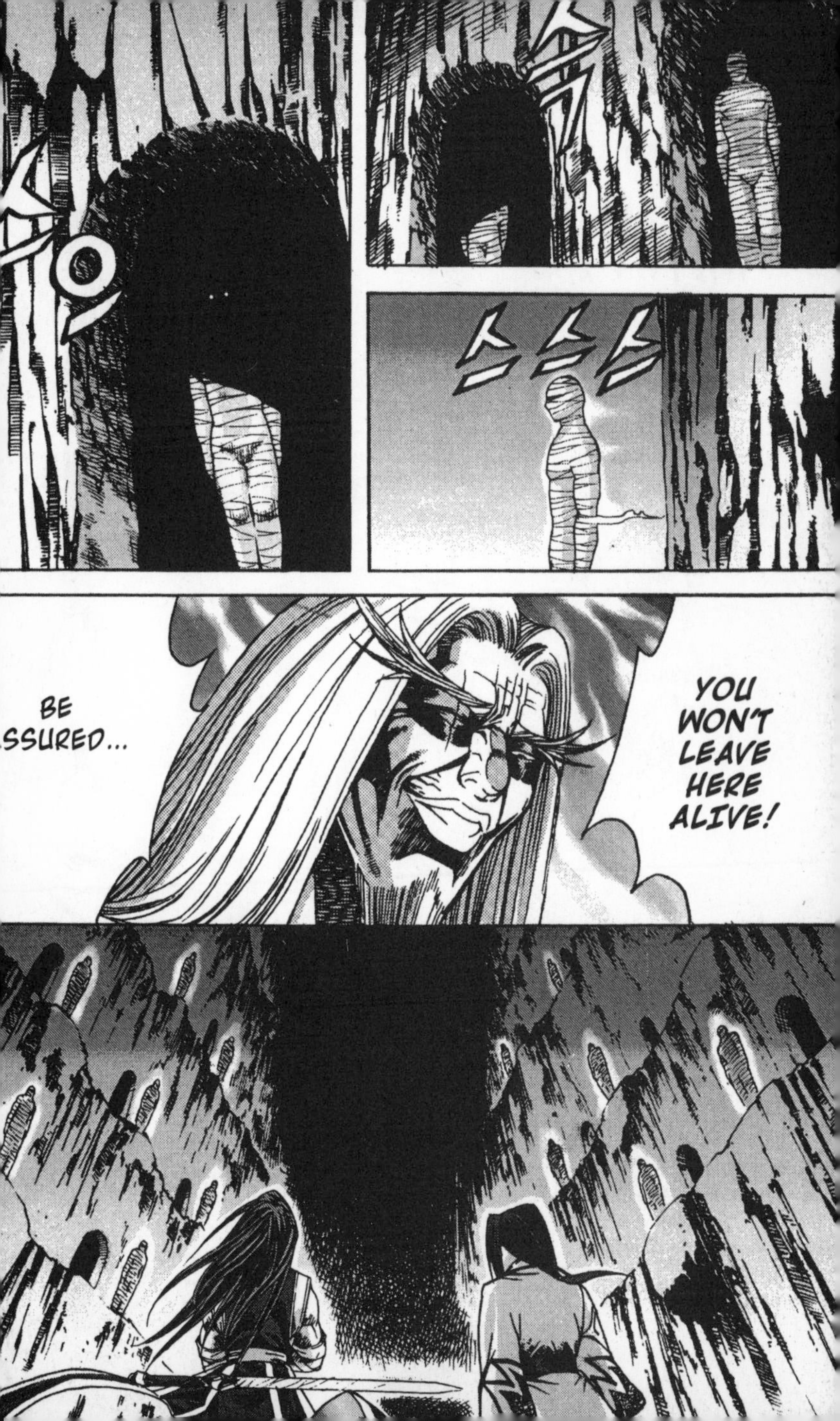
BE
SSURED...
YOU WON'T LEAVE HERE ALIVE!

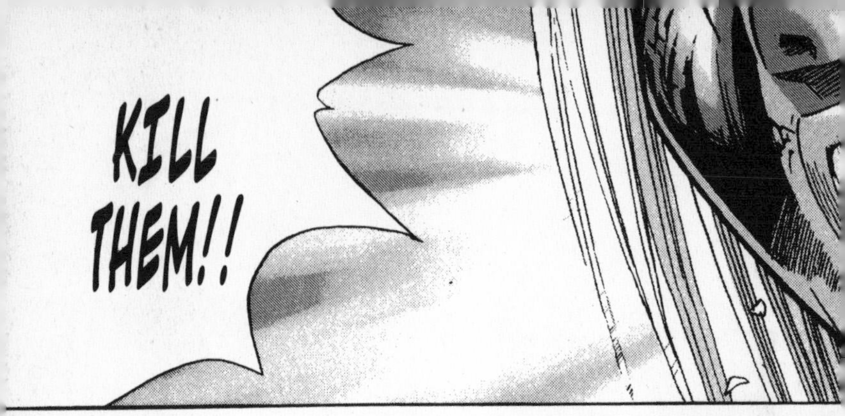
KILL THEM!!
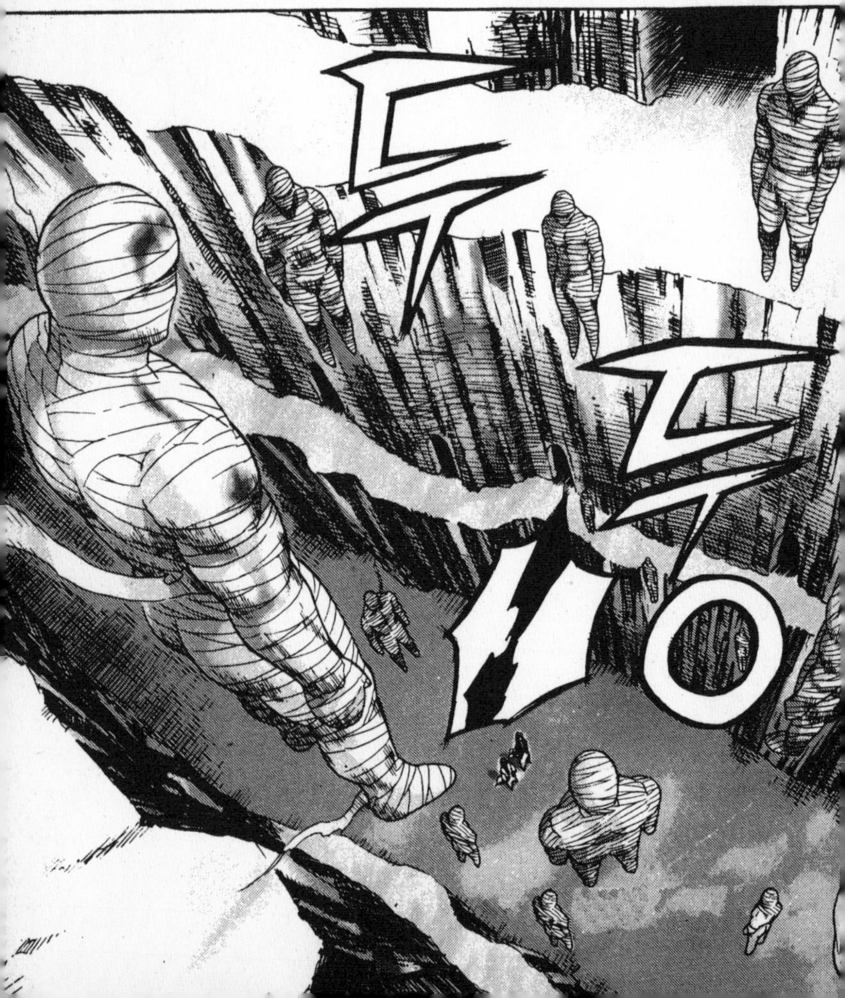

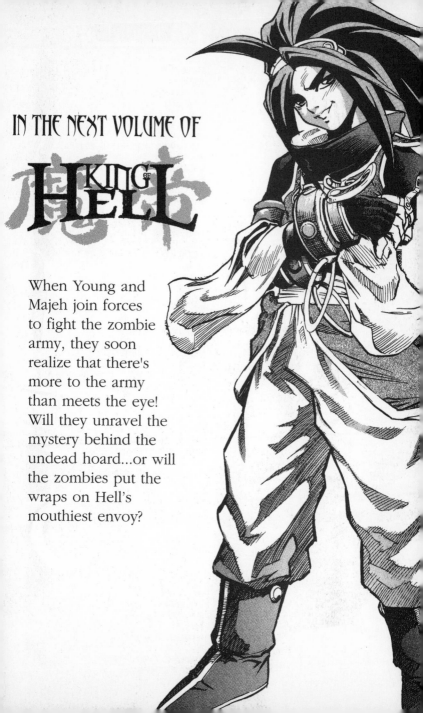

IN THE NEXT VOLUME OF

KING OF HELL

When Young and Majeh join forces to fight the zombie army, they soon realize that there's more to the army than meets the eye! Will they unravel the mystery behind the undead hoard...or will the zombies put the wraps on Hell's mouthiest envoy?

ALSO AVAILABLE FROM  TOKYOPOP®

MANGA

.HACK//LEGEND OF THE TWILIGHT
@LARGE
ABENOBASHI: MAGICAL SHOPPING ARCADE
A.I. LOVE YOU
AI YORI AOSHI
ANGELIC LAYER
ARM OF KANNON
BABY BIRTH
BATTLE ROYALE
BATTLE VIXENS
BOYS BE...
BRAIN POWERED
BRIGADOON
B'TX
CANDIDATE FOR GODDESS, THE
CARDCAPTOR SAKURA
CARDCAPTOR SAKURA - MASTER OF THE CLOW
CHOBITS
CHRONICLES OF THE CURSED SWORD
CLAMP SCHOOL DETECTIVES
CLOVER
COMIC PARTY
CONFIDENTIAL CONFESSIONS
CORRECTOR YUI
COWBOY BEBOP
COWBOY BEBOP: SHOOTING STAR
CRAZY LOVE STORY
CRESCENT MOON
CROSS
CULDCEPT
CYBORG 009
D•N•ANGEL
DEMON DIARY
DEMON ORORON, THE
DEUS VITAE
DIABOLO
DIGIMON
DIGIMON TAMERS
DIGIMON ZERO TWO
DOLL
DRAGON HUNTER
DRAGON KNIGHTS
DRAGON VOICE
DREAM SAGA
DUKLYON: CLAMP SCHOOL DEFENDERS
EERIE QUEERIE!
ERICA SAKURAZAWA: COLLECTED WORKS
ET CETERA
ETERNITY
EVIL'S RETURN
FAERIES' LANDING
FAKE
FLCL
FLOWER OF THE DEEP SLEEP, THE
FORBIDDEN DANCE
FRUITS BASKET

G GUNDAM
GATEKEEPERS
GETBACKERS
GIRL GOT GAME
GRAVITATION
GTO
GUNDAM SEED ASTRAY
GUNDAM WING
GUNDAM WING: BATTLEFIELD OF PACIFISTS
GUNDAM WING: ENDLESS WALTZ
GUNDAM WING: THE LAST OUTPOST (G-UNIT)
HANDS OFF!
HAPPY MANIA
HARLEM BEAT
HYPER RUNE
I.N.V.U.
IMMORTAL RAIN
INITIAL D
INSTANT TEEN: JUST ADD NUTS
ISLAND
JING: KING OF BANDITS
JING: KING OF BANDITS - TWILIGHT TALES
JULINE
KARE KANO
KILL ME, KISS ME
KINDAICHI CASE FILES, THE
KING OF HELL
KODOCHA: SANA'S STAGE
LAMENT OF THE LAMB
LEGAL DRUG
LEGEND OF CHUN HYANG, THE
LES BIJOUX
LOVE HINA
LOVE OR MONEY
LUPIN III
LUPIN III: WORLD'S MOST WANTED
MAGIC KNIGHT RAYEARTH I
MAGIC KNIGHT RAYEARTH II
MAHOROMATIC: AUTOMATIC MAIDEN
MAN OF MANY FACES
MARMALADE BOY
MARS
MARS: HORSE WITH NO NAME
MINK
MIRACLE GIRLS
MIYUKI-CHAN IN WONDERLAND
MODEL
MOURYOU KIDEN: LEGEND OF THE NYMPHS
NECK AND NECK
ONE
ONE I LOVE, THE
PARADISE KISS
PARASYTE
PASSION FRUIT
PEACH GIRL
PEACH GIRL: CHANGE OF HEART
PET SHOP OF HORRORS
PITA-TEN

07.15.04T

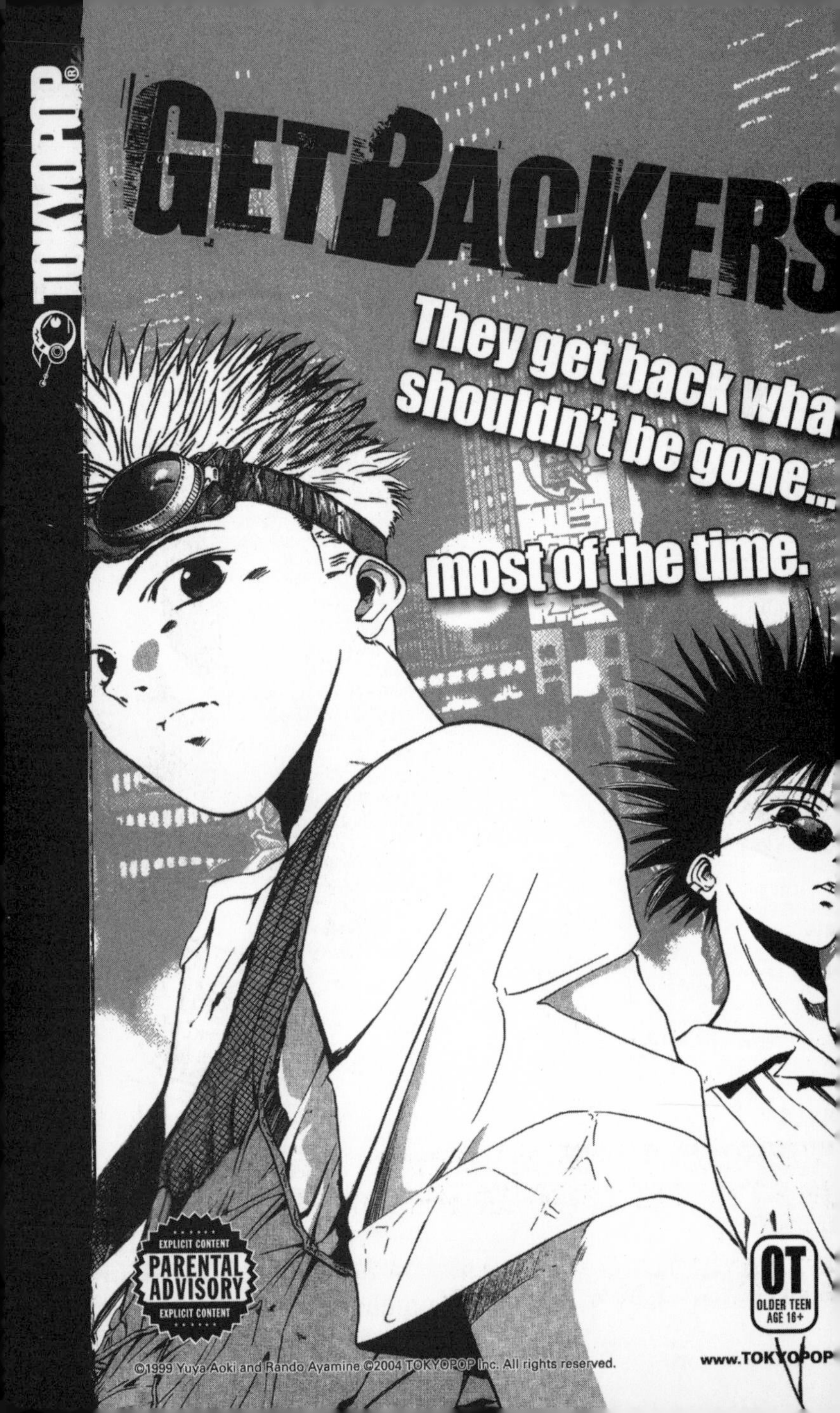
TOKYOPOP
GETBACKERS
They get back wha
shouldn't be gone...
most of the time.
EXPLICIT CONTENT
PARENTAL ADVISORY
EXPLICIT CONTENT
OT
OLDER TEEN AGE 16+
©1999 Yuya Aoki and Rando Ayamine ©2004 TOKYOPOP Inc. All rights reserved.
www.TOKYOPOP

TOKYOPOP®

CHRONICLES OF THE
CURSED SWORD

BY YEO BEOP-RYONG

A living sword forged in darkness
A hero born outside the light
One can destroy the other
But both can save the world.

Available Now At Your Favorite
Book And Comic Stores.